LIFE IN THE VIKING GREAT ARMY

LIFE IN THE VIKING GREAT ARMY

RAIDERS, TRADERS, AND SETTLERS

DAWN M. HADLEY

AND

JULIAN D. RICHARDS

*With contributions by Dave Haldenby,
Gareth Perry, and Mark Randerson*

OXFORD
UNIVERSITY PRESS

OXFORD
UNIVERSITY PRESS

Great Clarendon Street, Oxford, OX2 6DP,
United Kingdom

Oxford University Press is a department of the University of Oxford.
It furthers the University's objective of excellence in research, scholarship,
and education by publishing worldwide. Oxford is a registered trade mark of
Oxford University Press in the UK and in certain other countries

Published in the United States of America by Oxford University Press
198 Madison Avenue, New York, NY 10016, United States of America

British Library Cataloguing in Publication Data
Data available

Library of Congress Control Number: 2024938111

ISBN 978–0–19–884855–4

Printed and bound by
CPI Group (UK) Ltd, Croydon, CR0 4YY

The manufacturer's authorised representative in the EU for product safety is Oxford
University Press España S.A. of el Parque Empresarial San Fernando de Henares, Avenida
de Castilla, 2 – 28830 Madrid (www.oup.es/en).

Acknowledgements

This book is the culmination of over a decade of work on the Viking Great Army, involving many colleagues, to whom we owe a great debt of gratitude. Mark Randerson undertook comparative analyses of the metal-detected finds from both Torksey and Aldwark, and enhanced the artefact catalogues for both sites, during his MPhil research at the University of York, supervised by JDR and DMH; he co-authored Chapters 3 to 6. The strap-ends discussed in Chapter 4 were studied by Dave Haldenby, an independent researcher who has a long collaboration with JDR, commencing in 1993 at Cottam. Dave helped refine some of the PAS identifications, and contributed to Chapters 4 to 7. Gareth Perry at the University of York undertook new analysis on the Torksey and Stafford pottery industries and co-authored the wider review of pottery industries in Chapter 8.

In turn, each of our contributors wishes to acknowledge help from others. Mark Randerson would like to thank Adam Parsons for his willingness to discuss dress accessories, George Easton for sharing his thoughts on the fake hack-gold, Matt Bunker for his help in identifying the Torksey scabbard fitting, and Kitty Fisher for her support, encouragement, and assistance in checking numerical data. Dave Haldenby thanks Paula Gentil of the Hull and East Riding Museum for assistance and encouragement, and Dave Hirst, Steve Foster, Roy Doughty, Chris Hannard, and Christian Whitehead for sharing information on East Yorkshire sites. Gareth Perry is grateful to Jane Young for help with Lincolnshire pottery, Lorraine Mepham of Wessex Archaeology for advice on pottery production in southern England, Berni Sudds of Pre-Construct Archaeology for discussion of East Anglian pottery, and Joseph Perry of The Potteries Museum & Art Gallery, Stoke-on-Trent for access to the pottery from Stafford. DMH and JDR would like to thank David Parsons of the University of Wales for assisting us in interpretation of the runic and rune-like inscriptions discussed in Chapters 4 and 5, Aleks McClain of the University of York for providing us with the new radiocarbon dating evidence for Goltho, and David Roffe of the Institute of Historical Research who kindly provided us with a copy of the forthcoming report on the excavations at Stamford Castle by the late Christine Mahany and others. We are grateful to Keith Wade, formerly of Suffolk County Council Archaeological Service, for his feedback on

Chapter 8 and his advice on the Ipswich excavations. We would like to thank Mark Laurie at Nottingham University Museum for facilitating access to the Maurice Barley Archive, and Mark Noel and Ann Wilkinson of the University of Bradford for answering our questions about archaeomagnetic dates. We are grateful to Andrew Woods and Lucy Moore, undertaking doctoral research at the University of York, for updated identifications of the Torksey stycas, and to Johanne Porter for giving us access to her unpublished University of East Anglia doctoral thesis on the St Edmund coins. Michel Groothedde and Bert Fermin (both of Archeologie Zutphen), Bart Van den Bossche, and Wolfram Giertz drew our attention to comparative evidence in the Netherlands and Germany and provided bibliographic advice; Wolfram also assisted with identification of the Carolingian metalwork from both camps. An analysis of lead inset weights was undertaken by Rebekah Hiett, as a University of York Master's dissertation supervised by DMH, and some of her findings are mentioned in Chapter 3. A study of the Torksey iron hoard was undertaken by Lily Carhart, as a University of Sheffield Master's dissertation supervised by DMH, and we draw on her identifications in Chapter 6.

JDR and DMH would also like to thank the various metal detectorists and collectors who have shared information with us over many years. For Torksey they include Dave and Pete Stanley and Neil Parker. The late Roger Thomas took us to see his find spots at Catton, with other members of Witan Archaeology. Ian Briggs and Ricky Brelsford provided information about Spofforth; Paul Robbins, Paul Greenwood, and other members of the Grimsby and District Metal Detecting Club discussed their finds from Swinhope and Binbrook with us. Geoff Bambrook, Richard Bourne, Jon Mann, and Lee Toone provided invaluable information and images for finds from Aldwark, which Mark Ainsley showed JDR around, many years ago. Gary Johnson provided valuable additional information on Aldwark finds and on lead inset weights from across England. We are grateful to Michael Lewis at the British Museum for permission to use data and images from the PAS, as well as several current and former Finds Liaison Officers, notably Martin Foreman, Adam Daubney, Wendy Scott, Rebecca Griffiths, Amy Downes, and Lisa Brundle. Christine McDonnell and Eleanor Drew provided access to the York Archaeological Trust archive for Aldwark and gave permission for image re-use. Andrew Woods provided us with images of finds from Aldwark in possession of York Museums Trust. For permission to reproduce other images included in the book we are grateful to Andres Dobat (Aarhus University), Kevin Leahy (National Finds Advisor for early medieval metalwork for the PAS), Samantha

Parker (Lincolnshire County Council), Hannah Brown, Bert Fermin, and Lee Toone. Torksey team members Andrew Woods, Samantha Stein, Hannah Brown, Andrew Marriott, and Lizzy Craig-Atkins (University of Sheffield) gave generously of their time and expertise in earlier stages of the project, and reports on their analyses are available on the original Torksey archive hosted by the Archaeology Data Service (https://doi.org/10.5284/1018222).

Helen Goodchild, Reb Ellis-Haken (both University of York), Drazen Tomic, and Chloe Watson produced maps and plans, artefact drawings, and photographs. We have been fortunate to receive funding for our research at Torksey and other sites visited by the Great Army from the British Academy, the Society of Antiquaries of London, the Robert Kiln Trust, and the Universities of Sheffield and York. Finally, we are grateful to Charlotte Loveridge at Oxford University Press for her encouragement and support.

Contents

List of Illustrations

List of Tables

PART I

Introduction

The Viking Great Army landed in East Anglia in late 865 and over the following fifteen years fought numerous battles in all four Anglo-Saxon kingdoms, contracted and broke peace treaties, and deposed or killed at least four Anglo-Saxon kings, replacing them with its own appointees from the local elite. It had a major impact, initiating extensive transformations in Anglo-Saxon society, culture, economy, and political organisation. Previous Viking armies had raided only in the summer months, but the Great Army was a constant presence, overwintering at various locations in northern and eastern England. The Army divided in 875 and many of its members subsequently settled in Northumbria (876), eastern Mercia (877), and East Anglia (880), and its leaders adopted Anglo-Saxon styles of kingship, converted to Christianity, and engaged in political diplomacy. This paved the way for generations of Scandinavian settlement, as later migratory groups were drawn to these pioneer settlements, whose leaders had created a template for political conquest and acculturation, embedding new modes of cultural expression. The activities of the Great Army brought to an end the royal lines of three kingdoms and set in motion a series of events that had a long-term impact on craftworking, manufacture, and urban development.

Historiography

The Great Army has featured in several studies over the last decade, with insights transformed by new fieldwork, datasets, analytical methods, and theoretical framing. The conceptualisation of the Army, its structure, motivations, and impacts, have accordingly varied enormously. In 2014 Shane McLeod published a monograph-length examination, adopting an explanatory framework borrowed from Migration Theory.[1] Building on initial work by Alfred Smyth which had been refined by Clare Downham, he examined the close connections between Viking leaders in Ireland and England, but he put equal emphasis on the continental antecedents of the Army.[2] His study was largely based on written sources, as archaeological evidence was still limited, but it presented an important assessment of the economic impact and innovation of the earliest generation of Scandinavian settlers and the high degree of acculturation that ensued, including conversion to Christianity. He also explored the nature of kingship, both client kings established by the Great Army in the early phases of raiding and the first generation of Scandinavian kings. McLeod concluded that the earliest settlers would have been knowledgeable about the culture of Anglo-Saxon England and 'that many arrived prepared to adapt to its political, religious and economic cultures'.[3]

Since the publication of McLeod's book, the archaeological record has expanded considerably, not least through our fieldwork at the Great Army camp of 872–3 at Torksey (Lincolnshire), first published in 2016, and which will be discussed at length in the current volume.[4] Cat Jarman has revisited the evidence from the camp of 873–4 at Repton (Derbyshire), reassessing the scientific dating evidence for the burials excavated there in the 1970s and 1980s including a mass grave. She has also undertaken stable isotope analysis to better understand the origins of the individuals buried there and conducted new excavations. In the light of our evidence from Torksey, and a re-appreciation of the relevance of the exceptional Viking cremation cemetery at Heath Wood, Ingleby it has also been possible to set Repton within the wider landscape, including new metal-detector evidence at Foremark, reported by Jarman.[5] Research on the Repton finds also led her to consider the long distance connections of Viking armies via the Russian river systems and beyond.[6] Most recently she has collaborated with Jane Kershaw to investigate a potential Great Army site at East Thirston (Northumberland).[7] Kershaw was also one of the first scholars to make extensive use of metal-detected evidence for Viking settlement in England and her recent studies of the sources of Viking silver have included Viking Great Army material.[8]

1. McLeod 2014
2. Smyth 1977; Downham 2007; McLeod 2014, 109–71
3. McLeod 2014, 283
4. Hadley and Richards 2016; 2021
5. Jarman 2018; 2019; Jarman *et al.* 2018; 2019; Richards *et al.* 2004
6. Jarman 2021
7. Kershaw *et al.* 2023
8. Kershaw 2013

Gareth Williams has a long-standing interest in the Viking Great Army and, as a numismatist, has published several papers on associated coins and hoards. Most critically for this volume was his involvement, on behalf of the British Museum, in recording and bringing to publication the metal-detected finds from the Great Army camp at Aldwark (North Yorkshire). This followed the untimely death of Richard Hall who had led excavations there on behalf of York Archaeological Trust.[9] The publication of the excavations of a Viking camp at Woodstown, near Waterford in Ireland, appeared after McLeod's book had gone to press, and this has also provided context for the activities of the Great Army in England, since some of them came from raiding in Ireland.[10]

Neil Price and Ben Raffield have used ethnographic analogy to illuminate the character and activities of Viking armies, ranging from ritual deposits in water, to slavery and the influence of male–female sex ratios on the causes of the Viking Age.[11] Viking armies, including the Great Army, have also been likened to eighteenth-century pirate groups by Price. Through this analogy, he has interpreted ninth-century Viking armies as a 'social experiment unfolding in a context of itinerant violence...not on the way to anywhere, nor were they a means to an end, but rather they were objectives in themselves'.[12] Price highlighted the fluid organisation of pirate communities, and employed the concept of the hydrarchy to describe the network of independent pirate groups who were nonetheless 'attached to a larger and deeply dangerous body'.[13] He suggested that material culture, related to ships and clothing, or even bodily manipulation, such as tattoos and filing of teeth, may have been adopted to distinguish pirate groups.[14]

Christian Cooijmans has built on Price's concept of Viking armies as operating within a hydrarchy in his study of Francia. His work provided a valuable survey of the evidence from a wide range of chronicles, exploring the scale, and changing motivations, of Viking armies active in Francia, and tracing the range of activities in which they engaged, including trade and political collaboration, as they took advantage of the political turmoil in the Carolingian Empire in the ninth century.[15] A particular focus was on the places where armies camped, and

9. Williams (ed.) 2020
10. Russell and Hurley (eds.) 2014
11. Price 2014; 2016; Raffield 2014; 2016; 2022; Raffield *et al.* 2016; 2017
12. Price 2016, 170
13. Price 2016, 157
14. Price 2016, 167–9
15. Cooijmans 2020

the logistics of supplying them.[16] Cooijmans argued that Viking activity changed over time, according to its scale, the prevailing politico-economic circumstances of both the places they raided and Scandinavia, the nature of economic and political engagement, and the extent to which the armies had control over land in Francia. His conclusion was that Viking activity was purposeful, requiring a high degree of planning, and good intelligence about the Carolingian realm.[17] This study was also important in tracing the interconnectedness of Viking activity over wide areas of the Continent.

In another monograph-length treatment, Tom Horne has explored the economic activities of towns and camps in the late ninth and early tenth centuries, emphasising the connections between Britain, Ireland, and southern Scandinavia in the development of a 'market kingdom' alongside 'socially embedded redistribution of looted wealth'. He has argued that 'sophisticated commercial understanding arrived in Britain at least partially formed before developing its own adaptations', and that the economic network of which the Great Army was a part pivoted through southern Scandinavia.[18]

Most recently, a collection has appeared focusing on the camps of Viking armies across Europe and Scandinavia, edited by Charlotte Hedenstierna-Jonson and Irene García Losquiño. This includes contributions from most of the main researchers in the field, with syntheses of previous research, surveys of the wide range of historical sources from Ireland and the Continent, updates on recent archaeological investigations at key sites, and presentations of the findings of new fieldwork. The volume also features studies of issues that have received minimal previous discussion, including the religious life of Viking armies, as well as a broadening of the geographical context in which Viking camps are found.[19] The study of Viking armies and their camps is clearly a vibrant field of investigation, attracting diverse approaches, emphases, and conceptualisations, and this is valuable context for our discussion of the Great Army.

Outline

The perspective of the present volume is directed towards the people of the camps of the Great Army: where they were from, how they expressed their identities, the activities they undertook to resource themselves, their interactions

---

16. Cooijmans 2020, 123–35, 141–65; 2021, 991–4; 2023, 157–9
17. Cooijmans 2020, 211–28, 234–7
18. Horne 2022, 77
19. Hedenstierna-Jonson and García Losquiño 2023

with local communities, and the impact of the settlement of members of the Army over the following decades. It provides the first comprehensive comparison of the two camps with the most extensive archaeological datasets—Torksey and Aldwark. Chapter 1 places the activities of the Great Army in the wider context of previous Viking raids and Viking activity in Ireland and on the Continent, highlighting similarities with the activities of other Viking armies but also drawing out the distinctiveness of the Great Army. There has been a recent tendency to aggregate evidence relating to Viking armies operating across wider areas over hundreds of years, and while providing essential context and points of comparison, it risks losing sight of the chronologically and regionally specific activities. Where the Great Army arrived from, and where those who did not settle went, are also addressed.

In Chapter 2 we examine the scale, form, and location of Great Army camps, and the communication networks which were used by the Army, drawing on both historical and archaeological evidence. The places where it overwintered are recorded in contemporary texts, but they do not identify their precise locations, which requires archaeological investigation. We review the results of such studies, many of them very recent, including investigations of Torksey and Aldwark, reinforcing that the assemblages from these sites are not only distinctive but different from both those found elsewhere in the ninth century and at later camps. Having established the locations of the camps, we are able to address why they were chosen, typically at nodal points in transport networks, and what they reveal about the ambitions of the Great Army to conquer and settle in Anglo-Saxon England.

Part II commences with an overview of the datasets that form the core of this book, including how they were assembled. There is an introduction to the accompanying illustrated artefact catalogues, which are available as Open Access datasets from the Archaeology Data Service at https://doi.org/10.5284/1115933 for Aldwark, and https://doi.org/10.5284/1115932 for Torksey. In Chapters 3 to 6 we examine the rich artefactual evidence from the camps at Aldwark and Torksey to establish the range of activities that took place during the overwintering of the Great Army. In the 2020 Aldwark report, Gareth Williams expressed a hope that there would eventually be a detailed comparison between the finds with those from Torksey; publication of Aldwark, and the intelligence we have gathered on previously unreported finds, now allows detailed comparison with Torksey for the first time.[20] This has revealed the

20. Williams 2020h, 85

operation of a bullion economy (in the form of silver, gold, and copper-alloy ingots, hack-metal, and weights), minting of coins imitative of local and continental issues, wood-, metal-, and textile-working, fishing, and board-gaming. The assemblages are similar and both are quite unlike those from contemporary Anglo-Saxon settlements. We address the range and nature of craftworking practices, manufacturing, and forms of exchange that characterised the camps. This will enhance our understanding of their occupants, how they were provisioned, and their interactions with local communities. Comparative evidence from other camps, especially the burial evidence from Repton and nearby at Heath Wood, and from Irish and continental chronicles recording the behaviour and composition of ninth-century Viking armies is integrated with the findings from Anglo-Saxon written sources and insights from the archaeological record. Taken together these reveal that the Great Army was not simply a military force, but a community of men, women, children, craftworkers, and merchants. We can also see that it comprised multiple groups from diverse backgrounds and with competing agendas.

In Part III we examine the wider impact of the Viking Great Army in the countryside and on the development of towns and industry. Having identified the artefactual signature of the Army at Torksey and Aldwark, in Chapter 7 we investigate its presence at other rural settlements in eastern and northern England. Chapter 8 examines the longer-term impact of the Great Army on the development of industry. We conclude that late ninth- and early tenth-century transformations of production and supply of wheel-thrown pottery were introduced by continental potters, arriving in England in the wake of the Great Army. In doing so, we address major debates of the period concerning the impact of the Vikings, how to use archaeological evidence to trace migration, and the origins of medieval industry and its links to the growth of towns. Dynamic proliferation of urban places has been identified in eastern England, where Scandinavian settlement was extensive in the late ninth and tenth centuries, but the connection between these two developments remained disputed. Finally, Chapter 9 provides an epilogue in which we introduce what happened next, including those who settled in England, whilst returning members of the Great Army introduced aspects of their identity back to their homelands. This concluding chapter also reflects on agendas for future research and emphasises the importance of data sharing and application of standardised data recording protocols.

1

The Great Army in context

The origins of the Great Army are not recorded in any contemporary sources, but the disparate forces that joined it undoubtedly included those armies recorded as being active in continental Europe and Ireland in the mid-ninth century, as well as fresh forces arriving direct from Scandinavia.[1] Moreover, traditions—whether real or invented—about the actions and encounters of these armies must have been widely known, and influential on members of the Great Army. Viking raiders had become a regular presence across much of Ireland and the northern part of the Continent by the mid-ninth century, and acquisition of land had commenced. Contemporary accounts reveal that raiding groups rarely cooperated for any great length of time, and rivalries between them were as characteristic of Viking behaviour as were attacks on churches, towns, and centres of political power. Archaeological evidence is limited but contributes to the picture that emerges from the written sources of the diverse origins and areas of activity of the raiders. In this chapter, we provide an outline of the range of Viking attacks and interactions with local rulers and communities in Ireland, on the Continent, and in England, and we introduce Scandinavia in the decades before 865 to provide context for the actions of the Great Army.

Viking armies in Ireland: the *longphuirt*

Viking armies had been a year-round presence in Ireland since at least the early 840s, when bases described as *longphuirt* (singular *longphort*) are first documented on Lough Neagh, at Linn Duachaill (Co. Louth), and Dublin.[2] The term

1. McLeod 2014, 109–71
2. Mac Airt and Mac Niocaill 1983, 299–305

derives from two Latin loan-words, *[navis]longa*, meaning [war]ship, and *portus*, a harbour or haven, and they were, indeed, located close to accessible harbours.[3] Whether the *longphuirt* were a specific type of settlement has been extensively debated; the use of the term broadened over time, and not all Viking bases or camps were described in this way.[4] Irrespective of what they may have been called, archaeological evidence for Viking camps in Ireland remains limited, but it suggests the presence of sizeable communities, with access to extensive resources. In 841 Viking raiders were described in the *Annals of Ulster* as being based at the *longphort* of Linn Duachaill, which has been located archaeologic-ally at Annagassan ('the ford of Ath na gCasan'). Survey and trial trenching revealed a ditch and internal bank, *c.*245m long, defending a peninsula over a kilometre long between the River Glyde and the Irish Sea, effectively creating an island of *c.*64ha. The artefacts recovered include clench nails, an iron knife, two pieces of hack-silver cut from a Scandinavian arm-ring, two plain discoidal lead weights, a balance arm from a weighing scale, a belt buckle attachment, and the shaft of a ringed pin, of a type that the Scandinavians adopted from Irish forms.[5] A tinned copper-alloy boss with an inlaid trefoil motif, a binding strip, a mount with a central boss, and gilded interlace decoration, and another with a yellow enamel inlay, may be fragments of ecclesiastical items and reflect the proceeds of raiding. Burning and smithing hearth cakes suggest ironworking took place. Food resources available to the raiders included cattle, pig, and sheep/goat, while a lead line sinker, fishbones, and seashells suggest other local resources that were exploited. The *longphort* was the base for plundering in the kingdoms of north and south Tethba and an attack on the monastery of Clonmacnoise, yet collaboration between the raiders and some local communities is suggested by the record that in 842 'Comán, abbot of Linn Duachaill, was killed and burned by heathens and Irish'.[6] Other *longphuirt* were similarly located close to the borders between kingdoms, and the influence of the local political geog-raphy led John Sheehan to suggest that 'rather than being primarily regarded as assault bases, [they] should be viewed as a result of cooperation between the Scandinavian leaders and some Irish kings' (Figure 1.1).[7]

Extensive excavations in Dublin have illuminated the Scandinavian impact, but the majority of the evidence dates to the late ninth and tenth century, and

3. Ó Floinn 1998, 161–2; Sheehan 2008
4. Downham 2013, 4–9
5. Clinton 2013–14; Kelly 2015, 82–3
6. Mac Airt and Mac Niocaill 1983, 298–301; Downham 2007, 11–12
7. Sheehan 2018, 106

Figure 1.1. Approximate domains of Irish dynasties in ninth-century Ireland

for a long time the precise location of the *longphort* first recorded in 841 was unclear. It is now believed to have been largely focused around the Black Pool east of the River Poddle, a tributary of the River Liffey, where evidence for ninth-century Viking activity has been excavated over the last twenty years (Figure 1.2).[8] Occupation layers, represented by post-holes and hearths, have

8. Simpson 2005; Sheehan 2008, 289; Purcell 2015, 42–4

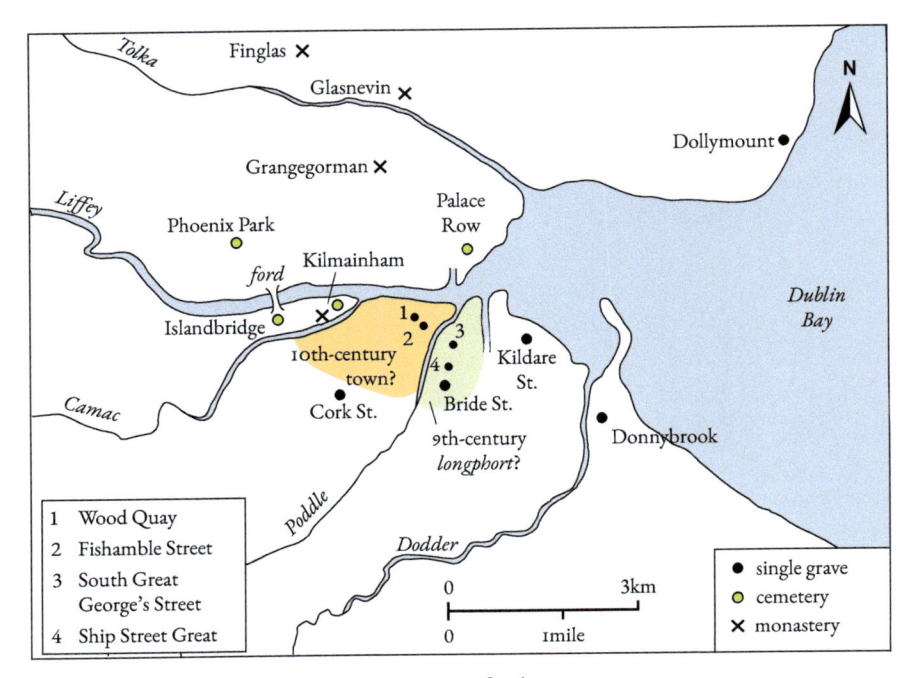

Figure 1.2. Dublin, showing known areas of Viking activity

been excavated at South Great George's Street, accompanied by refuse pits and animal remains, with finds including an axe head, a pair of iron shears, iron nails, and two lead weights. The burials include the grave of an adult male (aged *c.*20–30) from Golden Lane, just beyond the boundary of the large early medieval cemetery of the church of St Michael le Pole. It contained a spearhead, buckle, strap-end, a knife, and two flat cylindrical lead weights near the waist where 'a faint organic stained soil' suggested that they had been contained within a leather belt pouch. The grave of an adult female accompanied by a bone buckle, and two other unfurnished and badly disturbed graves were found nearby.[9] Immediately east of this site, excavation at Ship Street Great revealed the grave of an adult male aged 25–29 containing two silver fingerrings, an unidentified iron disc, and a bead. A sword blade found *c.*30m to the south may have been associated with it, given the lack of other Viking-age material in this area.[10] Around 200m to the east, other furnished burials have

9. O'Donovan 2008; Harrison and Ó Floinn 2014, 219, 537–43, where a tenth-century date for the strap-end and buckle are mentioned, but as shown in Chapter 4, these can now be assigned ninth-century origins.
10. Simpson 2005, 32–4; Harrison and Ó Floinn 2014, 572–6

been excavated at South Great George's Street. The burial of an adult male aged 25–29 contained a shield boss, a knife, carbonised wood, and a horn core. Stable isotope analysis suggested that he had spent his early years in the Western or Northern Isles of Scotland. A badly disturbed grave of a young adult male aged 17–20 contained a shield boss and carbonised wood; it had been placed on one of the hearths excavated at the site, although the remains were not burnt. Stable isotope analysis suggested that he had spent his early years in Scandinavia. A third burial contained an antler comb, bone pin, two iron knife blades, an iron rivet, and hammerscale, with stable isotope analysis suggesting that this adult male, aged c.17–25, had also spent his early years in Scandinavia. Only the lower part of a fourth grave survived and produced no grave goods, although 151 animal bone fragments were scattered around the skeleton, which could be assigned only an age of less than 25 years. Stable isotope analysis suggested this individual had also spent their early years in the Western or Northern Isles.[11]

The radiocarbon dates from these burials span the late seventh to early tenth centuries, presenting the possibility of Scandinavian settlement in Dublin before 841, although typological analysis of the grave goods has suggested that this is unlikely. Some of these dates may be affected by Marine Reservoir Effects, whereby marine food consumption can produce radiocarbon dates which appear older than those produced by terrestrial food consumption.[12] The stable isotope analysis has suggested that these individuals had spent their earliest years in diverse locations. For some this was somewhere in western Britain, which indicates Scandinavian bases in this region, earlier than indicated by the documentary sources.[13] The wider burial record from Ireland comprises over 100 burials revealing Scandinavian influences in their grave goods, most of which are in Dublin. These can generally only be broadly dated to the ninth century based on the grave goods, but many may pre-date the activities of the Great Army in England. It has been noted that the burials containing the earliest datable artefacts are at Dublin, where c.80% of Viking burials in Ireland are found.[14] The burials at Kilmainham and Islandbridge, around 2km to the west of the city centre, were uncovered in the nineteenth and early twentieth centuries, and while recording was often limited, the artefacts recovered are known to have included swords, shield bosses, spearheads, axe heads, dress accessories

11. Simpson 2005, 52; Harrison and Ó Floinn 2014, 576–84
12. Harrison and Ó Floinn 2014, 219; Griffiths 2010, 76
13. Russell and Hurley 2014
14. Harrison and Ó Floinn 2014, 220

and brooches, weights and balances, textile-working equipment, tools, and horse equipment. While many are of Scandinavian origins, others were forms adopted or manufactured in Ireland.[15]

Archaeological investigations at Woodstown (Co. Waterford) during construction of the N25 Waterford City Bypass between 2003 and 2007 revealed what appears to be the long-lived base of a Viking army on the banks of the River Suir (Figure 1.3).[16] The 6000 artefacts recovered suggest that activity was focused in the second half of the ninth century, with some material possibly extending into the first decades of the tenth century, although the paucity of coins hampers any greater precision.[17] The site is not mentioned in any written sources, but Downham suggests that it may be linked to an increase in raiding in the Barrow and Nore valleys in the 850s–860s.[18]

Two adjacent D-shaped enclosures encompassing c.2.91ha were identified by geophysical survey, and although archaeological features were truncated by ploughing, remains of a rectangular building (5.4 × 8.4m), with two phases of construction, were excavated. The survey suggested there were further structures,

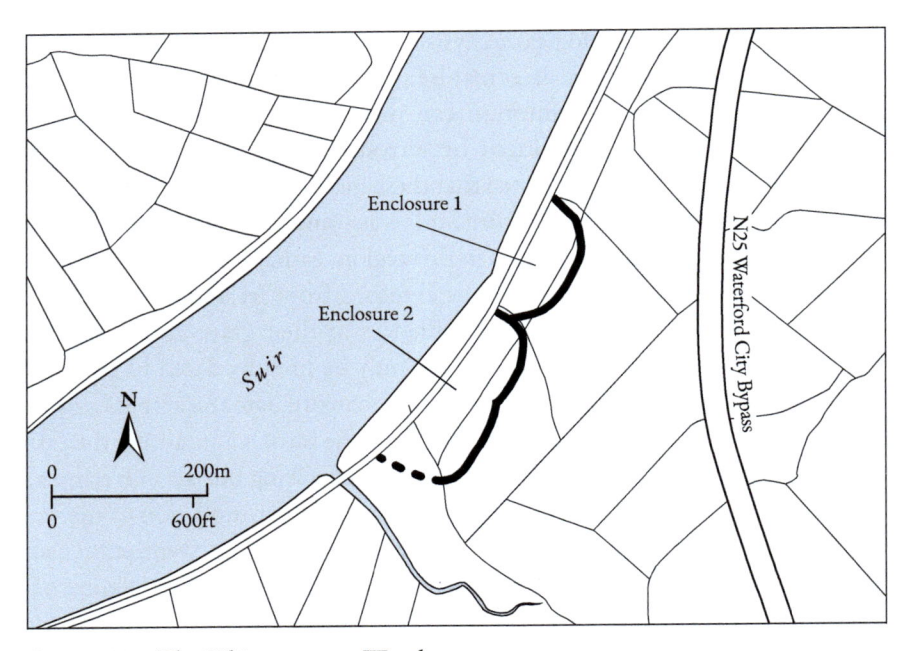

Figure 1.3. The Viking camp at Woodstown

15. Harrison and Ó Floinn 2014, 73–221, 305–503
16. Russell and Hurley 2014; Russell 2023
17. Harrison 2014a
18. Downham 2004, 77–80

and this was confirmed by a Ground Penetrating Radar (GPR) survey in 2018. This indicated the presence of at least six sub-rectangular structures across both enclosures, some of which were quite substantial, up to 17m in length.[19] Evidence for metalworking was uncovered by a combination of excavation and metal-detecting—which is only legal in Ireland with state permission—including 47 crucible fragments from the area of the building, along with fragments of furnace linings and bases, and 23 whetstones.[20] The recovery of 212 partial or complete clench nails indicates that boat repair was being undertaken alongside the river.[21] Other artefacts retrieved by metal-detecting of the plough soil included four Viking-age knives, various dress accessories including buckle and brooch fragments, and weapons, comprising two sword pommels, a spearhead, a possible axe head, and a number of conical and domed copper-alloy mounts which may have decorated shields.[22] Twenty-six whole or fragmentary silver ingots, 199 lead weights, and fragments of two Islamic dirhams indicate trading activity using bullion.[23] A single grave was excavated beyond the north-eastern end of the enclosures, and while no human remains survived, the grave goods suggest that it was the burial of a male. The grave contained a sword, which had been broken into four pieces before deposition, spearhead, shield boss and mounts, axe head, knife, whetstone, and a copper-alloy ringed pin, which had probably been used to fasten a cloak. Large sub-angular stones at one end of the grave suggest it had originally been covered by a stone cairn.[24] Woodstown provides the closest parallel to the camps of the Great Army in England, although it is much smaller, differs in the apparent duration of its occupation, and, as we shall see, has produced an artefact assemblage with a rather different profile.

Viking raiders in Ireland: coordination, rivalries, and ambitions

The written sources record multiple groups of Viking raiders active in Ireland in the 850s and 860s, sometimes working together but often in conflict with each other. For example, the *longphuirt* at Dublin and Linn Duachaill were

19. Russell 2023, 139
20. Young 2014a; 2014b
21. Bill 2014, 145
22. Scully 2014; Harrison 2014b
23. Sheehan 2014; Wallace 2014; Rispling 2014
24. Harrison 2014b; Harrison and Ó Floinn 2014, 663–8

attacked in 851 by a newly arrived group of raiders described by the *Annals of Ulster* as the *Dubgaill* ('dark foreigners'), who went on to defeat the *Finngaill* ('fair foreigners') the following year at Carlingford Lough.[25] Viking raiders regularly found local allies amidst the complex political situation in Ireland, where over 150 different kingdoms were subject to the authority of six regional overkings of Connaught, Ulster, Munster, Leinster, Northern Uí Néill, and Southern Uí Néill. Internecine disputes were extensive and ripe for exploitation, while Viking armies could prove useful allies in fighting off other groups of raiders.[26] For example, Mael Sechnaill, overking of the Southern Uí Néill, allied with Viking raiders but was also on the receiving end of another such alliance. In 856 he allied against a band of 'heathens' with the *Gallgoídil* ('foreign Gaels'), a group thought to have been of mixed Scandinavian and Gaelic origins in both Scotland and Ireland.[27] In 859, however, his lands were invaded by a force led by the Viking leaders Olaf and Ivar and the king of Osraige, Cerball; although Cerball and his overking Mael Sechnaill were, however, soon reconciled and fighting against Ivar and Olaf.[28] Following the death of Mael Sechnaill in 862 the raiders exploited the ensuing political instability, allying with Lorcán against a rival ruler of Meath, Conchobar, who was drowned by Olaf, his former ally.[29]

In 863 Viking raiders led by Olaf, Ivar, and Auisle plundered ancient tumuli at Knowth, Dowth, and Brú na Bóinne (Co. Meath), within the territory of the Southern Uí Néill and where the kings of North Brega were based. These Neolithic passage tombs were striking features in the landscape, but they were not, however, simply ancient burial locations, as early medieval burials dating to between the seventh and early ninth centuries have been excavated at Knowth. While it may no longer have been in use as a burial ground, it certainly contained the remains of individuals who would have been within the living memory of local communities.[30] A small settlement of late ninth- to tenth-century date developed at Knowth, with evidence for subsequent Scandinavian presence, including amber and glass beads, pegged gaming pieces made of antler and bone, a copper-alloy balance beam of a weighing scale, and two copper-alloy bells of a type found in numerous Scandinavian settlement and burial contexts in Britain and Ireland.[31] The plundering recorded in 863 can, then, be seen in a

25. Mac Airt and Mac Niocaill 1983, 310–11; Downham 2007, 13–14
26. Downham 2007, 12
27. Mac Airt and Mac Niocaill 1983, 249–51, 315; Jennings and Kruse 2009
28. Mac Airt and Mac Niocaill 1983, 316–17; Downham 2007, 17–19
29. Mac Airt and Mac Niocaill 1983, 317–19
30. Byrne *et al.* 2008, 10–15
31. Eogan 2012, 45–71, 85–156, 226–7, 244, 248–58

wider context of engagement with internecine disputes and it was not to be the last encounter for Scandinavians at this location in Ireland.

There is also evidence for the impact of Viking raiders from silver hoards. Ireland did not have a coin-using economy and silver hoards of the second half of the ninth century contain, instead, silver ingots, jewellery, and hack-silver. While it is difficult to assign a close date to such hoards, the majority have been recovered from Irish settlements, such as ringforts, crannogs, royal sites, and churches, having been acquired through various means including tribute, gift-giving, payment of ransoms, and other economic transactions.[32] The influx of silver into Irish hands caused by Viking activity became an embedded fixture in Irish politics. The clustering of hoards in the vicinity of the *longphuirt* is another indication of Viking impact, and the creation of a silver-based economy was one of the major economic innovations introduced by the Scandinavians into ninth-century Ireland.[33] A silver hoard discovered in 1841 at Coughlanstown West (Co. Kildare) contained at least eleven Carolingian coins, providing an indication of the interconnectedness of mid-ninth-century Viking activity.[34]

Viking leaders active in Ireland clearly had wider ambitions. For example, Olaf and Auisle crossed the Irish Sea and 'plundered the entire Pictish country' in 866, while in 870 Olaf and Ivar spent four months besieging Dumbarton Rock, the stronghold of the Strathclyde Britons, 'and at the end of four months they destroyed and plundered it'.[35] The site is at the confluence of the rivers Clyde and Leven, and rises to 74m above Ordnance Datum, with two summits separated by a deep cleft; this naturally defensible site, surrounded by crags and water, may have effectively been an island in the early medieval period. Excavations in the 1970s of an early medieval timber and rubble rampart on the eastern summit of the rock recovered a sword pommel bar and two lead weights, one inset with a fragment of an Irish glass bangle.[36] While the excavation report acknowledged that these items could have arrived there at any time in the ninth century or even later, it seems probable that they were associated with this recorded event, not least because the use of inset weights is a specifically late ninth-century phenomenon among Viking raiders.[37] Evidence of burning of the rampart may also have been associated with this siege.[38]

32. Sheehan 2018, 105–7
33. Sheehan 1998; 2007; 2008
34. Shearman 1872; Dolley 1961, 60–2
35. Mac Airt and Mac Niocaill 1983, 869–70; Downham 2007, 1–9, 12–23; McLeod 2014, 114–15
36. Alcock and Alcock 1990, 99, 113, 117; Lathe and Smith 2015
37. Williams 2020e
38. Alcock 1976, 111

Viking raiders took captives and either ransomed them or sold them into slavery. The most extensively documented instance of this occurred to Findan, an Irish nobleman from Leinster, who was first taken captive in 836 and then freed but was captured again in the 840s and sold on as a slave. Findan eventually arrived in Orkney, from where he escaped and travelled to the island monastery of Reichenau (now on the Swiss-German border), where his *Life* was written later in the century.[39] After the siege of Dumbarton Rock, Olaf and Ivar returned to Dublin 'with two hundred ships, bringing away with them in captivity to Ireland a great prey of Angles and Britons and Picts'.[40] These examples further demonstrate the interconnectedness of Viking activity in Britain and Ireland in the mid-ninth century. As we will see later, Ivar also joined the Great Army in England, and it is important to place the activities of the Great Army in this wider context of raiding, plunder, and attempts to exploit the local political situation. Furthermore, although the written record makes only scant reference to interactions between the raiders in Ireland and England in the ninth century, as chroniclers often lose sight of specific individuals when they leave their area of interest, assemblages of material culture associated with the Great Army also serve to connect them.

Viking armies on the Continent

Written accounts of the impact of Viking raids on Frankish territory are extensive and comparatively detailed, and much that emerges is consistent with what occurred at this time in Ireland. Viking raiders fought with and against each other, allied with Frankish rulers, made and broke their pledges, and found a myriad of ways to provision themselves through plunder, trade, and tribute. The archaeological record is, however, much thinner than that from Ireland, with hoards of metalwork providing the most important insights.

Continental chronicles provide detailed accounts of Viking activity in the mid-ninth century, especially in what is now France and the Low Countries, including the places Viking armies raided, their tactics, and the manner and extent of their involvement with local communities and regional rulers. As in Ireland, there is evidence for Scandinavian settlement on the Continent in the first half of the ninth century, with Frankish rulers seeking to use it to protect

39. Somerville and McDonald 2014, 195–8
40. Mac Airt and Mac Niocaill 1983, 869–70

their lands in Frisia. Emperor Louis the Pious received an exiled Danish king called Harald in 814 and provided him with military assistance to regain his position, but, having been exiled again, Harald accepted baptism at the behest of the Emperor in 826 in Mainz (Germany) and was granted land at Rüstringen in Frisia.[41] In 837 one of those who died defending the island of Walcheren (Netherlands), at the mouth of the River Scheldt, from Viking raiders was a certain Hemming, described as 'of the Danish race, a most Christian leader'. The raiders then 'stayed on the island for a while, levying as much tribute as they wanted'.[42] In 841, Emperor Lothar granted Walcheren 'to secure the services of Harald' who had been 'imposing many sufferings on Frisia and the other coastal regions of the Christians'. There has been debate about whether this was the same Harald dealt with by Lothar's father Louis, but either way a pattern was emerging of granting land to Danes in Frisia.[43] There is some limited archaeo-logical evidence for Scandinavian influence in Frisia at this time. For example, some of the ninety mounts with animal-style decoration recovered from near Domburg on Walcheren indicate ninth-century Scandinavian influence.[44] Alex Woolf notes that one of the terms used in the eleventh-century *Historia de Sancto Cuthberto* to refer to the Great Army is *Scaldingi*, which he suggests is a reference to the River Scheldt, implying that some of those forces making up the Great Army had been based on Walcheren.[45] Coin hoards from Frisia dating to the 830s and 840s correspond with the recorded Viking raids on Dorestad and surround-ing areas, with the *Annals of St Bertin* recording in 846 that 'Danish pirates went to Frisia, extracted as large a tribute as they wanted and then fought a battle which they won. As a result, they gained control of nearly the whole province.'[46]

In 850 a Viking leader called Roric 'laid waste Frisia and the island of Betuwe and other places in that neighbourhood'. Lothar responded by receiving him 'into his allegiance and granted him Dorestad and other counties'. It was expected that Roric would defend them from other Viking raiders and 'handle the taxes and other matters pertaining to the royal fisc'.[47] Roric, 'the nephew of Harald', appears to have retained control over land in Frisia, eventually accept-ing baptism, but periodically trying to regain power in Denmark.[48] Being

41. Nelson 1991, 51, 75; Coupland 1998, 89–90
42. Nelson 1991, 37; Coupland 1998, 87
43. Nelson 1991, 51; Coupland 1998, 90–1; Cooijmans 2020, 174–7
44. Coupland 1998, 89–92; Roxburgh *et al.* 2018
45. Woolf 2007, 72
46. Coupland 2006, 143–8; 2021; Nelson 1991, 62
47. Nelson 1991, 69; Coupland 1998, 97; Cooijmans 2020, 173, 175
48. Nelson 1991, 61; 2003, 14–15; Coupland 1998, 95–101

under Roric's control did not protect Dorestad from subsequent raids such as those in 857 when he was temporarily absent in Denmark, and 863 when raiders came along the Rhine 'sacking the emporium called Dorestad and also a fairly large villa at which the Frisians had taken refuge, and after slaying many Frisian traders and taking captive large numbers of people'.[49] In 867 Roric was expelled from Frisia, and his forces may have joined the Great Army in England, although he returned in 870 and seems to have remained in Frisia until his death c.880.[50]

Coins continued to be minted in Dorestad in the name of Lothar after Roric received it, but there was a sharp decline in output, while the poor quality of coins has been assigned to Scandinavian control of the mint.[51] It has also been argued that Scandinavians were responsible for minting imitations of Frankish coins widely found in Frisia, including gold *solidi* of Louis the Pious, which are thought to have been used as bullion. Coin hoards continued to be hidden into the 860s reflecting the ongoing disruption caused by Viking raiders.[52] Nonetheless, there are very few ninth-century finds from excavations in Dorestad that can confidently be assigned to Scandinavian influences, a rare exception being an arm-ring of twisted gold rods and an oval brooch.[53] In addition, a complete set of bone gaming pieces recovered from one of the huts near the harbour jetties, alongside tools, leather, glass and an amber bead, and a conical glass gaming piece from elsewhere in Dorestad, led Mark Hall to argue that their form 'certainly feels like it looks north to Scandinavia'.[54] There is tentative evidence of a furnished grave containing a sword, spearhead, and glass beaker that may date to the period of Roric's control but it was not recovered by archaeological investigation and little more can be said about its context.[55] The silting up of the river around the site saw a gradual mid-ninth-century decline in the economic vitality of Dorestad, which is not documented again after 863.[56]

Two Viking silver hoards found in the 1990s from Westerklief, on what was once the island of Wieringen (Netherlands), have provided strong evidence for Scandinavian activity in Frisia. The first hoard comprised six penannular arm-rings of Carolingian manufacture, a twisted arm- and neck-ring of

49. Nelson 1991, 104; Coupland 1998, 100–1
50. McLeod 2014, 168; Coupland 1998, 99–100
51. Coupland 2001, 173–5; Cooijmans 2020, 76
52. Coupland 2006, 254–5; 2016, 265; 2021, 129
53. IJssennagger-van der Pluijm 2021
54. Hall 2021, 43
55. Willemsen 2021, 107–10
56. Coupland 1988; Nelson 1991, 165, 177

Figure 1.4. The earliest of two ninth-century Viking hoards from Westerklief (National Museum of Antiquities, Leiden)

Scandinavian type, a Carolingian strap-end, three brooches set with coins of which one was a dirham and two were Sassanian issues, 17 ingots and 78 Carolingian pennies, typical of those circulating in Frisia, contained within a Badorf-ware vessel (Figure 1.4).[57] It has been dated from the coins to *c.*850.

57. Besteman 2004, 95

A second hoard of Scandinavian type found nearby, again in a Badorf-ware vessel, comprised a complete ingot, 24 pieces of hack-silver, 39 Carolingian coins, a cast silver imitation of a gold *solidus* of Louis the Pious mounted in a brooch, and 95 Islamic dirhams. It is dated to *c.*880, suggesting a long period of Scandinavian activity on the island. Wieringen would have provided a strategic location from which to control the navigation route from central Frisia across Lake Almere to Dorestad, and a well-protected base for wider raiding activities.

As was the case in Ireland, there were numerous Viking forces active on the Continent in the mid-ninth century, with multiple leaders. Sometimes separate groups came together for a short period to launch an attack, as occurred in 856 when according to the *Annals of Fontenelle* the forces of Bjørn and Sidroc combined to create 'a great deal of carnage and destruction' on the Seine. Although the latter left shortly afterwards, Bjørn was described two years later by the *Annals of St Bertin* as leader of only 'a part of the pirates based on the Seine' revealing the ongoing complexity faced by Charles the Bald, to whom Bjørn was persuaded to submit and 'swore fidelity after his own fashion'.[58] A series of events that began in 861 shows Viking raiders in conflict with each other, when a force led by Weland arrived on the Seine and 'besieged the fort built by the Northmen on the island of Oissel with those Northmen inside it too'. While Weland temporarily collaborated with Charles the Bald, receiving a substantial payment of 5000lb of silver, livestock, and corn, to desist from his raids, his forces were soon reinforced by another group. They continued to besiege those on Oissel, near Rouen, who were 'forced by starvation, filth and general misery to pay the besiegers 6000lb made up of gold and silver and to make an alliance with them'. Afterwards the raiders departed but, unable to set out for sea due to the approaching winter, they split up 'according to their brotherhoods into groups allocated to various ports, from the sea-coast right up to Paris'. The significance of these 'brotherhoods' (*sodalitates*) for the organisation of Viking armies has recently been emphasised by Raffield.[59] The involvement of Viking raiders in internal disputes was not uncommon, such as in 862 when rival groups were paid by either side in a regional dispute, led by Salomon, duke of the Bretons, and Count Robert of Anjou. Those hired by Salomon were captured on the Loire by the forces of Robert who 'slew every man in the fleet, except for a few who fled into hiding', and made an alliance with another group of raiders who had just left the Seine, 'before Salomon

---

58. Nelson 1991, 82, 86; Cooijmans 2020, 123–6; 2022, 10
59. Nelson 1991, 95–6; Coupland 1988, 104–7; Raffield 2016

could ally with them against him', which involved the exchange of hostages and a payment by Robert of 6000lb of silver.[60] This episode reveals not only the complex internecine disputes in which Viking forces became involved, but also the extent to which regional rulers were willing to make use of them while simultaneously, and, evidently quite rightly, distrusting them.

The continental sources make repeated references to Viking armies basing themselves on islands, revealing something of the communities that they established there and the activities in which they were engaged. For example, when a Viking force raiding in western Aquitaine 'landed on a certain island' in 843, perhaps Noirmoutier at the mouth of the Loire, the *Annals of St Bertin* record that they 'brought their households over from the mainland and decided to winter there in something like a permanent settlement'.[61] Similarly, a Viking army on an island in the Loire near the monastery of St Florent in the 850s is described by Abbot Adrevaldus of Fleury Abbey as erecting huts 'in a sort of village in which to keep their gangs of prisoners in irons, and to rest their bodies from their labours for a time, ready to serve on campaign'.[62] Other islands recorded as being occupied by Viking forces in contemporary sources include Biesse, opposite Nantes on the Loire (853), Oissel on the Seine (857 and 861), the Camargue on the Rhône (859), and one near Xanten on the Rhine (863), where they 'built a defence and stayed there for a while'.[63] The *Annals of St Bertin* report that Viking raiders based at Angers in 873 were besieged by the forces of Charles the Bald with whom they struck a deal concerning an island in the Loire where they 'requested to be allowed to stay until February...and to hold a market there' before departing. Many of those present then agreed to accept baptism and subsequently submitted to Charles while 'the rest would depart from his realm, never more...to return to it with evil intent'.[64] There is little archaeological evidence to correlate with these recorded activities, although some Scandinavian weapons have been recovered from along the Seine valley.[65] More recently, a collection of material—including weapons, tools, and a weight inset with Irish metalwork—from near Taillebourg on the River Charente (France) has been interpreted as deriving from a possible Viking camp, perhaps related to that recorded on the river in 865 in the *Annals*

---

60. Nelson 1991, 99; Cooijmans 2020, 172
61. Nelson 1991, 56
62. Coupland 1995, 196; Cooijmans 2020, 140
63. Nelson 1991, 75 (n.1), 82, 87–8, 90, 95; Cooijmans 2020, 146–9
64. Nelson 1991, 185
65. Périn 1990

of St Bertin.[66] Cooijmans has observed that slightly later accounts describe Viking camps using such terms as '*saepire, circumsaepire,* and *circumdare*–all signifying the act of encircling or surrounding', suggesting enclosures constructed against rivers, although archaeological evidence for this form of camp is lacking.[67]

Contemporary sources provide some further insights into how Viking raiders provisioned themselves for the lengthy campaigns on the river systems of Francia. For example, in 862, a group based at Jumièges 'decided to repair their ships and await the Spring equinox. When the ships had been repaired, the Danes made for the open sea, and split up into several flotillas which sailed off in different directions according to their various choices.'[68] In 866 a group departed an island near St-Denis and 'sailed down the Seine until they reached a place suitable for making repairs to their ships and for building new ones'.[69] A Frankish fleet was captured during a siege of a Viking camp on the island of Oissel in 858, and in 862 Carolingian ships were 'taken over by the Northmen' on the River Marne, and this may have been another, if challenging, means of provisioning Viking forces.[70] Viking forces were able to acquire gold and silver in tribute, typically paid to persuade them to leave a region or to desist from attacking churches, and also from the taking and ransoming of captives.[71] For example, in 857 'a great ransom was paid in cash' to save some of the churches in Paris from being burned. Shortly afterwards, Abbot Louis of St-Denis, a grandson of Charlemagne, and his half-brother were captured by raiders who 'demanded a very heavy fine for their ransom'; an indication of its scale is suggested by the fact that even draining dry church treasuries was insufficient and Charles the Bald had to rely on large sums being provided 'by all the bishops, abbots, counts and other powerful men' to rescue his kinsmen.[72] In 864, Rodulf, the nephew of Roric, received from Lothar II, king of Lotharingia, both cash and 'a large quantity of flour and livestock and also wine and cider...all this being termed a payment for service'.[73] Legislation issued by Charles in 864 at Pîtres reveals another means by which the Vikings were provisioned as it

---

66. Nelson 1991, 128; Dumont and Mariotti (eds.) 2013, 137, 186; Deutsch-Dumolin 2023, 174–5
67. Cooijmans 2020, 143
68. Nelson 1991, 98
69. Nelson 1991, 131
70. Nelson 1991, 98; Cooijmans 2020, 127
71. Nelson 1997, 36–8; Cooijmans 2020, 138–40
72. Nelson 1991, 85–6
73. Nelson 1991, 112; Lothar II was son of Lothar I who had previously engaged with Roric.

outlined punishments for anyone who provided them with weapons or a horse, stating that they 'shall pay with his life…as a traitor to his country and as one who sells Christianity to the heathen for its destruction'.[74]

Viking raiders attacked churches and towns, doing great damage and taking away extensive amounts of booty.[75] In 856 raiders sailed up the Seine and 'ravaged and plundered the *civitates*, monasteries, and *villae* on both banks of the river, and even some *civitates* further away'.[76] In 861 'traders who were fleeing back up the Seine by ship were chased and captured' by a Viking force who had just burned churches in Paris, and in 863 Vikings 'plundered everything they found within and around the sanctuary' of the church of St Victor in Xanten.[77] Viking forces had good intelligence about the places they raided, often turning up on the feast days of local saints, when resources would have been handily gathered together.[78] Writing early in the tenth century, Regino of Prüm observed that 'the Northmen became excited by the pillaging of a few [*civitates*] and territories and realised from the plunder available in each how much wealth they could get from all of them'.[79] Excavations in Rouen have identified evidence for extensive burning near to the cathedral which has been dated to the mid-ninth century and assigned to Viking activity, as have traces of burning at the church of St Victor in Xanten.[80] It is, however, difficult to date such events closely and the interpretations offered can only be tentative, if plausible.

The disruptions caused by the Viking raids can be partially traced through coin hoards. These typically comprise locally available coins and so probably represent the activities of local communities rather than hoarding by Viking raiders. An increase in hoarding has been noted from the 840s onwards, which is consistent with the recorded intensification of Viking attacks on the Frankish realm. For example, the hoards from Langon and St-Émilion are thought to have been associated with the recorded siege of Bordeaux in 847 and 848, and one from Orléans can be dated to the raid on the town recorded in 856, while Coupland has shown a close link between Viking raiding and the deposition of hoards in Frisia.[81] However, some cannot be directly linked with recorded

74. Coupland 1985; 2014
75. Coupland 2014
76. Nelson 1991, 82
77. Nelson 1991, 94; Cooijmans 2020, 137
78. Cooijmans 2020, 132–4
79. MacLean 2009, 168; Cooijmans 2020, 131
80. Le Maho 1994, 28–9; Borger and Oediger 1969, 74–8; Cooijmans 2020, 136–40
81. Armstrong 1998, 142; Nelson 1991, 65, 82; Coupland 2006, 249–50

raids, and although not all Viking raids would be recorded in contemporary sources, other factors are potentially relevant to the increase in hoarding. These include Frankish military activity, the raising of taxes, and expansion of the amount of coinage in circulation, while Coupland has argued that there were fewer silver hoards in Frisia from the 870s partly as a result of a decline in the amount of silver in circulation in that region.[82] Coins from elsewhere are rarely found in hoards in France, which has been seen as an indication that any currency brought into the region was driven out of circulation very quickly. It has recently been suggested by Cooijmans that the ransoms and payments of tribute to Viking forces were made in coin rather than bullion partly because the Carolingian rulers anticipated that it would soon return into circulation as the raiders used it to acquire the supplies they needed. This would also explain the rarity of Carolingian coins in later ninth-century hoards in Scandinavia.[83] The paucity of hoards of Scandinavian type, containing coins from multiple regions and hack-metal, is a striking contrast with other regions of Scandinavian activity and has been interpreted as revealing that 'the Scandinavian practice of using silver by weight seems never to have got a foothold'.[84]

The Frankish sources also provide a great deal of detail about the responses Viking raiders encountered. In particular, control over rivers and bridges was crucial to Frankish attempts to defend their lands (Figure 1.5). For example, the forces of Lothar and Charles the Bald stopped Viking raiders on the Seine in 852 by blockading it from either bank of the river.[85] Arriving in Senlis (Oise) in 862, Charles the Bald planned to prevent Viking raiders from plunder by placing his forces along the banks of the rivers Oise, Marne, and Seine. However, having received news of another group on its way to Meaux (Seine-et-Marne), Charles and his forces set off in that direction but were unable to catch up with them 'because the bridges had been destroyed' and so he 'rebuilt the bridge across to the island by Trilbardou, thereby cutting the Northmen's access to the way down the river. He also assigned squadrons to guard both banks of the Marne.' This proved sufficient to cause this group to depart, being required to provide hostages and return their Frankish captives.[86] Charles moved to Pîtres later in the year, where he ordered his leading followers to assemble 'with many workmen and carts' to build bridges on the Seine, although the extent of the

82. Armstrong 1998, 148–57; Coupland 2006, 253–4, 261–2
83. Cooijmans 2020, 181
84. Blackburn 2009, 65
85. Nelson 1991, 75
86. Nelson 1991, 98; probably Isles-lès-Villenoy in the River Marne.

Figure 1.5. The western part of the Frankish Empire in the ninth century. The dotted line indicates the boundary between the kingdoms of Charles the Bald and Lothar agreed in 843

bridge-building that followed may have been limited. Work commenced on a bridge at Pont-de-l'Arche, where the Seine met the Eure and the Andelle, which seems to have been the most important piece of bridge construction at this time.[87] In 864, Charles issued the Edict of Pîtres, which, among many other things, legislated that those who could acquire a horse should join the fight against the Viking raiders, and those who could not should contribute work on 'fortifications, bridges and swamp crossings'.[88] The following year, when Charles arrived at Pîtres again to deal with another Viking threat, he ordered that bridges over the Oise and the Marne should be repaired, as the local people had not been able to repair them due to Viking attacks.[89]

It may have been the success of Charles the Bald in dealing with Viking armies in Francia that led to them turning their attention to England. In 866 he paid off a fleet stationed on the Seine. According to the *Annals of St Bertin* they repaired their ships and built new ones, and then dispersed, some going to the Ijssel district of Frisia.[90] It has been suggested, however, that others sailed to East Anglia, joining the Great Army in time for the attack on York.[91] Indeed McLeod suggests that the Frisian group may also have sailed for England after they were unsuccessful in making an alliance with Lothar II in order to gain land.[92]

Viking armies in England in the 840s and 850s

There are a few accounts of Viking raids on England in the mid-ninth century, suggesting periodic activity that had begun to intensify. In 840 there were recorded raids on Wessex. In one encounter a force led by Ealdorman Wulfheard was victorious against a raid comprising thirty-three ships, but shortly afterwards Ealdorman Æthelhelm was killed in a defeat against a 'Danish army' at Portland (Dorset). Viking raids occurred in Kent, East Anglia, and Lindsey in 841, and two years later King Æthelwulf of Wessex was defeated in battle at Carhampton (Dorset) 'against the crews of 35 ships'. In 845 a West Saxon force led by two ealdormen and a bishop was victorious against a raiding party at the mouth of the River Parret (Somerset).[93] Around 850 the food rents from an estate at Brabourne (Kent) were granted by one Ealburh to St Augustine's,

87. Coupland 1991
88. Coupland 2004
89. Nelson 1991, 127
90. Nelson 1991, 131
91. McLeod 2014, 132–3; Sawyer 1998, 92
92. McLeod 2014, 133
93. Whitelock 1961, 42

Canterbury in return for prayers, allowing for provision for non-payment for up to three years 'because of heathen attacks', among other factors. This suggests a recognition of the risks of Viking raids causing local disruption.[94] In 851 there was intensified Viking activity, with an encounter between the men of Devon and a Viking army at *Wicganbeorg*, an unidentified location. There followed raids on both London and Canterbury, when '350 ships came into the mouth of the Thames', after which the Mercians were put to flight, but the West Saxons, under King Æthelwulf were victorious. A force from Kent also engaged in a naval encounter off Sandwich. This was also the year in which 'for the first time, heathen men stayed through the winter on Thanet' in Kent.[95]

A battle between the people of Kent and Surrey and a 'heathen army' on Thanet is recorded in 853, which saw 'many men on both sides…killed and drowned there' and the deaths of two ealdormen. The overwintering of an army at Sheppey is recorded in 855.[96] While the events of the mid-ninth century are largely coastal or restricted to the estuaries of major rivers, a raid on Winchester (Hampshire) is recorded in 860, although the raiders were put to flight by West Saxon forces from Hampshire and Berkshire. An army camped on Thanet again in 864, but despite making peace with the people of Kent in return for a payment, 'the army stole away inland and ravaged all eastern Kent'.[97]

These accounts provide little sense that the impact of Viking raids on England was on anything like the scale that it was in Ireland and on the Continent at this time. By the mid-ninth century we have documented examples of armies overwintering, significantly in locations described as 'islands', but in estuarine or coastal locations. Raiding armies were not penetrating deep inland; nor were they apparently staying in England over multiple years. Most importantly, there is no archaeological evidence that we can clearly associate with any of these recorded events, which also suggests they were not of the scale and did not have the impact that we will encounter in the 870s.

Scandinavia on the eve of the arrival of the *micel here*

Changes in southern Scandinavia in the ninth century provide the backdrop for Viking expansion and the quest for overseas wealth out of which the Great Army emerged.[98] From the late eighth century there are occasional references

94. Downham 2017, 11
95. Whitelock 1961, 43
96. Whitelock 1961, 43
97. Whitelock 1961, 45
98. McLeod 2014, 158–62; Horne 2022, 210–21

in continental sources to individuals described as kings, who apparently controlled large territories.[99] The foundation of international trading ports, or *emporia*, was intrinsically linked to the growth of royal power and the establishment of the early Scandinavian states. These trading sites must also have served as communications hubs that conveyed news about opportunities for wealth abroad.[100] The major centres were at Hedeby (now northern Germany), Ribe (Denmark), Birka (Sweden), and Kaupang (Norway), which have all seen extensive campaigns of excavation. All had been established in at least the early to mid-eighth century, and by the mid-ninth century were thriving trading centres, in receipt of goods from Scandinavia and further afield. It was once thought that Scandinavia was largely non-urban, but with excavations of recent decades it is unquestionable that there were towns in the ninth century, albeit not of the scale of those of later centuries.

Ribe was the first to emerge, a substantial *emporium* from the early eighth century, and closely linked to maritime trade, located on a navigable river at one of the few good natural harbour sites on the North Sea coast of Denmark. Excavations have revealed a market street, laid out with a series of plots, and earlier excavations suggested that initially Ribe hosted a periodic market, and reconstruction illustrations depicted temporary tent-like structures. However, the most recent excavations, in 2016–18, have confirmed that there were substantial post-and-wattle buildings and permanent settlement from the early 700s.[101] Ribe was part of a network that included Dorestad and Domburg in the Low Countries and Quentovic in Northern France, as well as London, *Hamwic* (Southampton), and Ipswich in England. Craftworking was undertaken from the outset, by both men and women, and included iron smithing, textile production, bone- and antler-working, and glass bead-making, and the emergence of trade was facilitated by the minting of silver sceattas. By the ninth century some crafts disappeared, including bead-making, but clusters of non-ferrous metalworking emerge, with a range of brooches cast in adjacent workshops. These activities continued uninterrupted well into the Viking Age, until at least 900. There were imported lava querns, pottery from the Rhineland, whetstones and reindeer antler from Norway. From the early ninth century Ribe was surrounded by a ditched enclosure, although this is not thought to have had defensive capacity until the tenth century. Nearly fifty

---

99. Cooijmans 2020, 22–31
100. Sindbæk 2008, 155
101. Sindbæk 2022, 435–63

burials have been excavated around the edge of the settlement, which were mainly cremations.[102]

Hedeby developed thanks to its commanding position at the foot of the Jutland peninsula. The earliest activity dates to the eighth century, when the first jetties were built and workshops came into use, but its rise is marked by the historical account of the militarisation of the Danish border by Godfred, a king of the Danes, and the relocation c.808 of merchants and possibly craft-workers from the Slavic trading settlement of *Reric* (thought to be near Groß Strömkendorf, Germany).[103] During the ninth century streets were laid out in Hedeby at right angles, parallel to a stream, defining fenced building plots of regular size. The settlement was enclosed by a semi-circular rampart and defended by a small fort in the tenth century, but before this there may only have been an enclosure ditch, while the harbour was protected by a semi-circular arrangement of piles.[104] There were over 10,000 graves in Hedeby, of which c.1350 have been excavated; these were spread across at least six cemeteries and included both cremation and inhumation graves, and while grave goods are rare they became more frequent from the ninth century. It has been estimated that the settlement had a population of c.1500, including both traders and craftworkers.[105] Imported materials supported a range of industries: iron-working with Swedish ore; the dressing of lava querns; bronze jewellery production; antler-, bone-, leather- and woodworking; and the manufacture of glass and amber beads. From the early ninth century Hedeby also minted its own sceattas.[106]

The earliest trading centre in Sweden lay at Birka, situated on the island of Björkö in Lake Mälaren, near modern Stockholm. On the neighbouring island of Adelsö, separated from Björkö by a narrow strait, stand the remains of a royal estate centre. It is tempting to see this as the power base from which Birka was controlled and taxed, at a distance. Birka was fortified, on land and water, from its foundation in the mid-eighth century. It was enclosed by a semi-circular rampart from the ninth century, which at its northern end extended out into the harbour in Lake Mälaren as a series of piles. Like Ribe, Birka appears to have been permanently occupied from the start. At Birka there are six separate but at least partly contemporaneous cemeteries, with the majority

---

102. Feveile 2008, 128–9
103. Roesdahl 2008, 655; Cooijmans 2020, 23
104. Hilberg 2009; Kalmring 2011
105. Eisenschmidt 2011
106. Andersson 2003; Armbruster 2004; Andersson Strand 2011; Hilberg 2011; Merkel 2016

of burials under mounds. In the main one at Hemlanden, north-east of the settlement area, there are at least 1600 graves.[107]

The earliest Norwegian *emporium* was at Kaupang (literally, 'market-place'), on the west side of the Oslo fjord. Excavations have revealed that the laying-out of individual plots was preceded by a very short-lived phase of itinerant craft production. Permanent buildings, for year-round use, were then constructed on each of the plots, probably in the early ninth century.[108] Kaupang had wide-ranging trading connections, with pottery and glass drinking vessels imported from the Rhineland. Its inhabitants were also melting down precious metals and the excavated finds include ingot moulds, and pieces of gold and silver jewellery which may have derived from raiding activity.[109] There are at least eight cemeteries, including both inhumation and cremation burials, many under mounds, and over sixty high-status boat burials. It has been suggested that the cremation graves reflect the local burial rite, but that the boat burials may indicate Danish merchants.[110] Dendrochronological dating of the jetty proves that it was erected after 803.[111] It is therefore argued that, like Hedeby, Kaupang may have been founded by Godfred in the early ninth century, as southern Norway was under the control of Danish kings at this time.

If these settlements can be described as towns, then they would have been quite small by medieval standards, with perhaps 500–1500 inhabitants. Most of the Scandinavian population still lived in the countryside in farming settlements, although there were also high-status residences, such as Tissø, on western Sjælland in Denmark. Here an exceptional lakeside settlement has been discovered, 7km from the sea and accessible via river.[112] Tissø was not an agricultural estate—there are few stalls for cattle. Instead, it was sustained by tribute, trade, and manufacture, and supplied with food by dependent farms in the area, and may have been an aristocratic or even royal residence. By the ninth century there was a substantial bow-sided timber hall set within an enclosure, where weapons and riding gear, including spurs, bridles, and a large number of arrowheads and sword mounts, are concentrated. Frankish and Carolingian drinking vessels were also found around the central hall. Miniature amulets,

107. Gräslund 1980; Ambrosiani 2008
108. Skre 2007; (ed.) 2008; Pilø 2007
109. Hougen 1969; Blindheim 1976; Hårdh 2008; 2011b; Kilger 2008a; 2008b; Gaut 2011; Pedersen 2008; 2016
110. Skre 2007, 39; Stylegar 2007, 65–101
111. Skre 2007, 220–2; Bonde 2007, 280
112. Jørgensen 2008

including Thor's hammers and tiny lances, recovered from this part of the site may indicate a small enclosed cultic area. Tissø means 'Týr's Island' and was named after the war god Týr; some fifty swords, axes, and lances were found on the lake bottom. There was also a craft and market area with workshops and small booths, where metalworking took place, and other craftworkers made combs, and glass and amber beads. Over 100 coins have been found at Tissø, including eighth-century Scandinavian and Frankish coins, although most are later Islamic issues; their distribution suggests that trading was taking place. A mid-ninth-century lead seal bears the name of Theodosius, head of the Byzantine armoury, and is identical to examples from Ribe and Hedeby; it has been suggested that Theodosius may have been buying iron or recruiting mercenaries from Scandinavia, showing another dimension of the wider links of Scandinavia.[113]

It is also apparent that from the eighth century Scandinavia was already integrated within long distance trading networks across the North and Baltic Sea, and with connections to Eastern trading routes. Whilst such early trading sites may not have been on the scale of the late ninth-century camps, they contained the seeds of later urban development. Whilst only around 1–2% of the Scandinavian population lived in a town during the Viking Age, the layout of the towns reflected organisation and rights to land and should, as Dagfinn Skre argues, 'be read as a manifestation of the ideas the founders had about what an urban community was and how it should function'.[114] There was a shared template in terms of plots, streets, refuse areas, and a focus on access to water, which Skre believes may have influenced the later layouts of Dublin and York. In addition, craft production became more uniform in the towns, marking a transition from making things on demand for known customers, to catering for a wider more commercial market. Towns led the movement for paying for goods in silver rather than other forms of exchange, and the camps of the Great Army also played a part, as we will see in this book, in transforming economic activities.

Conclusions

The written accounts provide important insights into the nature of the intensive Viking activity in Ireland and on the Continent in the mid-ninth century,

---

113. Nelson 1991, 44
114. Skre 2008, 88

and how the armies kept themselves on campaign for so long, including their interactions with local rulers and communities. In contrast, archaeological evidence for Viking activity in these regions is comparatively slender, in part because amateur metal-detecting, which has transformed our picture in England, is illegal in both the Republic of Ireland and France. Nonetheless, the material culture recovered from archaeological excavations and hoards discovered by chance provides a precursor of what we find associated with the Great Army in England, including hack-silver comprising both fragments of ingots, arm- and neck-rings, Islamic dirhams, and Carolingian metalwork. Similarly, Viking burials, mainly from Ireland, yield examples of weaponry that we find on the camps. We have also seen that Viking armies in Ireland and on the Continent were developing a pattern of behaviour, including choosing strategic island locations for their camps, and undertaking trade and craftworking, that later became characteristic of the Great Army in England. From the late 860s there was a sharp decline in the number of recorded raids on the Continent. Whereas the *Annals of St Bertin* record almost fifty Viking raids on Frankish territory in the 850s, in the 860s they refer to fewer than thirty, and by the 870s this had plummeted to fewer than five, before returning to double figures in the 880s.[115] Those warriors who were to make up the Great Army were turning their attention to England, where they would join up with raiders who had been in Ireland in recent years.

---

115. McLeod 2014, 168; Cooijmans 2020, 124, 135, fig. VI.1

2

The Great Army on the move

This chapter outlines the movements of the Great Army around the English landscape between 865 and 880. The places where the Army spent the winter are recorded in the *Anglo-Saxon Chronicle* and Asser's *Life of King Alfred*, and this broadly contemporary evidence provides a framework for its activities. However, these sources do not identify the precise locations of the camps, nor do they have much to say about the activities that may have taken place there, how the Army was provisioned, or its impact on the wider landscape, while the routeways taken by the Army are largely unrecorded. Archaeological evidence, much of it only recovered in recent years, both nuances and considerably expands the insights from the written sources (Figure 2.1). It has much to reveal about the regions affected by the Army's activities, many beyond the focus of the written sources, the strategic positions it occupied, the responses of local communities to the threat it posed, and the wealth that the Army had accumulated. The evidence includes metal-detected assemblages, excavated defences, and burials. The burials have provided important insights into the ritual practices of the Great Army, the construction of identity through funerary practices, and aspects of its material culture. There have also been attempts to track the movements of the Army through hoards of metalwork deposited during the 860s and 870s. There is a notable increase in hoarding in this period, some presumably hidden to safeguard wealth from the Army, but those that include imported coins, ingots, or hack-silver were probably deposited by members of the Army.[1] The evidence recovered and reported on in recent years from the documented camp of 872–3 at Torksey, and another undocumented camp at Aldwark, have transformed our understanding of the nature and extent of the Army's camps. They have also unlocked the potential of a more extensive body of archaeological evidence for the impact

---

1. Blunt and Dolley 1959; Pagan 1965; 1966; Brooks and Graham-Campbell 1986; Williams 2020f, 36–7

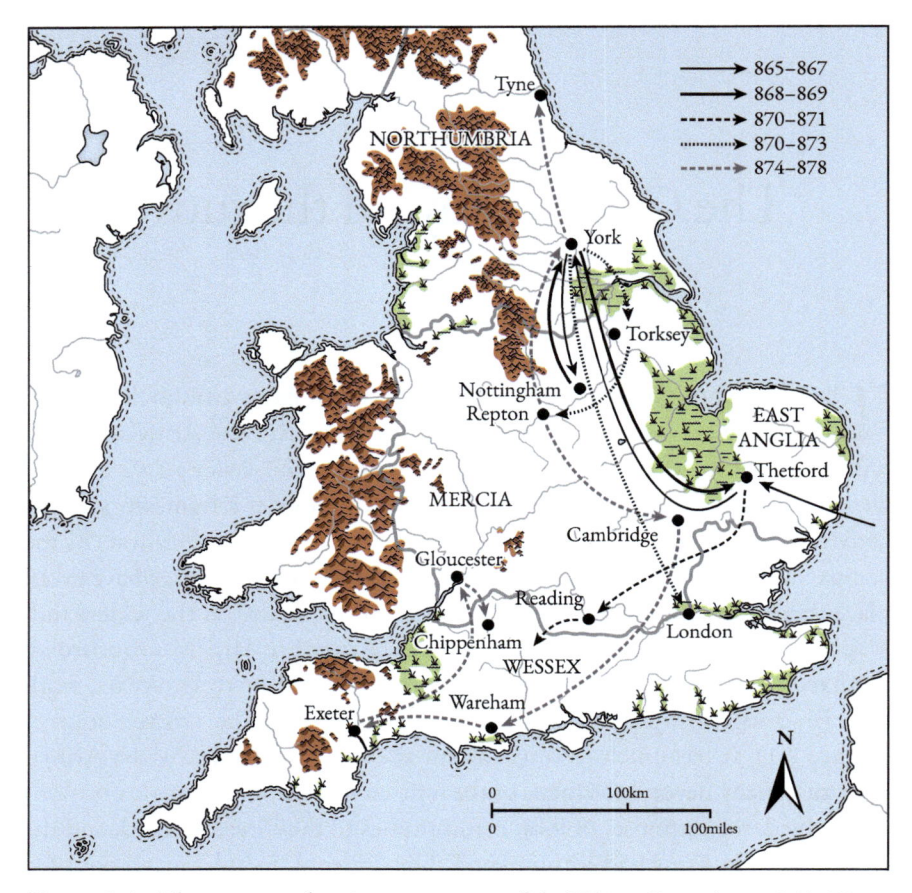

Figure 2.1. The camps and major movements of the Viking Great Army, 865–78

of this force on the wider landscape, as they have helped to identify an archaeological 'signature' for the Army, which will form the basis for the new insights to follow later in the book.

The following overview is structured broadly chronologically around the places at which the Army is recorded as overwintering, which are consistently shown to be key locations in the regional transport network. As Williams has recently observed, while 'winter camp' is a reasonable enough translation of the term *wintersetl* from the *Anglo-Saxon Chronicle* it may obscure the likelihood that the camps were occupied from one winter until the next.[2]

---

2. Williams 2023, 12

865–6 East Anglia

The *Anglo-Saxon Chronicle* records that in late 865 'a great heathen army [*mycel hæþen here*] came into England and took up winter quarters in East Anglia; and there they were supplied with horses, and the East Angles made peace with them'.[3] This heralded a fifteen-year period that transformed England. The origins of this Army are not specified by the *Chronicle*, and the claim by Asser that it had come from the Danube is probably a confusion of *Dania* with *Dacia*.[4] However, the Great Army is likely to have seen disparate forces come together from the wide arena of Viking activity at this time, including Scandinavia, Ireland, and Francia.[5] As we saw in Chapter 1 it seems likely that some of the Army arrived from Frisia, where there is evidence for a stronghold on the former island of Walcheren. A tradition recorded in the *Historia de Sancto Cuthberto* claims that the attack on York in 866 was led by Ubba, 'duke of the Frisians'.[6] Whilst we do not know where the Army first made landfall in East Anglia, a fleet sailing due west from Walcheren and the Scheldt estuary would reach the Essex coast and it is entirely plausible that its ships would head for one of the wide estuaries which would take them quickly inland, notably the Stour and the Orwell. The Orwell in particular would have provided well-charted waters as it would take them directly to the well-known trading site (*wic*) at Ipswich, which had Frisian connections. East Anglia more broadly had strong connections with Frisia in the ninth century; Rosie Weetch has drawn attention to similarities in ansate brooch styles of this date in the two regions, suggesting 'the two-way nature of maritime contact in this period'.[7] Ipswich had been under the control of King Edmund of East Anglia since 855 and the *Anglo-Saxon Chronicle* records no battle for control but, on the contrary, that the Army made peace and immediately overwintered, so must have negotiated a food supply.[8] Maybe the supply of horses was part of the deal intended to encourage the land forces to leave as soon as conditions for overland travel improved in the spring, whilst the supporting fleet continued up the coast to the Humber estuary.

3. Whitelock 1961, 45
4. Keynes and Lapidge 1983, 74; Downham 2007, 64
5. McLeod 2014, 109–71
6. Johnson South 2002, 50–1; McLeod 2014, 133–41; Williams 2020i, 93
7. Weetch 2014, 258–9; Pestell 2017
8. McLeod 2014, 61–3

866–7 York

The *Chronicle* records that in 866 the Army headed to Northumbria, travelling 'across the Humber estuary to the city of York', the first of annual movements between the various English kingdoms. Here they encountered 'great civil strife going on in that people', with Osberht having been deposed in favour of Ælla, a king 'with no hereditary right'.[9] The internecine dispute taking place in Northumbria delayed a military response; when it came, almost five months later, it resulted in an 'immense slaughter' of the Northumbrians, with both of their kings killed. The survivors made peace with the raiders, a pattern that we find most years, although what such 'peace' may have entailed is rarely recorded. Later chronicles record that following the deaths of Osberht and Ælla, a certain Egbert became king and reigned for six years 'in subjection to the Danes'. It is not certain that he was based in York, with Symeon of Durham recording that he ruled only 'beyond the Tyne', but nonetheless this suggests that the Army kept some sort of control in Northumbria through a local ruler.[10]

Whilst there is no direct archaeological evidence for the Viking takeover of York, there are some indications of disruption that can be linked to the events of this period. For example, substantial hoards of stycas, both in York and more widely in Northumbria, once seen as reflecting the civil war within Northumbria in the 860s, may in some cases have been responses to the arrival of the Great Army.[11] In particular, coins found *c.*1760 on Coney Street in York, included not only stycas, but '100 silver Saxon coins' and Carolingian silver pennies, and while once seen as two separate hoards, more recently they have been interpreted as part of the same hoard, probably deposited by members of the Great Army who had previously been on the Continent.[12] It may also have been the Viking attack that saw an elaborate, but carefully dismantled, Anglian helmet buried close to what would soon become the street of Coppergate.[13] The *wic* site at Fishergate seems already to have been in decline before the Army arrived and it was certainly abandoned by the late ninth century. None of the ubiquitous late ninth-century pottery known as York ware has been found at Fishergate but there is plausible evidence for the presence of the Great Army in

9. Whitelock 1961, 76
10. Giles 1849, 190; Whitelock 1979, 309
11. Pirie 2000
12. Williams 2020j, 104–6
13. Hall *et al.* 2014, 707

a terminal from a penannular brooch and a silver penny of Æthelberht of Wessex, the latest coin from the site.[14] At Coppergate, the famous house and workshop plots were not laid out until at least *c*.900, but there is some late ninth-century activity including a scatter of haphazard burials, one of which is of a male aged 36–45 who was dumped unceremoniously in a pit, and could have been a victim of the Great Army.[15] A styca of Eanred (*c*.810–40/41) and sherds of Ipswich ware pottery also suggest some activity, but it is impossible to say if they pre- or post-date 866, although two oblate-spheroid weights of types found in Scandinavia must post-date the arrival of the Great Army and there are two lead inset weights in later deposits.[16] Another ninth-century lead weight, inset with a cut fragment of Anglo-Saxon enamel, must also be one of the earliest Viking finds from within the city. It was found in a much later demolition layer at Clementhorpe nunnery, on the south bank of the River Ouse, suggesting activity linked to the Great Army (Figure 2.2). A fragmentary styca of Osberht (862–6) and a silver penny of Æthelwulf of Wessex, *c*.839–58 were found on the same site, where it has been suggested there was an Anglo-Saxon church.[17]

Figure 2.2. Re-used Anglo-Saxon enamel in an inset weight, recovered during excavations at Clementhorpe, York (YAT)

867–8 Nottingham

In 867–8 the Army overwintered at Nottingham, a strategically important place in Mercia, on a major north–south routeway, described as the *via versus Eboracum* in Domesday Book. King Burgred sought assistance from Æthelred I of Wessex and his younger brother Alfred. The Army was besieged but,

14. Rogers 1993, 1358, no. 5333; Abramson 2018, 103, 150
15. Hall *et al.* 2014
16. Mainman and Rogers 2000, 2561–4
17. Brinklow 1986

according to Asser, 'protected by the defences of the stronghold, refused to give battle, and since the Christians were unable to breach the wall' peace was made.[18]

The western edge of medieval Nottingham rises some 30m above the water meadows of the rivers Trent and Leen, and the east of the town is flanked by a stream, the Beck.[19] Excavations between 1969 and 1980, which have never been fully published, revealed several early medieval ditches cut into the underlying Bunter Sandstone. An enclosure has been reconstructed from excavated sections of three ditches, one of which was shown to be c.5m wide and up to 1.5m deep; this has been dated broadly to between the seventh and ninth centuries, based on pottery from the ditches. Sherds of a single Ipswich-ware pitcher of the early to mid-ninth century, typically found on high-status sites, provide the only indication of the nature of activity within the enclosure.[20] However, at just 2ha the enclosure is far too small to have been the documented fortification that defended the Great Army, and it is overlooked from the west so is not particularly defensible. A second enclosure of c.13.75ha has been reconstructed from a series of excavated flat-bottomed ditches, with a profile of c.45 degrees, and an internal bank, which can be dated only broadly to the ninth century.[21] Even if this enclosure was utilised by the Great Army, we probably need to look further afield for the full extent of the camp of 867–8. Around 200m north-east of the site of this enclosure 'two skulls and other human remains' were found in 1851 with weapons, including a ninth-century spearhead and two swords, although the latter are types usually thought to be of later date.[22] Recent excavations nearby have revealed parallel ditches, aligned north-west to south-east and roughly 16m apart, which contained hammerscale suggesting industrial activity, although this could not be closely dated.[23]

869–70 Thetford

In late 868 the Army returned to York and spent a year there, although the *Anglo-Saxon Chronicle* provides no further details. Then, in late 869 the Army 'rode across Mercia into East Anglia', spending the winter at Thetford

18. Whitelock 1961, 46; Keynes and Lapidge 1983, 77
19. Haslam 1987, 47–8; Hadley and Richards 2023, 89–91
20. Davies *et al.* 2019, 57, 61
21. Hall 1989, 189–92
22. Anon. 1851, 424
23. Davies *et al.* 2019, 62

(Norfolk), at a fording point over the rivers Thet and Little Ouse, where they were crossed by the Icknield Way.[24] A battle followed, with later sources naming the leaders of the Army as Ivar and Ubba. King Edmund of East Anglia was killed, although neither the *Chronicle* nor Asser explicitly state how he died.[25] Later traditions elaborate on the death of Edmund, who is described as meeting a particularly gruesome fate, tied to a tree, tortured and beheaded.[26]

The church of St Peter, situated on the north banks of the River Thet in a curvilinear enclosure, has been identified as a pre-existing minster, while the distribution of the coins of King Edmund in the vicinity has suggested that they were minted at Thetford, which was effectively the 'capital' of East Anglia by the mid-ninth century; these factors may account for the decision of the Army to base itself there.[27] After his death the names of two otherwise unknown kings, Æthelred and Oswald, appear on coins that have similarities with those of Edmund, even minted by three of his moneyers, while the coins of Æthelred used some of the designs of Edmund's coins, suggesting continuity of minting at Thetford. The poor control over literacy indicates Scandinavian influence, as does the minting of coins featuring a temple based on Carolingian issues from Italy, perhaps brought through Frisia where such coins were common. This suggests that Edmund was succeeded by two kings of local origins, perhaps appointed by the Great Army to rule in East Anglia, in a move that replicates what they had done previously in Northumbria.[28]

There have been numerous excavations within the tenth- and eleventh-century town of Thetford, an area of *c.*60ha surrounded by a ditch, but few potential indications of late ninth-century activity have emerged. Two burials found just outside the enclosure ditch may be of this date. One was accompanied by an Anglo-Saxon sword of uncertain type but deliberately bent as a possible act of ritual destruction; the other was accompanied by a fragmentary and undatable socketed spearhead and a knife, which was subsequently lost. A few unfurnished burials nearby may have been associated with them.[29] Indications of Scandinavian activity from Thetford include a Borre-style brooch, a trefoil brooch, four brooches of continental type, a lead Thor's hammer, possibly a model for use during the casting process, and fragments of steatite, from either

24. Whitelock 1961, 46; Hadley and Richards 2023, 91–2
25. Whitelock 1961, 46; Keynes and Lapidge 1983, 77–8
26. Winterbottom 1972, 65–87
27. Andrews and Penn 1999, 39–40; Blair 2018, 277; Porter 2021, 344–5
28. Blackburn 2001, 127; 2005, 23–5; 2009, 51–2; Williams 2014, 23; Porter 2021, 42–9, 345–6
29. Rogerson and Dallas 1984, 53, 105–6

Norway or Shetland, but these cannot be closely dated. However, some of the coins recovered are unusual finds, outside of their areas of normal circulation, and may have arrived in Thetford through Great Army agency, including five Northumbrian stycas, a mid-ninth-century denier of Lothar I minted in Dorestad, and two deniers of Charles the Bald.[30]

Just 6km north-west of Thetford, at Santon Downham, two furnished burials were excavated close to the church and the River Ouse. The surviving grave goods include an Anglo-Saxon sword and a pair of Scandinavian oval brooches, suggesting the burial of a male and female. Around 11km east of Thetford another furnished grave was excavated in a ditch at Middle Harling. The grave goods included four knives, a whetstone, a copper-alloy ear-scoop and a prick spur; the individual appears to have been buried clothed and wearing a belt as there was a copper-alloy buckle with iron plate on the left leg and an iron buckle near the left knee.[31] A hoard of three West Saxon and Mercian coins of the 'Lunettes' type from Carlton (South Cambridgeshire) has also been associated with Viking disruption in this region.[32]

870–1 Reading

The winter of 870–1 was spent in Wessex, at the royal estate of Reading (Berkshire). With the West Saxon focus of Asser and the *Chronicle* we have much more detail about what ensued in this year than for any other. Asser records that some of the Army began to build a rampart (*vallum*) between the rivers Thames and Kennet, while 'two of their earls, with a great part of the force, rode out for plunder'.[33] While probably a common practice, this is the first clear account of how the Army provisioned itself, perhaps recorded because it ended badly as the force encountered the army of Ealdorman Æthelwulf, at Englefield (Berkshire). Æthelred and Alfred brought reinforcements to Reading, and in the ensuing battle there was 'great slaughter' on both sides and Ealdorman Æthelwulf was killed, but the Great Army prevailed.[34] Another battle took place four days later at Ashdown (Berkshire), thought to have occurred near

---

30. Rogerson and Dallas 1984, 58, 68; Andrews and Penn 1999, 38; Wallis 2005, 38–40, 115; Atkins and Connor 2010, 40–1, 117; EMC 1984.0022, 2000.0091
31. Rogerson 1995; Graham-Campbell 2001, 110–12; Pestell 2019, 34–7
32. MacKay 2018; CAM-D6710C
33. Keynes and Lapidge 1983, 78
34. Whitelock 1961, 46

Kingstanding Hill in the Berkshire Downs, close to the Icknield Way. According to the *Chronicle* the Great Army was in two divisions: one led by the kings Bagsecg and Healfdene, and the other by the earls (*jarls*). Bagsecg was killed along with five of the *jarls*—Sidroc the Old, Sidroc the Younger, Osbearn, Fræna, and Harold. Numerous battles occurred over the coming months, with the Great Army mainly victorious, although at least another four *jarls* were lost. In this same year, Æthelred died and was succeeded as king of Wessex by Alfred, who would have started his reign alert to the threat posed by the Great Army, which had recently been reinforced by 'a great summer army' from overseas.[35]

Archaeological evidence for the Reading camp is largely limited to three burials and a hoard.[36] A burial discovered in 1831 in water meadows by the Thames was accompanied by a sword, which was apparently bent

Figure 2.3. Sword with decorated hilt, found in Reading in 1831 (Akerman 1867)

into the ribs of a complete horse skeleton (Figure 2.3). The sword is unfortunately now lost, but a surviving drawing shows 'gripping-beast' ornament on the hilt and it has been dated to the early Viking Age, *c.*800.[37] In 1966, *c.*300m north of the present bank of the Thames, at Playhatch, Sonning (Berkshire), gravel extraction recovered human bones along with a sword, a ringed pin, an iron knife, six arrowheads, and a piece of iron strip with a rivet, of unknown purpose. Examination of the bones indicated that they were from two adult males.[38] A group of coins was found in 1839 in a stone coffin to the south of St Mary's

35. Whitelock 1961, 47; Keynes and Lapidge 1983, 78–80
36. Hadley and Richards 2023, 86–7
37. Akerman 1867, 460–3; East 1986; Graham-Campbell 2001, 115
38. Evison 1969

church in Reading, and while our record is partial, the eleven known coins comprise seven of Burgred of Mercia, one of Edmund of East Anglia, and two of Æthelberht (860–5) and one of Æthelred I of Wessex. Their likely date of deposition is consistent with the Great Army's overwintering.[39]

It has been proposed that the most likely site for the Viking camp would have been on a gravel ridge, $c.0.5$km east of St Mary's, overlooking the confluence of the Thames and the Kennet (Figure 2.4). This prominent position was chosen as the site of an abbey built for Henry I in the early twelfth century, and Grenville Astill suggested that the west wall of the monastic precinct may have followed the line of the camp's defences.[40] This promontory location, overlooking a major waterway, is a familiar one for Great Army camps. The water meadows where the Viking burial was found is known as the *Vastern*, an Old English word meaning stronghold, reinforcing the likelihood of there being an early medieval defensive location.

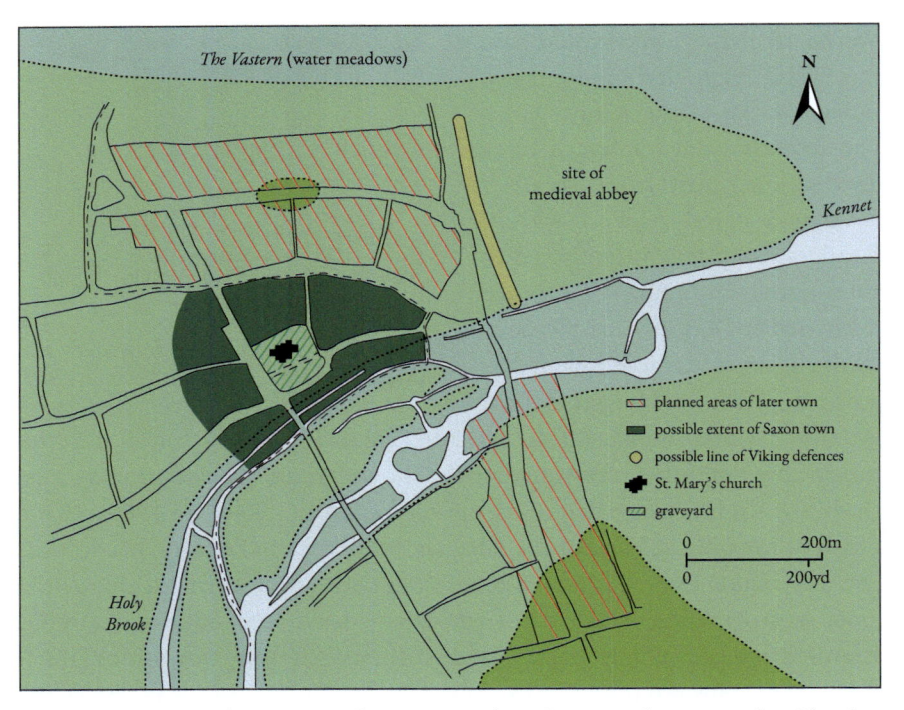

Figure 2.4. The Viking camp of 870–1 may have been on the peninsula of land at Reading which became the site of the medieval abbey, with the Anglo-Saxon town to the west

39. Sherlock 1956, 395–6; Graham-Campbell 2004, 38
40. Astill 1984, 30–1

871–2 London

In late 871 the Army returned to Mercia and took up winter quarters in London, where peace was made.[41] How this was facilitated is illuminated by a charter of 872 in which the Bishop of Worcester agreed to lease land to a king's thegn because of 'an immense tribute' paid from Mercian lords 'when the pagans had made a base at London'.[42] In our recent work we have pieced together evidence from London to suggest that the Army overwintered on Thorney Island, a small gravel island on which Westminster Abbey and the Houses of Parliament now sit (Figure 2.5).[43] While Westminster Abbey was not founded until the tenth century, there is a written tradition of an earlier

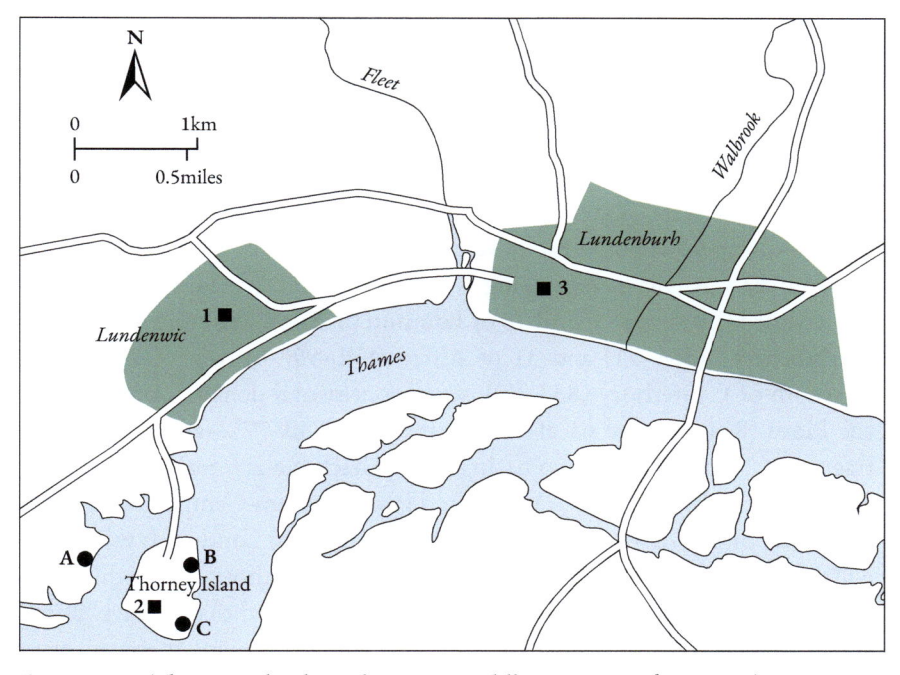

Figure 2.5. Thorney Island in relation to Middle Saxon *Lundenwic* and Later Saxon *Lundenburh*. 1. Royal Opera House site; 2. Westminster Abbey; 3. St. Paul's Cathedral; A. find spot of a possible gaming piece; B. likely site of Westminster Bridge hoard; C. find spot of Westminster sword

41. Whitelock 1961, 47
42. Whitelock 1979, 564; Blackburn 2007, 57–9
43. Hadley and Richards 2021, 175; 2023, 87–9

church, and archaeological evidence for eighth- and ninth-century activity.[44] The island was surrounded by marshy alluvium, through which two branches of the River Tyburn passed before joining the Thames.[45] Discoveries that may have been associated with Great Army activity include a hoard found *c.*1895 near Westminster Bridge which contained at least seven coins of Burgred and has been dated to after 871.[46] An eighth-century Insular drinking-horn mount recovered from the foreshore on the opposite banks of the Thames is of a type found in some Viking-age graves in Norway.[47] During excavations for a new boiler-house for the Houses of Parliament in 1948, a sword was found at what would have been the southern end of Thorney Island; two horse skulls and limb bones were found nearby, and while the sword has been dated to *c.*800, the similarities to the sword and burial context at Reading have been noted.[48] Other swords recovered from the Thames in London can be broadly dated to the late ninth or early tenth century.[49]

Other hoards can be associated with the movement of the Great Army to London. One from Croydon (Surrey), found in 1862, comprised at least four silver ingots, four pieces of hack-silver—three fragments of a spiral arm-ring and one of a broad-band arm-ring—and a corroded mass of some 250 coins, many of which were quickly dispersed into private hands (Figure 2.6). Despite its fate, the hoard is known to have included 94 coins of Burgred of Mercia, 24 from East Anglia—comprising two of Æthelstan (*c.*824–*c.*845), four of Æthelweard (*c.*845–*c.*855) and 18 of Edmund (855–69), 56 from Wessex—25 of Æthelred I (866–71) and 31 of Alfred (871–99)—a coin of Archbishop Ceolnoth of Canterbury (833–70), seven continental deniers—one of Louis the Pious (814–40) and six of Charles the Bald (840–77)—and three dirham fragments.[50] The mixture of coins, ingots, and hack-metal reveals a collection in Viking hands, which Nicholas Brooks and James Graham-Campbell assigned to the winter of 871–2 when the Great Army was based in London. It was reportedly found in a 'canvas' bag placed in a 'stone coffin without a lid', which they deem more likely to have been concealed in a churchyard than a grave. Such a collection of coins may partly have come together from having spent the previous years in East Anglia and Wessex, and from the 'immense tribute' gathered

44. Cowie 1988; Thomas *et al.* 2006, 40–6
45. Sloane *et al.* 1995
46. Pagan 1965, 24; MacKay 2015, 106
47. LON-EFCF31
48. Dunning and Evison 1961
49. Wilson 1965, 52; Cowie 1988; Naylor 2015, 132
50. Blunt and Dolley 1959, 222–34; Brooks and Graham-Campbell 1986

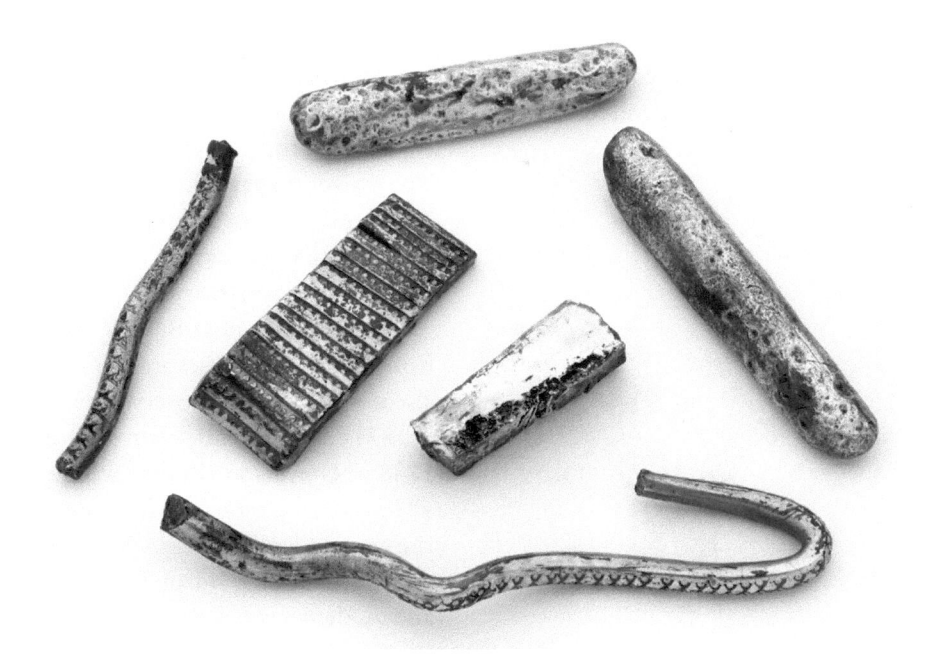

Figure 2.6. Silver ingots and hack-silver from the Croydon hoard, discovered in 1862 (Ashmolean Museum)

by Burgred as he made peace with the Army when it arrived in London. Other elements of the hoard, including the dirhams and fragments of Permian style spiral arm-ring are, however, thought to have been acquired in southern Scandinavia; the broad-band arm-ring is of a type often described as 'Hiberno-Norse', and believed to have been manufactured in Ireland, but prototypes occur in southern Scandinavia in the mid-ninth century.[51]

Precisely where the hoard was found is unknown, but Brooks and Graham-Campbell have noted that Croydon was an estate of the archbishops of Canterbury, which was granted to Ælfred, an ealdorman of Surrey, by Archbishop Æthelred (870–88). Ælfred and his wife, Werburg, donated to Christ Church, Canterbury, an eighth-century illuminated gospel book, the *Codex Aureus*, which contains an inscription recording that they had bought it from an 'army of heathens' with pure gold, as they did not wish it any longer to remain in heathen hands. Ælfred had been ealdorman since perhaps as early as 853, so they

---

51. Brooks and Graham-Campbell 1986, 97; Kilger 2008a, 234; 2008b, 321; Graham-Campbell and Sheehan 2011, 98; Horne 2022, 78

did not certainly acquire it from the Great Army, but, as Brooks and Graham-Campbell conclude, it seems a remarkable coincidence that a Viking hoard of the early 870s was deposited on the property of an ealdorman known to have engaged with a 'heathen army'. They also suggest that the Great Army may have been exploiting local estate organisation to acquire resources to support itself.[52]

Other coin hoards recovered from along the Thames are probably also a response to the overwintering of 871–2. A hoard recovered in 1838 at Gravesend (Kent) included 428 Mercian pennies (all but one of Burgred), 61 of Wessex, 49 of East Anglia (including 44 of Edmund), and a denier of Louis the Pious (Figure 2.7). Given only a single coin of Alfred it is thought to be a little earlier than the Croydon

Figure 2.7. Silver pendant cross from the Gravesend hoard, discovered in 1838 (Trustees of the British Museum)

hoard, possibly buried in the autumn of 871 when the Army first entered London. The hoard also contained a silver pendant cross with a central glass roundel of English manufacture, which, along with the denier, may suggest a collection acquired by members of the Great Army.[53] In 1882 digging of the foundations for the new Waterloo Bridge recovered a hoard of 96 Burgred pennies, with just one West Saxon coin of Æthelred I, and perhaps another of Alfred's Lunettes type. A hoard discovered at Wandsworth (Surrey) c.1913 contained at least four coins of Burgred, and an unspecified number of Lunettes of Alfred, while a hoard of 'several Saxon coins' was found in 1724 at Barking (Essex) including at least one of Burgred.[54] Excavations in 1996 in advance of re-development of the Royal Opera House in Covent Garden, recovered a hoard of 22 stycas, along with a small fragment of copper-alloy sheet with punched triangles similar to those found on Scandinavian silver arm-rings. They came from within the rampart of a defensive ditch, probably dug in

52. Brooks and Graham-Campbell 1986
53. Graham-Campbell 2002, 54; Naylor 2022b, 158
54. Pagan 1965, 24; MacKay 2015, 104, 145

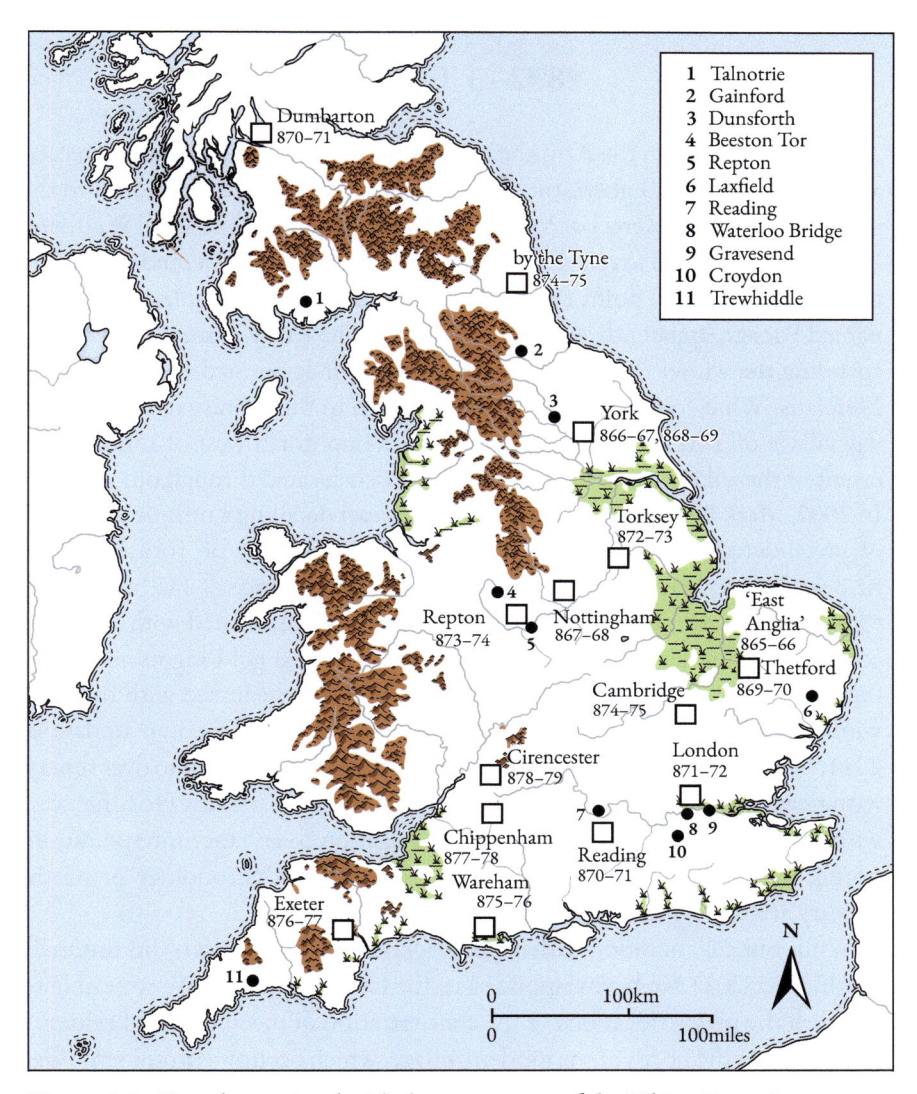

Talnotrie
Gainford
Dunsforth
Beeston Tor
Repton
Laxfield
Reading
Waterloo Bridge
Gravesend
Croydon
Trewhiddle

Figure 2.8. Hoards associated with the movements of the Viking Great Army

response to Viking attacks. The date profile of the stycas is of the 850s, but their recovery far outside their area of usual circulation may reflect the actions of a member of the Great Army after the occupation of London in 871 (see Figure 2.8).[55]

55. Malcolm *et al.* 2003, 278–84; Hadley and Richards 2021, 81

872–3 Torksey

After leaving London the Army headed to Northumbria. Later sources record a revolt against King Egbert, the Army's appointee, who had fled south to the court of Burgred of Mercia, accompanied by the Archbishop of York, Wulfhere. If the Army intended to reinstall Egbert, this did not materialise, and he appears to have died at some point that year. Later sources record a subsequent king named Ricsige, apparently another local lord.[56] The Army retreated to Lindsey, spending the winter of 872–3 at Torksey, where it again made peace with the Mercians. While long assumed to have occurred in the vicinity of the present-day village of Torksey on the River Trent, c.14km north-west of Lincoln, the extent of the Viking camp has only been precisely located through our research. In 2002, Mark Blackburn published a short paper detailing a unique collection of metal-detected artefacts from near the modern village of Torksey, which he described as betraying 'a strong Scandinavian presence'.[57] He highlighted the concentration of ninth-century coins, and finds associated with a bullion economy, including eleven Islamic dirhams, silver and gold ingots and hack-metal, and both copper-alloy and lead weights, which he linked with the over-wintering of the Great Army in 872–3. Blackburn published an update in 2011, by which time the numbers of dirhams recorded had risen to over ninety, with newly recorded evidence suggesting metalworking activity. He concluded with a hope for future archaeological investigation to enhance interpretation, noting the potential for the assemblage to refine the chronology of ninth-century artefact types.[58]

While our collaboration with Mark Blackburn was cut short by his untimely death, since 2011 we have responded to the challenge he set. We were able to establish the precise locations of the concentration of metal-detected evidence as six fields to the north of the modern village, which occupy a prominent ridge of high ground adjacent to the Trent. Although modern drainage has transformed the landscape, our project's geomorphological analysis revealed that to the east was a wet, marshy environment, deriving from a former channel of the Trent which had begun silting up in the Bronze Age, when peat deposits began to form. Sediment mapping revealed a build-up of silt to the north and south

---

56. Giles 1849, 209; Johnson South 2002, 62–3
57. Blackburn 2002
58. Blackburn 2011, 221

of the site, suggesting that these areas had remained open to the Trent, which would have provided naturally occurring seasonal tidal ports below the higher ground of the camp.[59] The camp at Torksey was, then, effectively on an island, providing both protection and a good vantage point over the local landscape (Figures 2.9, 2.10). The nature of the landscape may be reflected in the Old English place-name 'Turoc's [or Turc's] island (ēg)'.[60] This was a strategically important location, close to a crossing point over the Trent of a Roman road now known as Till Bridge Lane, which runs from Ermine Street just north of Lincoln, and proceeds north-west towards York. Torksey was also located adjacent to the Foss Dyke, a canal widely regarded as being of Roman construction, which connects the Trent to Lincoln. Whilst it is uncertain if the Foss Dyke was navigable in the ninth century, it has been suggested that it was used to transport Torksey ware in the tenth, and Alan Vince linked its later usage to the late tenth-century refurbishment of quaysides in the Wigford area of Lincoln.[61]

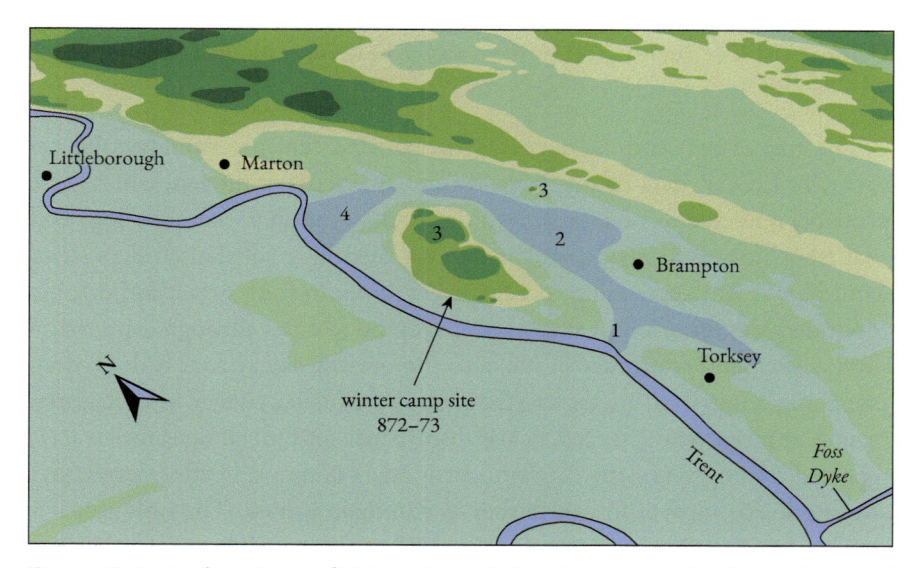

Figure 2.9. In the winter of 872–3, bounded to the west by the River Trent and surrounded by wet and marshy ground, the site of the Viking camp at Torksey was effectively an island. Sediment mapping south [1] and north [4] of the site revealed river silts, suggesting that these areas remained open to the Trent; low ground east of the camp was a peaty wetland [2]; sandy dunes provided high points in the landscape [3] (after Stein 2014)

59. Stein 2014; Hadley and Richards 2016
60. Cameron and Insley 2010, 122–6
61. Sawyer 1998, 197; Vince 2003, 240–1; Hadley *et al.* 2023, 3

Figure 2.10. The camp at Torksey from across the Trent, with the floodplain below (Hannah Brown)

The area of the camp is roughly 55ha, with no evidence from geophysical survey or LiDAR data of any defensive embankments or ditches, which were probably rendered unnecessary given the island location. Geoarchaeology and trial trenching established that the site is sealed by a substantial deposit of wind-blown sand, extending to a thickness of 4m in some areas, and this has precluded identification of many archaeological features through geophysical survey. The sand continues to move to the present day and, as it does, deep ploughing brings fresh artefacts to the surface, although a change in agricultural regime in recent years has led to less disturbance and metal detectorists have reported finding very little. In some areas any Viking occupation levels have already been removed; in others they may remain buried. The only features clearly identified in the geophysical survey were traces of a Roman farmstead, explaining the concentrations of Roman pottery and other artefacts found there during fieldwalking.[62] On the western edge of the centre of the site, our fieldwalking recovered fragmentary human remains; excavation retrieved further remains but revealed that any burials in this location had long since been ploughed out. Two radiocarbon dates indicate that these date to the late ninth century. Analysis of the remains was able to identify a minimum number of only two adults, both probably male, aged 18–25 and 25–35 years, respectively. A fragment of occipital, consistent with the human cranium, shows evidence

62. Hadley and Richards 2016, 31–6; 2021, 96

of two separate blows from a sharp implement, suggesting a violent, perhaps fatal, encounter. A further human cranial fragment was recovered c.200m to the north-east, which may indicate a second burial area within the camp, possibly associated with another warband within the Army.[63]

In 2016 we released an online catalogue of the metal-detected finds from Torksey, which then comprised over 1500 early medieval artefacts, including 124 dirhams, 40 silver English pennies, 174 Northumbrian stycas, over 70 pieces of silver and gold hack-metal and ingots, 12 copper-alloy ingots, over 350 copper-alloy and lead weights, 270 gaming pieces, over 200 mainly copper-alloy dress accessories, and evidence for metalworking.[64] The coin dating has a good fit for a deposition date of 872–3, and we believe that the bulk of the assemblage was deposited at the same time, within the single overwintering. This assemblage, which has continued to expand, provides an 'archaeological signature' of the Great Army, the first detailed analysis of which forms the core of this book.[65] The evidence from Torksey also has had considerable implications for our understanding of the size of the Viking Great Army. While not all of the 55ha is likely to have been as densely occupied as a later town, the scale of the camp is much greater than the four major urban places known in Scandinavia, even at their maximum extent in the tenth century: Birka c.6ha; Kaupang c.5.4ha; Ribe c.12ha; and Hedeby c.24ha. It is also much larger than the Viking camp at Woodstown (2.91ha) which must therefore represent a much smaller force. Given the size of the camp it is clear that the Great Army and its followers comprised thousands of people. We can never know exact numbers camped at Torksey, but if a fleet comprised 50–100 longships, and each ship had a crew of 30 to 50 warriors, then an army within the range 1500–5000 is not implausible and could easily have been accommodated on the island at Torksey. There is likely to have been an impact on the wider landscape during the overwintering, as the Army provisioned itself; this is explored in detail in subsequent chapters. However, wider disruption in Lindsey at this time is suggested by a hoard of nine Mercian and West Saxon coins recovered in 1985 at Walmsgate (Lincolnshire), some 50km from Torksey. This has been dated to c.873 given the absence of the latest issues of Burgred.[66] It was found close to Barton Street, the major north-south route through the Lincolnshire Wolds, which is probably of prehistoric origins. Since West Saxon and Mercian coins circulated together, we cannot easily say whether this was a hoard in local possession or had been hidden by a member of the Army; although the former seems

63. Hadley and Richards 2016, 56–7
64. Richards and Hadley 2016
65. Hadley and Richards 2016; 2018; 2020; Richards and Haldenby 2018
66. Pagan 1986, 209; Blackburn 1998

more likely given its small size and absence of hack-metal or ingots, as we will see, there are similar-sized hoards from burials associated with the Army at Repton.

873–4 Repton

The Army stayed in Mercia the following year, moving on to Repton *c.*115km up the Trent. The *Anglo-Saxon Chronicle* provides an unusually detailed account of the ensuing events:

> In this year the army went from Lindsey to Repton and took up winter quarters there, and drove King Burgred across the sea, after he had held the kingdom 22 years. And they conquered all that land.... And the same year they gave the kingdom of the Mercians to be held by Ceolwulf, a foolish king's thegn; and he swore oaths to them and gave hostages, that it should be ready for them on whatever day they wished to have it, and he would be ready, himself and all who would follow him, at the enemy's service.[67]

Again, the Army had intervened in local politics to appoint a king to rule in collaboration with them. Depiction of Ceolwulf as little more than a 'foolish king's thegn', appointed according to Asser 'by a wretched arrangement', is, however, a perspective from Wessex, written after his demise. In fact, Ceolwulf ruled for several years and seems to have been well established with the local aristocracy and was acceptable enough to Alfred for the pair to embark on a joint reform of their coinage. He was probably a member of a rival branch of the Mercian royal family to Burgred, perhaps descended from a Ceolwulf who had reigned earlier in the ninth century.[68]

Prior to recovery of metal-detected evidence from Torksey, our understanding of the camps of the Great Army was largely informed by excavations undertaken between 1974 and 1988 at Repton by Martin Biddle and Birthe Kjølbye-Biddle.[69] These were focused on the major Mercian monastery of St Wystan, which was located on a promontory, where a low cliff rises *c.*6m above a remnant of the former course of the Trent. To the east of the crypt, excavation revealed the butt end of a substantial V-shaped ditch, over 4m deep, which had been filled in from its north side, probably through the casting in of an internal bank. Dating evidence was limited to two pottery sherds from the bottom fill, and a copper-alloy dress pin with a faceted head decorated with ring-and-dot

67. Whitelock 1961, 48
68. Blackburn and Keynes 1998; McLeod 2006, 151; Naylor 2022a
69. Biddle and Kjølbye-Biddle 1992; 2001

ornament, all of late ninth- or early tenth-century date. Resistivity survey located the course of the ditch east of the church, while magnetometer survey was employed in the churchyard to the west. Excavation was undertaken where the ditch joined the cliff above the Old Trent Water, which revealed four successive ditches, the earliest of which was V-shaped with a flat narrow bottom, but no dating evidence was recovered. Extrapolating from this evidence, it was proposed that the Army constructed a D-shaped enclosure, with its straight edge along the cliff edge above the Old Trent Water and incorporating the church as a gatehouse. The area enclosed was published as 1.46ha, although recalculation has shown it was no more than 0.4ha (Figure 2.11).[70]

Given that the course of the ditch was largely extrapolated from a resistivity survey and three excavation trenches and that dating evidence was recovered from only one trench, there remains significant room for doubt over the interpretation of the D-shaped enclosure.[71] The primary publication of the excavations illustrates a complex sequence of earthworks, with the Viking enclosure succeeded by the bailey of the Earl of Chester's castle of the early to

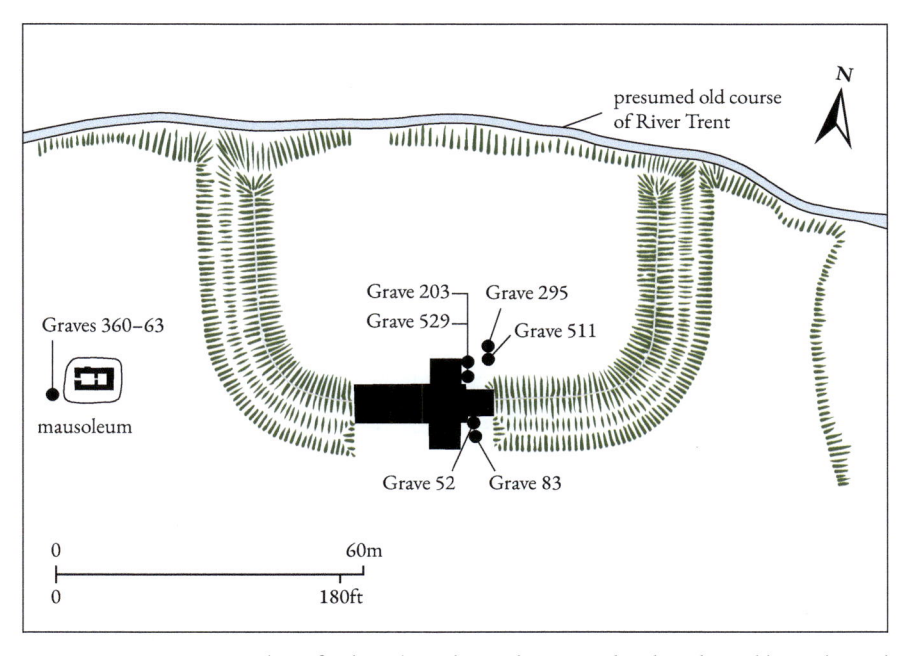

Figure 2.11. Repton: plan of Viking burials in relation to the church, and hypothetical plan of the enclosure, previously thought to represent the Viking camp of 873–4

70. Biddle and Kjølbye-Biddle 1992, 40; 2001, 59; Stein 2014, 43; Hadley and Richards 2021, 85
71. Hadley and Richards 2021, 113–16

mid-twelfth century.[72] An alternative view is that the scale and profile of the ditch are more in keeping with medieval castle defences, in which case, and as was first suggested by the excavator in an interim report: 'We thus have the classic situation of a Norman castle with a church "at the castle gate" included within its defences.'[73]

The excavations also revealed five burials believed to have been associated with the Great Army's overwintering (Figure 2.12).[74] Grave 511 contained an adult male, 35–45 years old, interred with a sword, placed in a fleece-lined wooden scabbard covered with leather, with a copper-alloy buckle for a suspension strap, adjacent to which was an iron key. He had been buried wearing a necklace of two glass beads and a silver-alloy Thor's hammer amulet, with a leaded bronze gilt fastening; a copper-alloy buckle at the waist bore traces of

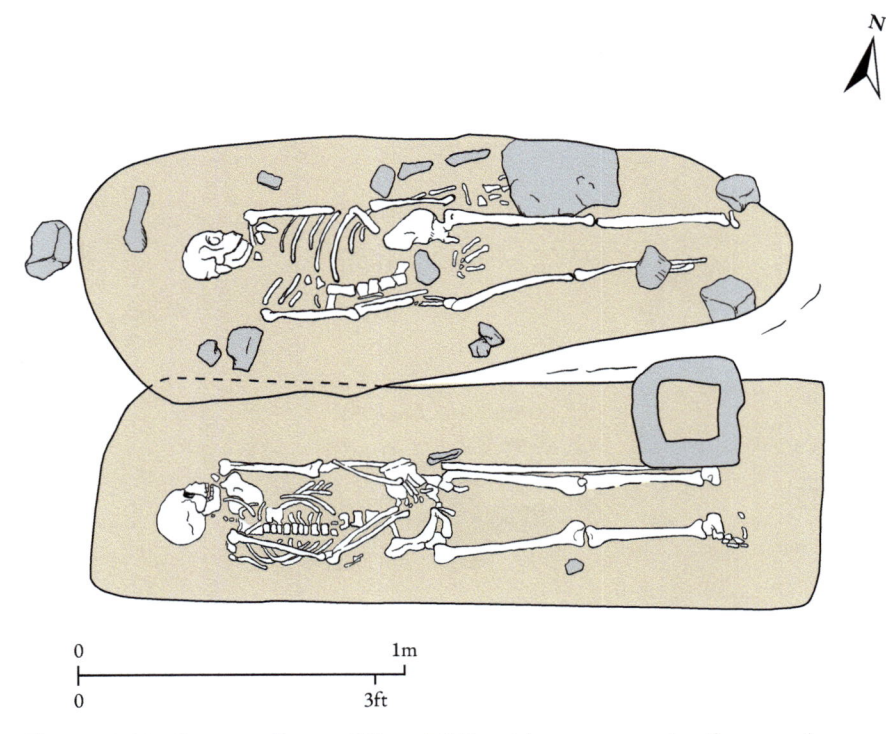

0 ————————————— 1m
0 ————————————— 3ft

Figure 2.12. Repton: Graves 295 and 511, with a stone setting for a marker post placed between them

72. Biddle and Kjølbye-Biddle 2001, 51, fig. 4.3
73. Biddle and Kjølbye-Biddle 1988, 7
74. Biddle and Kjølbye-Biddle 1992; 2001

textile and leather suggesting there was a belt, from which were suspended two iron knives. Between his thighs was the tusk of an adult wild boar, while the humerus of a jackdaw was found in a square area of softer earth that suggested the former presence of a box or bag. This male had evidently met a violent end; he had received two injuries commensurate with spear wounds just above the eyes and there was a sword cut into the head of the left femur suggesting that the femoral artery had been severed, and perhaps also that the genitalia had been mutilated. In this context, the boar's tusk has been interpreted as having an amuletic role.[75] This was the first burial north of the chancel, and partially cut into its north side was the grave of a second adult male, aged 17–20 years (Grave 295), accompanied by an iron knife at the waist. A cut to the right side of the skull may have been related to his manner of death. Given that the Army had arrived in England eight years earlier, this individual may have been travelling with it since the age of 9–12 years. A stone-lined base for a grave marker was placed centrally at the east end of the two graves, suggesting there was an expectation of a second interment when the individual in Grave 511 was buried. Both graves were then covered over with a cairn of broken stones (c.1.8m square), including fragments of a ninth-century stone cross-shaft.

The close association between these males has been reinforced by analysis of oxygen and strontium stable isotopes, suggesting that both probably spent their early years in southern Scandinavia, while dietary stable isotopes indicate that both experienced a change of diet in later life from 'marine towards more terrestrial foods, possibly an indicator of a mobile lifestyle as might be expected for two warriors'.[76] More recently, aDNA analysis has led to a claim that the two males were 'related in the first degree on the paternal side…either father and son or half-brothers'. Jarman has suggested that they may have been Olaf who is recorded in Irish sources as raiding in Ireland from 853 and in Scotland, and his son Eysteinn. Olaf was killed by King Constantine of the Scots in 874, while Eysteinn was killed the following year by Healfdene.[77] Irrespective of these speculative identifications, the funerary tableau certainly indicates the loss of two individuals of great significance to the Great Army.

Other furnished graves adjacent to the church include Grave 529, the burial of a male aged 25–35 years at death, placed within a wooden coffin to the north of the crypt. The grave contained a gold ring and five silver coins, which had been placed near his head; areas of dark staining suggest they may have been

75. Richards 2003, 388; Jarman 2019; Ratican 2020, 210–11; Hadley and Richards 2021, 148–52
76. Jarman 2019; Jarman et al. 2019
77. Jarman 2019

deposited in a leather or textile bag. The coins comprised two of Burgred, from late in his reign c.871–4, and three of Alfred, one of which could date to a few years after the overwintering. Given their placement within the coffin the coins were probably an offering rather than a hoard hidden with the intention of subsequent retrieval.[78] Grave 83 was of a male aged c.50 years, interred in a wooden coffin and with a copper-alloy ring on the third finger of his left hand. Recent stable isotope analysis yielded a strontium value at the higher end of what might be expected for someone with origins in Britain, but consistent with inland Scandinavian regions. Buried to his left in a wooden coffin in the same grave pit, was a younger man, aged around 20 years; this is a striking parallel with Graves 511 and 295 to the north of the church, which may also suggest a family connection.[79] A spearhead found to the north of Graves 295 and 511 may have come from a disturbed grave, as may have an axe found in 1923 close to Grave 52 immediately south of the crypt, and which later excavation suggests came from a coffined burial.[80] That there were unfurnished graves containing individuals of Scandinavian origins is suggested by stable isotope analysis of two individuals buried next to each other to the south of the crypt (Graves 43 and 44), who had strontium results similar to the individuals in the furnished Graves 511 and 295.[81]

Excavation of a mound c.60m west of the church revealed the remains of a late seventh- or early eighth-century mausoleum containing a substantial charnel deposit, in the eastern of two chambers.[82] The floor of this chamber was covered with a thick layer of Mercia mudstone, and an antiquarian account suggested that the chamber had been roofed with stones resting on timber joists. The excavation revealed the whole structure had been sealed beneath a low stone cairn, covered by an earth mound, its edges defined by stones. It was a substantial structure c.11m × 13m. When first discovered c.1686 it was claimed that a central burial had been seen, but modern excavations encountered no such thing, although the charnel had clearly been heavily disturbed during antiquarian investigations. Nonetheless, a stack of sorted long bones in the north-east corner may represent the remains of an originally more orderly arrangement. Amidst the deposit were such objects as an axe, a fragment of a sword, two large and several smaller seaxes, knives, a chisel, a barrel padlock key, and other iron objects. There were also fragments of seventh- or eighth-century

78. Biddle, Blunt et al. 1986, 16–19; Biddle and Kjølbye-Biddle 2001, 65
79. Jarman et al. 2019, 86
80. Biddle and Kjølbye-Biddle 2001, 65
81. Jarman et al. 2019, 86
82. Biddle and Kjølbye-Biddle 2001, 67–8

silver and silver gilt with cloisonné work, possibly from a sword hilt, and six pins. Five silver pennies comprised a complete coin and one cut in half struck for Burgred of Mercia, an imitative coin struck in the name of Æthelred I of Wessex, and one naming Alfred on the obverse, although the reverse had been struck from a die usually used on Burgred coins minted in London. These were all struck no later than c. 872, while the fifth coin in the name of Alfred, struck by a moneyer usually associated with Burgred coins, was dated to 873–4.[83] It has been suggested that some of these artefacts may have been associated with the putative central burial.[84]

The coins provided important dating evidence for the charnel deposit. Some of the radiocarbon dates from the charnel initially seemed to be too old, and it was thought that the deposit may have also included remains from much earlier burials even though the taphonomy of the deposit suggested it was more homogenous.[85] These dates have recently been recalibrated to take account of Marine Reservoir Effects. The need to do so was reinforced by Grave 529 which contained coins of the 870s yet had yielded a radiocarbon date of AD 670–770. The revised dates are now consistent with the charnel having derived from the remains of individuals deposited in the late ninth century.[86]

Stable isotope analysis indicates that the charnel remains were of individuals from various locations, although it is not possible to establish where based on the strontium values. Previous results from analysis of oxygen isotopes have been adjudged problematic because of inaccurate conversions between the values measured and drinking water equivalences, but promised new analyses of the oxygen and lead isotopes are not yet published.[87] Therefore, while current results have to be regarded as partial, the diversity of the values yielded is, nonetheless, consistent with what we can surmise of the Army's composition from the range of material culture discussed in this book. Osteological examination revealed that the charnel deposit comprised the remains of at least 264 individuals, including 253 adults and 11 juveniles, and over 80% were robust males in the age-range 18–45 years. The paucity of small bones of the hands and feet has led to the suggestion that much of the deposit had originally been buried elsewhere. There has been much speculation over the origins of these remains, with the initial report noting 'little surviving evidence of terminal trauma'.[88]

83. Biddle, Kjølbye-Biddle et al. 1986, 111–19
84. Biddle and Kjølbye-Biddle 2001, 68
85. Biddle and Kjølbye-Biddle 2001, 78–9
86. Jarman et al. 2018, 188–9, 192–3
87. Jarman et al. 2019, 81–4
88. Biddle and Kjølbye-Biddle 2001, 79–80; Richards et al. 2004, 102–31

More recent analysis has apparently demonstrated that 'the charnel bones do in fact show evidence of trauma…consistent with a burial of battle dead exhumed from other locations', although a full osteological report is not yet published.[89] Cut into the south-west corner of the mound was the burial of four young individuals: the supine burial of an individual aged 8–12 years, above which were three bodies crouched on their sides, two aged 8–12 years and another aged c.17 years (Graves 360–63). There was a sheep's jaw at the foot of the grave, and a stone base suggested the burial had been marked above ground. It was initially interpreted as a sacrificial deposit marking the completion of the charnel mound, and although no osteological evidence has been published to support this deduction, Jarman has recently reported that two of the individuals had experienced weapon trauma.[90]

For a generation, the findings from Repton gave the impression of a relatively small camp, but more recently, in the light of the findings from Torksey, new insight into the overwintering has emerged. Excavations at Repton conducted by Jarman outside the enclosure recovered an iron arrowhead, the tip of an iron axe head, two clench nails, and four lead gaming pieces, like types from Torksey. At Foremark, 3km to the east, many finds that we now know to be indicative of the presence of the Great Army have been recovered by metal-detecting (Figure 2.13). Unfortunately, they were not reported by the finder, but Jarman was able to establish that they included gaming pieces, dirhams, Anglo-Saxon strap-ends and brooches, cubo-octahedral weights, and a Thor's hammer pendant. Additional objects, including a gaming piece, a sceat, and a strap-end were found by another metal detectorist in 2021 and are now in a private collection.[91] Small-scale excavations in 2019 recovered another lead gaming piece and an iron ploughshare, near what may have been a building which had evidence of burning, radiocarbon-dated to the late ninth or early tenth centuries. While no traces of any defences have been located, the place-name notably derives from Scandinavian *forn* ('old') *-verk* ('defensive fortification').[92] In the light of the new evidence from Torksey and Foremark, Martin Biddle has accepted that the scale of the camp at Repton was much more extensive than suggested by the D-shaped enclosure.[93]

89. Jarman *et al.* 2019, 84
90. Biddle and Kjølbye-Biddle 2001, 73–4; Jarman paper presented to 2022 Viking Congress
91. Gary Johnson pers. comm.
92. Jarman 2019, 24–5
93. Biddle 2023, 70, fig. 3.2

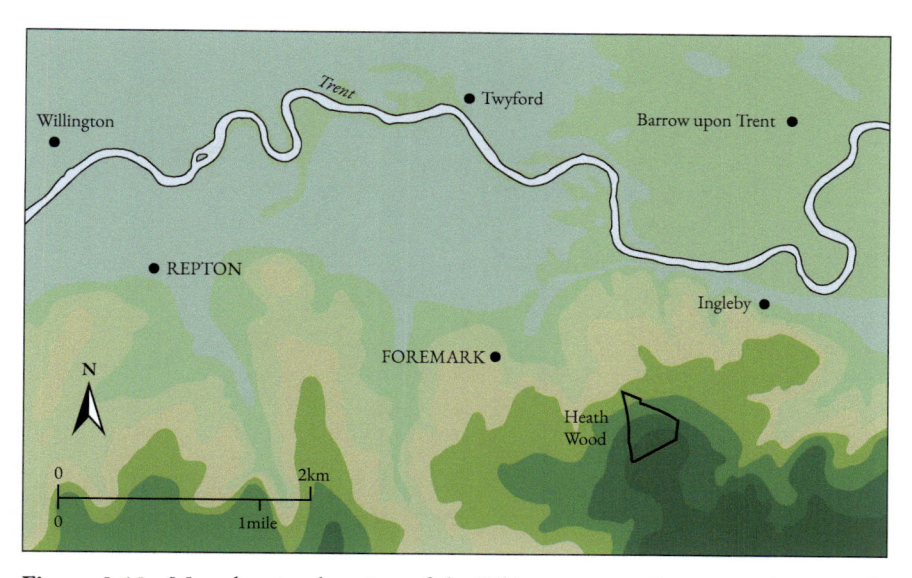

Figure 2.13. Map showing location of the Viking camps at Repton and Foremark, and the Viking cremation cemetery in Heath Wood

Foremark is on low-lying land, bordering the edge of the Trent floodplain, about 1km north-west of the only Viking cremation cemetery in Britain, on the higher ground at Heath Wood, Ingleby (Derbyshire). It comprised 59 barrows, around a third of which have been excavated, recovering cremated human and animal remains, and grave goods including weaponry and dress accessories.[94] The two mounds excavated under modern conditions are the best understood. In Mound 50 the cremated remains of an adult, possible female, and a juvenile or infant were recovered, along with cremated remains of horse, dog, pig, sheep/goat, and cattle (Figure 2.14). The uncremated jaw of a cow lay above the cremation layer. Artefacts recovered included a sword hilt grip, a small knife, and a hinge pivot, perhaps from a chest in which the body was interred, and at least four iron clamps, probably from a shield rim. There were also over twenty nails, some of which were domed or tinned, suggesting a decorative function, perhaps deriving from a chest or casket, although some may have come from timber used for fuel. The excavation of this mound was important in suggesting the presence of women and children amongst the Army, which is consistent with accounts in contemporary continental sources.

94. Richards *et al.* 2004

Figure 2.14. Mound 50 under excavation at the Viking cremation cemetery, Heath Wood (authors)

For example, Regino of Prüm recounts the arrival of a Viking army at the deserted town of Angers in the Loire valley, where the raiders based themselves in 873 'with their wives and children', while the late ninth-century Latin poem *Bella Parisiacae Urbis* refers to the presence of women alongside the Viking army that besieged Paris in 885 and 887.[95] Excavation of Mound 56 recovered the cremated remains of an adult and a pig, and a ringed pin. There were no pyres beneath some of the mounds and it has been suggested that the cremated remains were of members of the Great Army who had died in battle and been cremated elsewhere. Their remains were then transported for interment at Heath Wood, in an act of burial and commemoration that served as 'a reminder of comradeship', and which provides a parallel with the charnel deposit at Repton, albeit involving different funerary rites. It is now apparent that the Great Army occupied a wide area along the Trent, and not simply the site mentioned in the contemporary written sources.

Stable isotope analysis of the cremated remains has provided some new insights into both the life courses of those buried at Heath Wood and the potential places of origin of some of the animals.[96] Analysis of oxygen and

95. MacLean 2009, 168; Dass 2007, 35, 83–5
96. Löffelmann *et al.* 2023

strontium isotopes of the adult and juvenile buried in Mound 50 suggested that these two individuals had 'spent most of their lives in different places'. The remains of the juvenile yielded strontium values closer to those of the adult from Mound 56, suggesting that they may both have grown up locally or 'in southern or eastern England—or even large parts of Europe. For Scandinavia, Denmark or southwestern Sweden would also be a possible place of origin'. In contrast, the horse, dog, and a possible pig from Mound 50 yielded results that suggested origins in Norway, or central or northern Sweden; these were closer to the results for the Mound 50 adult. Taken together this evidence reinforces the impression that members of the Great Army had diverse origins and differing life histories. It also reveals a new aspect of the provisioning of the Army. The *Anglo-Saxon Chronicle* records that the Army was given horses on its arrival in East Anglia in 865 but this new analysis demonstrates that at least one treasured horse and dog had travelled with their owner across the North Sea. It provides an archaeological demonstration for the scene, depicted in the Bayeux Tapestry, of horses being disembarked from the Norman fleet at Hastings, some 200 years later.

A hoard recovered in the early twentieth century from a cave at Beeston Tor (Staffordshire) has been linked to disturbances attendant on the overwintering in the Trent valley around Repton, 42km to the southeast (Figure 2.15). It comprised 49 coins, including 20 of both Alfred and Burgred, eight of earlier West Saxon kings and one of Archbishop Ceolnoth, along with one gold and two bronze rings, a bronze binding and two silver brooches decorated with niello. It was found loose but the hoard may originally have been in a bag or purse, since the accounts

Figure 2.15. Silver Anglo-Saxon disc brooch from the Beeston Tor hoard, discovered in a cave system in the Peak District in 1924 (Trustees of the British Museum)

of its recovery report traces of skin and leather, while the largest brooch was still attached to some fabric with gold thread. The coins suggest that the hoard is unlikely to have been deposited later than 875.[97]

97. Blunt and Dolley 1959, 220–1; Graham-Campbell 2004, 37

874 The Great Army divides

After the winter of 873–4, the Army divided in two, with one part led by Healfdene heading north and taking up winter quarters on the River Tyne. The *Historia de Sancto Cuthberto* records that Healfdene's army 'entered the Tyne and sailed as far as *Wircesforda*', and while this does not survive among local nomenclature, it was clearly at a fording point over the river.[98] The location of Healfdene's camp near the Tyne is yet to be discovered, although a metal-detected site at East Thirston (Northumberland) has been suggested as a historically undocumented camp associated with his raiding of the Picts and Strathclyde Britons.[99] The artefacts were distributed across *c.*15ha, on a promontory overlooking the floodplain of the River Coquet. The finds indicate Roman and early Anglo-Saxon activity but there are also Viking finds which fit the Great Army signature, including over twelve lead gaming pieces, three pins, seven strap-ends, a glass inset lead weight, and four stycas, one of which appears to have formerly been attached to a weight.[100] Excavation revealed the remains of an Anglo-Saxon weaving shed, but nothing which could be assigned to a phase of Viking occupation.[101]

What is known of Healfdene's subsequent career reinforces that factions of the Great Army were active over wide areas. The *Chronicle* records that he 'often ravaged among the Picts and the Strathclyde Britons', and the following year 'Healfdene shared out the land of the Northumbrians, and they proceeded to plough and to support themselves'.[102] The process of settlement by members of the Great Army had commenced, but Healfdene appears to have left Northumbria for Ireland shortly afterwards. He is believed to be the Albann who, according to the *Annals of Ulster*, killed the son of Olaf 'king of the Norsemen' in 875, but was himself killed in 877 in a battle between 'the fair heathens and the dark heathens' at Strangford Lough (Co. Down).[103]

A hoard recovered at Talnotrie (Dumfries and Galloway) in 1912 contained six Northumbrian stycas, four pennies of Burgred of Mercia, a cut Carolingian coin of Louis the Pious, and two dirham fragments, a large inset weight, and several pieces of Anglo-Saxon and Insular metalwork, as well as two Insular

---

98. Johnson South 2002, 53
99. Kershaw *et al.* 2023
100. Hadley and Richards 2018, 14; Kershaw *et al.* 2023
101. Anon. 2023
102. Whitelock 1961, 48
103. Mac Airt and Mac Niocaill 1983, 331–3; Ó Cróinín 2013, 254

Figure 2.16. The Talnotrie hoard (National Museum of Scotland)

pins and a strap-end (Figure 2.16).[104] The inclusion of a cake of wax led to the suggestion that it was a local metalworker's hoard, but given the similarities with the Torksey assemblage it is likely that it was deposited by a former member of the Great Army. The Burgred coins have been taken to suggest a date of 870–1, which would associate the hoard with the campaigns of Ivar and his kinsman Olaf among the Strathclyde Britons, when he captured the stronghold of Dumbarton Rock, but it could equally be associated with Healfdene's ravaging among the Picts and Strathclyde Britons in 874–5.[105]

104. Maxwell 1913; Graham-Campbell and Batey 1998, 109, 227
105. Brooks and Graham-Campbell 1986, 90

A major camp which can be associated with Healfdene was identified by metal-detecting in North Yorkshire, and first reported in 2003. It may have been first occupied when the Army was reportedly in York in 866–7 and 868–9, but the coinage demonstrates it was still in use in the later 870s. The site was initially known as Ainsbrook, a portmanteau of the surnames of the metal detectorists who discovered it, Mark Ainsley and Geoff Bambrook, and subsequently published as 'A Riverine site near York'. It has since been revealed as being to the north of the village of Aldwark, *c*.20km north-west of York, on the River Ure.[106] The finds assemblage recovered has much in common with that of Torksey, including a heterogeneous collection of coins and ingots of both copper alloy and silver, hack-silver and gold, a collection of scale weights, metalworking debris, craftworking equipment, and large amounts of metal-work gathered together for processing (Figure 2.17).[107] The coin assemblage, in particular, suggests occupation between the late 860s and mid-870s, although there is also evidence for some activity continuing at Aldwark into the late ninth or even early tenth and eleventh centuries.[108] This includes two Anglo-Scandinavian bells, which are generally to be dated to a Scandinavian settlement phase in the early tenth century, and an Irish crutch-headed ringed pin of the eleventh–twelfth century, but the absence of tenth-century pottery has

Figure 2.17. Finds from the Viking camp at Aldwark (Gary Johnson)

106. Hadley and Richards 2016, 26; Hall 2020a; Williams 2023
107. Williams 2020a–f
108. Williams 2020g, 81; 2020h, 84

been taken to indicate that later occupation was small-scale and short-lived. Some of the Aldwark assemblage was published in 2020, although it is clear that a lot of what had been recovered was sold without being recorded.[109]

Targeted trial trenching was conducted by York Archaeological Trust, supported by geophysical and LiDAR surveys by English Heritage, revealing a poorly-defined sub-rectangular earthwork enclosure orientated along the north-eastern bank of the Ure (Figures 2.18, 2.19). No western side was identified, and although this may have been obscured by modern field boundaries or lost through erosion, it is probable that the natural escarpment of the river was its boundary.[110] Excavation exposed elements of a double ditch defining this

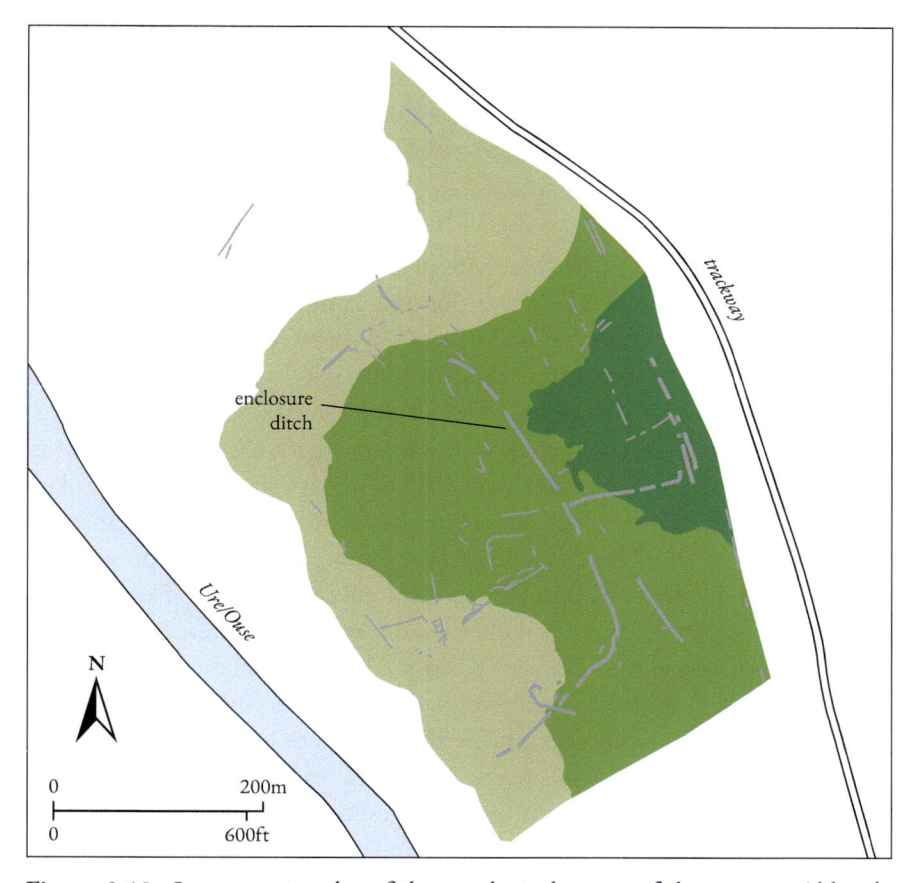

Figure 2.18. Interpretative plot of the geophysical survey of the camp at Aldwark, showing the enclosure ditch

109. Williams 2020a
110. Hall 2020b, 9; Howard 2020

Figure 2.19. The area of the camp at Aldwark, from across the River Ure (authors)

enclosure to the south, possibly set with posts, and an entrance was identified in the centre of the eastern side. The enclosure encompasses 31ha, and the place-name may refer to this feature: Old English '*ald*, *weorc*', or 'old fortification'.[111]

Radiocarbon dates from charcoal in pits indicate a first phase of occupation between AD 610 and 770 (95% confidence level), suggesting that some features, including the enclosure ditch, may reflect earlier activity, reinforced by a collection of early Anglo-Saxon metalwork.[112] The report suggests that the date range of the bulk of the activity on the sites is consistent with the settlement of Northumbria by Healfdene's faction of the Army, a force which presumably fractured and divided further as they spread across the conquered kingdom.[113] However, it may also be that when the *Chronicle* records the Great Army in York that some elements of the force were based at Aldwark given the coincidence of the dating with these recorded activities, the proximity to York, and the fact that evidence for the Army's presence within York itself is archaeologically very limited (Figure 2.20).[114] The smaller size of the camp in comparison with Torksey would be consistent with either suggestion.

111. Hadley and Richards 2021, 115–16
112. Hamilton *et al.* 2020
113. Williams 2020g–i
114. Hadley and Richards 2021, 204; 2023

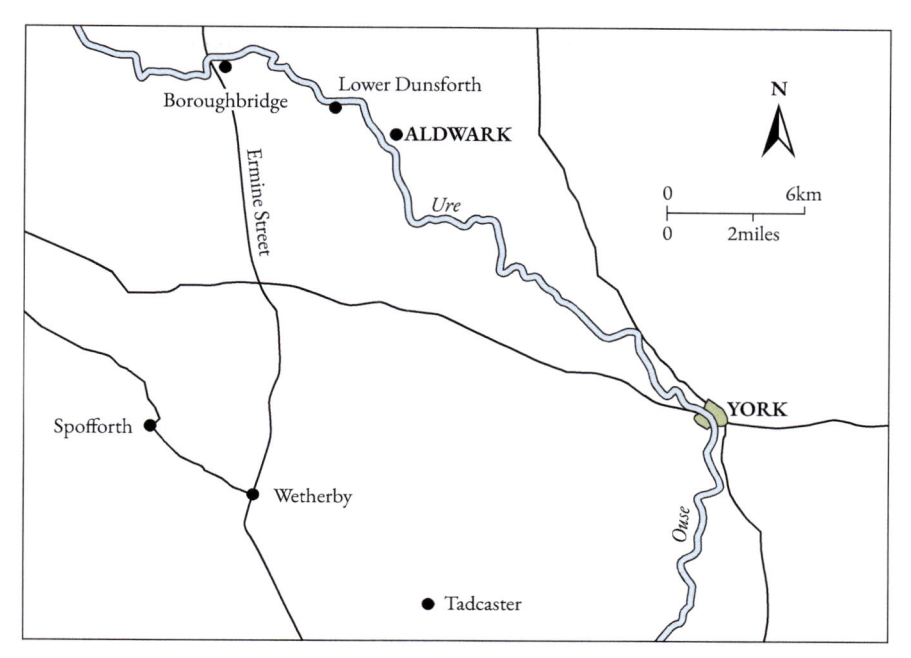

Figure 2.20. Map showing the location of Aldwark in relation to York, with key Roman routeways

Now that the location of the camp has been revealed, it also helps to contextualise a small hoard discovered in 1861 at Lower Dunsforth (Yorkshire) on the opposite bank of the Ure to Aldwark, close to the next crossing point upriver. It comprised around thirty coins, but we only have a record of six of Burgred, two of Æthelred I of Wessex, and seven of Alfred, suggesting it dates to the mid-870s.[115]

874–5 Cambridge

While half of the Army went north with Healfdene, the other half, under its kings Guthrum, Anwend, and Oscetel, had headed back to eastern Mercia, close to East Anglia, spending a year at Cambridge. We do not know whether these kings, previously unrecorded, had been with the Great Army since it arrived in 865, or had joined, as has been speculated, with the 'summer army'

---

115. Blunt and Dolley 1959, 221; Brooks and Graham-Campbell 1986, 106; Williams 2020j, 106

in 871.[116] The location of the camp is not known, although Paul Everson and David Stocker propose it was on the 'strand' north of the River Cam, adjacent to the Roman crossing point and former Roman enclosure.[117] They believe this was already a focus for seasonal markets, reflected in small quantities of Ipswich ware, but that it became an enclave of Scandinavian merchants in the late tenth and eleventh centuries. Excavations have not yielded anything to confirm this, although there are a few finds which may be linked to the 874–5 overwintering outside Cambridge, such as three gaming pieces and a weight from Little Wilbraham, 11km to the east.[118]

875–6 Wareham

Late in 875 the southern force moved into Wessex, to Wareham (Dorset), described by Asser as a fortified site and the location of a nunnery.[119] McLeod suggests that they probably entered Wessex near Reading, a familiar area having used it as a base in 870–1. The journey from Reading to Wareham would have been c.180km if using the Roman roads via Old Sarum and Badbury Rings, requiring multiple overnight stops.[120] That the Great Army apparently achieved this without hindrance highlights the difficulty that the West Saxons had in raising and moving an army before Alfred's military reforms and the Burghal Hidage system. The *Chronicle* provides an unusual level of detail about the ensuing peace, reporting that the Army gave Alfred hostages and swore oaths on a 'holy ring' to leave the kingdom, although Asser claims that they swore oaths on Christian relics.[121] Two weights inset with West Saxon Lunettes from Kingston (Dorset) and a Carolingian silver gilt mount perhaps from a sword or harness, have been associated with activity at the camp at Wareham in 875–6.[122]

876–7 Exeter

Subsequently, Guthrum's force headed to Exeter (Devon), where it spent the winter of 876–7, losing some 120 ships to a great storm while at sea near

116. Abels 2003, 276
117. Everson and Stocker 2022, 58
118. SF-1CB627, -6F5256, -6F7361, -50B784, -B137C2
119. Keynes and Lapidge 1983, 82
120. McLeod 2023, 212
121. Whitelock 1961, 48; Keynes and Lapidge 1983, 82
122. Archibald 1998; Williams 1999, 29; 2023, 26; McLeod 2014, 143

Swanage (Dorset). Although Alfred was unable to catch up with the land-based force before they reached Exeter, nonetheless 'they gave him hostages there, as many as he wished to have, and swore great oaths and then kept a firm peace'. The Trewhiddle hoard found near St Austell in Cornwall appears to have been a collection of church treasure, hidden from a Viking raiding party but never recovered. It was once thought to have been deposited in the mid-870s, and linked to the Exeter camp but it has now been re-dated to c.868.[123] Two gold ingots found on the route between Wareham and Exeter, at Loders (Dorset) and Kilmington (Devon) respectively, may also be associated with the Army's activities in this year.[124] In August of 877, this force 'went away into Mercia and shared out some of it, and gave some to Ceolwulf', in another move to settle in one of the English kingdoms.[125]

877–8 Chippenham

Guthrum's part of the Great Army returned to Wessex, spending the winter of 877–8 at the royal residence at Chippenham (Gloucestershire). Some of the West Saxons now submitted to the Army, while others were driven 'across the sea', except for Alfred who 'journeyed in difficulties through the woods and fen-fastnesses with a small force'. The situation facing Wessex became even more grave with the arrival in Devon of another Viking force, which had been overwintering in Dyfed (Wales), led by 'the brother of Ivar and Healfdene', who later sources identify as Ubba. He was killed in an ensuing battle at Countisbury Hill (Devon), with the victorious West Saxon force seizing from the raiders 'the banner which they called "Raven"'.[126]

After gathering his forces, Alfred left the marshes in early May of 878 and headed to 'Egbert's stone' where he was met by 'all the people of Somerset and of Wiltshire and of that part of Hampshire which was on this side of the sea'. The precise location is unknown but has been suggested as being to the east of Selwood Forest, on the border of Dorset, Wiltshire, and Somerset.[127] Two days later Alfred's forces arrived at Edington (Wiltshire), put the Army to flight, and then besieged them in their fortress, which was probably at Chippenham. After a two-week siege, 'thoroughly terrified by hunger, cold and fear, and in

123. Wilson and Blunt 1961; Brooks and Graham-Campbell 1986, 109; Graham-Campbell 2004, 37
124. SOM-E7F945, -BFD27A
125. Whitelock 1961, 48
126. Whitelock 1961, 49; Keynes and Lapidge 1983, 84
127. Baker and Brookes 2013, 201–3

the end despair' according to Asser, those inside the fortress sought peace. Three weeks later Guthrum and thirty of his men arrived at Aller, near Athelney (Somerset):

King Alfred raised him from the holy font of baptism, receiving him as his adoptive son; the unbinding of the chrisom on the eighth day took place at a royal estate called Wedmore. Guthrum remained with the king for twelve nights after he had been baptised, and the king freely bestowed many excellent treasures on him and all his men.[128]

Two hoards found in 2015 date to the late 870s and this final phase of Great Army activity. The first from a field near Watlington (Oxfordshire) comprised fifteen complete silver ingots, two complete and two fragmentary silver arm-rings and fragments from two different neck-rings, a single fragment of hack-gold from a twisted rod, a fragment of an Anglo-Saxon hooked tag, and 203 coins (Figure 2.21).[129] The Scandinavian character of the hoard is clear from two Carolingian deniers alongside coins from both Mercia and Wessex while the complete silver rings and ingots correspond to the Scandinavian weight unit of 25g, with the cut pieces about one-third of that, with most pieces nicked, as the silver content had been tested when the items changed hands.[130] The bulk of

Figure 2.21. Ingots, hack-silver, and silver coins from the Watlington hoard (Ashmolean Museum)

128. Keynes and Lapidge 1983, 85, 248
129. Naylor and Standley 2022
130. Kershaw 2022, 133–4

the hoard comprises 13 coins of the Two Emperors and 186 Cross-and-Lozenge varieties, for both Alfred and Ceolwulf, and largely minted in London and Canterbury, suggesting this part of the hoard was brought together in the Thames Valley or south-east England. Other items had been brought from southern Scandinavia, where the closest parallels for the arm- and neck-rings are largely found, as well as the specific D-shaped profile of the ingots. The two deniers, of Louis II (855–75) and Charles the Bald (875–7), were both minted in Pavia (Italy), but are thought to have been acquired in the Netherlands, where such coins have been found in hoards, some clearly in Scandinavian ownership, including the second Westerklief hoard of c.880.[131] The Watlington hoard is coin-dated to the late 870s, after the Battle of Edington. It is thought unlikely that the Anglo-Saxon coins were acquired through economic transactions locally since they are rare as single finds; rather it was concluded that the coins were more likely acquired as tribute, perhaps from the large payments made to the remnant of the Great Army that continued to raid in Wessex and Mercia.[132] The hoard was found close to a major estate centre at Benson (Oxfordshire), and the likely meeting place for the hundred of Ewelme.[133] It was also close to the Icknield Way, the traditional boundary between Wessex and Mercia.[134]

The second hoard found in 2015 presents more challenges given its chequered history of recovery and reporting, leading to the prosecution and jail of four metal detectorists and a coin dealer.[135] It was originally dubbed the Leominster hoard, but has been renamed as the Herefordshire hoard, and is believed to have contained around 300 coins although most were illegally sold off. Among thirty-one to have been recovered are examples of the Two Emperors and the Cross-and-Lozenge types minted for both Alfred and Ceolwulf, a single later coin of Alfred of c.879, a coin of Archbishop Wulfred of Canterbury (805–32), a denier of Louis the Pious, and a dirham. Other items recovered from the hoard include a crystal sphere mounted in a frame of four gold strips, of Frankish workmanship and dated to the sixth to seventh century, a ninth-century gold finger-ring of Anglo-Saxon manufacture with octagonal exterior set with rosettes against a niello background, an arm-ring of probable ninth-century Anglo-Saxon manufacture, and at least one silver ingot (Figure 2.22). On the basis of the coins recovered the hoard has been dated to c.879–80, and

131. Naylor and Coupland 2022, 116–17; Kershaw 2022
132. Naylor 2022b, 167
133. Mileson and Brookes 2014, 5
134. Naylor and Standley 2022, 2
135. Hoverd *et al.* 2020

Figure 2.22. Selection of finds from the Herefordshire hoard: a sixth- to seventh-century crystal sphere mounted in a gold setting, of Frankish origins, a ninth-century gold finger-ring with eight external facets decorated with an alternating pattern of rosette or flower petals set in a black niello background, and the obverse and reverse of a coin of the Two Emperors type (Trustees of the British Museum)

can be placed in a similar context to the Watlington hoard. Its location may be explained by the fact that Leominster was the location of a major Anglo-Saxon monastery.[136]

After his acceptance of baptism, Guthrum stayed at Cirencester (Gloucestershire) for a year. At this time another Viking army arrived at Fulham near London and made contact with Guthrum's part of the Great Army, but soon headed back to the Continent. While we do not know where it came from, it left for Ghent (Belgium) suggesting links with forces in Frisia.[137] In 880 Guthrum's forces went to East Anglia, 'settled there and shared out the land'.[138] A treaty drawn up between Alfred and Guthrum in the following years legislated for their respective areas of authority, making arrangements for legal disputes, trade and the movement of people between each other's territories, prohibiting their followers from joining each other's armies. The treaty also defined a boundary between the two realms, which ran 'up the Thames, and then up the Lea, and along the Lea to its source, then in a straight line to Bedford, then up the Ouse to Watling Street'.[139] This boundary seems not to have lasted very long, nonetheless the treaty is important not only for dividing out areas of responsibility but for integrating Guthrum into the legal, social, and economic structures of the society within which he and his followers now lived.[140] It was also an opportunity for Alfred to speak on behalf of the *Angelcynn*, a stage in the

136. Hoverd *et al.* 2020; Naylor 2022b, 155–7
137. Whitelock 1961, 50; McLeod 2014, 139–40
138. Whitelock 1961, 50
139. Keynes and Lapidge 1983, 171
140. Kershaw 2000

creation of a notion of Englishness that emerges strongly through Alfred's career.[141] Guthrum ruled in East Anglia until his death in 890, and while nothing more is recorded of his activities, coins were minted during his reign that were copies of those of Alfred, while others were in his baptismal name of Æthelstan.[142]

Conclusions

The ability of the Viking Great Army to move freely and at speed over long distances was key to its success, as when it rode from East Anglia to Northumbria in 866, or across Mercia into East Anglia in late 869. The ability of the annual food rents from any single Anglo-Saxon kingdom to provide for a force in the thousands would have severely tested local treaties and alliances and this is surely one reason why the Army moved between kingdoms each year.[143] The other would have been to seek new sources of plunder and to probe regional weaknesses. The Army was clearly well-informed about the geography of England as well as about geopolitical rivalries. One of the key differences from earlier raiding forces was the ability of the Great Army to attack deep within enemy territory, a tactic developed in Francia.[144]

It seems likely that when on the annual move between camps scouting parties travelled ahead of the Army, probably with local guides. The movements of the Army often appear to correlate with the course of Roman roads and prehistoric routeways. Each spring, as land travel became easier, it is probable that the land forces went first, travelling light and on horseback. A horse and rider can travel 80km in ten hours, and it is worth noting that in 1066 Harold moved his forces from London to Stamford Bridge (Yorkshire)—a remarkable journey of 300km—in four days. But the Great Army was not generally under such pressure so it is likely that a more leisurely pace was adopted, conserving energy, and warriors on foot were unlikely to travel more than 30km in a day.[145] Meanwhile, the Viking fleet would have followed by sea and navigable rivers, carrying reinforcements and supplies, as well as women, children, slaves, and treasures to be safeguarded. We can also make use of information for how the Anglo-Saxon forces travelled to better understand how Viking armies moved, particularly if accompanied by local guides. The *Anglo-Saxon Chronicle* recounts that in the lead up to the Battle of Edington, Alfred's forces rode to

141. Foot 1996
142. Whitelock 1961, 53; Blackburn 2005
143. McLeod 2006; 2023, 207–10
144. Baker and Brookes 2013, 137
145. McLeod 2023, 211–12

'Egbert's Stone', which must have been a known mustering point as Alfred had to wait only a day for the arrival of forces from Somerset, Wiltshire, and Hampshire, also demonstrating that travel times were well understood.[146]

When in 876 the Army moved between its camps at Wareham and Exeter, both coastal locations, the *Anglo-Saxon Chronicle* makes a distinction between the 'mounted raiding-army' and the 'raiding ship-army', indicating that though they were working in concert they were regarded as separate forces.[147] Similarly, when the Army travelled from East Anglia to Northumbria in 866 many travelled on horseback, but it seems likely that to cross the Humber they joined up with their ships in order to ferry a large force across the Estuary, using the known ferry crossing points. Continental sources similarly distinguish between forces moving on land and by river.[148] Our ability to map the extent of waterborne mobility in this period is limited by the lack of reliable written evidence for navigation and whilst some models of river navigation may be too generous as they depend upon thirteenth-century and later sources, the upper reaches of rivers would probably have been reachable in late autumn and spring when river levels were higher.[149] The known camps are all at coastal or riverine locations, as was also the case in Francia, and information about the crossing points with land routes must therefore have been critical to planning the next overwintering site. The journeys from Reading to London in 871 and from Torksey to Repton in 873 would have been accomplished most easily by boat, but the camps are also sited at the meeting points between the waterways and major land routes. The camp at Torksey is just south of the east-west Roman crossing over the Trent at Till Bridge Lane. Fords and bridges would have been strategic locations for the control of movement through the landscape. It is probably no coincidence that these places are still controlled through the operational toll bridges near both Aldwark and Torksey. Aldwark is the closest crossing point to York of the Ouse and its tributaries and at Repton a later causeway crosses the floodplain of the Trent.

The Irish and continental sources discussed in Chapter 1 provide much more detailed information about a range of interactions with Viking armies not mentioned in the Anglo-Saxon sources. On the other hand, the rich metal-detected information for England provides us with insights generally unavailable for Ireland and France. When taken together we can begin to build up a rich picture of Viking armies on the move. In Part II a detailed comparative analysis of the assemblages from the camps at Torksey and Aldwark is presented.

146. Whitelock 1961, 49; Baker and Brookes 2013, 202
147. Whitelock 1961, 48; McLeod 2023, 211
148. Cooijmans 2020, 128
149. Baker and Brookes 2013, 172–3; Edwards and Hindle 1991; Langdon 1993

PART II

Life in the camps

The Viking camps at Torksey and Aldwark provide an unprecedented opportunity to study life in the Great Army in detail. They are the only camps to have been extensively metal-detected, yielding large artefact assemblages: $c.3580$ finds from Torksey, and $c.1500$ from Aldwark. Both camps were initially identified through amateur metal-detecting, and unstratified metal-detected artefacts form the bulk of both assemblages, but archaeological trial trenching has been undertaken at each location, with some artefacts recovered from secure, discrete contexts.

The Torksey dataset was originally based on the finds catalogued and, in many cases, acquired by the Fitzwilliam Museum, which were initially reported to Rachel Atherton at Derby Museum (Figure II.1). In addition, there was a hoard of ironwork recovered by metal-detecting, which was given to the then City and County Museum in Lincoln (now Lincoln Museum) in 2002.[1] This catalogue has been substantially expanded by archaeological fieldwork on the site, including excavation and fieldwalking, and particularly by further metal-detector surveys, undertaken under archaeological supervision and using hand-held GPS to plot finds. We have also amalgamated these artefacts with detector finds recorded with the Portable Antiquities Scheme (PAS), a scheme run by the British Museum to enable metal detectorists to report their finds to local Finds Liaison Officers, as well as some finds made before recording began which were sold at auction. Therefore, some items are known to us only from brief descriptions, including some without images. Artefacts recorded by Kevin Leahy at North Lincolnshire Museum have also been added to the Torksey catalogue; but only when it can be credibly established that they are from the camp, as many were reported before the site was identified. Thus, this

---

1. Carhart 2014 recorded the provenance of the hoard as the 'Millfield, Torksey', but we have subsequently confirmed with the finders that this was within the area of the Viking camp.

Figure II.1. Selection of metal-detected finds from Torksey (Fitzwilliam Museum)

study includes finds unavailable to all previous publications. An earlier version of the catalogue was released by the Archaeology Data Service (ADS) in 2016 but an extensively cleaned, updated, and expanded dataset has been published to coincide with this volume.[2] Where possible we have included photographs of all artefacts, supplementing those taken for the Fitzwilliam Museum and the PAS with our own photographs, as well as X-rays of iron objects. This catalogue describes the largest assemblage of metal-detected finds records from any site, of any period, anywhere in England.

For Aldwark, the catalogue was established by using the small finds (sf) numbering system created by York Archaeological Trust (YAT), now trading as York Archaeology, which was employed in the site report published in 2020, and included items recovered up to 2008.[3] The 2020 report separated the discussion of 121 closely grouped finds, which allegedly came from a hoard, from that of the rest of the metal-detector finds. However, we have merged the

2. Richards and Hadley 2016; Richards *et al.* 2023a
3. Hall 2020a, 3; Williams (ed.) 2020, 11

two in our catalogue, on the basis that excavation of the area from which the supposed hoard was recorded provided no indication that it was a distinct deposit.[4] We have also extended the finds catalogue published in the 2020 report with artefacts reported by the same finders described in a number of British Museum Treasure Reports and which we know to be from Aldwark. Information from both YAT and the Yorkshire Museum has also been incorporated into the Aldwark catalogue, including some finds not described in the 2020 site report. We have expanded on the identifications provided by Nicola Rogers, Catherine Mortimer, and Penelope Walton Rogers for YAT, undertaking new comparative analyses. In addition, the dataset has been supplemented with the records of collectors, who have been willing to place this information in the public domain. Care had to be taken as the name of Ainsbrook, by which the site was first known (Chapter 2), became so well known that it seems to have been used as a provenance to provide cache value to finds which may have been recovered elsewhere, so finds have only been included where they can be associated with Aldwark with some confidence, based on their collection history. One collector provided measurements and photographs of finds he had acquired from one of the original detectorists before reporting commenced, and which are therefore not included in the 2020 report. We have supplemented YAT drawings and X-rays with photographs from other collectors and dealers, as well as some from online sale sites, such as eBay, but again not all artefacts have images, and only brief descriptions exist in some cases.[5]

Figure II.2 compares the sources of information for each dataset. For Aldwark 8% of the finds were catalogued by the British Museum as Treasure and information for an additional 27% was also derived from the published report. The largest group (45%) comprised metal-detector finds catalogued by YAT; some, but not all, of these were also discussed in the 2020 published report, and the majority were returned to the finders, who later sold them *en masse* to a UK buyer. These have subsequently been dispersed amongst numerous private collectors from whom we gained information about a further 9% of finds, although some of these have now been acquired by the Yorkshire Museum. Finally, 11% of the overall assemblage was recovered during the excavations and are held by YAT.

4. Hall 2020c, 66, fig. 27
5. Richards *et al.* 2023b

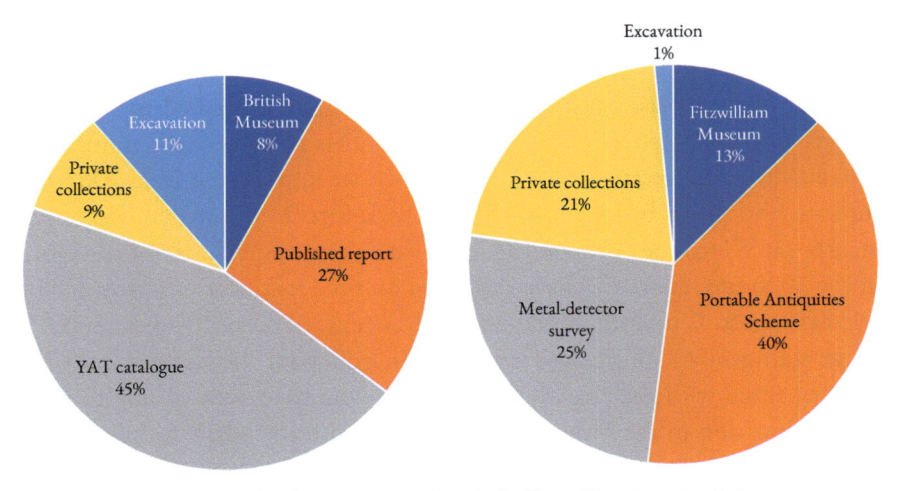

Figure II.2. Sources of information: Aldwark (left) and Torksey (right)

For Torksey, 13% of the finds were purchased by the Fitzwilliam Museum from metal detectorists and recorded and given accession numbers. The largest group (40%) are recorded in the PAS database, although many of these came from our metal-detector survey but were recorded by the PAS on our behalf. A further 25% of finds also came from our survey but are logged only in our project catalogue. An additional 21% were recovered before the advent of our survey but have subsequently been added to the catalogue. Finally, the smallest fraction (1%) was recovered during our excavations.

Entries into both catalogues have been organised on a progressive numbering system: whilst artefacts have been categorised according to a series of criteria, all finds have been added in the order in which they were reported and recorded. Both catalogues therefore operate the same basic cataloguing system, using a 'Catalogue Number' to identify individual items, prefixed with the site name. Finds from either catalogue are referred to here using this system. For clarity, finds from Aldwark are identified by the prefix 'A', with Torksey catalogue numbers prefixed with a 'T'. For Aldwark, the 'A' numbers equate to the published 'sf' numbers for the finds catalogued by YAT, but the sequence has been extended to accommodate the additional finds. For Torksey, artefacts had been catalogued according to a combination of Fitzwilliam Museum accession numbers, PAS identifiers, and survey numbers from our recording project. Both catalogues facilitate a concordance with the previous numbering systems. A cut-off date of November 2023 was applied for the addition of new finds to both datasets. In the chapters to follow we will discuss evidence for artefacts that had been recycled on the camps, and sometimes transformed into new object types, but for the purposes of the catalogues, artefacts are generally categorised according to their original function.

Recovery and recording biases

The site at Torksey was reported relatively early in its history. Nonetheless, detecting had been in progress in the area for many years prior to this point, with descriptions of finds of 'Viking' material circulating within the metal-detecting community. By contrast, the reporting of Aldwark occurred very late in the history of the site, after substantial amounts of material had been removed over the course of several years. On both sites, significant, and unassessable, amounts of material are known to have been removed and distributed without being recorded. As illustration, although ninety stycas have been published from Aldwark, it has been claimed that 'hundreds' were found, but subsequently sold.[6]

This dispersal of material may also promote a further bias in the available data. As noted, many artefacts have been recovered from the sites, recorded, and returned to their finders. In some instances, particularly for many of the earliest finds, this recording is only partial, with significant gaps in the information. These omissions cannot now be corrected, as these finds have passed into private ownership, typically without any details of the new owner, while others have been discarded. In the case of the ferrous material from Aldwark, over one hundred items are recorded in the YAT database merely as 'Objects' and 'Returned to Owner'. No further information is available, and thus over 35% of this assemblage cannot be subject to any form of analysis. Whilst no other lacuna is so pronounced, similar omissions occur throughout the two archives.

Finds of several periods were recovered at each site, as might be expected when any fields in lowland England are intensively detected for many years (Figure II.3). Only those believed to be linked to the Army's occupation of the camps are discussed in the following chapters, but all finds are catalogued in the searchable datasets made available via the ADS. For Torksey they have been categorised by period where possible, whereas for Aldwark this has generally not been attempted for finds which do not derive from the camp phase, so a greater proportion are simply 'Unknown'. From Torksey there are roughly

6. Hall 2020a, 3; Kelleher and Williams 2020; Hadley and Richards 2021, 208, 214

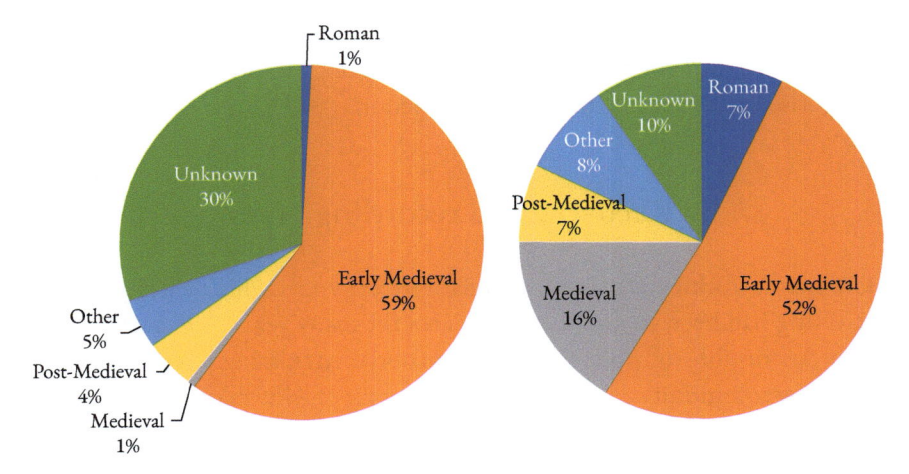

Figure II.3. All finds by period: Aldwark (left) and Torksey (right)

equal proportions (7–8%) of 'Other' (largely prehistoric) and Roman finds, the latter reflecting the farmstead located within what became the camp. There are also 17% medieval, and 7% post-medieval artefacts, representing later activity within the area of the camp (Figure II.3).

Good preservation, and a predominance of recognisable shapes and surface decoration, is believed to positively affect the recovery and recording of Viking artefacts.[7] In contrast, heavily corroded material, or items which cannot be easily identified, are more likely to be discarded. In the instance of the Foremark site near Repton (Chapter 2), anecdotal evidence suggests that several of the distinctive lead gaming pieces, a key element in the Great Army 'signature', were disposed of by a detectorist unaware of their significance.[8] Nonetheless, at Aldwark and Torksey there is a very similar proportion of early medieval finds. At Aldwark the proportion is 59% (888 objects); at Torksey it is 52% (1845 objects). The higher absolute number of finds recorded from Torksey reflects the length of detecting and extent of recording, but probably also the larger area of the camp. At Aldwark the camp was almost half the size, but we are also aware that many artefacts were disposed of without recording.

Most of the early medieval items fall within a late ninth-century date range and derive from the occupation of the camps, and therefore it can be safely assumed that less diagnostic objects with broadly early medieval characteristics are contemporary with them. However, at Aldwark small-scale activity has

7. Kershaw 2013, 14
8. Jarman 2021, 85

been inferred potentially pre-dating the camp, associated with the enclosure. Equally, the broader dating of several categories of artefacts may indicate that intermittent activity continued at both sites into the early tenth century, but there is nothing to suggest extensive or continuous occupation.

The recovery rates of ferrous items are also an issue with metal-detected data. Detectorists routinely programme their machines to exclude iron, or they discard iron finds, allowing them to focus on items which have more personal interest. Archaeological involvement with Torksey has served to counter both these factors, reducing the recovery bias. This was not the case for the first eight years of detecting at Aldwark. Although ferrous material was later catalogued, many of the artefacts are categorised as 'hedgerow finds', collected from field boundaries where they had previously been abandoned by the detectorists.[9] This material discrimination has had an effect on the assemblage, with iron objects either under-represented or poorly recorded. Nonetheless, the proportions of the materials of the early medieval finds are remarkably similar (Figure II.4). The proportion of precious metals are almost identical, with 1% gold at each camp; 19% silver at Aldwark and 20% at Torksey. The ratios of copper-alloy and lead objects show greater variation. At Aldwark copper-alloy objects make up 33% of the total, and lead 40%, whereas at Torksey it is the other way round, with 39% copper-alloy and 34% lead. The reason for this is unclear. It could be a recording bias as we know that at Aldwark many

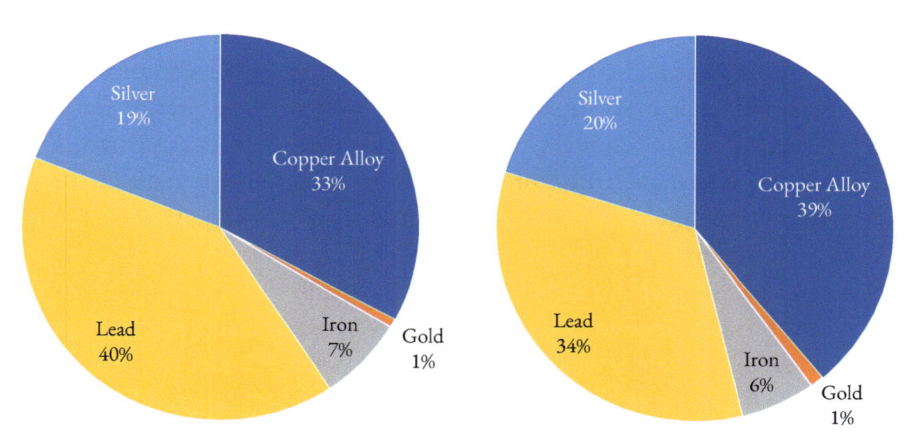

Figure II.4. Proportions of early medieval finds by main materials: Aldwark (left; n= 850) and Torksey (right; n=1833)

9. Hadley and Richards 2021, 209–10

copper-alloy stycas were sold without recording, although equally lead gaming pieces were not retained, so the difference may be real. Finally, the iron objects, whilst under-represented, were recovered in similar proportions; they comprise 7% of the Aldwark assemblage and 6% of that from Torksey (Figure II.4).

A comparison is made with Woodstown, where metal-detecting was also undertaken but as part of the archaeological investigations. From a total of 6007 finds, over 90% were metal. More than 5000 finds were recovered from the topsoil, some of which were identified through a sieving programme, but the ratio of metal to other materials is noted as being 'disproportionately high', primarily due to the use of detectors.[10] With over 3560 items, iron represents roughly 59% of the total assemblage. Not all these iron objects are of archaeological significance, and the proportions may have been affected by a railway line bordering the Woodstown site, but, nonetheless, this indicates the extent of the probable bias in recovery and recording at Aldwark and Torksey, given the very different proportions of ironwork reported.

Summary

Despite having incomplete information from both Aldwark and Torksey, viewed together the finds assemblages are large enough to be representative of the nature of the Viking camps and the range of activities undertaken there. They also indicate what we should expect to find at other camps of the Great Army. We can be confident that the finds represent the activities of members of the Army whilst it overwintered: processing of loot, trade, production and repair, acquisition of resources, and preparations for the next campaign. The assemblages are characteristic of Viking activity, comprising material from diverse locations, much of it cut up for its bullion value, and quite unlike those from contemporary Anglo-Saxon sites. The periods of occupation can be closely dated, uniquely for early medieval settlements.

The sheer quantity and value of the metalwork assemblages forces a radical reappraisal of the scale of wealth amassed by the Army. Plunder was being processed on a massive scale. There was intensive trade and exchange, in goods and probably in slaves. The unusual concentration of people in such camps may have given many of the members of the Viking armies their first taste for urban living.[11] Other urban features included a range of industries, comprising the

---

10. Scully 2014, 125
11. Williams 2013, 17–19

processing of precious metals and other metalworking, including smithying, and other forms of craftworking, including textile- and wood-working. In Chapters 3–6 we address the range and nature of craftworking practices, manufacturing, and forms of exchange that characterised the camps. This enhances our understanding of the occupants of the camps, how they were provisioned, and their interactions with local communities. We have structured the following discussion around four key themes: the portable wealth acquired by the Army; the objects worn and processed on the camps; metalworking and forms of production including minting; and the provisioning of the Army. As will become clear, however, many of the forms of evidence reveal complex stories, reflecting the people on the camps, the places they had previously travelled, and the activities in which they engaged, including some of the symbolic and ritual practices of the Army, in the way that the assemblages from the camps had been collected, transformed, and deposited.

3

The spoils of war and peace

Members of the Great Army were clearly engaged in trade and exchange whilst camped at Aldwark and Torksey. This may have been for provisioning and re-supplying the Army, or converting slaves or goods that had been acquired via raiding into more easily portable wealth. This should not be surprising, since continental texts provide examples of late ninth-century Viking armies trading from their camps in Francia. For example, the *Annals of St Bertin* record that in 873 a Viking army besieged by Frankish forces at Angers was permitted to hold a market on an island in the Loire before departing, while the *Annals of Fulda* describe Franks entering a Viking camp on the River Meuse at Asselt (Netherlands), for the purposes of trade in 882.[1] Such accounts are valuable but for the nature of Viking trade and exchange in the camps we need to turn to archaeological evidence. This chapter explores the evidence for multiple means of exchange at Torksey and Aldwark, identifying the similarities and differences between the camps. While there have been previous studies of aspects of each site, this chapter provides the first extended comparative analysis and draws on a more complete dataset than was available to any previous work.[2] It also compares the assemblages from the two camps with that from Woodstown, a longer-lived ninth-century Viking camp, as well as highlighting comparable finds from elsewhere in Britain and Scandinavia.

Bullion played an important role in exchanges by weight, and involved use of ingots and hack-metal, but coins may have been used at face value, given the lack of fragmentation of English coins.[3] The use of bullion alongside a managed currency has been dubbed a 'dual economy'. It has previously been

---

1. Nelson 1991, 183–5; Reuter 1992, 92; Cooijmans 2021, 202
2. Important studies include those by Blackburn (2002; 2011), Hadley and Richards (2016), and Woods (2020) on Torksey material, and on the coins (Kelleher and Williams 2020; Williams 2020a), bullion (Ager and Williams 2020), and weights (Williams 2020b) from Aldwark.
3. Blackburn 2011, 230–5

assumed that this did not emerge until coins began to be minted for Scandinavian rulers from the 880s/890s, but it now appears that it existed from the very outset of Viking settlement.[4] The picture that emerges from Aldwark and Torksey is, however, not so much of a dual economy as of multiple metal economies operating simultaneously, with gold, silver, and copper-alloy all used in both coined and bullion form. This was doubtless in part to facilitate economic exchange with communities in the vicinity of the places where the Army overwintered, but distribution of precious metals was also one of the means by which Viking leaders maintained their status and secured the loyalty of their followers, and was another form of economic transaction in the camps. The chapter begins with a discussion of the coins from the two camps, as these also provide the dating for the activity, which is especially important in the case of the undocumented camp at Aldwark. It then explores the evidence for ingots and hack-metal, followed by the weights and balances that would have been required for the operation of a bullion economy.

Coins

The Great Army had acquired a diverse range of coins, and this clearly distinguishes Aldwark and Torksey from contemporary settlements. There are broad similarities between the coins from the two camps, including the ways in which they had been treated, but also subtle differences relating to their chronology, the locations of the camps, and collecting and recording biases at each. Other than two dirham fragments, no coins were recovered from Woodstown, reflecting the lack of any monetary economy operating in Ireland in the late ninth century, and emphasising a clear distinction between Viking activity in Ireland and England.

Anglo-Saxon and continental silver coins

There are 14 'broad' silver pennies from Aldwark and 41 from Torksey, 38 of which can be identified to a ruler (Table 3.1). The coins cluster in the 860s and early 870s, and largely comprise the Lunettes type of Burgred of Mercia and Alfred of Wessex, which ceased production c.875.[5] Given that coin finds of the early ninth century are generally more prolific than those of the middle and

---

4. Graham-Campbell 2002; Blackburn 2009; Kershaw 2017
5. MacKay 2015

Table 3.1. 'Broad' silver pennies

Issuer		Reign dates	Aldwark	Torksey
Mercia	Offa	757–96		1
	Coenwulf	796–821		2
	Burgred	852–74	9	13
	Ceolwulf II	874–c.879	1	
Wessex	Æthelberht	860–5		1
	Æthelred I	865–71		1
	Alfred	871–99	2	10
Continental	Lothar I	814–40		1
Later	Æthelred II	978–1016 (two reigns)		2
	Cnut	1016–35		4
	Harold I	1035–40		1
	Edward the Confessor	1042–66	2	2

later parts of the century, this marks out the sites as distinctive.[6] The assemblage from Aldwark suggests that it was occupied slightly later than Torksey, given the presence of a coin of Ceolwulf II of the Cross-and-Lozenge type which replaced the Lunettes series, and was minted after the Army had divided in 874.[7] Although a small sample, among the late ninth-century coins there is a higher proportion of West Saxon silver pennies from Torksey (12 out of 29; 41%) than from Aldwark (2 out of 12; 17%), which may reflect the association of the Aldwark assemblage with a faction of the Army that had headed north after several years in Mercia. In contrast, the overwintering at Torksey occurred after several years in which the Army had been raiding in Wessex, overwintering at Reading in 870–1. Having said this, we know that Lunettes from both Mercia and Wessex circulated widely south of the Humber and so the Army would have been in possession of a mixture of coins from both kingdoms wherever it acquired them.[8] As was discussed in Chapter 2, there are many hoards dating to the 860s and 870s comprising coins from both Mercia and Wessex, mainly Lunettes, that were either local collections of coins hidden in the wake of the activities of the Army or in its possession. The profile of these silver pennies provides critical dating evidence. It suggests that Torksey was

6. Blackburn 2011, 225; Hadley and Richards 2016, 43; Williams 2020a, 12
7. Williams 2020g, 80–1; Naylor 2022a
8. MacKay 2015

occupied in the early 870s, perhaps just over 872–3, while Aldwark seems to have had a slightly longer period of occupation from the late 860s to mid-870s.[9]

These coins are largely unfragmented; a Burgred Lunette from Torksey (T2204) was broken, and one of Alfred from Aldwark (A147) had been bent and snapped but this appears to be later accidental damage rather than a product of Viking-age activity.[10] Otherwise, their completeness suggests these coins were being used in monetary exchange, especially in the area around Torksey, which was in Mercia and where Lunettes of both Burgred and Alfred are likely to have been in contemporaneous use. In contrast, by the time they arrived at Aldwark such coins are unlikely to have been viable mediums for local exchange, being far outside their normal area of circulation; indeed, three coins of Burgred had been pierced, indicating that they had been demonetised, perhaps for use as insets in lead weights.[11] A coin of Lothar I minted in the 840s or 850s at Dorestad (T1134) from Torksey was also out of place and must have been used as bullion, and it is intriguing that both of the early ninth-century coins of Coenwulf of Mercia were fragmentary, and one was certainly cut suggesting it was used for bullion (Figure 3.1).

There are no coins dating to between the early 870s and the late tenth century, but there are a few of both earlier and later dates (Figure 3.2).[12] The greater number of eleventh-century coins from Torksey is almost certainly

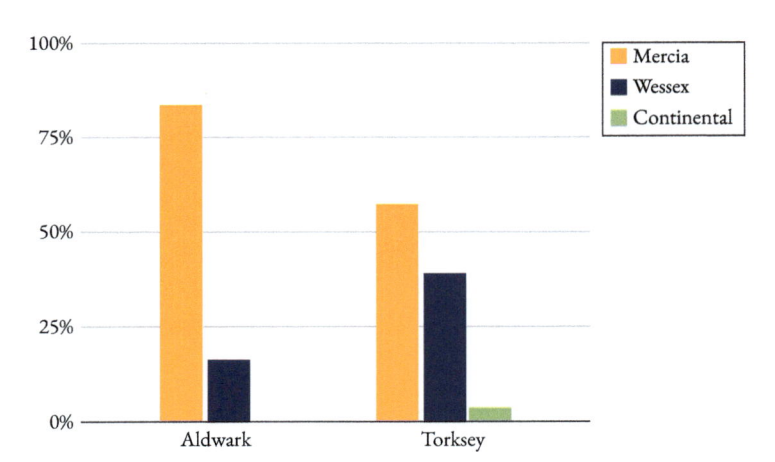

Figure 3.1. Comparison of the proportions of eighth- and ninth-century silver pennies (n=40)

9. Williams 2020g, 81
10. Williams 2020a, 11–12
11. Williams 2020a, 12
12. Woods 2020, fig. 19.1; Hadley and Richards 2021, 98; Naismith 2017, 159–60

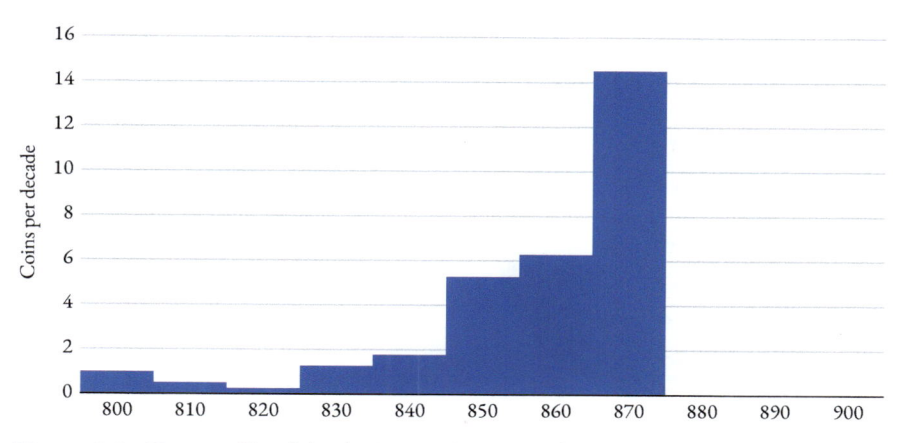

Figure 3.2. Date profile of Anglo-Saxon silver coins from Torksey (after Woods 2020)

linked to the prosperous borough of that date immediately to the south.[13] There are fourteen sceattas of the late seventh or eighth century. One is a Series D coin (T712), whilst a further eleven are Series E 'porcupine' sceattas; both series were minted in Frisia, but are common in England, with a wide distribution.[14] Two others were minted in Northumbria (T713 and T2152). Although these have not previously been considered contemporary with the period of overwintering, the concentration is curious, given that there is little other evidence for settlement of this early date at Torksey.[15] That the Army was in possession of comparatively 'antique' items can be clearly shown from other evidence, such as the Frankish gold and crystal pendant dating to between the sixth and seventh centuries deposited as part of the Herefordshire hoard of the late 870s.[16] Such artefacts may have been curated in ecclesiastical treasuries for several centuries. More directly relevant to understanding the presence of the sceattas at Torksey are a handful of lead weights inset with sceattas. Williams has highlighted a Series E 'porcupine' sceat inset in a lead weight, believed to have been found in Lincolnshire.[17] A weight inset with a gilt Series D sceat of Frisian origin, reportedly found in Norfolk in the 1980s, and another inset with a Series K type 32a sceat of *c.*720–45 from Kent were auctioned in 2015 and 2016, respectively (Figure 3.3).[18] There is no clear evidence for the use of such

13. Hadley *et al.* 2023
14. Naismith 2017, 87–90
15. Hadley and Richards 2016, 45
16. Hoverd *et al.* 2020
17. Williams 1999, 23
18. Classical Numismatic Group Auction 100, Lot 2259 (2015), https://issuu.com/cngcoins/docs/cng_mbs_100_virtual_catalog/277 (last accessed 21 January 2023): Auction 102, Lot 1421 (2016), https://www.cngcoins.com/Coin.aspx?CoinID=310646# (last accessed 27 August 2023)

Figure 3.3. Inset weight with Series K type 32a Kentish sceat of *c.*720–45. The circumference shows impressions of a type of die used in silver jewellery manufacture (Gary Johnson)

weights in economic activities in the seventh and eighth centuries, and while none has come from the camp they lend support to the argument that the Army may have had access to sceattas; the one from Kent inset in a weight was reportedly in mint condition and may have been acquired from a Treasury by the Great Army. The wolf-headed serpent depicted on the reverse of the sceat may have appealed to Viking raiders because of a perceived association with Scandinavian mythological beasts. In the light of this evidence, it is potentially significant that an eighth-century Northumbrian sceat of King Eadberht from Cottam (East Yorkshire) displays a distinctive peck mark, signalling that it was tested for silver content in the late ninth century, presumably when a faction of the Great Army visited the site.[19] Furthermore, an early eighth-century Series J sceat was found in the late ninth-century burial of an adult at Repton (Grave 524). While the excavators thought it may have been residual, it was noted that the coin, an imitation of possible continental origins, was 'found among the bones of the left hand' and so may have been a deliberate inclusion of an item *c.*150 years old.[20] If sceattas were available to the Army, then they must have been used as bullion.

Stycas

There are 204 copper-alloy Northumbrian pennies, known to numismatists as stycas, now recorded from Torksey and 106 from Aldwark, an increase from the

19. Hadley and Richards 2020, 117
20. Biddle, Blunt *et al.* 1986, 29; Biddle and Kjølbye-Biddle 2001, 91

totals reported in previous studies, which were 174 and 90 respectively (Figure 3.4; Table 3.2). Although it had long been thought that stycas ceased being minted in Northumbria by the mid-860s, if not earlier, this new evidence demonstrates their continued circulation well into the 870s. Their presence at Aldwark is consistent with their usual area of circulation.[21] In contrast, it is more surprising at Torksey, as stycas did not circulate widely outside Northumbria and are generally only recovered in Lincolnshire as single finds.[22] They must have been brought there directly from Northumbria, where the Great Army had been before overwintering at Torksey. A smaller concentration of 25 stycas was discovered 2km downriver of Torksey, where the prehistoric trackway Till Bridge Lane crosses the Trent at Littleborough, the 'little fortification', referring to a Roman fort.[23] This may indicate an outpost guarding the approach to the camp.

Andrew Woods has recently compared the relative proportions of stycas from Torksey with those from hoards dated to the 850s or 860s, two from York (St Mary's Abbey and St Leonard's Place) and two from Bolton Percy, which were found on different occasions but possibly part of the same hoard.[24] To this we can add information from Aldwark to extend the comparison, as well as additional stycas from Torksey (Figure 3.4). On the basis of the names of the

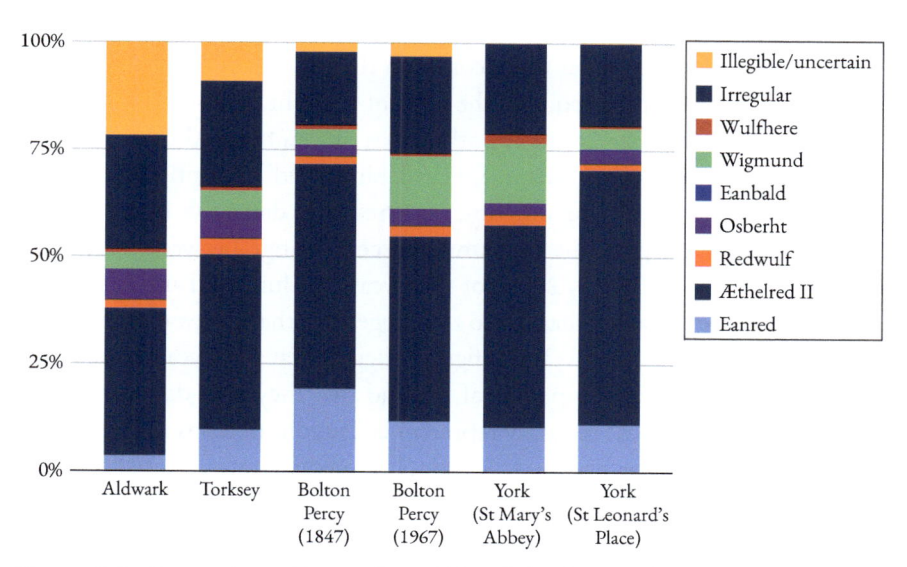

Figure 3.4. Proportions of stycas from Aldwark, Torksey, and contemporary hoards (based on Pagan 1987, 157; Woods 2020, 401)

21. Blackburn 2004, 344; Kelleher and Williams 2020, 36
22. Pirie 2000; Abramson 2018
23. EMC-2009.0195-0222
24. Woods 2020

Table 3.2. Numbers of stycas from Aldwark and Torksey

	Issuer	Dates	Aldwark	Torksey
Kings	Eanred	*c.*810–41	4	20
	Æthelred II	841–*c.*849 (two reigns)	36	83
	Redwulf	844	2	8
	Osberht	849–67	8	13
Archbishops	Wigmund	837–54	4	10
	Wulfhere	854–900	1	1
Other	Derivative/blundered	850s/860s?	27	49
	Double reverse		1	1
	Illegible/uncertain		23	19

moneyers, it can be seen that stycas of the second reign of Æthelred II (844–9) were found in greater numbers than those from his first reign (841–4) at Torksey (21.3% and 16.1% of the total number of stycas respectively), whereas at Aldwark the coins of the second reign were found in roughly equal proportions to those of the first reign. In contrast, in the hoards the coins of the first reign are three or four times more common than those of the second reign.[25] There is also a lower proportion of the coins of Osberht (849–67) in the hoards (between 2.8% and 4.2%) than at both Torksey (7.5%) and Aldwark (7.5%).[26] Many of the stycas in these assemblages had 'blundered' inscriptions, which are often nonsensical; these are sometimes referred to as derivative issues. Among the hoards the proportions of blundered coins range between 17.4% and 22.24%, whereas at Torksey 28.2% of the stycas are blundered and at Aldwark the figure is 25.5%, which has led to the suggestion that stycas may even have been minted by the Army.[27] These figures suggest that the stycas at the camps were collected late in their period of use and that they post-date the hoards; nonetheless they almost certainly represent collections of coins in contemporary circulation in Northumbria. Although the comparatively smaller size of stycas would probably have prevented them being fragmented, the number recorded at both camps points to them being used in monetary exchange.

25. Woods 2020, 402
26. Kelleher and Williams 2020
27. Williams 2015, 99, 113; Kelleher and Williams 2020, 36; Woods 2020, 400

Dirhams

A total of 35 dirhams are now known from Aldwark and 147 from Torksey, including 21 from Aldwark and 26 from Torksey unavailable to previous studies (Figure 3.5). The Aldwark camp did not necessarily have more restricted access to dirhams, which are likely to be under-represented as many are believed to have been sold off to private collectors without proper recording.[28] That is less likely at Torksey, where the majority have been identified, making it possible to assess more reliably the age structure of the assemblage. The numbers from both sites are considerably greater than from Woodstown, which was also subject to metal-detecting, and where just two dirham fragments were recovered, only one of which could have been at the site in the late ninth century as the other probably dates to the early tenth century.[29]

Blackburn observed that the date profile of the Torksey dirhams is similar to that of several sites in Scandinavia, including Kaupang, but with an obvious divergence in the latter part of the ninth century (Figure 3.6). The sharp cut off in the late 860s provides key confirmation of the date of activity in the camp.[30] The latest dirham (T525) was struck in 866–8, which demonstrates the

Figure 3.5. Selection of Islamic dirham fragments from Torksey. Two fragments had been pierced suggesting that they may have been previously worn as pendants (Fitzwilliam Museum)

28. Historia Detectum pages on eBay and pers. comm. Gary Johnson
29. Rispling 2014
30. Blackburn 2008, 52–3; Woods 2020, 398–9

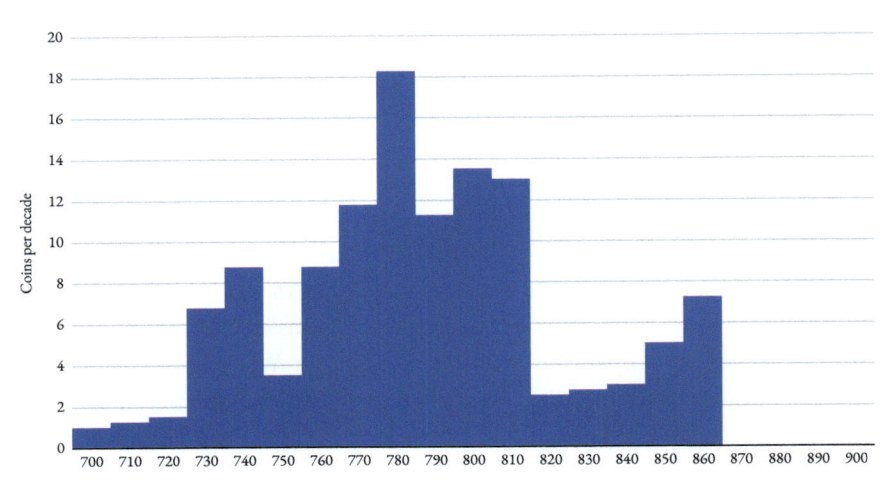

Figure 3.6. Date profile of dirhams found at Torksey (after Blackburn 2011, fig. 1)

speed with which Islamic silver could arrive in western Europe.[31] It also carries implications for both the composition and connections of the Great Army; this coin, struck after the Army arrived in England, was presumably brought from Scandinavia by one of the groups which periodically joined the force. In contrast, most of the dirhams from Aldwark are either too worn or fragmentary to identify, although one (A155) is an Umayyad dynasty coin dating from 661–750; four eighth-century Umayyad coins were also found at Torksey.[32] The date range of the three dirhams in the Croydon hoard similarly spans over a century, with two dating to 786–809 and the third to 842–7. This date range mirrors assemblages from Scandinavia and hoards from the Baltic and Russia: dirhams might circulate for centuries before deposition, with comparatively antique issues used for everyday transactions.[33]

All the dirhams from both Torksey and Aldwark are fragmented, which is not invariably the case for dirhams recovered in early medieval England. A survey by Rory Naismith of dirhams recorded up to 2004 in both hoards and as single finds revealed that, setting aside the finds then known from Torksey, more than half were whole. A more recent survey by Kershaw has listed more fragmentary single finds recovered by metal-detecting, but, nonetheless, comparison with these studies highlights the particularly fragmented nature of both camps' assemblages. While the whole dirhams from England largely date to the tenth century, the Croydon hoard is of a similar date to the camps and all three dirhams are notably

31. Blackburn 2011, 258
32. T603, T620, T622, T628
33. Naismith 2005, 194–5; Gustin 2011, 241

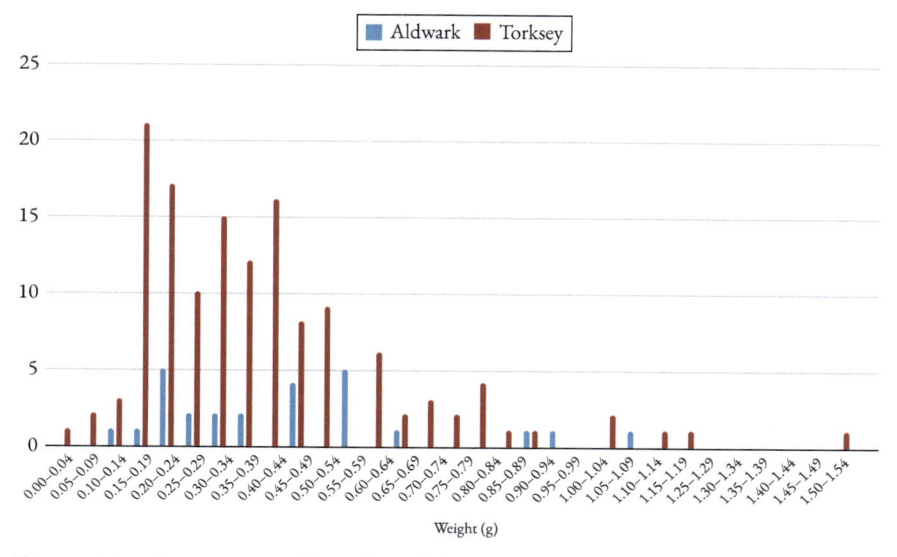

Figure 3.7. Comparison of weights of fragmented dirhams from Aldwark (n=26) and Torksey (n=138) for which weights are recorded

whole, as is the single dirham recovered from the Herefordshire hoard of the late 870s.[34] This reveals that the Army had access to whole dirhams and suggests that they became especially fragmented during their use on the camps.

The known weights of dirham fragments from both Aldwark and Torksey are compared in Figure 3.7. The weight range of the Torksey assemblage is affected by a small number of fragments above 1.25g, but even with this distortion, the average weight of the 138 for which it is recorded is low in comparison with the weights of dirhams from Scandinavian sites (Table 3.3). Blackburn has warned against comparing fragmentation between different sites, since variations in preservation and recovery will affect the results, with silver adversely affected by soil conditions at Kaupang and so reducing the weights of many of the coins.[35] In other ways, however, the 1998–2003 fieldwork at Kaupang provides a good comparison as the site was subject to intensive controlled metal-detector survey as well as metal-detecting and sieving of the topsoil of the excavated areas.[36] It is therefore significant that the average weight of dirhams from Kaupang is still greater than those from either Aldwark or Torksey. The lower average weight, coupled with the lack of whole coins, demonstrate that the dirhams from the camps are more fragmented than

34. Naismith 2005, 212–17; Kershaw 2017; Hoverd *et al.* 2020
35. Blackburn 2008, 65
36. Skre 2007, 144–8, 156–7

Table 3.3. Comparative assemblages of dirhams (Blackburn 2008, 66, table 3.14; Merkel 2016, Appendix A, table 1; Rispling 2004, 43–56)

Site	Number of dirhams	Number of whole coins	Number of fragments of known weight	Mean weight of fragments
Aldwark	35	–	26	0.45g
Torksey	147	–	138	0.40g
Kaupang (pre-833)	51	8	43	0.63g
Kaupang (834–90)	16	1	15	0.74g
Hedeby	49	6	42	0.68g
Birka (1990–5 excavations)	86	18	65	0.58g

those found in Scandinavia, becoming increasingly fragmented with circulation and use.[37]

The Army was clearly used to fragmenting silver coins and this makes the retention of the English pennies as whole coins even more striking. As Woods has pointed out, many of them have weights greater than the dirham fragments and could have been cut into smaller pieces if required for use in bullion exchange.[38] This reinforces that the silver pennies were retained whole to be used by tale rather than in bullion exchange.

Ingots and hack-metal

In the following discussion we deal first with ingots, showing that in the cases of all three metals—silver, gold, and copper—we can see the use of both complete and fragmentary ingots, and then fragmented items of precious metals. One of the essential characteristics of ingots is that they are portable stores of metal, reworked from a range of items, obscuring their origins. This quality has prompted the suggestion that complete, regularly sized, ingots were 'primitive money', with their form rendering them a practical medium for higher-level, possibly inter-regional, exchange.[39] However, as we will see, the ingots from Aldwark and Torksey were very fragmented, which more strongly implies lower-level transactions within the camps (Figure 3.8).

37. Hårdh 1996, 89
38. Woods 2020, 408
39. Gaimster 1991, 119; Thurborg 1988, 303; Sindbæk 2001, 51

Figure 3.8. Selection of silver ingots and hack-silver from Torksey (Fitzwilliam Museum)

Silver ingots

Ingots of silver are the most numerous at both camps and are mainly fragmented; 35 out of 40 at Aldwark and 41 out of 43 at Torksey (Figure 3.9). There are six complete ingots (A144.1, A1267, A1772, A1773, A1774, T1717) of Type 1 according to the scheme devised by Kruse, which are cast, unworked, or minimally-worked bars of varied cross-section.[40] In Scandinavia the distribution of this form is centred on historically Danish territories, Oslofjord, and Gotland, but they also occur in Ireland and England, including in the Watlington hoard.[41] Sheehan has identified a hammered and rolled bar (T79) as an early 'bullion ring', fulfilling roughly the same economic function as an ingot.[42] Whilst previously seen as originating in Ireland, prototypes are now believed to have emerged in southern Scandinavia. There are also several fragments of Kruse Type 4 ingots, where the metal has been reworked and hammered, from both Aldwark (A1244, A1262,) and Torksey (T417, T418, T866). Blackburn notes that these are common in Scandinavia but more unusual amongst English finds.[43]

---

40. Kruse and Graham-Campbell 2011, 74
41. Wiechmann 1996; Hårdh 2008, 104; Williams and Ager 2010; Williams and Naylor 2016
42. Sheehan 2011, 398–9
43. Blackburn 2011, 260

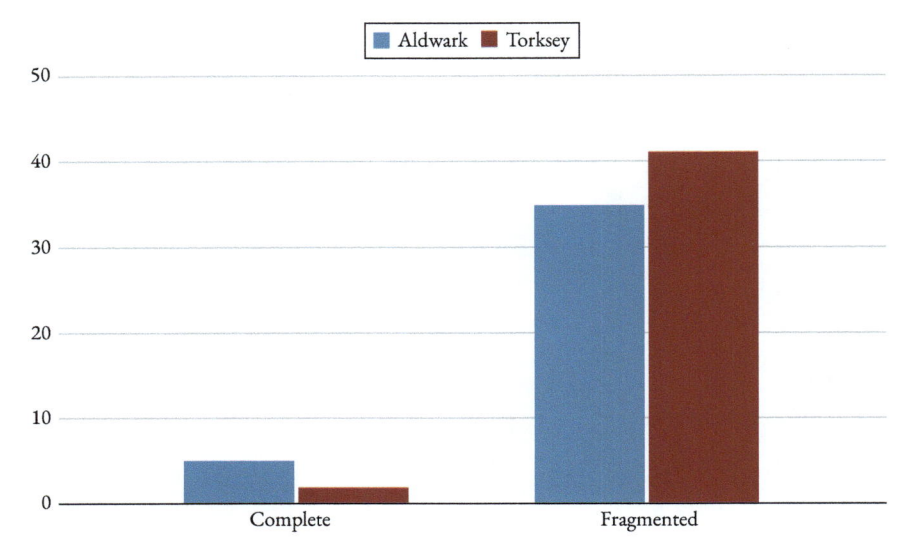

Figure 3.9. Complete and fragmented silver ingots (n=83)

Several metrological assessments have attempted to determine a weight standard in Viking-age bullion, but no universal measure has yet been established. Kruse and Sheehan have both proposed a rough target weight of approximately 25–26g for the bullion economy in Britain and Ireland.[44] A144.1 (6.96g), A1267 (6.74g), and T79 (6.38g) might be positioned within such a unit, each being a very approximate quarter of the proposed target weight,

Figure 3.10. Selection of ingots (not to scale; left to right): two complete ingots from Aldwark (A144.1; PAS) and Torksey (T1717; authors), a hammered and rolled bullion ring (T79; Fitzwilliam Museum), and a fragmented bullion ring (T1301; PAS) both from Torksey

although none of the values seem particularly convincing; T1717 (4.7g) does not appear to conform with it, and all four are small in comparison with the majority of hoard finds (Figure 3.10). While it is possible that none of the complete ingots was made to any particular weight standard, meaningful analysis will always be frustrated if more than one weight unit is present in an assemblage, as Kruse has noted.[45] The Type 1 and

44. Kruse 1988, 294; 1993, 193; Sheehan 2011, 402
45. Kruse 1988, 293

Type 4 examples appear, in any case, to be what Hårdh has categorised as 'workshop ingots'; suitable for storing silver, but not intended as measured means of payment.[46]

The fragmentary ingots mainly comprise terminal or central sections cut from straight bars, although a curved section of sub-square bar, approximately 6mm thick, was probably a fragmented bullion ring (T1301). There are similar numbers of cut ingot fragments from both camps, with the majority in the 0.5–2.9g range, although Aldwark has yielded a much larger number in the lightest category, of 0.5–0.9g, perhaps reflecting a higher degree of fragmentation, or smaller transactions there. The forty fragments of known weight from Torksey produce an average of 3.40g, while those from Aldwark have a lower value of 2.77g. Only two ingot fragments at each of Torksey and Aldwark are heavier than 10.0g and these are clearly outliers (Figure 3.11).

Few hoards from late ninth-century England contain silver ingots, which are more common in contemporary Irish and Danish assemblages, and in tenth-century English hoards.[47] With the exception of those from the Silverdale (Lancashire) hoard of c.900–10, ingots in hoards tend to be whole, in marked contrast to the assemblages from Torksey, Aldwark, and Woodstown where

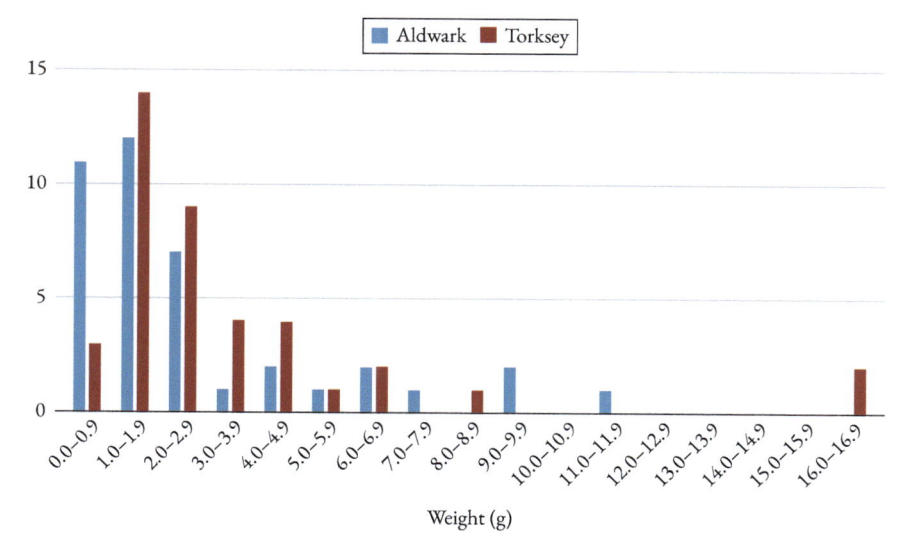

Figure 3.11. Weights of silver ingot fragments from Aldwark (n=40) and Torksey (n=40)

---

46. Hårdh 2011a, 284–5
47. Kruse 1986, 80; Sheehan 2014, 197

Table 3.4. Assemblages of whole and cut silver ingots from Aldwark, Torksey, Woodstown, and four hoards (after Brooks and Graham-Campbell 1986; Williams and Naylor 2016, 11; Kruse 1986, 79–80; YORYM-CEE620; LANCUM-65C1B4; Sheehan 2014, 198–200)

Location	Complete ingots	Fragmented ingots	Mean weight of fragments
Croydon (871–2)	4	1	14.80g
Torksey (872–3)	2	41	3.40g
Aldwark (866–post 874)	5	35	2.77g
Watlington (late 870s)	15	–	N/A
Silverdale (c.900–10)	13	107	11.46g
Bedale (North Yorks.) (late 9th to early 10th centuries)	23	6	79.91g
Woodstown (c.850–950)	2	24	6.00g

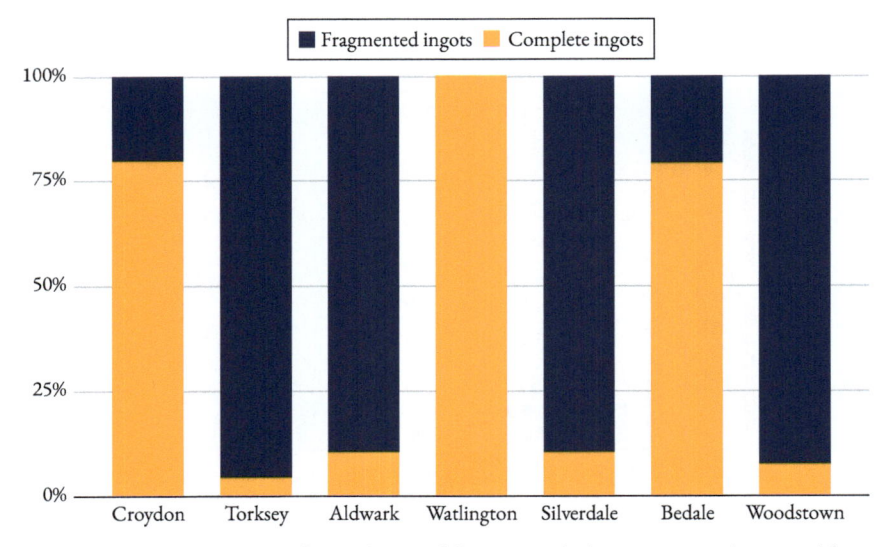

Figure 3.12. Proportions of complete and fragmented silver ingots in the assemblages presented in Table 3.4 (n=258)

fragmentary ingots dominate (Table 3.4; Figure 3.12).[48] The mean weight of the fragmented ingots in hoards is also far greater than those from the two camps.

48. Kershaw 2014, 155–6

This again emphasises the particularly high degree of fragmentation of silver finds from Aldwark and Torksey, and suggests that at the camps ingots were used as a form of currency, rather than solely as a mechanism for storing silver. The mean fragment weights are very close to those from Woodstown, suggesting that silver ingots played similar roles in the economies of all three sites.[49] One of the two complete ingots from Woodstown was found in the fill of a smithing hearth, suggesting silver smelting with a possible focus on ingot production.[50]

Gold ingots

The recovery of gold from both Torksey and Aldwark offers important insight into Viking activity because gold in any form is rare in Viking-age hoards in England. It is more common in Irish hoards, although neither gold ingots nor hack-gold were recovered from the camp at Woodstown.[51] The Torksey assemblage contains one complete and six fragmentary gold ingots. The complete ingot (T857; 1g) is hammered and folded and appears to be a reworked bullion fragment (Kruse Type 4) rather than deliberately cast (Figure 3.13). This suggestion is reinforced by the fact that the few complete gold ingots from elsewhere are typically much heavier. For example, a cast gold ingot recovered with the Galloway hoard weighed 28.90g, whilst a review of examples recorded by the PAS revealed weights ranging from 3.11g to 39g.[52] The mean weight for the

Figure 3.13. Hammered and folded complete gold ingot (T857) from Torksey (PAS)

Torksey fragmentary ingots is 2.08g and the heaviest is 4.97g, while the one gold ingot fragment now known from Aldwark (A1770) weighs 1.2g. This assemblage suggests the use of gold in economic activities by the Great Army, serving as a form of 'commodity money', and seemingly used in relatively small-scale exchange, to judge from the light weights.[53]

49. Horne 2022, 164
50. Sheehan 2014, 197; 2015, 165
51. Johnson 2014
52. Goldberg and Davis 2021, 56; Randerson 2023, 90
53. Williams 2020f, 43–4; Kershaw 2019, 246

Copper-alloy ingots

Whole and fragmented copper-alloy ingots have been recovered from both camps. There are two whole examples and fifteen fragments from Torksey, with a range of 0.29–13.79g, but generally *c.*2–9g in weight and with a mean weight of 4.16g, and six whole ingots from Aldwark, ranging in weight from 7.5–12.74g, with a mean of 10.08g. Assemblages of apparently standardised copper-alloy bars have often been interpreted as hoarded stocks of raw materials for metalworking, without direct economic function.[54] However, Sindbæk suggested that similarly-shaped cast brass bars from Viking-age hoards on Gotland and at Hedeby could have fulfilled a role as a medium of exchange, 'reflecting increasingly routinized procedures for handling the exchange of coloured metal'.[55] More recently, their use as an economic medium within the sphere of activity of the Great Army, has been prompted by the association of cut ingots with similarly-fragmented copper-alloy metalwork and copper-alloy stycas on the camps, implying their inclusion in a metal-weight economic system.[56] Blackburn noted that two out of three copper-alloy ingots sold online, and later confirmed as Aldwark finds (A1221.2, A1221.3), displayed the characteristic transverse hammer marks often seen on silver bars; he interpreted this as a deliberate attempt to make these pieces resemble precious-metal ingots, reinforcing their inclusion in a three-tier exchange system alongside silver and gold (Figure 3.14).[57] A fourth Aldwark copper-alloy ingot (A1807) showed clear evidence of hammering; whilst a fifth (A145) with square cross section and chamfered edges was reported as having been found with a selection of silver items as part of the so-called Aldwark hoard.[58]

Figure 3.14. Three copper-alloy ingots believed to be from Aldwark (A1221.3, A1221.2, A1221.1); this 2001 auction catalogue photograph is the only known image (Fitzwilliam Museum)

Fragmented copper-alloy ingots have been recovered from elsewhere in England, including Coppergate and Fishergate in York, Flaxengate in Lincoln, and

54. Ulbricht 1992, 252; Bayley *et al.* 2014, 128
55. Sindbæk 2001, 59
56. Blackburn 2011, 235–6; Williams 2011, 354; Woods 2020, 406–7
57. Blackburn 2011, 235–6
58. Ager 2020, 15

the Royal Opera House site in London, and Tim Pestell has noted an increasing number of individual finds from across East Anglia.[59] While such individual finds are not closely datable, the possibility arises that some are associated with the activities of the Great Army.[60] A cut fragment from Fishergate (no. 5290) shows evidence of characteristic transverse hammering and surface working, with transverse hammering present on ingots from both Bawsey and Billingford (Norfolk).[61] There were four copper-alloy bar ingots from Woodstown, three complete and the fourth broken at one end; the weight of only one of the complete examples is recorded, which at 6g is lighter than the whole ingots from Aldwark and Torksey.[62] They have also been found more broadly across the Viking world in several hoards, such as one from Spillings on Gotland with a *terminus post quem* of 874.[63]

Post-depositional damage can sometimes make it difficult to be certain that the fragmented ingots from Torksey were all deliberately cut, although some fragments (e.g. T245) had been partially cut and then broken. Nonetheless, the weights of the fragmented Torksey ingots group relatively closely, suggesting that many were intentionally cut to a target weight range, rather than being the result of more random fragmentation during craft processing (Figure 3.15).

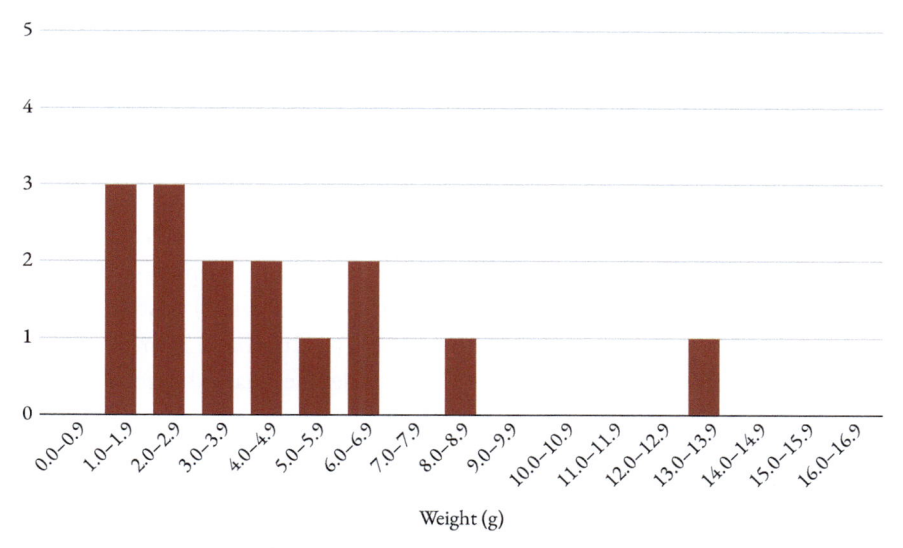

Weight (g)

Figure 3.15. Weights of copper-alloy ingot fragments from Torksey (n=15)

59. Bayley 1992, 781; 2008, 22; Rogers 1993, 1237–8; Blackmore and Dennis 2003, 274; Pestell 2013
60. Williams 2011, 354; 2015, 113
61. Rogers 1993, fig. 610; Pestell 2013, 249
62. Johnson 2014, 116–17 (E2964:600:732; E2964:600:4775); Scully 2014, 126–7 (E0441:600:466; E0441:2353:9)
63. Westholm 2009

Table 3.5. Numbers of hack-silver and jewellery fragments

Location	Hack-silver fragments	Jewellery fragments			Total
		Broad-band arm-rings	Other arm-rings	Other jewellery	
Aldwark	28	5	4	1	38
Torksey	26	2	6	3	37

Furthermore, the weight distributions are reasonably close to those of fragmentary silver ingots, implying the existence of roughly equivalent processes.

Hack-silver

Cut pieces of jewellery and fragments of worked silver were found at both Aldwark and Torksey (Table 3.5). Examples include fragments of a penannular brooch (T700), a disc brooch (T808) (discussed in Chapter 4), and finger-rings with bezels decorated with Trewhiddle-style beasts, broadly indicating a ninth-century English origin (A1266 and T1727).[64] A piece of silver from Aldwark (A1768) decorated with a stylised version of an acanthus bud appears to have been a book clasp (lower left in Figure 2.17). It probably dates to the first half of the ninth century and may be paralleled by a piece provenanced to the Seville region of Spain, which was raided by Vikings in 844 and 859.[65] There is also potentially some significance in the cultural origins of the fragments of arm- or neck-rings recovered from both camps. Two spiral-striated and stamped rods (T3346, T1715) appear stylistically to be from 'Permian'-type rings, which have origins in the regions of Perm and Vyatka (Russia) west of the Ural mountains. However, with cross-sections of only 4.2mm and 3.7mm, respectively, they are closer to types from the Duesminde (Denmark) hoard, which are imitative of the eastern Permian type, but appear to have been manufactured in Scandinavia to a lighter, weight-adjusted standard of c.50g.[66] Fragments of similar rings are included in the Croydon hoard.[67] There are also five broad-band arm-ring fragments from Aldwark and two from Torksey, of a type closely associated with Hiberno-Scandinavian production, although Sheehan

64. Thomas 2006, 156–7
65. Wolfram Giertz pers. comm.; Schulze-Dörrlamm 2009, 744, fig. 1.2
66. Hårdh 2008, 113; 2011a, 286; 2016
67. Brooks and Graham-Campbell 1986, 95–6

has argued that it too derives from a southern Scandinavian prototype.[68] Three broad-band arm-rings were recovered at Woodstown, amongst six fragments of arm-rings and other pieces of hack-silver.[69] With Irish production commencing *c.*880, the dominance of broad-band arm-rings at Aldwark, while a small overall number, may indicate increased contact with the Irish Sea region.[70] The hack-silver from Woodstown is less diverse than the assemblages from Aldwark and Torksey, which was restricted to the arm-rings and a fragment of an Irish brooch, but with no examples of Carolingian or Anglo-Saxon origins.[71]

The weight ranges for the hack-silver are presented in Figure 3.16. In both assemblages most fragments fall within the 0.1–1.9g ranges. Figure 3.17 compares the weights of these fragments with those of assemblages from Kaupang and Uppåkra, a trading, manufacturing, and religious centre in southern Sweden which was occupied until the eleventh century. Again, a high degree of fragmentation, centred towards low weight ranges, is visible at both camps. Whilst the economic use of hack-silver mirrors the practice in Scandinavia, the evidence from both camps suggests that more frequent, smaller-scale

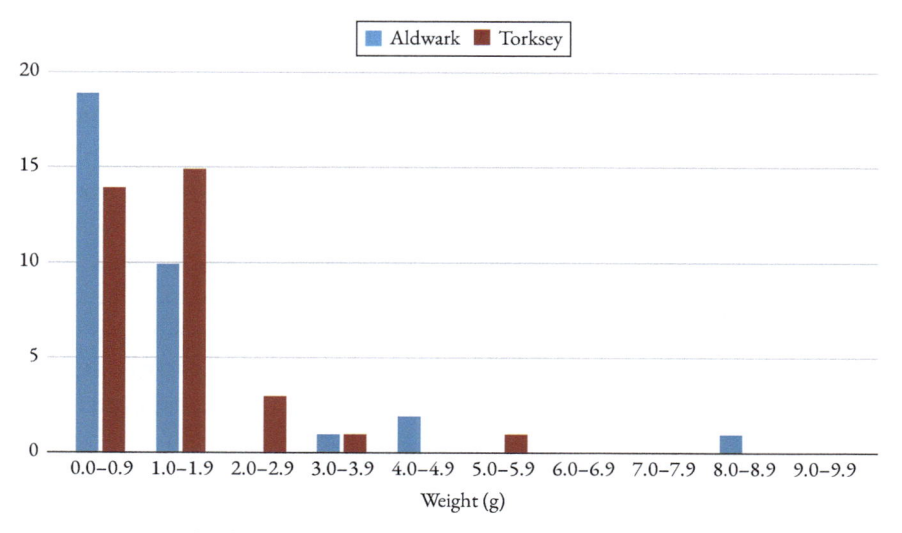

Figure 3.16. Hack-silver with known weights from Aldwark (n=33) and Torksey (n=34)

---

68. Sheehan 1998; 2009; 2011
69. Sheehan 2014, 194, 200–2; Sheehan 2015, 163
70. Sheehan 2009, 61
71. Sheehan 2014, 196–210

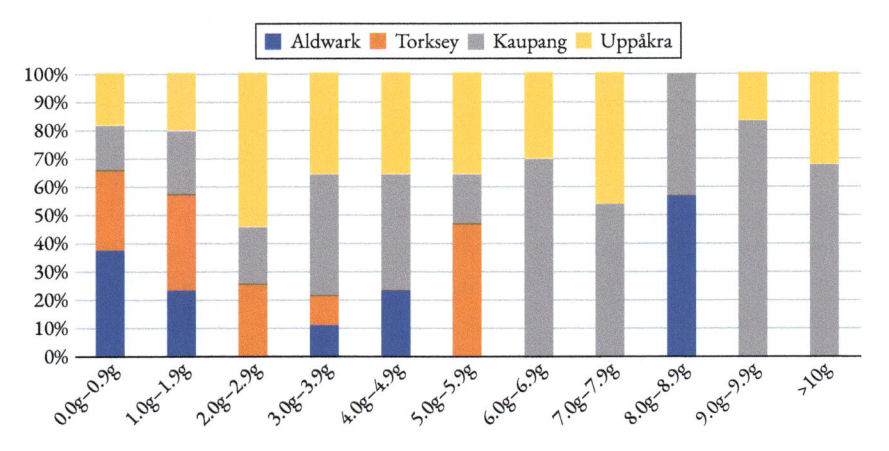

Figure 3.17. Weight distribution of hack-silver fragments from Aldwark, Torksey, Kaupang, and Uppåkra (Hårdh 2008, 101, tables 5.3–5.4) (n=290)

transactions were enacted than at Kaupang and Uppåkra.[72] This pattern mirrors that of the weights, and therefore usage, of the silver ingots.

Hack-gold

Nine pieces of hack-gold have been recovered from Torksey and three from Aldwark (Figure 3.18). Due to their highly fragmented nature, only tentative identifications of the objects can be offered. A fragment of Anglo-Saxon filigree work from Aldwark (A1717) may have been from an item of jewellery, such as a brooch, while a punch-decorated and shaped piece from Torksey (T82) appears to be an off-cut from a thin appliqué foil, presumably from a decorative fitting.[73] Part of the bezel of a flat-band finger-ring, decorated with overlapping punched circles (T743), has cut marks on either side and on the reverse, demonstrating deliberate fragmentation. Graham-Campbell

Figure 3.18. Selection of hack-gold from Torksey T80–T82 (Fitzwilliam Museum), T586, T743 (PAS)

72. Pestell 2013, 245; Woods 2020, 405–6; Horne 2022, 226–7
73. Ager 2020, 13; the example from Torksey is mentioned in Blackburn 2011, 234 (n.25) but not otherwise described.

has suggested that annular finger-rings of this form were a comparatively early and short-lived fashion in Viking-age Britain, possibly connected with the Great Army. For example, a punch-decorated gold ring was recovered from Grave 529 at Repton and a further, contextless, example is known from Thetford, the site of the Army's overwintering in 869–70. In addition, the description of a now lost silver finger-ring from the Laxfield (Suffolk) hoard of the late 870s suggests it was of a similar design; since the hoard also contains deniers and a silver arm-ring, it is likely to have been in Scandinavian hands.[74] A short piece of circular-section rod (T306) with a slight spiral twist was probably cut from a Scandinavian-style arm- or neck-ring. Four further short sections of rod or bar may represent very highly fragmented neck- or arm-rings (T419, T1312, T1688, T2469), although it is possible that they were workshop waste. Finally, there are two fragments of different *solidi* of Louis the Pious at Torksey, one an official issue (T1696) and the other an imitative type (T38); both have been deliberately cut, suggesting that they were also intended to be used as bullion.

While it is unwise to draw firm conclusions from such a small sample, the low weights of the hack-gold (Figure 3.19) echo the high degree of fragmentation

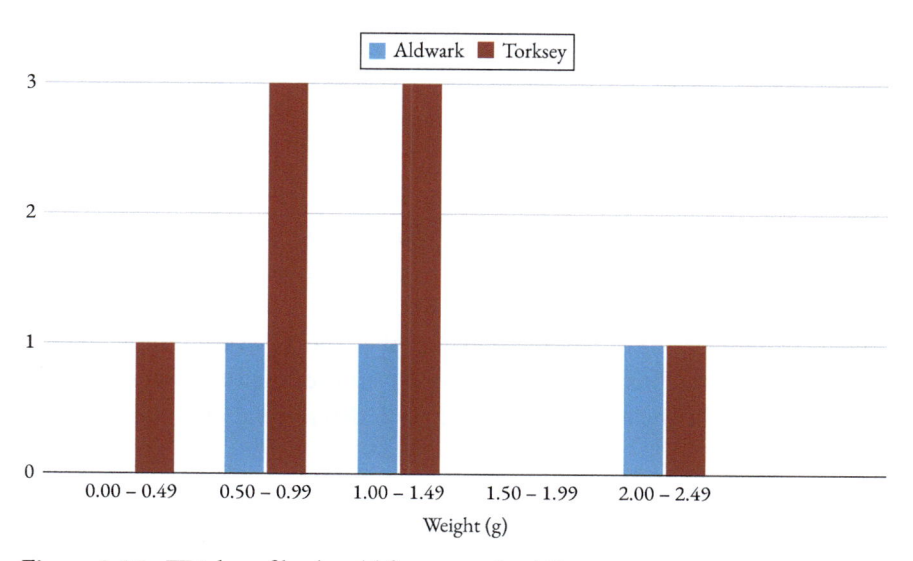

Figure 3.19. Weights of hack-gold fragments (n=11)

74. Graham-Campbell 2011, 106; Biddle and Kjølbye-Biddle 2001, 67; A.R. Goodall 1984, 68

observed amongst the hack-silver. The mean weight for the Torksey fragments is 1.09g, less than the mean of 1.48g at Aldwark. Both are below the mean weight of the fragmented gold ingots, potentially demonstrating that hack-gold from jewellery was used in a different way to that cut from ingot bars.

Gold is thought to have typically functioned as a medium for prestige jewellery throughout the Viking Age. Hårdh has noted that in Scandinavia gold objects tend to be recovered complete, without any fragmentation, and either singly or in conjunction with other gold objects, rather than alongside objects of other materials.[75] This suggests that gold did not commonly have a direct economic role. Therefore, as Blackburn observed it is striking that gold appears to have experienced a period of increased use in later ninth-century England, where hack-gold forms a higher proportion of all recorded gold finds than anywhere else within the sphere of Scandinavian influence.[76] References to gold in Anglo-Saxon charters also increase in the 860s and 870s.[77] In addition to the finds from Aldwark and Torksey, a single curved fragment from a gold arm- or neck-ring was recovered as part of the Watlington hoard of the late 870s.[78] This connection has led to the deduction that single finds of hack-gold from England reported to the PAS are likely to relate to Scandinavian activity in the late ninth or early tenth century.[79] The employment by the Great Army of such a high-value medium for what are clearly small-scale payments is exceptional, and is not paralleled by any other recognised economic activity in mainland Europe or Scandinavia.[80]

Fake gold

It appears to have been worth going to some effort to try to pass off base metal as gold, with seven pieces of fake gold from Torksey. These are in the form of gold-plated copper-alloy, comprising two ingots, three rods, and two gilded, copper-alloy forgeries of Frisian imitative *solidi* of Louis the Pious. One of these (T1695) may be of Frisian origin, but the other (T2147) appears to be an English copy of a Frisian imitative coin, given the English influence on the portrait.[81] Unlike the two genuine gold *solidi* described above, both coins are

75. Hårdh 1996, 132
76. Blackburn 2007, 77–8
77. Blackburn 2007, 57
78. Williams and Naylor 2016, 12, 29–30; Standley 2022, 181; Kershaw 2019, 234–6
79. Blackburn 2007, 75
80. Kershaw 2019, 246
81. Blackburn 2007, 82, no. A17; 2011, 228, 252 originally published as coming from 'near Gainsborough', but now known to be from Torksey.

complete. Any fragmentation would, obviously, reveal the base-metal cores of such coins, indicating that they were intended to be passed as single, high-value items.

Torksey is unique in producing fake hack-gold of this period, which cannot have been intended for metalworking, and therefore must have served some economic function.[82] One of the ingots (T1788) has clearly been manufactured to be a convincing forgery; it takes the form of a terminal from an octagonal-section ingot, cleanly cut with a chisel, and with gilding applied to all faces, obviously intended to disguise the copper-alloy core. The other (T738) is sub-rectangular and less than 9mm long, with no signs of cutting. Gold plating is only preserved on what appears to be the upper face; whilst gilding may have corroded off other faces, it is equally possible that it is unfinished. Three thin rods (T335, T2097, T3518) are all either bent or curved, presumably with the intention of making them appear as if they were waste offcuts or had been fragmented from a Scandinavian-style neck- or arm-ring.

Given their form, it seems that these were intended to be passed off as fragmented gold bullion, although they would have been far lighter since copper-alloy is typically one-third of the weight of 90% pure gold. This would have marked them out as clear fakes or, at best, as heavily-debased alloys with low grades of purity.[83] They may, however, have been accepted by people who were unfamiliar with gold, and the increased use of gold in economic transactions identified by Blackburn must provide the context for the production of such fakes.[84] The presence of these forgeries supports the suggestion that the camp saw a comparative glut of gold, with the metal suddenly available as a medium for trade. The fact that it was considered worthwhile to counterfeit both ingots and smaller items clearly testifies to a role for gold in exchange, but also suggests a status at Torksey as a relatively new, less familiar currency metal.

Weights

A bullion economy required the weighing of metal, and 315 weights have been recorded from Aldwark and 291 from Torksey. These fall into three broad categories: copper-alloy cubo-octahedral; lead; and inset lead. There are also a few oblate-spheroid weights, with copper-alloy shells and lead cores (Figure 3.20).

82. Blackburn 2011, 234
83. G. Easton pers. comm.
84. Blackburn 2007, 78

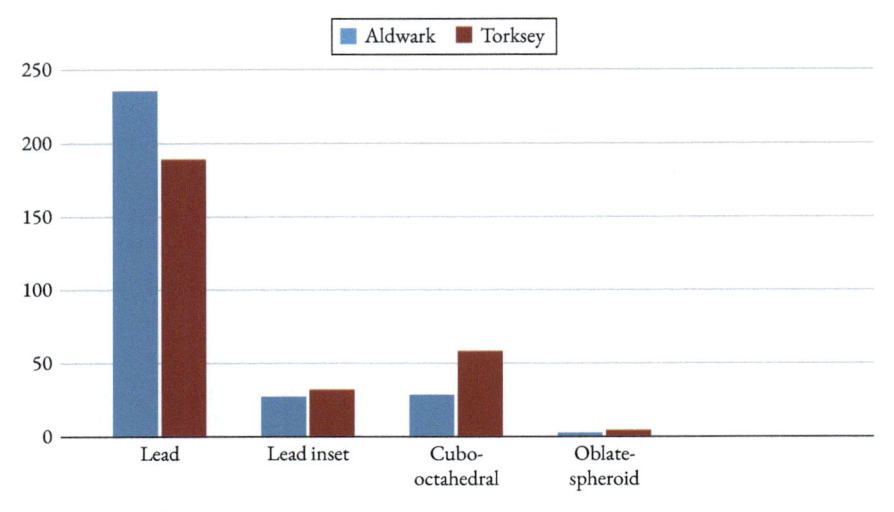

Figure 3.20. Numbers of weight types from Aldwark and Torksey

In the following sections we explore whether the differing proportions of weight types at the two camps is a real pattern or can be accounted for by differences in collecting practices and classifications employed in their study. We will also compare their profile with assemblages of weights from contemporary Viking-age trading sites in Scandinavia and Woodstown.

Cubo-octahedral weights

Cubo-octahedral weights are now widely regarded as having appeared in Scandinavia in the 860s and 870s, and it is the Great Army that introduced them to England.[85] Their design is generally seen as being based on an Islamic system of measurement, and closely connected to the trade in dirhams (Figure 3.21).[86] However, there is also some evidence, from Birka, and the island of Gotland, that they were being manufactured there.[87] Kilger has argued that the introduction of cubo-octahedral weights to Scandinavia involved a new method of measuring value, intrinsically linked to the ability to weigh to a calibrated standard.[88] Whilst the exact unit used remains open to debate, the adoption of a widely-accepted weight system is seen as necessary for the proliferation of dirhams and fragmented hack-silver as trade media from

85. Pedersen 2008, 132; Williams 2020e, 20; Horne 2022, 176
86. Mikkelsen 1998, 45
87. Pedersen 2008, 121, 132–40
88. Kilger 2008b, 325

the 860s.[89] In this respect, the use of a recognisable and reliable weight type served to ensure trust in metal-weight transactions, enabling international trade.[90] Twenty-nine cubo-octahedral weights are recorded from Aldwark and 57 from Torksey, which represent 9% and 20% respectively of the total number of all weights from each site. The higher numbers and proportions at Torksey may be linked to the greater numbers of fragmented dirhams, and can tentatively be

Figure 3.21. Selection of cubo-octahedral weights from Aldwark (PAS)

taken as an indication of differences in the economic transactions at the two camps. It may also perhaps reflect the closer links of Torksey with southern Scandinavian and Baltic economies, where they were common items, when compared to Aldwark.[91] There are, notably, no copper-alloy cubo-octahedral weights from Dublin, despite the large assemblage of Viking-age weights. There is a single example from Woodstown, which in the absence of X-ray fluorescence analysis has been described as an unusual silver example.[92] In neither of these places are dirhams found in any concentration, reinforcing their link with cubo-octahedral weights.

Cubo-octahedral weights are typically classified according to the number of dots, or annulets, punched onto each face; as weights increase with these markings, they are usually assumed to indicate a weight unit, although they may merely have signified a place within a set.[93] The weight ranges are widely recognised as being normalised around a shared weight unit derived from Islamic systems.[94] Analyses of the target weight have arrived at several options, but no universally-accepted range has emerged. The weights from both camps are compared in Table 3.6, arranged against three possible units offered by Blackburn and Sperber.[95] The overall mean weight per annulet at Aldwark is 0.61g, lower than any of the suggested units. At Torksey, the overall mean weight per annulet

89. Horne 2022, 107
90. Kershaw 2013
91. Horne 2022, 5, 20–5
92. Sheehan 2014, 205
93. Pedersen 2008, 149–50
94. Holland 1986
95. Blackburn 2011; Sperber 2004; Geake 2010

Table 3.6. Comparison of cubo-octahedral weights from Aldwark and Torksey (based on Williams 2020e and Blackburn 2011)

Number of dots/ annulets	Weight ranges	Count	Mean weight	Standard deviation	Mean weight per marking	Target weight at 0.65g per marking	Target weight at 0.71g per marking	Target weight at 0.8g per marking
6	Aldwark 3.13g–4.05g	8	3.59g	0.26	0.60g	3.9g	4.26g	4.8g
	Torksey 2.02g–8.87g	10	4.16g	1.90	0.69g			
4	Aldwark 1.29g–2.89g	8	2.33g	0.52	0.59g	2.6g	2.84g	3.2g
	Torksey 2.06g–3.62g	15	2.60g	0.41	0.67g			
3	Aldwark 1.81g–1.99g	6	1.92g	0.06	0.64g	1.95g	2.13g	2.4g
	Torksey 1.66g–2.62g	10	1.99g	0.31	0.66g			
2	Aldwark 1.25g–1.51g	5	1.38g	0.12	0.69g	1.3g	1.42g	1.6g
	Torksey 1.16g–1.62g	14	1.41g	0.14	0.71g			
1	Aldwark –	–	–	–	–	0.65g	0.71g	0.8g
	Torksey 0.73g–1.08g	5	0.85g	0.20	0.85g			
0	Aldwark 0.58g	1	0.58g	0	–	–	–	–
	Torksey –	–	–	–	–			

is 0.69g and whilst the mean of 0.71g for weights with two annulets accords exactly with a unit proposed by Sperber, the comparatively high standard deviation of the six annulet weights casts doubt on there being a single standard. Blackburn proposed that two different weight units might be present in the Torksey series, with lower-value weights conforming to a 0.8g standard.[96] This may be supported by the low standard deviations recorded for the one and two annulet weights on both sites, suggesting that they were manufactured to closely controlled targets. Whilst other standard deviations remain comparatively low, even amongst larger datasets such as the three and four annulet weights from Torksey, all the weight ranges vary and overlap to a notable degree. This suggests that different weight series are probably present at both locations.

An unmarked weight from Aldwark (A1449) is unusual. Whilst cubo-octahedral weights can be prone to corrosion, with pitting occasionally removing dots and annulets, this example is in good condition and the faces are not obscured.[97] Rather than indicating an unfinished condition, Williams has commented that its small size and low weight suggests that the lack of marking is deliberate, signifying that it was manufactured to lie below the ranges of one annulet weights.[98] No deliberately unmarked cubo-octahedral weights have

96. Blackburn 2011, 237
97. Sperber 2004, 70–1
98. Williams 2020e, 32

been securely recorded at Kaupang or Hedeby, with a few that lack markings being heavily corroded and much heavier than the examples from Aldwark.[99] The same is true of three examples from Birka, but two others from this site lie close to a weight of 0.5g, very similar to the 0.58g recorded for the Aldwark example, suggesting that the unmarked Aldwark weight does reflect a known, if rare, element of the Scandinavian cubo-octahedral weight system.[100]

Lead weights

Lead weights were used by metalworkers before evidence emerges that they were used by traders in commercial transactions and they remained a common component of metalworkers' toolboxes into the tenth century.[101] Those recovered from a bronze-caster's workshop at Birka date to the first half of the ninth century, and isotope analysis revealed that they were made of lead from the British Isles; the majority were made of lead originating in Derbyshire where medieval lead mining is well documented, although two appear to have been made of lead from Leadhills in Scotland, and one is consistent with lead from the Mendips.[102] At Kaupang lead weights are recorded alongside the first appearance of hack-silver in the second quarter of the ninth century, leading to the suggestion that they were intrinsically connected with the metal-weight economy.[103] Similarly, a set of lead weights from Cottam are not associated with any evidence of metalworking, and Wallace observes that the Woodstown hack-silver appears to have been targeted on the same unit as the weights, suggesting that both were used in economic transactions.[104]

There are 235 plain lead weights recorded from Aldwark and 193 from Torksey, although some of these have recesses or piercings and may originally have held insets (Figure 3.22). The Aldwark weights were categorised by Williams according to a proposed typology for all Viking-age weights, which primarily identifies weights by shape, with sub-classifications dependent on material and decoration.[105] We have classified the Torksey weights according to Williams' typology for ease of comparison (Figure 3.23). It is possible that the Type F (domed), G (conical), and H (pyramid) weights at Aldwark include

99. Pedersen 2008, 149 and table 6.11
100. Sperber 2004, 74–5
101. Gustin 2004, 21; Pedersen 2008, 119, 166–7; Haldenby and Kershaw 2014, 118; Williams 2020e, 30
102. Ambrosiani 2013, 236; Stos-Gale 2004
103. Pedersen 2008, 133, 162
104. Haldenby and Kershaw 2014, 119; Wallace 2013, 208
105. Williams 2020e, 20 and table 1

Figure 3.22. Selection of weights from Torksey (not to scale; Fitzwilliam Museum and PAS)

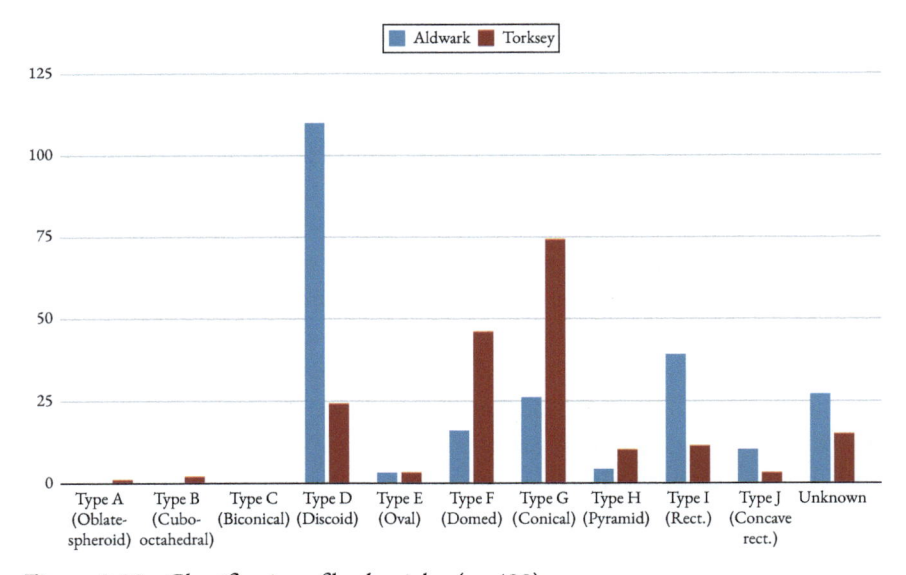

Figure 3.23. Classification of lead weights (n=428)

fourteen items that would have been classified as gaming pieces at Torksey, as these commonly also take domed or conical shapes (discussed below). Nonetheless, even allowing for some of what we would have described as gaming pieces being labelled as weights, by far the most common type of weight at Aldwark, representing almost half of all examples, are those of simple cylindrical and discoid shapes (Type D), which are mostly undecorated. Whilst gaming pieces are believed to have been discarded by the detectorists at Aldwark, which may have contributed to the lower proportions of the similar looking Type F, G, and H weights, it seems highly unlikely that discoidal lead weights would have been disproportionately rejected by those detecting at Torksey. In sum, neither classification systems nor patterns of retention satisfactorily explain the contrasting proportions of lead weights of differing types, which therefore seem to be a meaningful pattern.

Lead weights are common finds on Viking-age sites in Scandinavia, particularly in urban contexts. Although differing classification terms are used, the cylindrical/discoid form is almost universally described, allowing comparisons of the distribution of this type (Figure 3.24). The proportion of such weights at Aldwark is in line with Scandinavian patterns, as they are in the majority among lead weights at Birka and Kaupang, which reinforces the impression that the low numbers of discoidal weights at Torksey is unusual. Pedersen suggests that the discoid shape represents an early form in Scandinavia, with both lead and copper-alloy discoid weights dominating the assemblages on Migration Period sites including Helgö (Sweden). Whilst they continue to appear in large numbers on Viking-age sites, such as Kaupang and Birka, there is a decline in

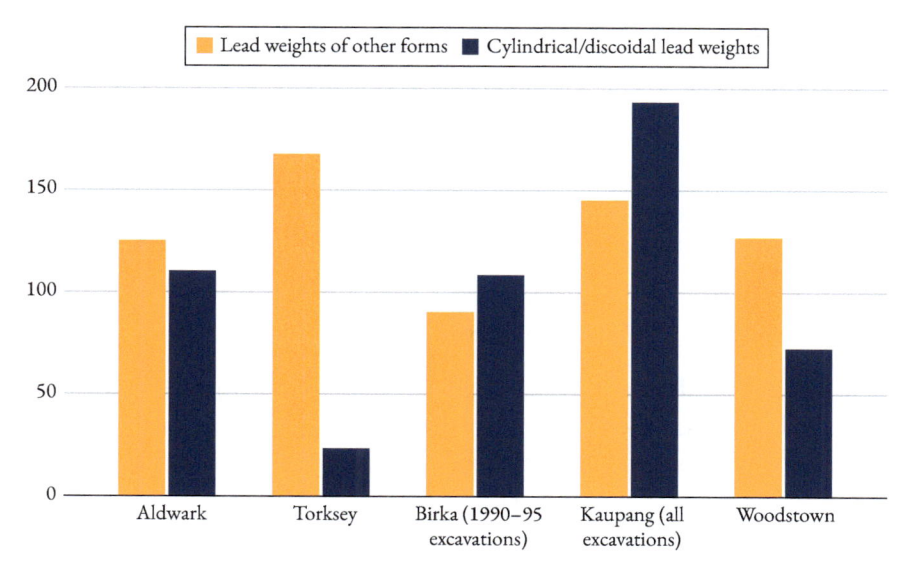

Figure 3.24. Comparative numbers of cylindrical/discoidal lead weights and lead weights of other forms (Gustin 2004, 19, table 1; Pedersen 2008, 123, table 6.4; Wallace 2014, 226)

copper-alloy examples but an increase in the variety of other weight forms.[106] At Woodstown, around a third of the lead weights are of the discoidal form, and Wallace suggests that they cluster close to half- and whole-units of a potential standard of 26g. He also proposes that complete runs of the form can be observed from below 20g to around 36g, including specific weights which are not represented by other forms.[107] This may indicate that at Woodstown this discoidal shape was reserved for a specific use.

At Torksey the cylindrical/discoid weights of Type D have a weight range of 2–24g. The mean weight is 8g, and whilst there is no clear standard, four out of 23 examples are c.3g and 12 are within the 5–9g range. At Aldwark there are 106 Type Ds with recorded weights, ranging from 1–28g, apart from two outliers of 71g and 86g. Thirty-one fall within the 5–9g range. The domed Type F weights also show no evidence of a single weight standard. The 45 Torksey examples range from 1–51g with a mean of 16g, with 35 clustered between 12 and 26g; only two are less than 5g and there are two outliers at the top end, with weights of 49g and 51g. At Aldwark there are only 15 Type Fs, all within the range of 2–23g with a mean weight of 9g. Finally, the third large group of Torksey weights comprises the conical Type G weights, of which there are 74 examples, with a range of 4–49g and a mean of 15g, but there is a single large weight of 49g and the remaining 73 seem to show an almost continuous gradation from 4–30g with no sign of clustering around any specific values. At Aldwark there are 26 Type Gs, with a range of 2–28g and mean of 14g. Again, there appears to be a continuous gradation within the range, although it may be significant that the means for Aldwark and Torksey are so similar. Overall, however, the most striking feature of the weights is the lack of any weight standard, reinforcing that these are personal sets, and if used in weighing out qualities of other metals in trading or metalworking there was no concept of a weight system and it only mattered that the user knew what they represented.

Conical weights and gaming pieces

The comparative dearth of discoid weights at Torksey is hard to explain, but it may be linked to the casting of the gaming pieces produced at the site. Among the lead objects from Torksey are 346 conical forms, typically 20–30mm in height, which we have classed as gaming pieces (Figure 3.25). They are discussed here as there may have been some degree of interchangeability in the use of these objects in

106. Pedersen 2008, 132
107. Wallace 2014, 229

both gaming and trade, and indeed permeability between gaming and trading activities. The Torksey gaming pieces were crudely manufactured; some had been cast in a mould—one (T122) retains a moulding flange—but others appear to have been pressed into shape from pieces of lead sheet. The majority are domed and hollowed; at Torksey one was found stacked inside another, but cylindrical base holes in otherwise solid pieces may have been designed to hold wooden pegs.[108] Some pieces have little spikes or knobs on the top, like crowns, presumably to mark out king pieces. In contrast, solid pieces lacking decoration were classified as

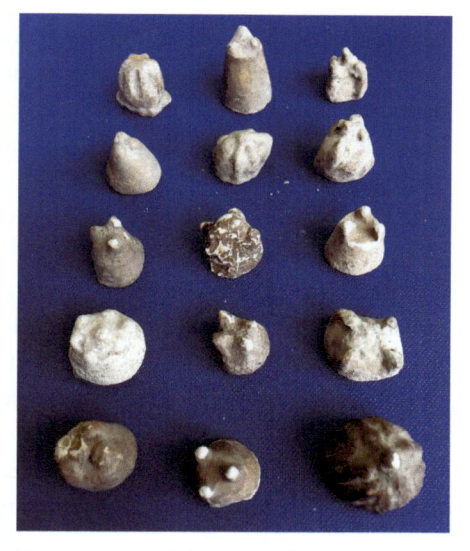

Figure 3.25. Selection of gaming pieces from Torksey (authors)

weights.[109] The fourteen probable gaming pieces from Aldwark are a much lower number than at Torksey, and whilst we know that unrecognised gaming pieces were discarded at Aldwark there is no reason why this would have affected the proportions of types of lead artefacts that were retained.[110] It is possible that the most common weights from Aldwark, of Type D cylindrical/discoid form, were also used as gaming pieces; such counters, often described as 'tablemen', are a widely-recognised form of medieval gaming piece, manufactured from stone, reworked pottery sherds, or bone and antler, although these tend to be later in date.[111] While undatable, there are over twenty water rounded pebbles of discoid form, one of which had been glazed (T1251), from Torksey, which may have been used as playing pieces as alternatives to such forms in lead.

Gaming pieces have been found in high-status burials in Scandinavia and areas of Scandinavian settlement, including Balnakeil (Sutherland), Scar and Westness (Orkney), and the Île de Groix (Brittany).[112] This has led to game-playing being interpreted as an elite occupation connected to the display of an aristocratic

108. Blackburn 2011, 238, fig. 9i
109. Williams 2020e, 30
110. Hadley and Richards 2021, 115–18, 217
111. MacGregor *et al.* 1999; MacGregor 1982, 7728, fig. 940; Mainman and Rogers 2000, 2564–7
112. Batey and Paterson 2013, 650–1; Owen and Dalland 1999, 127–32; Maldonado 2021, 52; Du Chatellier and Le Pontois 1908–9, 150–1

lifestyle, and an aspect of military training, versing the player in 'tactics and strategy'.[113] However, a recent review of the gaming evidence from Dorestad, including what is believed to be a complete set of bone gaming pieces from a harbourside or jetty in the Hoogstraat area, concluded that the low-grade and improvisational nature of some gaming pieces shows that board games were also played in a mercantile context by all levels of society.[114] The lead examples from the camps appear to have been perceived as low-value items, and their crude manufacture, leading to short use and casual disposal, is one of the main contributing features towards their inclusion in the archaeological signature of the Great Army.

Although they are unusual in being made in lead, the Torksey gaming pieces were clearly manufactured following established forms in other materials. For example, the basic conical or domed forms, and decorative grooves and protrusions, have numerous parallels across early medieval Europe in bone, antler, amber, and glass. Some of the pieces from Torksey were evidently skeuomorphs of gaming pieces made of more than one material, such as the bone examples inset with iron or copper-alloy to mark out king pieces. Blackburn observed that the 'crowned' domed pieces, decorated with three to five pinnacles, are unknown in Scandinavia, but more recently Hall has identified two glass parallels from British contexts: the Pictish hillfort at Dundurn (Perthshire) and Lindisfarne (Northumberland).[115] Both are conical, topped with five small glass nodules evenly distributed across their crowns, and such types seem likely to have informed the crowned lead gaming pieces. The Great Army was a heterogenous force, and it is tempting to read the diversity of the skeuomorphs as a deliberate attempt to provide players from diverse backgrounds with familiar pieces, which fitted their own cultural norms. This also carries the strong implication that individuals from various regions, including a Northumbrian or northern British cultural background, were present on the camp at Torksey. Finally, this diversity, along with the sheer number, reinforces our belief that lead gaming pieces were first manufactured at Torksey, re-using lead from either the preceding Roman villa or plundered from churches.

Gustin suggests that various routines and rituals accompanied trade in the late Viking-age and early medieval Baltic with the aim of establishing a social relationship, and trust, between trading partners.[116] Gaming may have served such a function, because, as Hall observes, north-western Europe appears to have had a network of shared gaming practices; accordingly, mutually-understood

113. Solberg 2007, 268; Hedenstierna-Jonson *et al.* 2017, 854
114. Hall 2021, 38; Clason 1980, 240–2
115. Blackburn 2011, 241; Hall 2021, 41; Alcock *et al.* 1989, 216, illus. 14:26; Hall *et al.* forthcoming
116. Gustin 2015, 30

playing rules could cross boundaries created by cultural differences or the lack of a common language.[117] Game-playing may have similarly served as a means of cross-cultural communication and facilitation of trade across the widely-drawn, multinational populations of the camps. It was also a way of familiarising participants with the domed and conical (Type F and G) weight forms and establishing them as trustworthy whilst simultaneously removing them to a more relaxed social setting. The Great Army gaming pieces thus effectively bridge a divide between two classes of object, combining lead, the material of metal-weight trade, with the common, easily recognised shapes of playing equipment, and we suggest that the mutable connection between gaming pieces and Type F and G lead weights was deliberate. The differences in proportions of the common discoid form of weights at Aldwark and Torksey may indicate that certain weight/gaming piece forms were specifically endorsed at the two camps, which raises the possibility of central control of the Great Army markets. These weights and gaming pieces may have been introduced by leaders of different factions of the Army, acting as overseers of trade at the two camps; temporary market sites require regulation, if only in the form of an authority who can guarantee peace. Beyond this guarantee, further central control to promote easy trade corresponds well with Horne's suggestion that elements of the Great Army were involved in the creation of a 'market kingdom', formalising silver trade between the east and west.[118] Those with the authority to mint coins—for which we have evidence from Torksey (discussed in Chapter 5)—could equally guarantee weights, with reliability reinforced through use of familiar types, potentially to the extent of mandating the use of specific weight forms. Both actions accord strongly with the political and economic vision seen in many aspects of the Great Army's activities.

Lead inset weights

There are twenty-seven lead weights from Aldwark and thirty-four from Torksey that are inset with decorative metalwork, coins, or other materials. The dating evidence from a variety of contexts suggests that lead inset weights emerged in the late ninth century. For example, there was a weight inset with Insular metalwork in the Talnotrie hoard, which contained coins suggesting a deposition date of the early or mid-870s (see Chapter 2).[119] Similarly, the richly

117. Hall 2021, 43
118. Horne 2022, 49, 89
119. Maxwell 1913

furnished late ninth-century burial at Kiloran Bay (Colonsay) contained a lead weight inset with a fragment of Anglo-Saxon metalwork.[120] Two inset lead weights from the enclosed settlement near Llanbedrgoch (Anglesey) are ascribed a late ninth- or early tenth-century date.[121] Weights inset with coins seem to have been 'concentrated in the first decade or so after the arrival of the *micel here* in England in 865', including three from Aldwark (A1566, A1567, A1757) and one from Torksey (T3636) inset with stycas.[122] Among lead weights incorporating coins that have been reported to the PAS or elsewhere are more than ten which contain a type of coin commonly found at both Aldwark and Torksey, including stycas, Lunettes, and other mid-ninth-century coins from Mercia and Wessex, as well as a fragment of a Louis the Pious denier and coins of Charles the Bald.[123]

At least twenty-nine inset lead weights were found at Woodstown, although it is difficult to establish the total number as there are a much larger number (up to sixty-nine) which have indentations that may indicate they may once have contained an inset.[124] None of the Woodstown weights have coin insets, probably reflecting the fact that coins were not used in Ireland at this time.[125] Almost all of the insets are of Irish manufacture, with the possible exceptions of a silver brooch terminal, either of Pictish or Irish manufacture, and a mount of Anglo-Saxon manufacture bearing a Latin inscription. It was concluded that 'there is no reason to doubt that the majority...need not have travelled far before being cut down for re-use as decorative caps for lead weights', and so this is another way in which the assemblage of inset weights differs from those found at Aldwark and Torksey. Some of them were found in an area where excavation revealed non-ferrous metalworking, and which the absence of moulds or unfinished artefacts suggested probably involved melting down of copper-alloy objects to create ingots.[126] Other inset weights from Ireland include ten examples from the cemetery at Islandbridge in Dublin and twelve dredged from the River Blackwater between Blackwatertown and Lough Neagh (Northern Ireland) which have been dated to the later ninth or early tenth century.[127] The proportions of inset

120. Graham-Campbell and Batey 1998, 122
121. Redknap 2004, 158
122. Williams 2020e, 23; Blackburn 2002, 98–9; Williams 1999, 25
123. Williams 1999, 29–31; 2020e, 23 and table 2; Hiett 2020, Appendix 1; Mustchin and Walker 2016; DENO-FC3487; SWYOR-D00CF2; LIN-3DFD27; LVPL-5E4310; NLM-5766; NMS-16C428, -0D47D0; YORYM-8054B2, -01F58
124. Wallace 2014; Hiett 2020, 21–2, 146–60
125. Harrison 2014a, 16
126. Ó Floinn 2014, 172–4, 190
127. Bourke 2010; Harrison and Ó Floinn 2014, 174–7

weights from Aldwark, Torksey, and Woodstown are very similar, although the Woodstown total becomes much larger if the possible insets are included (Figure 3.26). In any case the numbers at all three camps clearly exceed those from Scandinavian trading sites. Overall, the evidence indicates that the use of inset weights developed in Britain and Ireland sometime in the second half of the ninth century, possibly from the 860s. They were later adopted on a more limited scale in Scandinavia, where many were inset with Insular material.[128]

Williams argues that the purpose of all forms of insetting was to personalise weights, making them recognisable to their owners.[129] The inset weights in ninth-century Scandinavian graves at Kilmainham and Islandbridge in Dublin, and Kiloran Bay may also reflect their specific personal associations, and it is notable that exotic items, including coins, or fragments of glass, are often featured as insets (Figure 3.27).[130] This practice represents an innovation in the Scandinavian metal-weight economy, with the insets reflecting the environment in which the weights were made; they also provide an example of

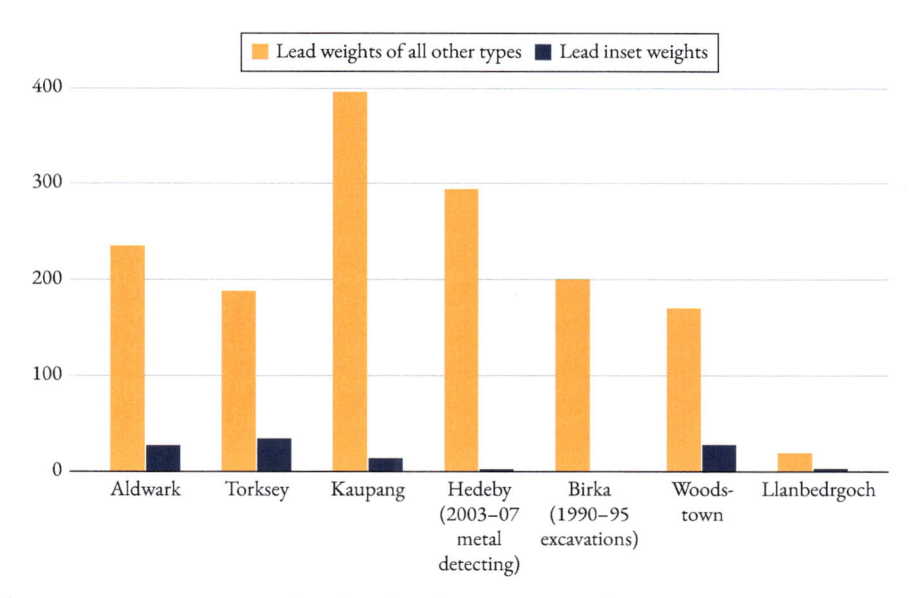

Figure 3.26. Number of lead and lead inset weights from Aldwark, Torksey, and other sites (Pedersen 2008, Appendix 1; Hilberg 2011, 218; Gustin 2004, 19; Wallace 2014, 233–55; Redknap 2004, 159)

128. Williams 2020e
129. Williams 1999, 34
130. Harrison and Ó Floinn 2014, 174–8

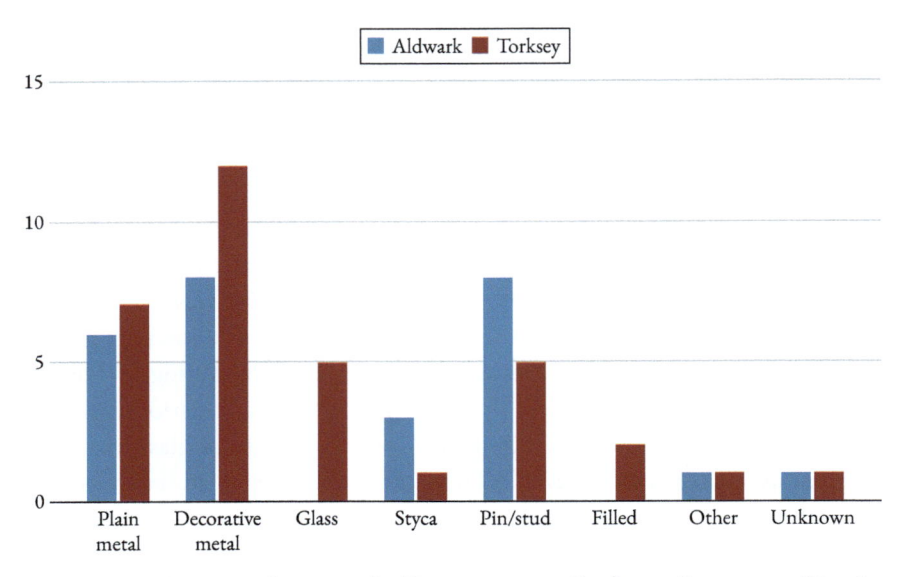

Figure 3.27. Inset weight materials. 'Decorative metal' refers to fragments of Insular fittings, generally embellished with chip-carved or interlaced designs, and 'Filled' describes copper-alloy objects into which lead has been poured (Williams' Type K) (n=61)

manufacturing during the earliest phases of Scandinavian settlement. Indeed, small decorative fragments of metalwork from Woodstown and Torksey appear to have been deliberately prepared as insets for weights (see Chapter 5), as do the pierced Burgred coins from Aldwark. The circumference of an unprovenanced weight inset with a sceat (illustrated in Figure 3.3) had been regularly stamped with a die commonly used in the decoration of Scandinavian arm-rings.[131] This suggests that the inset weights may have been made on the camps by the silver and goldsmiths. They would most likely also have had access to the tools and the offcuts of decorated metalwork and coins required for their decoration.

Some of the insets are comparatively roughly finished, particularly the fragments of glass and plain metal, suggesting the use of scrap material, with its decorative qualities apparently not a prime consideration. In the Torksey corpus, a single piece of decorated metalwork has been split and set into two separate weights (T1732 and T2088). This seemingly reflects the practice of random, comparatively careless fragmentation of decorative metalwork identified by Aina Margrethe Heen-Pettersen, in contrast with its apparently more careful fragmentation and repurposing when found in the Norwegian

131. Graham-Campbell 1995, fig. 28

assemblages she studied.[132] However, other insets seem to have been more carefully selected to reflect either elite materials or socially significant commodities, to project and display wealth or social standing, or to indicate the sources of wealth in the bullion economy.[133] Maria Baastrup has suggested that in Scandinavia weights inset with Irish metalwork may have signalled that the trader was familiar with distant cultures, both facilitating trade and also marking the status of the traders.[134] The insets could have also been loaded with symbolic messages of authority, especially in the case of coins which may have made the weights appear more official.[135] Where legible, coins inset in weights display the obverse depicting the name of the king rather than of the moneyer or mint, which may have carried implications of protection for the user and the transaction.[136]

The inset from one Torksey weight (T978) can be identified as the broken bottom of a funnel beaker or similarly shaped vessel. Another Torksey weight (T3611), and two recorded on the PAS from North Yorkshire and Leicestershire, also appear to contain insets from vessel glass, while a fragment of convex vessel glass was also part of the Talnotrie hoard.[137] Funnel beakers were the most common glass drinking vessels in the ninth century in both Anglo-Saxon and Scandinavian contexts, albeit rare.[138] They were associated with artisans and traders, and may also have been involved in the trading process as part of the rituals involved in generating trust between trading partners; later medieval Scandinavian laws indicate that deals were sealed with a drink.[139] Embedding a fragment of vessel glass into a weight may have been a way to symbolise this sort of ritual practice. Sherds of vessel glass from graves in Kaupang were probably amulets or tokens of whole vessels, reinforcing the symbolic significance of vessel glass.[140]

Balances

Balances were essential for everyday mercantile activity, with a Viking force on the Seine recorded as receiving a large silver payment 'according to their scales' in 866, although they would also have been required by metalworkers.[141] Two incomplete copper-alloy balances have been identified from Aldwark. One

132. Heen-Pettersen 2021
133. Harrison and Ó Floinn 2014, 178; Horne 2022, 204–6
134. Baastrup 2014
135. Pedersen 2008, 168–9; Williams 1999, 35; 2020e, 23
136. Pedersen 2008, 176; Hiett 2020, 35
137. YORYM-01F154; PUBLIC-57FD2D; Maxwell 1913, 15
138. Gaut 2011, 169–70, 174, 189; Broadley 2014, 22
139. Gaut 2011, 257; Gustin 2015, 30
140. Hiett 2020, 53–4; Hougen 1969, 131–2; Gaut 2011, 174
141. Westholm 2009, 146; Nelson 1991, 130

(A156) comprises the pointer, part of the central beam and stirrup, through which a knotted wire loop passed for suspension. The stirrup is fixed to the beam by means of a copper-alloy rivet, set at the base of the pointer, which would have acted as a pivot. The beam is rectangular in section, with a piercing and the remains of an iron rivet visible at the end of one of the arms. The opposite arm is broken at roughly the same length, with the item forming an inverted T-shape, which it has been suggested may have prompted a secondary use as a pendant (see Chapter 4).[142] It appears to have a long pointer, similar to the complete balance from Kiloran Bay.[143] The Aldwark balance has been categorised as belonging to Steuer's Type 6, which were all manufactured with folding arms, with recessed slots on the ends of the beam, to accommodate the foldable arms by way of a pivoting mortise and tenon joint.[144] However, this seems questionable as the equal length of the arms is a product of later damage, and there are no hinge recesses. If the rivet hole on the beam had originally been a hinge, another would have been required on the now-broken end, which would have rendered it asymmetric. Instead, this iron rivet may represent a repair, to what was a fixed-arm rather than folding-arm balance.

The single-piece central beam and pointer of another balance (A1159) is missing the stirrup, with the pivot-point marked only by a piercing towards the base of the pointer. The beam is sub-square in section, with vertical slots for the hinging arms visible in thickened collars on each terminal, and it is clearly of Steuer's folding Type 6. Kruse has suggested a preference for smaller sizes of balance in the late Anglo-Saxon period, and the beam is certainly large in comparison to tenth-century examples from Thetford and York.[145] However, the three folding balances recovered as grave goods from Dublin all have beams of equal or greater length, suggesting that the Aldwark example is broadly contemporary.[146]

There may be part of another incomplete balance from Torksey (T699), which also appears to be of the fixed-arm type (Figure 3.28). The cast, rectangular-section copper-alloy bar is broken at both ends, but retains a short, pierced triangular projection which may be the combined pointer and suspension hole for an absent stirrup. The upturned curve of the surviving arm is paralleled by a complete ninth-century balance beam from Ipswich.[147] In contrast, another upturned fixed-arm balance from Coppergate (no. 10415)

142. Ager 2020, 15
143. Graham-Campbell and Batey 1998, 120
144. Ager 2020, 15; Steuer 1987, Abb. 2; Horne 2022, 171
145. Rogers 2020a; Kruse 1992, 76–8; A.R. Goodall 1984, 69; Mainman and Rogers 2000, 2559–61
146. Harrison and Ó Floinn 2014, 172
147. Kruse 1992, fig. 2a

was recovered from a twelfth- to thirteenth-century context, but interpreted as residual from either the Roman or Anglo-Scandinavian period.[148] This illustrates the difficulties in dating such comparatively undiagnostic designs, but given the wider context at Torksey it seems likely to be contemporary with the Great Army's overwintering.

Figure 3.28. Probable balance arm (T699) from Torksey (authors)

Conclusion

Both camps have yielded evidence of complex, multi-faceted economies, with multiple metal economies and various weight and exchange systems operating simultaneously. This suggests that both camps operated as markets, where, as Williams observes, 'Forms of exchange were as varied as forms of wealth.'[149] While this variety may reflect diverse groups within the Army, the sharing of plunder and the need to engage with local economic systems must also have been factors in this diversity. It is principally the retention of Anglo-Saxon silver pennies as whole, in contrast to the highly fragmented dirhams, that suggests engagement in local exchange. As we will see in Chapter 5, these coins are accompanied by evidence for minting of similar issues, reinforcing their use in local exchange. Cooijmans suggests that market activity represents a secondary 'diversification' for Viking camps in the Frankish realm, but it seems to have been of primary importance at both Torksey and Aldwark, albeit that the nature of the available evidence from England and the Continent is quite different.[150] Portable wealth was doubtless not acquired solely through raiding and plunder, with tribute taking probably an element of the peace treaties that the Army repeatedly made when overwintering. As we saw in Chapter 2, the Church is known to have leased out land in the late ninth century as a means of raising tribute to pay Viking armies.[151] Irish and continental sources record the capture and sale of slaves by ninth-century Viking armies; indeed, prisoners

148. Mainman and Rogers 2000, 2561, 2646
149. Williams 2015, 105
150. Cooijmans 2020, 145
151. McLeod 2006; 2014, 186–98

held for ransom, or to be resold as slaves, or retained for domestic tasks were a less archaeologically visible part of the treasure that needed to be safeguarded in the camps, as testified by the flight of captives gathered on the French island of Noirmoutier in 843.[152] While slave-taking is not directly documented in contemporary sources in England, it must have occurred. The peace treaty between Alfred and Guthrum from the 880s notably contains a clause in which they agreed not to harbour the runaway slaves from the other's realm.[153] The ransoming of hostages was another means of acquiring wealth, which was also politically useful; following the arrival of the Great Army at Repton, the new ruler of Mercia, Ceolwulf, gave hostages and swore oaths that he would be ready 'at the enemy's service' whenever required.[154]

The fragmented dirhams, ingots, and hack-silver show clear connections to Scandinavian economic systems, but, as Williams notes, the Viking camps date to a period of major economic change, with fragmented silver a comparatively new medium of exchange.[155] Whilst casual loss almost inevitably prejudices the dirham, ingot, and hack-metal assemblages towards the smallest fragments, these are appreciably smaller than those recovered from trading sites in Scandinavia. The mean weights are remarkably similar for the two camps and may derive from a practice of 'topping up' larger weights for transactions, but the dearth of similar material in Scandinavia strongly suggests that this was not a routine occurrence there. These smaller, lighter fragments were probably used in transactions in their own right, showing regular, small-scale exchanges in fragmented silver at both camps. Hårdh observed that the intense fragmentation of silver is typically the final intermediate step between barter and coin.[156]

In assessing this evidence, we must remember that there will have been types of economic transaction and trade not archaeologically evidenced. This may have included exchange of other forms of portable wealth such as livestock, while barter, gift-giving, and food renders as part of tribute payments in peace treaties may all have been a means of provisioning the camps that remain beyond the archaeological evidence discussed here.[157] The significance of precious metals in an economy of display should also be acknowledged; while the archaeological traces comprise fragmentary items, such as arm-rings, complete

152. Deutsch-Dumolin 2023, 179
153. Pelteret 1980, 106–7; Keynes and Lapidge 1983, 172; Holm 1986
154. Whitelock 1961, 48
155. Williams 2015, 104
156. Hårdh 1996, 86
157. Williams 2015, 104–7

examples were available to the Army, such as those in the Watlington hoard. This chapter has also revealed something of the diverse cultures encountered by members of the Great Army, especially those engaged in trade. This was sometimes symbolised through such practices as the insertion of material from new environments into weights, reflecting a cultural agility essential to establish trading networks but also paving the way for integration into the communities among which many members of the Great Army were to settle.

4

Wearing and processing

This chapter examines the decorative metalwork from Aldwark and Torksey, including dress accessories and jewellery. The majority are of Anglo-Saxon manufacture, but some are of Scandinavian, Irish, or continental origin. The chapter nuances our understanding of the material culture of the camps by seeking to distinguish items that may have been used by members of the Great Army and its followers, finding their way into the archaeological record through casual loss, from those that represent the gathering together and processing of looted material. Deliberately cut fragments of decorative metalwork suggest an extensive range of metal processing and production, indicating that specialist metalworkers travelled with the Army, with loot being melted down and processed, turning it into bullion or new objects. The repurposing of jewellery to create new forms or for use as insets for lead weights is also evidenced. It is well recognised that there need be no direct relationship between the place of origins of forms of material culture and the individuals who wore or used them, and therefore deductions about the ethnic identity of individuals on the basis of material culture are hazardous.[1] Nonetheless, some items are so place-specific that their appearance at Aldwark and Torksey must reveal regions through which members of the Army had travelled, while some of the manufacturing practices at the camp are so regionally distinctive as to betray the presence of craft specialists from diverse origins. Most of the early medieval artefacts date to the ninth century and are contemporary with the activities of the Great Army, but some items of earlier date, especially where there is evidence for their repurposing, may also reflect activities undertaken during the overwintering (Table 4.1).

---

1. Hadley and Richards 2000; Hadley 2020

Table 4.1. Proportions of early medieval dress accessories

Site	Brooches	Pins	Strap-ends	Hooked tags
Aldwark	14	16	45	9
Torksey	23	64	156	29

Figure 4.1. Selection of strap-ends from Torksey (Fitzwilliam Museum)

Strap-ends

There are 45 early medieval strap-ends from Aldwark and 156 from Torksey, mostly copper-alloy, and these have been classified by Dave Haldenby, using the typology devised by Gabor Thomas (Figures 4.1 and 4.2).[2] The majority of the assemblages extend over a comparatively narrow, ninth-century, date range; *c.*20 later strap-ends from Torksey relate to subsequent settlement in the town to the south. The Class A strap-ends dominate, but the ratios of Classes B to E differ, reflecting a clear contrast between the camps. Some of the strap-end forms were once dated to the early tenth century but new evidence, including that from the two camps, confirms earlier origins.

2. Thomas 2000a

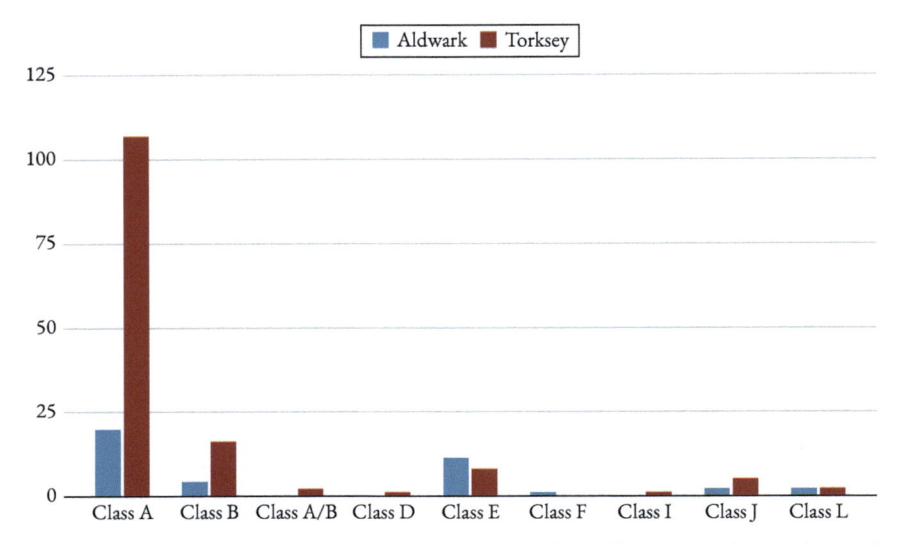

Figure 4.2. Strap-end types according to the typology devised by Gabor Thomas (n=182)

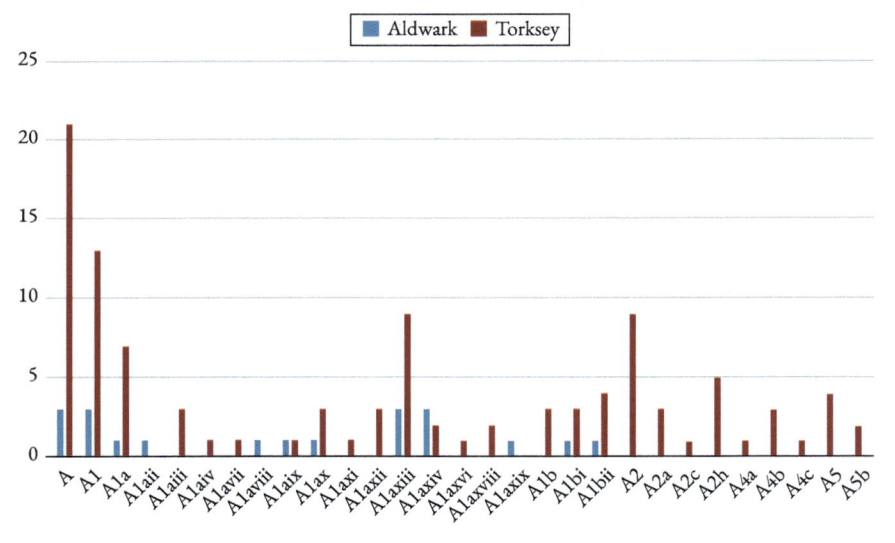

Figure 4.3. Class A strap-ends (n=126)

Class A strap-ends

Class A strap-ends are characterised by a convex form, with bifurcated butt-ends and zoomorphic terminals (Figure 4.3). These are divided into types according to their decorative schema including Trewhiddle-style artwork (A1), geometric designs (A2), anthropomorphic designs (A3), enamelling (A4), and embellishment with silver wire (A5).[3] The date range for the Class A series is reasonably narrow, with the Trewhiddle-style decorative artwork which characterises the A1 type commonly dated to the ninth century, and seen as passing out of use by *c.*900. It has, however, been argued that there was an extended date for Trewhiddle-style metalwork in northern England, with strap-ends of this form recovered from both settlement foci at Cottam (East Yorkshire), which has been seen as a survival in an 'artistically conservative' region.[4] The seven strap-ends recovered from East Thirston are all of sub-type A1a, as was the strap-end from the Talnotrie hoard, and each site has been associated with the activities of the Army (see Chapter 2).[5] Both A2 and A5 types can be dated to the ninth century on archaeological grounds, with an A5 strap-end recovered from the late ninth-century charnel deposit at Repton.[6] Type A4 strap-ends are less chronologically secure, but are also dated to the ninth century.[7] All these forms can therefore be assumed to derive from the occupation of the camps.

There are no Type A2, A4, and A5 strap-ends from Aldwark, probably reflecting the northern dominance of the A1 series observed by Thomas. Otherwise, the assemblages from both locations are generally unremarkable, distinguished from contemporary settlements only by the quantities of strap-ends when compared to other common categories of early medieval artefacts such as pins (discussed later in this chapter). The single sub-type A1avii strap-end from Torksey (T741) is, however, of note (Figure 4.4). This form is also known as a 'Wooperton type', after the Northumberland find spot of the first described example, and it features two backwards-facing beasts. The series is

characterised by a high degree of homogeneity, with Richard Bailey suggesting that their pronounced similarities pointed to manufacture in a single workshop, probably in York.[8] We have identified a concentrated northern bias for the distribution of the forty-four examples now known, with *c.*80% recovered from

Figure 4.4. A1avii strap-end (T741) and a lead model for an A1 strap-end (T1459; PAS)

3. Thomas 2000a, 69–99
4. Thomas 2006, 157; Hall 2000, 320
5. Kershaw *et al.* 2023, 106; Thomas 2000a, 74, 351
6. Thomas 2000a, 187
7. Thomas 2000a, 199–202
8. Bailey 1993, 90

Yorkshire.[9] Although the decorative scheme has English influences, the type was produced by casting, a Scandinavian method of manufacturing. The Torksey strap-end is a rare outlier south of the Humber, suggesting the presence of someone from Northumbria, and it was probably lost by its owner rather than being collected as a source of scrap. It also suggests that dress fittings produced in an English style, or which would appeal to Anglo-Saxon tastes, were worn by members of the Army or their local allies at Torksey. The A5 strap-ends from Torksey are also distinctive in being outliers in the distribution of this type, which is otherwise strongly concentrated in East Anglia, leading Thomas to suggest that they may have been manufactured in Ipswich where moulds for manufacturing strap-ends have been found.[10] A5 strap-ends have also been found at Repton and Cottam, other sites visited by the Great Army, suggesting both the agency of the Army and also perhaps that they had been adopted into the dress of some of its members.

Just under half of the Torksey Class A strap-ends are so fragmented as to make identification to type impossible, compared with only 20% of those from Aldwark. Furthermore, many of the fragmented Class A strap-ends from Torksey show signs of cutting, a feature absent in the Aldwark assemblage. Whilst corrosion and post-depositional damage make it difficult to be certain that this fragmentation is all deliberate, fragments with multiple cut lines (e.g. T1747 and T3545) confirm that in those cases this fragmentation was not accidental. Whilst the relative totals of collected strap-ends are similar, the higher degree of deliberate fragmentation at Torksey suggests that the material was being used differently at each camp. The significance of the fragmentation is reinforced by comparison with broadly contemporary assemblages from elsewhere, including Cottam, Cowlam (East Yorkshire), and Staunch Meadow, Brandon (Suffolk) and while seven of the 37 early medieval strap-ends from Flixborough (Lincolnshire) were damaged, there is no evidence that any of them had been deliberately fragmented.[11]

Part of a lead model for a strap-end has been found at Torksey (T1459) (Figure 4.4). Although only the proximal end remains, fashioned with a bifurcated terminal, the surviving trilobate palmette design indicates a Trewhiddle-inspired influence characteristic of the A1 type.[12] Whilst lead was occasionally used to produce wearable belt fittings, the Torksey example cannot have been

9. Haldenby *et al.* 2022, 104–6
10. Thomas 2000a, 141–2
11. Thomas *et al.* 2009, 13–16
12. Thomas 2000a, 193–4

worn as it lacks rivet holes. Lead models are widely seen as being used in the production of clay moulds, an intermediate stage in the creation of cast items, probably used to form basic mould shapes to which fine detail could be added.[13] The rudimentary trilobate palmette motif resembles the simplified design impressed on to a strap-end mould fragment from Carlisle, suggesting that the Torksey find could have been used as a master matrix in the manufacture of similar moulds.[14]

Class B strap-ends

Class B strap-ends are broadly defined by split butt-ends and zoomorphic terminals similar to the Class A series but distinguished by parallel-sided bodies and a longer, narrower form (Figure 4.5). Furthermore, in contrast to the almost entirely Anglo-Saxon decorative forms of the Class A series, Scandinavian art styles are prominent in some Class B strap-ends, with distinctive Borre-style animal masks on the B4 types and both Ringerike and Urnes designs on the B6 types. The Class B series spans a far wider date range than the Class A, with individual sub-types occupying quite different chronologies. The B1 and B2 types form the bulk of the Torksey assemblage, and they are characteristically

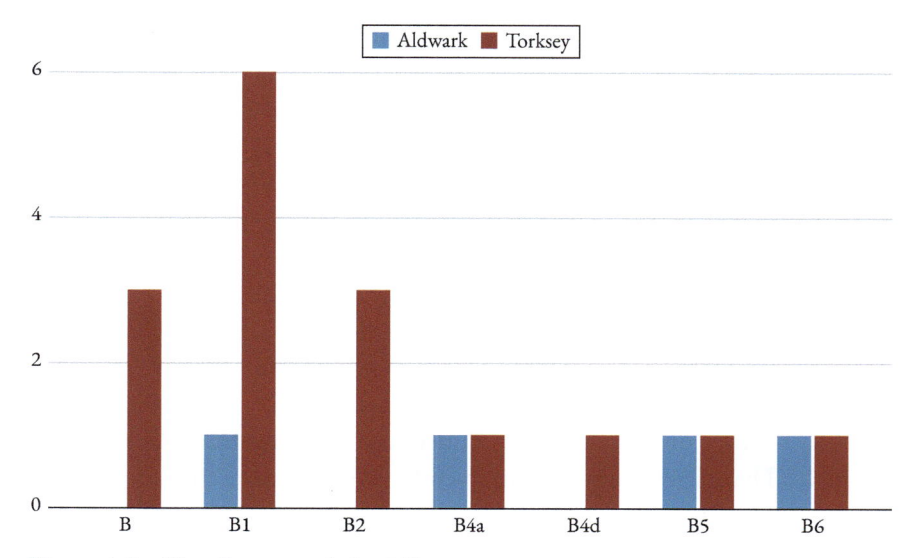

Figure 4.5. Class B strap-ends (n=20)

13. Coatsworth and Pinder 2002, 74; Ager 2006a, 248; Thomas *et al.* 2008
14. Taylor and Webster 1984, 179

Anglo-Saxon in design, with date ranges centred on the ninth century.[15] The distribution of these types is concentrated south of The Wash, and Thomas has therefore suggested that their production may have focused on centres such as Winchester and Canterbury.[16] It seems reasonable to conclude that these particular strap-ends derive from the occupation of the camp, but had been collected by members of the Army as a source of scrap, possibly whilst overwintering in London in 871–2. Their marked southern distribution may explain the recovery of only one B1 strap-end and no B2 forms from Aldwark. The single B6 forms from each camp date to the eleventh century, and must reflect later, casual losses.

The Borre-style animal masks which characterise the B4 type are strongly indicative of Scandinavian design, with the B4a sub-type particularly showing a heavy relief decoration which Thomas interpreted as being produced by casting. These elements, coupled with a distribution including both northern Scotland and the Irish Sea region, led him to suggest that the B4a strap-ends were developed and produced around the Irish Sea but widely adopted across northern England and eventually in Scandinavia.[17] Thomas identified 16 examples, greatly exceeded by the 62 now known, largely confined to Yorkshire, Lincolnshire, and East Anglia. As well as the finds from Aldwark (A943) and Torksey (T1579), examples come from both Stamford Bridge 2 and Cottam, each of which saw Viking activity from the ninth and into the tenth century (see Chapter 7).[18] The B4 type has a long period of use, with derivative examples distributed across eastern England and two possible lead casting models from Essex.[19] An equally broad date range can be proposed for the B4d sub-type, represented by a single find from Torksey (T365). The three B4 strap-ends recovered from the camps were almost certainly worn by members of the Great Army and illustrate some of its cultural affiliations within the wider Scandinavian milieu.

The parallel-sided, heavily-cast Type B5, produced with stepped butt-ends and occasional simple peripheral grooves decorating the reverse, likewise demonstrates cross-cultural and Scandinavian-influenced traits. We have proposed a narrow date range for this form, with Scandinavian colonists developing the series as a means of expressing a new identity distinctive from Anglo-Saxon designs.[20] The distribution of B5 strap-ends has a relatively compact northern

15. Thomas 2000a, 99–100, 202–5
16. Thomas 2000a, 244
17. Thomas 2000a, 245–6; 2001, 45
18. Haldenby *et al.* 2022, 109–10
19. Thomas 2000a, 147
20. Haldenby *et al.* 2022, 2

Figure 4.6. B5–3 strap-ends: A929 (YAT) and T745, front and rear (PAS)

bias, centred on York, the probable location of the manufacturing workshops; what appears to be a lead model for a B5 strap-end was recovered from Coppergate, indicating casting nearby.[21] The Aldwark example (A929) belongs to the new B5–3 sub-type we have proposed (Figure 4.6). This sub-type appears to be a development of slightly earlier B5 patterns, with a comparatively varied artistic repertoire incorporating aspects of both Anglo-Saxon and Irish design. The Torksey example (T745) is very eroded, but deeply-contoured interlace visible on its face suggests that it also belongs to the B5–3 sub-type, albeit that the split butt-end is irregular.[22] Although the eroded tip and ring-and-dot decoration near the butt has similarities with Type E4 strap-ends, Thomas' definition of the B5 type includes a split end.[23] It is possible that this is a very early version of the B5–3 design, carried south by a member of the Army, or it may be a later derivative model, made as a copy after production started in Northumbria.

Like the Class A strap-ends, the Class B forms are heavily fragmented. While deliberate cutting is not certain, it is the B1 and B2 types with Anglo-Saxon designs that are notably highly fragmented unlike the Scandinavian-influenced B4 and B5 types. This suggests a contrast between the material gathered for processing and those strap-ends being worn within the camps, where new forms of material culture, with Scandinavian-influenced decorative schema, were already being developed.

Class E strap-ends

The wide, tongue-shaped Class E series forms a point of departure from most strap-end forms (Figure 4.7). Whilst Anglo-Saxon fashions appear to have mainly favoured unbuckled textile girdles, fitted with pairs of Class A or B strap-ends, the broader, heavier Class E fittings were most probably attached to leather straps, worn with buckles and sometimes strap-slides. This style originated in the Carolingian realm and was widely adopted in Scandinavia. However, it did

21. Mainman and Rogers 2000, 2569
22. Haldenby *et al.* 2022, 7, fig. 4
23. Thomas 2000a, 104

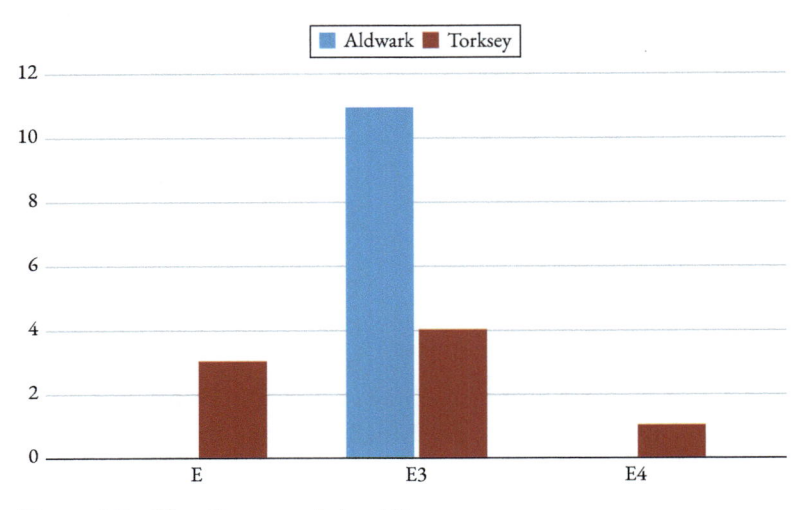

Figure 4.7. Class E strap-ends (n=19)

not appear in England until the late ninth century, with the bulk of the Class E series dated to the tenth and eleventh centuries.[24] Given that the Class E represents a divergence from local clothing styles, it must reflect a Scandinavian introduction. The majority will have functioned as dress items although two iron E3 strap-ends (A134, T2572) were probably used on horse harnesses.

Three Class E strap-ends from Torksey have no clear type, appearing to be generic tongue-shaped forms, with few further defining characteristics. One (T757) is an undecorated silver strap-end only 11mm wide. This may have had a similar use to other small examples of the Class E series, which are often associated with buckles fitted with strap guides, used to secure spurs or, more occasionally, garters or footwear.[25] The other examples are difficult to classify. One (T20) was catalogued by Blackburn but no detail was provided, while only the lower half of the body and tip of the other survive (T1759).[26] This section is sparsely decorated, with traces of a simple peripheral groove visible, possibly on the reverse to judge from its profile. Peripheral grooves are occasionally seen on the reverse of E3 and E4 strap-ends, but both these types also display heavy relief decoration on the front face.[27] This decoration is typically cast, and so this Torksey example is unlikely to be an unfinished version of either form. It may be a derivative item or a trial casting, used to test one side of a two-piece mould.

24. Thomas 2000a, 208, 278–9
25. Thomas 2000a, 269
26. Blackburn 2011, 231
27. Haldenby *et al.* 2022, 10

The single E4 strap-end from Torksey (T801) is truncated on all sides, but elements of a cast Borre-style ring knot visible on one side, along with two rivets aligned against a framing bar, enable it to be confidently identified. The E4 type was a long-lived design, which Thomas dates from the late ninth to tenth centuries, and so the Torksey example must be an early product in the series.[28] Whilst the cast production and Scandinavian-influenced design of the E4 has clear similarities with the B5, its longevity has created a far wider distribution, principally in eastern England but also to the west and in the Irish Sea region.[29] Therefore, not all examples of Type E4 can be associated with the Army, although such strap-ends were evidently worn by its members.

All Class E straps-ends recovered from Aldwark are of Type E3. An unfinished example (A920), with traces of casting flash on one side and a broken tip, seems to have been discarded during the manufacturing process (Figure 4.8). Another (A1151) retained a casting gate, the solidified lump of metal which forms at the entrance of a two-piece mould; they are extraneous and so cleaned off successful casts.[30] Three lead models relate to E3-style belt fittings, and like the Torksey lead model for an A1 strap-end, they lack rivet holes so would not have been wearable. Two are for strap-ends (A927, A1764), whilst the third is for a strap guide (A1155), and all bear the characteristic medial rib of this form. Leahy observes that models could be of very specific use in producing items with such pronounced ribs.[31] It seems highly probable that the models were used as patterns for mould-making, providing clear evidence for casting of E3

Figure 4.8. Failed castings and lead models for Type E3 strap-ends from Aldwark (left to right): A920, A1151, A927 (all YAT), A1764 (Lee Toone)

28. Thomas 2000a, 213–14
29. Thomas 2000a, 252; Haldenby *et al.* 2022, fig. 11
30. Rogers 2020c, 53
31. Leahy 2003, 143–4

strap-ends at Aldwark.[32] The volume of complete copper-alloy E3 strap-ends accords with this, as do nine strap guides with medial ribs, of a type believed to form a suite with the E3 fittings. Furthermore, several of the strap-ends and slides are scored with deep, parallel file marks and striations, suggestive of rough finishing; they were presumably lost or discarded at an intermediate stage of production, after casting but prior to final polishing.

The E3 type was previously seen by Thomas as having two distinct distributions. One was in the Irish Sea area, and included examples from burials at Carlisle Cathedral, Cumwhitton (Cumbria), Peel Castle (Isle of Man), and Golden Lane, Dublin. He also mapped a broader distribution of individual finds across eastern England.[33] Leahy later illustrated three more examples from Lincolnshire, one reworked into a pendant, and others are now known from Cottam, Cowlam, Ryther (Yorkshire), Swinhope and Binbrook (Lincolnshire).[34] Thomas proposed that the E3 type originated in Ireland and only spread to England after the taking of York by Hiberno-Norse raiders in 919. Whilst he suggested that instances of ring-and-dot decoration supported an attribution towards the later date, examples from Cottam now demonstrate that such designs can be found on late ninth-century artefacts.[35] Paterson has suggested that the concentration of the near-identical examples from Carlisle, Peel Castle, and Golden Lane indicates a manufacturing centre within Cumbria.[36] However, the assemblage from Carlisle Cathedral is now matched by the four E3 strap-ends from Torksey, whilst the twelve complete examples from Aldwark provide the densest concentration from a single location, presenting important new evidence for the dating and distribution of the E3 type.

A single, undecorated E3 strap-end with a raised medial rib (no. 307) from the *emporium* site at Walichrum, near Domburg, on Walcheren has strong parallels with several of the Aldwark finds and one from Torksey (T42). Whilst unstratified, it is probably of ninth-century date, since the Domburg *emporium* operated throughout the eighth and ninth centuries but decreased sharply in importance in the later ninth century after a period of Scandinavian overlordship. A recent review of the archaeological evidence from Walichrum has noted hack-silver, two dirham fragments, and a cubo-octahedral weight associated

---

32. Williams and Hall 2020, 82–3
33. Thomas 2000a, 251; 2001, 44; Paterson and Tweddle 2014; Paterson *et al.* 2014; Graham-Campbell *et al.* 2002, 90–1; O'Donovan 2008
34. Leahy 2007, fig. 68:1–3; Haldenby 1992, 31, fig. 3:9; Richards and Haldenby 2018, table 2; Hadley and Richards 2020, 123
35. Thomas 2000a, 213; 2001, 44; Haldenby and Richards 2016, section 4.4.2
36. Paterson *et al.* 2014, 149; Paterson and Tweddle 2014, 217

with this Scandinavian activity.[37] Two E3 strap-ends have also been recovered from Kaupang, one of which (C52517/844) has a doubled medial rib and features simple ring-and-dot decoration, similar to an Aldwark example (A924). The second strap-end (C52517/1724) is made of lead/lead-alloy, and although published as a functional fitting, it lacks a rivet or rivet hole in the split end.[38] The lack of any attachment point suggests that it was used as a casting model, like the example from Aldwark (A927), implying that E3 strap-ends were manufactured at Kaupang. All the E3-related material from Kaupang was found during field survey, and so lacks archaeological context, but the occupation dates suggest that craft production occurred in the mid-to-late ninth century, continuing into the early tenth century.[39] It can therefore be argued that stylistically, the plain or simply-decorated E3 strap-ends with raised medial ribs from both camps show ninth-century manufacture, pre-dating Thomas' suggested tenth-century introduction of the type to eastern England. In summary, rather than representing an Irish Sea style, it now seems possible to read the suites of E3 fittings as an introduction of the Great Army, derived from a continental model, and imported first into eastern England before being adopted in western Britain and Ireland.

Although some E3 strap-ends from both locations are broken, there are no signs of deliberate cutting, with the broken E3 fittings from Aldwark probably the result of casting flaws and faults. This suggests that Class E fittings, like the B4 and B5 types, were not broadly regarded as a suitable source of scrap metal; this presumably reflects their Scandinavian-inspired origin. It is tempting to see this evidence for production of E3 fittings as demonstrating a deliberate decision to focus on manufacturing this type at Aldwark, whereas Torksey has produced a wider range of fittings worn by members of the Army. The larger assemblage of the E3 type at Aldwark suggests that it was a form introduced, and manufactured, by the Great Army mainly in the years after the overwintering at Torksey.

Other strap-ends

A single Class F strap-end (A931) was recovered from Aldwark (Figure 4.9).[40] The Class F has a very distinctive form, with double-sided decoration, decorative roundels, and zoomorphic terminals.[41] Although it is heavily corroded,

37. Capelle 1976, 26, Taf. 18; Thomas 2000a, 115, 251; Nelson 1991, 51; Deckers 2022a
38. Wamers 2011, 71
39. Pedersen 2016, 14
40. Rogers 2020c, 53–4
41. Thomas 2000a, 120

Figure 4.9. Aldwark strap-ends, including a Type J2 (A956) with a crude bird motif scratched into the tinned surface and a Class F (A931) (YAT)

obscuring any surface decoration, X-rays reveal a piercing in the centre of the roundel, indicating that it is of the F1 type. Thomas suggested this was the original Class F form, manufactured in Ireland, with Dublin subsequently proposed as a production centre.[42] Although the series is broadly dated from the late ninth century to the first half of the tenth, Graham-Campbell suggests that what is now classified as the F1 type 'cannot be much later than *c*.900', with which Nicholson broadly concurred in discussion of a Class F buckle from Whithorn (Dumfries and Galloway).[43] Like the Type E3 material, Class F fittings appear to have been manufactured in sets, with a companion buckle also recovered from Aldwark (A925).[44] We have previously proposed that these paired buckles and strap-ends, alongside a corresponding series of fittings and distributors, were produced as sword-strap fittings.[45] This connection with specifically military usage signals that F1 strap-ends can be viewed as indicative of early Viking incursions, particularly those related to the Great Army. Whilst a solely martial connection might be questioned for some of the associated strap fittings, both this strap-end and the corresponding buckle are strong evidence for the presence at Aldwark of individuals who had been active in the Irish Sea zone.

The most numerous of the other identified strap-ends is the Class J, of which five were recovered from Torksey and two from Aldwark. Whilst this is an extremely long-lived form, the general volume of early medieval strap-ends recovered from each camp suggests that it is reasonable to associate them with the Great Army. A Class J strap-end was also part of the Beeston Tor hoard of

42. Thomas 2001, 45; Paterson 2021, 332
43. Thomas 2000a, 216; Graham-Campbell 1973, 131; Nicholson 1997, 623
44. Rogers 2020c, 54
45. Haldenby *et al.* 2022, 4

*c.*875.[46] A crude bird motif had been scratched into the tinned surface of an unpublished Type J2 strap-end from Aldwark (A956) (Figure 4.9). Although both the head and tail are obscured, it displays thin, curved-tipped wings and a lozenge-shaped body demarcated by horizontal lines. The design echoes the bird-of-prey or raven device often used in Scandinavian art, although tinned copper-alloy sheets are closely associated with Insular manufacturing. Whilst the Aldwark strap-end was probably marked with a *graffito* after conversion, rather than being decorated beforehand, both the design and the material shows obvious Scandinavian influence, connecting to a wider pattern of adapting Insular objects as dress accessories. It finds an intriguing parallel in a Type J2 strap-end (no. 66) from Flixborough, which also has a notched attachment end with a sub-triangular projection, but the bronze sheet from which it was cut was already ornamented with a finely incised pattern of flowing spirals and trumpets. This sheet was originally used to bind an Insular *situla* pail, like complete examples found in Viking-age graves in Norway and Sweden, before its re-use as a strap-end.[47]

Several unusual strap-ends were also recovered from both camps. Two are items converted for use as strap fittings. One (A948) is a sub-rectangular plate decorated with roughly cut longitudinal and transverse grooves, and with three irregularly spaced piercings for attachment points. Another (T1003) is more complex, made from two separate copper-alloy sheets, one partially decorated with a curving chip-carved design (Figure 4.10). These sheets are joined by two rivets and would presumably have been placed on either side of a strap, creating

Figure 4.10. Irregular strap-ends (left to right): A945 (YAT), A1719 (PAS), T1003 (authors)

46. Thomas 2000a, 218–19
47. Youngs 2001, 211–16; Thomas *et al.* 2009, 10–11

a fitting akin to a more conventional Class J strap-end. A similar fitting was recovered from Grave V at Peel Castle, composed of two shaped sheets, riveted together, and attached to a re-used mount decorated with a gilt interlace design. This Manx example was also interpreted as a strap-end, providing a parallel for the Torksey example, and a similar composite buckle plate is known from the Islandbridge cemetery in Dublin.[48]

Rogers identified an Aldwark strap-end (A945) as having been cut down from a larger fitting.[49] However, several near-identical strap-ends come from the Continent, and this artefact provides more evidence that some members of the Great Army had previously travelled through the Carolingian Empire. Two iron objects from the early tenth-century Île de Groix boat burial off the north-west coast of Brittany have similar decorative profiles; these have been identified as 'casket mounts', but their forms are far more characteristic of the suites of fittings used on Type III Carolingian sword belts.[50] A similar Carolingian strap-end from Wiltshire differs in having an incised foliate decoration, but shares semi-circular horizontal ridges and a stepped butt-end.[51] This step was previously identified as a partially-broken split on the Aldwark example, a confusion clearly caused by the fractured remains of a separate retaining plate; this break suggests that the fixing failed, and that the strap-end therefore shows a casual loss from a Carolingian-style sword belt, of a type common in Frisia.[52] Another strap-end from Aldwark (A1719) has similarities to Carolingian and 'Carolingian-type' fittings and with both Type E4 and E6 strap-ends.[53] A buckle plate from Aldwark features a Trewhiddle-style beast, of a type familiar to Class A strap-ends, to which Rogers has suggested may have been made as a companion piece, in a fashion for matching sets that was, however, more typical of Carolingian regions.[54] Although no equivalent Carolingian strap-ends have been recovered from Torksey, two sword-belt mounts (T580, T1633), and a silver strap guide (T805), are decorated in the distinctive florid acanthus designs which characterise mid-to-late ninth-century Carolingian metalwork, and particularly sword-strap and bridle fittings (see Figure 6.31).[55]

48. Graham-Campbell *et al.* 2002, 92–3; Harrison and Ó Floinn 2014, 448–9
49. Rogers 2020c, 54
50. Price 1989, 96; Robak 2018a, fig. 6
51. WILT-6E9825
52. Wolfram Giertz pers. comm.
53. Robak 2018b, figs 2–3
54. Rogers 2020c, 54
55. Wamers 2005a, 129–41; 2005b, 173; Mitchell 1994, 146; Thomas 2012, 498

Disc brooches

Seven disc brooches of both Anglo-Saxon and Scandinavian manufacture have been found on the camps, providing evidence for the presence of females (Figure 4.11). One example from Torksey (T773) was clearly made in Scandinavia (Figure 4.12). Although the pin-lug and catch-plate are abraded, and their exact forms were not recorded in detail, the remains of a small attachment loop, and the convex shape of the brooch, are characteristic of Scandinavian manufacture. The Borre-style decoration of inward-facing animal heads identifies this as a Jansson Type II A.[56] This has a wide distribution across southern and

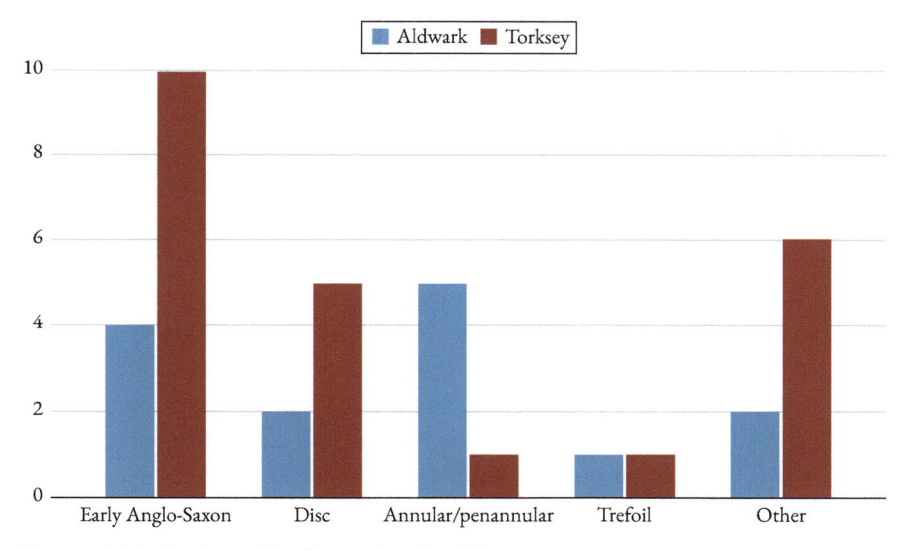

Figure 4.11. Early medieval brooches (n=37)

Figure 4.12. Torksey disc brooches (not to scale; left to right): T307 (authors), T773, T798, T808 (PAS)

56. Kershaw 2013, 23–4; Jansson 1984a, Abb. 8.2

eastern Scandinavia, with concentrations at Birka, Hedeby, and Uppåkra, while manufacturing remains have been discovered at Birka and on Gotland.[57] Of the three brooches of this style recovered from graves at Birka, two were accompanied by oval brooches, whilst the third was in the grave of a child alongside a needle, knife, and clay pot.[58] This suggests that a brooch with such gendered connotations from Torksey was worn as part of Scandinavian female dress, by a woman who came to England with the Great Army. The PAS description of another brooch (T790) suggests Scandinavian origins or influence as it notes the presence of an attachment loop on the reverse.[59] A similar design can be seen on a disc brooch (T798) classified as a variant of a 'Terslev' Type V, with the atypically large, flat form, coupled with its lead-alloy composition, indicating strong English influences in the manufacture.[60] This hybrid 'Anglo-Scandinavian' form dates to the mid-tenth century, clearly post-dating the occupation of the camp, but it indicates a continued Scandinavian influence in the area.

The body of another Torksey brooch (T307) was made from a re-used flat-headed pin, identifiable by two opposed piercings on the sides of the face, which would have held connecting chains. These indicate that the brooch originally formed the central part of a three-pin suite. The floruit of linked-pin suites is generally believed to be the eighth century, and a similar date is suggested by the design, which echoes the spiralling tendrils seen on eighth-century pin-heads from Yorkshire and Suffolk.[61] A long life is evident in the re-use of the pin-head as a brooch; the small catch-plate is secured by a rivet passing through a third piercing in the disc, the location of the original pin shank, whilst an adjacent area of discoloration presumably marks the former position of a soldered-on pin assembly. The twisted strip of the catch copies brooch fastenings of the eighth and ninth centuries, such as the brooches from Ixworth (Suffolk) and Beeston.[62] However, the Torksey brooch does not feature the full-width integral pin-and-catch-plate strips of these examples, even though it would have been possible to fit one using the opposed piercings on the plate. Whilst it is difficult to date this re-use, the conversion of discs of metalwork from Britain and Ireland into brooches by Scandinavians is an established phenomenon.[63]

There are three fragmented disc brooches. One from Torksey (T808) is the only silver disc brooch, which was apparently deliberately broken for

57. Kershaw 2013, 50
58. Arbman 1940, I, 151–2, 393, 458; II, Taf. 70
59. NLM7020
60. Kershaw 2013, 74–5, 148
61. Bailey 1970, 406; Hinton 1974, 24; Parsons 1992, 169
62. Wilson 1964, 120, 137
63. Bakka 1963, 6–7

use as bullion. The surviving decoration forms part of a Trewhiddle-style beast, indicating English manufacture. Two copper-alloy fragments from Aldwark

appear to be from disc brooches of earlier types and may reflect scrap collected for reprocessing. One was identified by Rogers as a mount (A1073), but is more likely to be part of a fragmented disc brooch, in which the central perforation held a bossed rivet, securing part of a one-piece pin plate (Figure 4.13).[64] The quartered, chip-carved interlaced tendrils of the design echo

Figure 4.13. Aldwark disc brooch fragments: (left) A1073 and (right) A1108 (YAT)

the Mercian-inspired brooches of the Pentney hoard (Norfolk), and a copper-alloy disc brooch from Leicester, all dated to the first half of the ninth century.[65] Another fragment (A1108) is probably from an openwork Trewhiddle-style brooch, suggesting that it was of late eighth- to ninth-century manufacture; there is a similar ninth-century copper-alloy brooch from Elmsett (Suffolk).[66]

Trefoil brooches

A fragment of a probable trefoil brooch has been identified at each camp (Figure 4.14). Trefoil brooches are a uniquely Scandinavian artefact, unknown in Britain and Ireland prior to the start of Viking activity. Although their form was adapted from elaborate Carolingian sword-belt fittings, the brooches were exclusively used as a component of female dress.[67] The Torksey example (T123) is heavily corroded, possibly burnt, and broken near to the junction at

the base of the arm, but the remains of a slightly offset pair of perforated cast lugs are visible on the reverse. Whilst these may have formed part of a series of identical lugs, positioned on each arm of a flat trefoil fitting, the raised centre is indicative of a brooch, suggesting that they

Figure 4.14. Fragments of possible trefoil brooches (not to scale): A923 (YAT) and T123 (authors)

64. Rogers 2020c, 61
65. Webster 2001, 275–7; Webster and Backhouse 1991, 228–9, no. 186
66. West 1998, 26 and fig. 24:6
67. Graham-Campbell 1980, 93

formed part of a Scandinavian-style pin assembly.[68] Although the corrosion makes identification difficult, the abraded remains of a parallel scrollwork design are visible, suggesting that it may belong to Maixner's Type P4.8.[69] The example from Aldwark (A923) is a similar tongue-shaped fragment with possible Borre-style animal heads, as seen on a trefoil brooch from Stallingborough (Lincolnshire), although the apparent lack of fittings and of the characteristic broadening which defines the arms of trefoil brooches means it could also be an E4 type strap-end.[70]

Penannular brooches

Whilst the penannular brooch form was adopted by Scandinavians from Irish dress, with distinct, locally manufactured types swiftly developing, the examples from Aldwark and Torksey appear to be of Irish or western British manufacture.[71] All are, however, fragmentary, indicating that they were probably broken up for re-use rather than employed as dress fasteners. The single Torksey find (T700), a silver-gilt fragment paralleled by a ninth-century brooch from Kilkenny (Ireland), may have been fragmented for use as bullion (Figure 4.15).[72] There is also a fragment of a penannular brooch of Graham-Campbell's

Figure 4.15. Penannular brooch fragments (not to scale; left to right): T700 (PAS), A1065, A1079 (YAT)

Type G3 from Aldwark (A1065). The Type G brooch is typically found across western Britain, with examples known from Cornwall to the Hebrides, but it is generally absent from Ireland.[73] There is a second possible example of a Type G3 brooch fragment (A1079), although its heavily corroded nature renders this identification tentative. Whilst four raised pellets are visible, the shapes of both their enclosing field and the terminal itself are obscured. Three other fragments (A1099, A1100, A1169) derive from either penannular or annular/pseudo-penannular brooches, with parallels from Co. Louth and Orkney.[74]

68. Blackburn 2011, 232; Paterson 1997, 654; Kershaw 2013, 15
69. Maixner 2005, 255
70. Rogers 2020c, 56–7; Haldenby *et al.* 2022, 18
71. Wamers 1998, 38
72. Youngs (ed.) 1989, 99
73. Dickinson 1982, 44–5; Edwards 1990, 135–6
74. Rogers 2020c, 56

Other brooches

A variety of other brooch forms have been found at both camps (Figure 4.16). A terminal and section of the bow survive of a copper-alloy ansate brooch (A1203), with an iron rivet indicating the location of the catch. The ring-and-dot decoration, coupled with the remains of an incised saltire, indicates that this is a Weetch Type XI.D, a ribbon-shaped brooch unique to England. Type XI brooches are generally seen as dating to the late ninth and tenth centuries.[75] T304 is difficult to assign to a type, although the presence of gilt, chip-carved interlace probably indicates an eighth-century date.[76] Two copper-alloy strip brooches with narrow, flattened plates (T1052, T1684) correspond to Weetch Type 31.B.[77] They are broadly dated to the eighth to early ninth century, although iron examples have been recovered from stratified tenth-century contexts at Flixborough.[78] Such brooches are densely concentrated in East Anglia and Lincolnshire, and Rosie Weetch suggests that a cluster at Flixborough indicates that it was a manufacturing centre.[79] There may be a fragment of another strip brooch from Torksey (T2997), broken from a lozenge form Type 31.C with a wider, highly decorated plate. Similar gilded 'Greek key' motifs can be seen on a brooch from Ilam (Staffordshire) and an unprovenanced example in the British Museum, and Weetch connects these designs with Mercian-style decoration.[80] The Type 31.C has a general distribution across eastern England south of the Humber, and although comparatively scarce within the Mercian

Figure 4.16. Other brooches (left to right): A1203 (YAT), T1052, T1684, T2997 (authors), T799 (PAS)

75. Weetch 2014, 40, 165, 185–6
76. Webster and Backhouse 1991, 220
77. Weetch 2014, 139
78. Weetch 2014, 138; Ottaway 2009a, 6
79. Weetch 2014, 186, 189
80. Weetch 2014, 140, 183–4

heartlands, one complete example was recently recovered during excavations at Repton.[81] These ansate and strip brooches were probably collected for recycling, with the gilded face of the Type 31.C (T2997) particularly valued.

Early Anglo-Saxon brooches recovered from both sites include fragments of cruciform, square-headed, annular, small-long, and button brooches, and they are probably residual. Nonetheless, in the light of the foot of a Salin Style I cruciform brooch used as a mount in an inset weight found by a metal detectorist 'near York' we should not discount the possibility that some earlier material was available and brought to the camps as scrap.[82] An early Anglo-Saxon wrist clasp (T799) seems to have been converted into a brooch as the remains of a pair of fittings on the reverse suggest it once had a pin, perhaps providing another example of the survival, and repurposing, of an antique piece.

Pins

Base-metal dress and hairpins are ubiquitous items of early medieval material culture in England. Substantial assemblages are known from Flixborough, York, and Southampton, with over 200 recovered from Staunch Meadow alone.[83] Whilst the dating of several classes of pins has been refined in recent

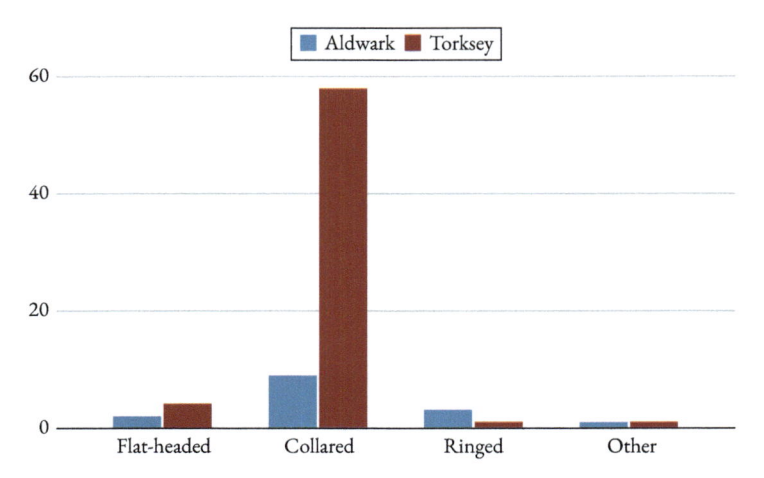

Figure 4.17. Early medieval pins (n=79)

81. Weetch 2014, fig. 4.6; Jarman 2019
82. Gary Johnson pers. comm.
83. Rogers *et al.* 2009; Mainman and Rogers 2000; Hinton and Parsons 1996; Riddler *et al.* 2014, 229

decades, there is no agreed naming convention or typology for many of them.[84] There are 64 early medieval copper-alloy pins from Torksey and 15 from Aldwark, one which is a trefoil-headed pin of fifth- to sixth-century date (A1110), and probably residual (Figure 4.17).[85] No iron pins were recovered from either site, which is probably a result of recovery bias given that iron pins are well represented at excavated sites such as Flixborough where they comprise 20% of all pins.[86]

Flat-headed pins

Terminology for pin types with flat heads is particularly confused and inconsistent.[87] The term 'flat-headed pin' is used here for pins with flat heads, typically between 20 and 35mm or 45–55mm in diameter, and often riveted to separate pin shanks, to distinguish them from later types sometimes described as 'disc-headed'.[88] The heads are generally highly decorated on one face, often with chip carving, and perforations on the plate edges, suggesting a use in linked pairs or suites; occasionally, pierced projecting lugs serve

Figure 4.18. Flat-headed pin (T1062; authors)

the same function.[89] Only one complete example has been identified (T1062), which has a circular head, separated from the pin shank by two triangular projections (Figure 4.18). Two small perforations are visible on one side of the head, one of which is broken; the smaller, cruder perforation was presumably intended as a replacement. As discussed earlier, another example (T307) is almost certainly derived from a pin suite of this type but was re-used as a brooch.

Five cut or broken fragments from discoidal copper-alloy plates, gilded on one decorated face, may represent fragments of flat-headed pins (Figure 4.19). The remains of a central rivet hole are visible on one (A1098), previously identified as a possible mount,[90] and a small, pierced projecting lug survives on another (T1543). Although no other perforations or remains of pin shanks

84. Haldenby and Richards 2016
85. Walton Rogers 2020a, 47
86. Rogers *et al.* 2009
87. Rogers *et al.* 2009; Haldenby 2012
88. Cramp 1964, 92; Rogers *et al.* 2009; Haldenby 2012; Haldenby and Richards 2009
89. Parsons 1992
90. Rogers 2020c, 61

Figure 4.19. Flat-headed pin fragments (left to right): A1071, A1098 (YAT), T873, T2417 (authors)

have been identified, their decoration and gilding is consistent with more complete examples of flat-headed pins from Flixborough. For example, the incised radial lines on one fragment (A1071) strongly echo those on a Flixborough silver pin (no. 673), while the cast, splayed-arm cross on another (A1098) and the 'speckled' border of a third (T873) parallel those of Flixborough nos. 562 and 560, respectively.[91] The chip-carved decoration on the other two fragments (T1543 and T2417) was commonly employed on pin-heads, and a similar rope-work border to one (T2417) can be seen on one of the outer elements of the pin suite from the River Witham (Lincolnshire).[92]

Pins of this type are usually recovered as single finds. Where multiple pins are recorded, such as at Flixborough, Meols (Cheshire), and Cottam, they tend to be complete, whereas most of those from Aldwark and Torksey are fragmented.[93] This suggests that the pins were not being worn in the camps but had been gathered and broken apart. The flat-headed pin form is generally dated to the eighth century, but with continuity into the ninth century, and so their presence on the camps is not particularly anomalous.[94] A matched pair of silver flat-headed pins in the Talnotrie hoard reinforces that late ninth-century Viking raiders had access to such items.[95]

Collared pins

Several forms of collared pins have been found on both camps (Figure 4.20). Polyhedral pins (sometimes termed 'faceted' pins) are characterised by cuboid,

91. Rogers *et al.* 2009, 67
92. Haldenby 2012, 3; Wilson 1964, pl. XVIII
93. Bailey 1970, 405–6; Hinton and Parsons 1996, 30; Rogers *et al.* 2009, 36–7; Griffiths 2007, 66
94. Webster and Backhouse 1991, 83
95. Graham-Campbell 1995, 4

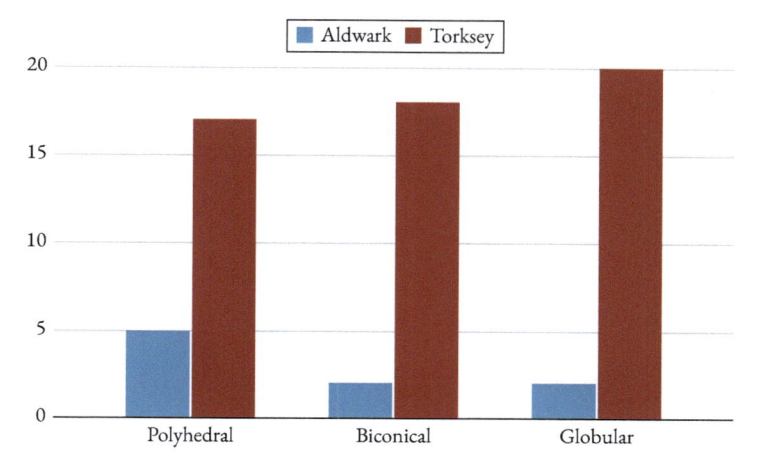

Figure 4.20. Collared pins (n=64)

chamfered heads, and while ring-and-dot or punched-dot ornamentation is typical, undecorated heads are known.[96] Decorated pin-heads, including the flattened sub-type, are the main form of polyhedral pin from Torksey. By contrast, 46% of collared pins recorded on the PAS database from East Anglia are undecorated, while the corresponding figures from excavated sites are 34% at Staunch Meadow, 23% at Flixborough, and *c.*19% at Southampton.[97] At just under 12%, the proportion of undecorated polyhedral pins at Torksey appears significantly lower, but higher than the mere 5% recorded at Cottam.[98] Given the established Great Army presence at these last two sites, these low percentages may show selective looting of the more eye-catching polyhedral pins with decorated heads.

Biconical pins are characterised by a 'double cone' head, with sub-groups displaying flat medial bands, flattened or rounded crowns, or a combination of both. The sub-group with a medial band and a conical top dominates the Torksey assemblage (Figure 4.21). In Haldenby's national survey of biconical pins 57% possessed a medial band, a similar figure to those recovered from Flixborough and Cottam.[99] At Torksey, in contrast, over 70% have medial bands, suggesting selectivity.

96. Haldenby 2012, 7
97. Riddler *et al.* 2014, 234; Rogers *et al.* 2009, 51–5; Hinton and Parsons 1996, 21–5
98. Richards 1999, 102–3
99. Haldenby 2012, 8; Rogers *et al.* 2009, 55–9; Richards 1999, 71, 102–4

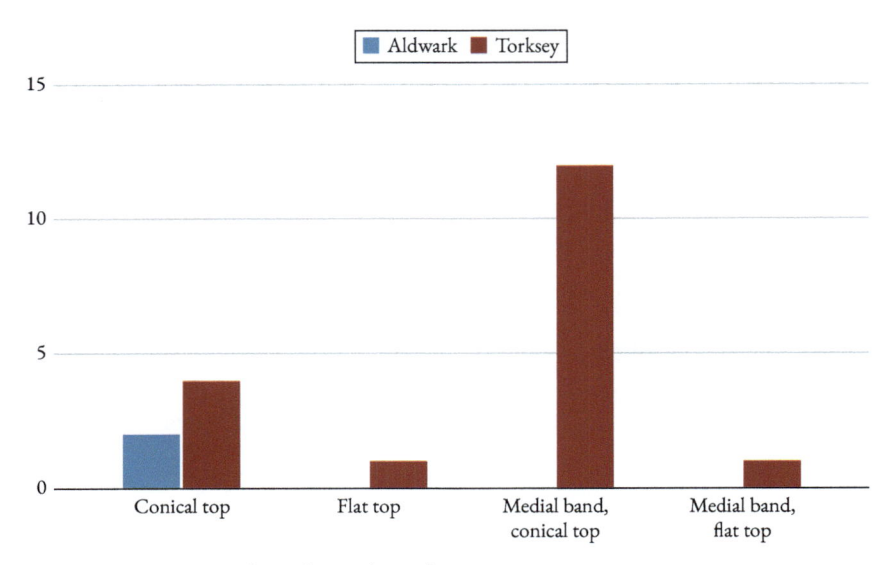

Figure 4.21. Biconical pin forms (n=20)

Globular pins are characterised by various spherical and sub-spherical head forms, sometimes with ring-and-dot decoration.[100] They are common on many Middle Saxon sites; for example, they were the second most frequent form at Flixborough, and dominant at Southampton, Fishergate, and Staunch Meadow.[101] The 15% of Torksey pins decorated with ring-and-dot is similar to the proportions at Staunch Meadow and Fishergate, with 15.9% and 15.3% respectively (Figure 4.22).

The low proportion of pins to strap-ends at Aldwark and Torksey stands out when compared to assemblages from contemporary settlements, where pins and strap-ends are found in broadly similar numbers. There are roughly twice as many combined Class A and B strap-ends to collared pins at both Aldwark and Torksey. The assemblages of pins are atypical in other ways, with only two silver pins, both globular forms (A1268, T135), with the Aldwark example being treated as hack-silver. At Torksey, this means that precious-metal pins comprise only 1.7% of the whole assemblage, which contrasts with 9% at Flixborough.[102] This may imply that silver pins were selectively collected for their specific alloy content for melting down. In the Middle Saxon Southampton assemblage, simple biconical pins and those with medial bands were made of brass, a different alloy than was used for other pin forms, and

100. Haldenby 2012, 8–9; Haldenby and Richards 2016, section 4.3
101. Rogers *et al.* 2009, 33; Riddler *et al.* 2014, 230
102. Rogers *et al.* 2009, 43; Riddler *et al.* 2014, 230–6

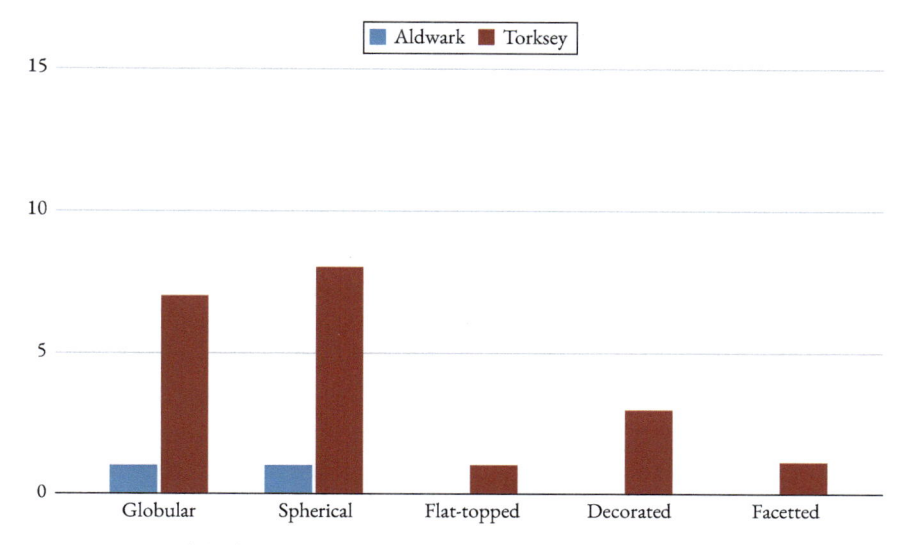

Figure 4.22. Globular pins (n=22)

brass was also one of the characteristic elements of Scandinavian jewellery.[103] In contrast, the two flat-topped biconical pins that lacked medial bands from Torksey were also the only gilded pins, suggesting that they may have been selected for other reasons.

Ringed pins

Ringed pins are defined by Fanning as any pin with a loose, swivel ring held captive by the pin-head. Like penannular brooches, they were adopted by Scandinavians from Insular dress, gaining popularity during the ninth century.[104]

The comparatively low numbers of ringed pins from the two camps suggests that they were casual losses from items of personal dress, rather than collected scrap (Figure 4.23).

A clear example of the earlier form of pin from Aldwark (A141) displays a plain ring and simple loop. One of the broken pin shanks from Aldwark (A1191) can also be safely assumed to

Figure 4.23. Ringed pins (top to bottom): A1191 (YAT), A141 (PAS), T1627 (authors)

103. Wilthew 1996, 67; Kershaw 2013, table 2.1
104. Fanning 1994; Wamers 1998, 38

represent this form, despite part of the loop and the ring being absent. The third Aldwark example (A1177) is a crutch-headed pin, an eleventh-century form deriving from later activity. A pin from Torksey (T1627) has a flattened, oval-shaped ring, suggesting Scandinavian influence, but no parallel has been found for its decorated shank. Horne suggested that this pin may 'indicate the presence of a *longphort*-based trader' at Torksey, but its decoration indicates a more complex story.[105] The biconical, octagonal swelling under the head was slotted onto the pin shank during manufacture, its position resembling the polyhedral swellings on the 'Vestfold type' pin form common in Kaupang, and possibly therefore expressing an element of Scandinavian identity.[106] However, additional resonances emerge from the development of faceted, cubo-octahedral decorations on weighing equipment in the late ninth century.[107] In the Baltic area, these decorations subsequently featured on penannular brooches, with faceted, weight-like knobs used as terminals; it has been postulated that they were intended to convey a social identity, signalling involvement in a common system of weight-trading across wider cultural divisions. Whilst these brooches were an eastern fashion, similar developments can be seen on Insular ringed pins, with the use of a faceted 'bead' appearing to reference cubo-octahedral weights introduced from the east into southern Scandinavian economies. The plain-ringed, polyhedral-headed pins became highly popular in the early tenth century and have been taken by both Fanning and Horne as markers of group identity, signalling membership of a mercantile class.[108]

The assemblages are too small to assign any meaning to the contrasts between them, but along with the ringed pins from burials that can be associated with the Great Army they reflect a range of influences. The Scandinavian influence on the Torksey pin and that from Mound 56 at the Heath Wood cremation cemetery contrast with the Insular influence on the pins from Aldwark and the Sonning burial.

Hooked tags

Early medieval hooked dress tags have received little study, largely proving resistant to classification. The triangular hooked tag is believed to be the earliest form, originating in the seventh century, with the circular type becoming popular in the late eighth century; both forms continued in use until the later eleventh

105. Horne 2022, 227
106. Blindheim 1976, 22
107. E.g. Gustin 2015, 33–5
108. Fanning 1994, 34–6; Horne 2022, 106, 227

Table 4.2. Hooked tags from Aldwark and Torksey

Location	Tag form				Total
	Triangular	Circular	Other	Unknown	
Aldwark	1	2	1	5	9
Torksey	10	16	2	1	29

century.[109] Whilst the use of hooked tags on garments is suggested by burial evidence, some forms appear too delicate to be used on clothing. Occasional finds from hoards and graves imply a connection between hooked tags and pouches. For example, two hoards of tenth-century English coins, one from the Forum in Rome and the other from Tetney (Lincolnshire), contained hooked tags that appear to have served as purse fasteners.[110] Larger assemblages of hooked tags have been associated with urban, commercial centres and market locations.[111]

The numbers of hooked tags from both camps are surprisingly high, particularly given that they are not seen as typically Scandinavian (Table 4.2). The Torksey assemblage comprises the largest corpus from a single site in Britain. More finds are recorded from the city of Lincoln as a whole, but include many unfinished examples from a probable workshop on Flaxengate. It seems improbable that these small items would have been collected by the Great Army for scrap given that pins had largely been discounted.[112] One possible reading of the high numbers of hooked tags is as signifying the presence of pouches and coin purses, linked to economic activity.

Amulets

The assemblages from both camps include items that must reflect personal belief systems of members of the Great Army. From Torksey there is a complete cast silver Thor's hammer amulet (T634), the tip of which had been bent back perhaps to form a suspension loop, a fragment of another silver example (T136), and one cast in copper-alloy (T308) (Figure 4.24). Thor's hammer pendants are known in Scandinavia and Viking colonies from Iceland and Normandy to Russia, in male and female graves, hoards, and settlement sites.[113]

109. Thomas 2009, 17
110. Graham-Campbell and Okasha 1991, 222–5
111. Griffiths 1988, 45–6; Webster and Backhouse 1991, 221
112. Ten Harkel 2018, 19–20
113. Pestell 2013, 238–44

Figure 4.24. Amulets (not to scale, left to right): T136, T308 (Fitzwilliam Museum), T634 (PAS), T1628 (authors), A156 (PAS)

They are widely distributed in eastern and northern England, mostly of silver and often crudely made, like the Torksey examples. A metal-detected example is known from Foremark, and Gareth Williams has recently identified forty-five examples, with over a dozen recorded on the PAS.[114] In some cases the shaft has been pierced for suspension, but often it has been bent to form a loop, as was the case with the Thor's hammer pendant recovered from Grave 511 from Repton, and another from the Cuerdale hoard.[115] It is impossible to say if T136 was originally similarly suspended since the end is missing, but there is no trace of a suspension loop on the complete copper-alloy example (T308). Examples without suspension loops are known from Scandinavia, and interpreted as being used in ritual, including sacrifice in the cult house.[116] If, alternatively, T308 was worn it must have been attached to clothing using thread, rather than hanging round the neck as a pendant. In Scandinavia, Egon Wamers catalogued *c.*75 Thor's hammers, with around 75% from hoards and just 10% from graves, mainly those of females. In several cases the Thor's hammer had been placed on top of the coffin or elsewhere in the grave, or strung from a belt, rather than around the neck of the deceased.[117] It has been suggested that parts of two balances from Aldwark may have been repurposed as hammer-shaped pendants (A156, A1159).[118]

The anchor-shaped amulet (T1628) has been variously interpreted (Figure 4.24). Examples from Dublin were initially interpreted as metrological

---

114. E.g. LEIC-94A679, -185125; NMS-BEBB91, -88D515, -8E57D8, -A388C5, -35FDF0, -B95003; PUBLIC-B8D647; YORYM-8425D2, -453; LIN-D3E540; SWYOR-489283; NMS-A9E816; LANCUM-ED9222; Jarman 2021; Pestell 2013, 238–44; Williams 2023, 48

115. Biddle and Kjølbye-Biddle 1992, 48–9; Graham-Campbell 2011, 123–6

116. Jensen 2010, 65

117. Wamers 1997

118. Ager and Williams 2004; Ager 2020, 15; Rogers 2020a; Williams 2023, 47–8

weights before being proposed as fishing weights, either sinkers for land-lines or 'grip' weights for line fishing, but then reclassified as 'functionless ornaments'.[119] However, a collection of eleven similar objects from Hedeby were interpreted as possible amulets, six having either single or double per-forations, with the closest parallel to Torksey (no. 9) displaying a short stem with a pierced, rounded terminal.[120] A similar item from Coppergate (no. 10583) was published as a pendant but re-interpreted as a metrological weight; it also has a short stem with a now-broken perforation at the terminal and, although decorated with incised lines, is morphologically very close to the Torksey find.[121] Two further items from Aldwark which were clearly designed to be hung around the neck may also have served some amuletic function (Figure 4.25). A tiny silver pendant (A1805) has what has been interpreted as a raven's head design. A fan-shaped silver pendant has incised lines radi-ating from an upper semi-circle with two ring-and-dot motifs (A1806); the symbolism, if there is any, is unclear and it may have been purely decorative.

Figure 4.25. Possible amulets from Aldwark (not to scale): A1805 and A1806 (Yorkshire Museum)

A lead-alloy sheet model of a female figure (A1222) has also been labelled as an amulet (Figure 4.26). Facing left, with hair tied up or knotted and hanging down her back, the figure appears to be hold-ing a shield. The object has been crudely made, lacking the detail found in comparable Scandinavian examples produced as silver brooches or pendants, and one from Wickham

Figure 4.26. Amulets in the form of a lead-alloy sheet model of a female figure, possibly a Valkyrie (A1222; YAT), and a fragment of a miniature sword (T2353; PAS)

119. Wallace 1987, 212; 1998, 13; 2015, 271–2
120. Koktvedgaard Zeitzen 2002, Taf. 2; Jensen 2010, 170–2
121. Axworthy Rutter 1985, 62; Mainman and Rogers 2000, 2563; Hall 1984, 106

Market (Suffolk).[122] Such figures are often interpreted as Valkyries, welcoming warriors to Valhalla, in their role in Norse mythology as 'shield-maidens'.[123] From

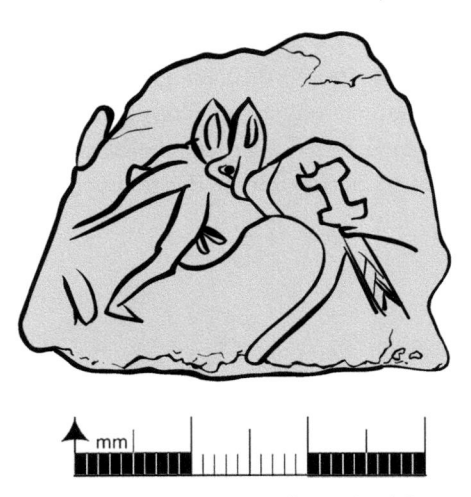

Torksey, there is a fragment of cast silver which, based on parallels from Uppåkra, appears to come from a miniature sword (T2353). Such miniatures are often found at cultic sites but may have been imbued with a broader protective purpose and this example was probably brought to England by a member of the Great Army as a personal talisman.[124] The same may be true of a crude drawing of the mythological Fenrir the wolf on both sides of a fragment of scrap lead (A1712), which clearly carried some ideological significance (Figure 4.27). Alternatively, it may have been graffiti or even a trial piece prior to some more accomplished depiction, in the same way that an incised lead disc

Figure 4.27. Fragment of scrap lead from Aldwark (A1712) depicting the mythological wolf Fenrir who is apparently carrying a sword; the legs of a human figure can be seen between his jaws (Drazen Tomic)

from the Brough of Birsay (Orkney) has been interpreted as a 'sketch' for working up a final design.[125]

Whilst those items very clearly evoke Scandinavian belief systems, a number of pendant crosses were also recovered, revealing a more complex situation among the occupants of the camps. These are unfragmented and may reflect the presence of members of the Great Army drawn from Christian regions, or, alternatively, early Scandinavian accommodations with Christianity. A silver cross with indecipherable lettering from Aldwark (A1711) seems to be an Anglo-Saxon object into which rune-like devices have been roughly carved (Figure 4.28). David Parsons suggests that it is vaguely imitative of a coin legend: MO is a common abbreviation for *moneta* on Anglo-Saxon coins, and further letters could be V or the inverted V, often used, without a cross-bar, for A.[126] A cross-shaped pendant cut from a sheet of gold (A1713) may be another

122. Williams 2014, 79
123. Rogers 2020c, 58–9; Gardeła *et al.* 2022
124. Capelle 2003; Jensen 2010, 45–9; Gardeła 2021
125. O'Meadhra 1993, 432–3
126. David Parsons pers. comm.

Figure 4.28. Pendant crosses (not to scale, left to right, top): A1711 (authors), A1713 (PAS), T223 (Fitzwilliam Museum); (bottom) T981, T2117 (authors), T3560 (Kevin Leahy)

converted Anglo-Saxon object; one of the arms has been perforated near the edge, probably to allow its use as a pendant. Whilst it has similarities with the Anglo-Saxon silver pendant cross from the Gravesend hoard (Chapter 2) it is much simpler; Anna Gannon suggested that it may have been unfinished, but signs of wear show it had been used.[127] Three much cruder lead crosses from Torksey may have been made by members of the Great Army. Two (T223 and T981) have a noticeably raised boss on one arm, which may have allowed their suspension by a thong of thread or leather, whilst the third (T2117)—which has raised ribs—had been deliberately pierced for suspension as a pendant. A cast lead disc with an equal-armed cross in the central field (T3560) has similarities with a failed pendant casting from tenth-century Period 4B deposits at Coppergate.[128] A styca (T488) had been pierced close to one edge, suggesting it was intended to be worn as a pendant, rather than for attaching to a lead weight, and the presence of crosses just below the piercing opens the possibility that it served an amuletic function. The variation in form of the amulets, and their obviously crude manufacture reinforces that these are personal items and reflects the diversity of ideologies represented within the camps.

127. Gannon 2004
128. Mainman and Rogers 2000, 2476, 4148

Conclusion

This chapter has demonstrated the value of examining not just the types of material culture associated with Viking activity but also the way in which they had been treated, in order to nuance our insights into the activities that took place on a site. Consideration of the proportions of dress accessories has also been shown to be important, with far more strap-ends than pins than would be expected on a typical settlement providing evidence for the selective gathering and processing of metalwork. In broad terms, the dress accessories discussed in this chapter illustrate two different aspects of life in the camps. The majority appears to have been collected by the Great Army for re-use and recycling, principally items of Anglo-Saxon origins, with some Irish material, especially penannular brooches. The types of collared pins, strip brooches, and sub-type A1, B1, and B2 strap-ends found at each camp largely reflect their broader regional distributions. However, rather than being a randomly gathered representative sample of common dress accessories in the environs of each camp, some objects were clearly collected selectively. Whilst strap-ends were presumably preferred over pinheads for the mundane reason of their greater metallic content, at Torksey, the apparent focus on collared pins with medial bands and conical tops may also show that specific alloys were identified and deliberately targeted. The higher proportion of annular/penannular brooch fragments at Aldwark may indicate that these items were collected for more symbolic purposes. Both actions demonstrate engagement with the material properties of the items collected, indicating that the assemblages do not merely show indiscriminate looting, but that both metal content and symbolic meaning may have also been factors in collection. A further symbolic element may be illustrated by the fragmentation of some of this material, with both the flat-headed pins and strip brooches suggesting that the Great Army preferred highly decorated and gilded metalwork. The fragmentary state of much of the material discussed in this chapter, with evidence of deliberate cutting rather than just accidental damage, reveals the processing of the metalwork.

A smaller subset of the dress accessories appears to have been worn or used by people within the camps. Some of these reveal the presence of women, reflecting periodic mentions of women, children, and 'households' among Viking forces in the continental sources discussed in Chapter 1. A few dress accessories are of Scandinavian manufacture, such as a Borre-style strap junction from Aldwark (A1718); others, such as the B4 strap-ends, reveal

Scandinavian stylistic influences. Wider influences from the broader Scandinavian cultural sphere can also be seen, such as the ringed pins of a type adopted from Irish fashions, the single Class F strap-end from Aldwark, a few Carolingian forms and others repurposed from Insular metalwork. The E3 series, which were also being manufactured at Torksey, are of Carolingian-influenced design, and can be said to reflect the fashionable 'military look' Wamers has identified as being more widely adopted, including into female dress accessories. These adapted belt fittings may have related to the 'currency of power' which Thomas saw as a process of cultural assimilation achieved through the adoption of Carolingian material.[129] Their use to signal group identity may have been equally important, either within a specific faction or across the camp as a whole. The production of A1 strap-ends evidenced at Torksey reveals that there was demand for new dress accessories of diverse types. It has been argued previously that the heterogeneous composition of Viking forces may have made the adoption of group-specific material culture a necessity, as a means of establishing solidarity and a collective identity. This may have been achieved through such means as the documented use of banners carried into battle, or the use of different burial practices, as seen at Repton and Heath Wood.[130] Cooijmans has also suggested that membership of defined military groups may have been signalled by adopting material derived from previous 'host cultures' encountered by these forces.[131] The archaeological evidence for such arguments has, however, been thin, but the assemblages from Aldwark and Torksey provide major new insights into these practices, albeit in a rather more mundane manner than recent depictions of them as pirate communities might suggest. Both the ringed pins and E3 strap fittings show the deliberate communication of group identity, with the Aldwark strap-ends being used to demonstrate group affiliation and a specific association with the Great Army. This signalling of Viking identity seems to contrast with the later years of Scandinavian settlement. Whilst introduced by Scandinavian agency, some of the dress accessories discussed in this chapter were adopted into regional dress styles, becoming longer-lived forms with a wide distribution across northern and eastern England.[132]

129. Wamers 2005b; Thomas 2012, 490, 507
130. Richards *et al.* 2004, 99–107; Price 2014, 62; 2016, 167; Raffield *et al.* 2016, 5–10; Raffield 2016, 320
131. Cooijmans 2020, 33
132. Hall 2000; Thomas 2000b; Kershaw 2013

5

Metalworking and minting

In the previous chapter we explored the rich assemblages of dress accessories and jewellery found at Aldwark and Torksey. These were shown to reflect the journeys of the occupants from the items they wore, and the loot they had acquired along the way, much of which was clearly being re-used for other purposes. In this chapter further evidence for metalworking is considered, including tools, the waste from manufacturing processes, trial pieces, models and moulds, offcuts and fragments. The evidence for the minting of coins on the camps is also discussed. The tools, in particular, provide insights into a much wider range of specialist metalworking being undertaken in the camps than is apparent from the finished artefacts alone. In many cases this would have been the production of iron objects which are under-represented from both sites given issues of both preservation, and, more importantly, recovery. The chapter also shows that some of the perceived differences between activities undertaken on the two camps are a product of the differing methods of investigation and recording, especially of ferrous material.

Metalworking tools

There are two early medieval hammerheads, an anvil, and nineteen punches from Torksey, and two punches from Aldwark. Both hammerheads (T1426, T2829) are small and sub-square in section, with squared striking faces (Figure 5.1). The bases and sides are parallel, whilst the tops display clear angles where they narrow to sub-rectangular cross-panes; the cross-pane of T1426 is broad, whilst T2829 is thinner and flatter. The eye of T1426 is narrow and sub-oval, whilst that of T2829 is not discernible. They are paralleled by a hammerhead from Coppergate (no. 2201), and so are almost certainly of early medieval date.[1] Early

1. Ottaway 1992, fig. 196

Figure 5.1. Hammerheads and anvil from Torksey (left to right): T1426, T2829, T2298 (authors)

medieval hammers generally conform to a standard shape, with a narrow, elongated body, long and straight cross-panes, and, commonly, raised cheeks on the upper face, bracketing the eye, with examples known from Thetford, Goltho (Lincolnshire), and Soham (Cambridgeshire).[2] Like the Coppergate find, the Torksey hammerheads are both atypical, suggesting that they may represent basic utilitarian tools not produced for any specific task. Arwidsson and Berg suggest a weight range of 400–750g for smiths' 'hand hammers', which Ian Goodall terms 'hand sledges'.[3] The Torksey hammerheads are lighter—at 270g (T1426) and 199g (T2829)—making it unlikely that they were used for welding, drawing out bars, or other heavy tasks. Given that neither hammerhead possesses the very elongated form seen on tools designed for more delicate work, it is also unlikely that either was used for chasing or shaping metal sheet. However, they would have been useful for light work in either iron or nonferrous metal, including shaping wires, driving nails, or striking other tools such as punches and chisels.[4] The striking faces of both hammerheads are burred, with that of T2829 dished in the centre, suggesting that it has been used to repeatedly strike narrow bars or rods. Its narrow cross-pane would also have been ideally suited to producing the thin, linear strike-marks seen on 'transverse hammered' Viking-age ingots, such as those reported from Aldwark.[5]

A substantial, nail-shaped object (94mm × 52mm) weighing 217g comprises a broad, wedge-shaped shank of sub-rectangular section, set orthogonally onto

2. Goodall 2011, 14–15; 1987, 177–8; Goodall *et al.* 1984, 76–7; Wilson 1976, 265
3. Arwidsson and Berg 1983, 30; I.H. Goodall 1984, 77
4. Ottaway 1992, 514
5. Kruse and Graham-Campbell 2011, 79–80; Blackburn 2011, 235

a wide, slightly domed sub-square head (T2298). Whilst it may be an extremely large nail or a hitch-pin, its identification as an anvil is supported by its similarity to the anvil from the seventh-century 'smith's grave' at Tattershall Thorpe (Lincolnshire).[6] This has been interpreted as the burial of an itinerant craftsman, travelling with portable equipment, and possibly with a pack-animal; such a description could equally apply to any metalworkers accompanying the Great Army, who would presumably value comparatively lightweight, transportable tools. The Torksey anvil would have been driven into a block of seasoned hardwood for use, suggesting that the Army expected to be able to procure such a suitable mounting.

Early medieval anvils are rare.[7] An iron anvil (no. 2200) from Anglo-Scandinavian levels at Coppergate is of an 'L'-shaped, 'beaked' form, as is the heavily-beaked anvil (no. 75) from the Mästermyr tool hoard on Gotland, which is of probable tenth- or eleventh-century date.[8] In contrast, a smaller anvil (no. 72) from Mästermyr is straight and wedge-shaped, lacking the wider head evident on both the Torksey and the Tattershall Thorpe examples; a similar anvil appears to be depicted on the front panel of the eighth-century Franks Casket.[9] A wedge-shaped, square-headed anvil with an additional narrow beak has also been recovered from Hedeby, and there is another of this form from the early tenth-century Île de Groix boat burial.[10] Practical considerations such as intended use almost certainly influenced the shape of any anvil. The Torksey anvil would not have been suitable for heavy blacksmithing work but would have been serviceable for lighter metalworking of the type suggested by the two hammerheads. The Tattershall Thorpe anvil has a pritchel-hole in one corner, showing that it could be used for punch-work and manufacturing nails; a projecting, flattened corner on the head of the Torksey anvil may indicate a similar feature.

There are nineteen punches from Torksey and two from Aldwark (Figure 5.2). These were not exclusively metalworking tools, although one of the Aldwark punches (A389) was recovered amongst metalworking debris in Trench 22.[11] Goodall lists punches amongst the equipment necessary for woodworking and stoneworking, and MacGregor *et al.* have argued that a double-pointed punch

6. Hinton 2000, 23–5
7. Hall (2020c, 74) reported a possible anvil stone at Aldwark, but this was subsequently deemed an incorrect identification by YAT.
8. Ottaway 1992, 512–13
9. Arwidsson and Berg 1983, 15, pl. 21; Webster 2012, 10
10. Armbruster 2004, 111; Langouët 2006, 97, fig. 9 (2)
11. Hall 2020c, 69

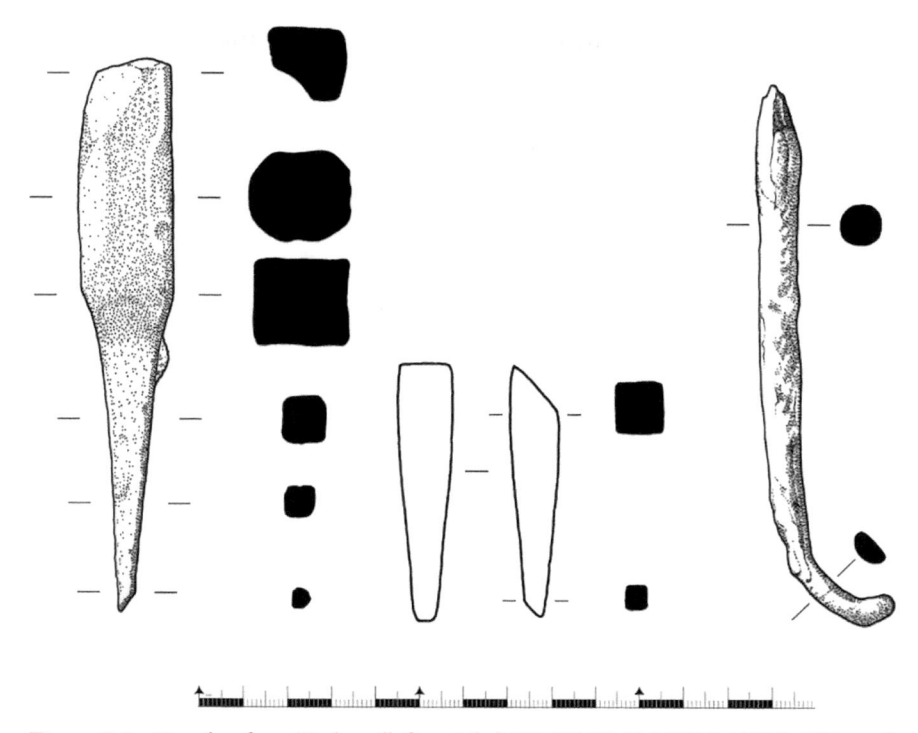

Figure 5.2. Punches from Torksey (left to right): T2474, T2552, T2834 (Chloe Watson)

was used to decorate rib-bones on a casket lid from Coppergate.[12] The identification of these tools as punches may be inexact, as the same basic form can encompass a variety of more specialised tools, including hot and cold tangless chisels, drifts, sets, and pritchels, although uses can be proposed for several of the Torksey examples. One (T2474) is almost certainly a pritchel. It is sub-square in section, with a long, tapering point extending from a wider, shouldered body, and the centre has chamfered corners, creating a roughly octagonal cross-section. Ottaway notes that this feature indicates that such tangless punches were designed to be held by tongs or rods, and so intended to be used hot. Pritchels are commonly used in forging horseshoes, although this object may have been employed in the manufacture of roves, matching the square-section clench nails recovered from the site. Eight wedge-shaped tools could be described as chisels, but Ottaway classifies very similar objects as punches. These would be useful when cutting up metal objects, or when making decorative

12. Goodall 2011, 27, 45; MacGregor *et al.* 1999, p. 1954

grooves, with several of the smaller examples most probably used on non-ferrous material.[13] Two of the Torksey punches (T2552, T2834) are thicker towards the centre and taper to the ends, suggesting that they were formerly set into organic handles; the remainder appear to have been tangless, with several showing clear burring and other signs of striking on the upper ends.

Punches are relatively scarce in early medieval contexts. Hana Lewis catalogues only seven definite, and three possible, punches in a sample of forty-five excavated non-elite rural settlements.[14] Only two punches were recorded from Thetford, and three from Winchester.[15] There is also a paucity of punches in Viking-age Scandinavia, although the tool collection from a tenth-century inhumation at Bygland, Telemark (Norway), demonstrates that punches were integral to the toolkits of specialised craftworkers.[16] Some larger assemblages are, however, also known in England from both high-status rural settlements and urban sites: for example, 12 tangless and 15 tanged punches were recorded at Flixborough, whilst the largest corpus comes from Coppergate, where 23 tangless and 16 tanged punches were recovered, many of which provide close parallels for the Torksey finds.[17] In assessing the Coppergate assemblage, Ottaway observed that a wider variety of designs would have been required, especially by smiths, than has been found through excavation; the production of coin dies was particularly noted as needing a broad range of tip forms.[18] The examples from Torksey can tentatively be linked with the evidence for minting discussed later in this chapter.

Metalworking waste

About 6.5kg of metalworking waste was recovered from the excavation trenches at Aldwark, including slag, furnace linings, five hearth bases, and casting waste.[19] These were distributed across the trenches, suggesting that different types of metalworking took place at various locations around the camp. Some of the assemblage may derive from earlier occupation, particularly given the comparatively early radiocarbon dates produced by a feature containing fragments of burnt clay oven lining in Trench 22 (cal AD 670–780 and AD 690–830, at the

13. Ottaway 1992, 516–17
14. Lewis 2019, Appendix 5.7.2
15. I.H. Goodall 1984, 77; 1990a, 199
16. Blindheim 1963, 34
17. Ottaway *et al*. 2009, 318; Ottaway 1992, 515–19
18. Ottaway 1992, 519
19. Mortimer 2020, 48

95% confidence level).[20] However, nothing from this trench confirms that metalworking pre-dates the arrival of the Great Army; indeed, the presence of slag deposits, a punch, clench nails, and roves suggests that these can be associ-ated with the activities of the Army.[21] At Torksey *c.*600g of ironworking slag has been recorded during metal-detecting and excavation. The ferrous slag from both camps may be classed as smithing waste, representing either metalworking by-products or broken-up hearth bottoms, but either way demonstrating that ironworking was practised at both locations.

Mortimer has catalogued four fragments of vitrified furnace lining amongst the Aldwark material. One contained copper-alloy deposits, but the others are non-diagnostic, and could have been used in any metalworking process.[22] The same is true for the fragments of slag, with only three metal-detected samples from Torksey being confidently attributed to non-ferrous working.[23] Although this waste material shows some differences between the two camps, the circum-stances in which it was found make it difficult to assign any significance to this. The detectorists did not routinely recover metalworking waste at either site, and the larger assemblage from Aldwark, especially the hearth bases and fur-nace lining, can be accounted for principally by the more extensive excavation conducted there (Figure 5.3). Furthermore, although no hearth or furnace material has been identified from Torksey, the thick overburden of wind-blown sand across the site could easily mask any metalworking remains from geomag-netic survey.[24] Nonetheless, the high-temperature working of both iron and copper-alloy was clearly practised at both locations.

Figure 5.3. Crucible base (A1808) with silver content from Aldwark (Yorkshire Museum)

Waste from melting and casting activity has been recovered from both camps, generally in the form of small, sub-rounded, irregular lenses of metal, in copper-alloy, lead, silver, and gold. The recording of droplets was, however, incomplete, with recovery practices introducing a considerable bias. In particular,

20. Hall 2020c, 70
21. Williams and Hall 2020, 83
22. Mortimer 2020, 48
23. T1323, T3467–8
24. Hadley and Richards 2016, 35; Hall 2020c, 66

small amounts or shapeless melts of copper-alloy are known to have been screened out or discarded by detectorists, when working without direct archaeological supervision. Similarly, high volumes of very small lead droplets are known to have been detected at Torksey, but neither counted nor weighed.

To contextualise this evidence, we can compare it with the findings from Kaupang, where Pedersen has observed a significant discrepancy in the relative proportions of cast metals suggested by different methods of archaeological investigation. For example, the droplets recovered from sieving and metal-detecting suggested that metalworking was almost exclusively conducted in copper-alloy and lead, with limited use of silver. In contrast, archaeometallurgical analysis of excavated crucible fragments revealed that silver was as abundant as copper-alloy. Therefore, even a comparatively well-recorded assemblage of droplets and melts may offer only a partial picture, reflecting the care with which craftspeople handled various metals, rather than providing an accurate record of which materials were cast. Pedersen argues that 'every tiny fragment of valuable gold was taken care of' at Kaupang, where just a single droplet was recovered, even though archaeometallurgical analysis suggests that gold was worked there almost as frequently as silver.[25] Although this droplet was recovered during excavations of a workshop plot, there is no reason why the craftworkers at Torksey would have been inherently less careful, and therefore, the four droplets from Torksey probably represent overspill from gold working, and suggest that gold was extensively used and particularly abundant in the camp.

Technical considerations require an over-allowance of molten metal when casting, and whilst spillage can obviously occur when filling the narrow inlets of closed, two-piece moulds, droplets can form even when casting ingots in open moulds.[26] Given the abundant evidence for metalworking at both camps, the recorded droplets probably indicate casting. It is, however, possible that their presence derives from economic activities, as silver droplets and 'bean-shaped' Kruse Type 2 ingots are sometimes found as components in silver hoards in Ireland, as well as in the Cuerdale hoard.[27] These assemblages suggest that silver droplets circulated in the Irish Sea area in the later ninth and early tenth centuries, perhaps incorporated into the range of low-weight,

25. Pedersen 2017, 128
26. Kruse *et al.* 1988, 90–1
27. Sheehan 2014, 206

fragmented silver used for small-scale transactions or to top up larger amounts. A few of the Torksey silver melts show signs of being flattened or pressed whilst semi-molten, and are similar to the Type 2 ingots discussed in Chapter 3, while the weights of fifty-three of the droplets lie between 0.1 and 1.9g, mirroring the weight range seen in the fragmented hack-silver.[28] This opens up the possibility that they would have been usable in everyday transactions, and may represent economic, rather than manufacturing, activity.

Metal-detecting recovered ten pieces of litharge at Aldwark (A1039–48). Litharge cakes are a by-product of cupellation, wherein silver or gold is refined through high-temperature oxidisation, which results in the creation of base lead litharge, partially absorbed into hearth material, with precious metal separated on the surface. Whilst cupellation can be performed to recover silver from freshly-smelted argentiferous lead, it is also used in the purification of debased silver, and is likely to have been the process undertaken at Aldwark.[29] Lead oxide litharge cakes would be easily identified by metal-detector, and so their absence from Torksey may suggest another difference in practice between the camps. No litharge cakes were found at Woodstown either, despite an extensive metal-detector survey, but cupellation has been identified there from four cupel fragments, small ceramic vessels usually used to assay the purity of silver, rather than to refine it.[30] Cupels have also been identified at Viking-age urban sites such as Kaupang, Birka, Hedeby, and Coppergate.[31] Early medieval litharge, indicative of larger-scale refining, is far rarer, with cakes found at Coppergate, Winchester, and at Fröjel on Gotland.[32] The ten litharge cakes from Aldwark have a combined weight of 1380g, and given that medieval treatises suggest a ratio of three parts lead to one of material for refining, this suggests that at least 340g of silver was purified on the site.[33] However, a greater proportion of lead is required for material which contains high amounts of copper, and Mortimer reported that several of the litharge cakes have a greenish tinge, indicating high levels of copper compounds which would have altered this ratio.[34] The scarcity of evidence for cupellation on Viking-age sites makes the Aldwark material unusual, and comparable to the nine fragments from

---

28. Kruse and Graham-Campbell 2011, 74
29. Merkel 2016, 24; Mortimer 2020
30. Young 2014b, 270–3
31. Bayley 1992, 750
32. Bayley 1992, 749; Bayley and Barclay 1990, 181; Kershaw and Merkel 2022, 127
33. Merkel 2016, 24
34. Mortimer 2020, 48

Coppergate Periods 3–6, although these span the mid-ninth to the later eleventh centuries.[35]

Cupellation is a skilled and labour-intensive process, which Merkel suggests would only be undertaken if completely necessary.[36] In the Viking Age silver was not routinely assayed by cupellation, with nicking or pecking far more common methods of assessing purity and debasement.[37] Although silver purity was of clear importance in the bullion economy, cupellation was not the sole available method to improve metal quality. Whilst silver coinage in England became increasingly debased throughout the third quarter of the ninth century, the Great Army was able to access dirhams, sources distinguished by extremely high levels of silver purity.[38] The routine melting and reworking of silver which characterised the Scandinavian economy would allow any low-grade metal to be purified by the addition of a higher-grade source such as dirhams, removing the necessity for refining. Cupellation is wasteful, with the resulting contaminated lead oxide rendered effectively unusable.[39] All purified silver is usually removed from this oxide waste, but several of the Aldwark litharge cakes retain fragments of precious metal, some 'visible to the naked eye'.[40] This betokens an abundance of silver. At Fröjel, large-scale cupellation has been linked to the casting of silver arm-rings and penannular brooches, and the production of broad-band arm-rings can be inferred at Torksey from lead trial pieces, but there is no such evidence to indicate what was produced following cupellation at Aldwark.[41] Cupellation can be a step in the process of coin making, frequently when old coin is re-minted, but there is no direct evidence for this from Aldwark either.[42] Even so, this evidence of a systematic programme of silver refining implies a centralised control over bullion quality and the market.

Metalworking moulds, models, and trial pieces

In Chapter 4, we highlighted the evidence for the manufacture of E3 strap-ends at Aldwark and casting of A1 strap-ends at Torksey, and there is further evidence for the casting of dress accessories from moulds and models. A fragment

35. Bayley 1992, 749
36. Merkel 2016, 31
37. Kershaw and Merkel 2022, 127
38. Metcalf and Northover 1985, 150
39. Hoffmann 2021, 34
40. Mortimer 2020, 48
41. Kershaw and Merkel 2022, 127
42. Merkel 2016, 31–2

Figure 5.4. Lead casting models from Torksey (not to scale): T281 and T280 (Fitzwilliam Museum)

of lead alloy, broken on all sides and with a flat reverse (T281) has the remains of a lozenge-shaped field divided by four raised arms on the front (Figure 5.4). These arms define a quatrefoil shape, with hollows which lead to piercings, arranged around an elliptical central projection, resembling a decorative openwork boss, a characteristic feature of several classes of Scandinavian jewellery. This lead model may represent the remains of a casting prototype for such an item. The low profile and clear framing field of the design mean that it is unlikely to have been intended for the production of the separately-cast bosses affixed to Type P51 oval brooches; whilst these were typically of a similar quatrefoil openform type they also exhibit a more rounded, uniform shape and are highly domed.[43] The lower, more angular pattern of the Torksey lead model suggests that it most probably formed the central boss of an equal-armed brooch, and there are similarities with the central fields of the Type III F:1 and Type III H:1 brooch forms identified at Birka.[44] There are also some similarities with the central bosses recorded on both the Type II B1 and II B2 large oval brooches from Birka, although the lead model has a slightly asymmetrical design.[45] In either case, this workshop material suggests the production of at least one item of classically Scandinavian jewellery associated with female dress, suggesting a market for Scandinavian female jewellery at the camp.[46]

A second possible lead model (T280) is formed of two small, conjoined, slightly flattened lead spheres, with a possible lip of casting flash passing around their circumference (Figure 5.4). They appear to have been cut at one end, suggesting that they were once part of a longer section of similar globules. The two spheres have a marked similarity to the cast rods used as 'beaded' border elements of early medieval metalwork, especially jewellery.[47] It was manufactured by either impressing or filing sub-spherical divisions into round-section wires, and these wires were typically narrow, resulting in granulated beads with diameters ranging from 0.5mm to 2.5mm, most commonly towards the lower end

43. Jansson 1985, fig. 56
44. Aagård 1984, 99
45. Jansson 1984b, 76
46. Hayeur Smith 2004, 71; Kershaw 2013, 171–2
47. Whitfield 1998, 57

of this range.[48] However, larger 'beaded' borders do exist, such as the gilded copper-alloy frames of the so-called Rupertus Cross housed at Bischofshofen (Austria), which is of eighth-century Anglo-Saxon origins.[49] Although it would have been inefficient and wasteful to produce thicker sections of beading by the techniques outlined above, a longer arrangement of the spheres seen in T280 could have been used as a model to cast large-diameter beaded rods. Experiments by Coatsworth and Pinder identified lead as being particularly suited to the production of such beaded borders, with its malleability producing results which were indistinguishable from Anglo-Saxon originals.[50] Beaded or pelleted borders were also featured on dress items such as buckle frames or hooked tags (e.g. T3566).[51] Therefore, sections of beaded lead rod, used to create larger models, would be a useful component of a craftworker's toolkit.

Viking-age lead models are not common. Pedersen catalogues them as only occasional finds from sites in Scandinavia, with the collection of twenty-six models from Kaupang deemed exceptional, although only two can be assigned to secure contexts; the majority have been broadly dated to 800–75 on stylistic grounds, although some may date to as late as 950. The Kaupang finds were principally collected through the use of metal-detectors; however, similar detector surveys at Hedeby have not produced a comparable assemblage, suggesting that there may have been a strong element of regionality in the use of lead models.[52] Whilst the numbers of lead models from Aldwark and Torksey are much lower than the total recovered from Kaupang, both assemblages appear substantial when viewed in an English context. For example, only a single lead model was recovered from Coppergate, the B5 strap-end model discussed in Chapter 4.[53] Lead casting models would have been suited to the mobile nature of the Great Army; they were durable and robust, convenient for storage and transportation, and available for use whenever a suitable workshop could be established. The portability of lead models is evidenced by an example from Kaupang (C52517/635) interpreted as a model for manufacturing base-frames for decorative glass studs, with its morphology suggesting an Insular origin, and isotope analysis indicating that the lead was probably sourced from Scotland.[54] Lead models may have been particularly attractive to

48. Duczko 1985, 17–22, 32–104
49. Wilson 1984, 133–4
50. Coatsworth and Pinder 2002, 75–6
51. Paterson and Tweddle 2014, 212
52. Pedersen 2016, 38–40, fig. 4.28
53. Tweddle 2004, 453, fig. 112
54. Pedersen 2016, 61–2

itinerant craftworkers, who may also have prized their ability to be used repeatedly. In contrast, wax is fragile and easily damaged, and any models for the 'lost wax' casting process would have been difficult to transport.[55] Models for equal-armed brooches appear to have been used in several distinct workshop areas at Kaupang in the early to mid-ninth century (Periods I and II). At that time, the occupation is believed to have been seasonal, reinforcing that the models were utilised by travelling traders.[56] The lead models from Aldwark and Torksey were similarly designed for repeated use, suggesting not only manufacturing, but also the serial production of closely related items.

Pedersen has observed that use of clay moulds for equal-armed brooches would require lengthy, complicated preparation, even with the use of lead models. She concluded that this timescale meant that such brooches were made in advance as stock for subsequent sale to consumers with whom the craftworker had limited contact, in contrast to the earlier practice or production of more individualised items to order. However, she also saw serial production as fundamentally representing a technical option, one of several from which the craftworker selected to adapt to a given market. Whilst complex items could be made in advance, the use of moulds also offered capacity to cast large volumes of more straightforward products, with closely-linked series of objects, such as harness mounts, produced individually to order.[57] Either way, whether the lead models were used on the camps for mass production for a wider market or for multiple items to order, this suggests something of the flexibility of production shown by the craftworkers at Torksey. In contrast, the simple forms of the Aldwark strap-end models all speak of easy, swift casting. Furthermore, the recovery of only Thomas Type E3 models from Aldwark suggests that manufacturing at the camp was focused on belt fittings, to the exclusion of other dress accessories; the fact that all three models are from the same type implies the production of a high volume of these objects.

Lead trial pieces have been recovered from Torksey, some of which had been used to test a variety of decorative punches. Blackburn noted that the punched designs on two of them (T85, T2087) were all common elements of decoration on Scandinavian silver jewellery (Figure 5.5).[58] A lead object (T2067) bearing 'C'-shaped punch marks can be tentatively interpreted as another trial piece.

55. Coatsworth and Pinder 2002, 75; Pedersen 2016, 70
56. Pilø 2007, 192–200; Pedersen 2016, 68
57. Pedersen 2017, 125–6, 129–30, 134
58. Blackburn 2011, 242

Figure 5.5. Lead trial pieces from Torksey (not to scale; left to right): T85 (Fitzwilliam Museum), T2067, T2087 (authors)

Similar punched decorations are occasionally used on Scandinavian jewellery, to form undulating, transverse grooves. Such designs are generally seen on Type A band arm-rings with sub-group (i) designs, characterised as 'Scandinavian and related' ornament. Their distribution is strongly centred on Scandinavia; in Britain they are limited to four fragments in the Cuerdale hoard, and another in the Dysart Island hoard (Co. Westmeath, Ireland). Similar crescent-shaped punched designs are also seen on the annular flat-band finger-rings that Graham-Campbell has associated with the Great Army.[59] Although the specific punches themselves have not been identified, it seems likely that all three trial pieces were produced on site, suggesting that Scandinavian-style rings and broad-band arm-rings were manufactured at Torksey.

An unfinished disc brooch or mount at Aldwark (A1080) was compared by Rogers to a disc-shaped blank from Bawsey with a single, central perforation and a demarcated quadrant with a Trewhiddle-style beast sketched out.[60] The latter was interpreted as a trial piece for a disc brooch, although it could similarly have been work in progress, lost or discarded before completion. The decoration in one quadrant of the unfinished Aldwark example indicates production in an Anglo-Saxon style (Figure 5.6). More broadly, it suggests the production of dress

Figure 5.6. Unfinished disc brooch or mount (A1080; YAT) and broken copper-alloy *pressblech* die (T2124; authors)

59. Graham-Campbell 2011, 91, 106, 146
60. Rogers 2020c, 56

accessories appealing to local tastes, presumably by a craftworker used to manufacturing in this style, but whether they were produced for members of the Great Army or for a market amongst the surrounding populations is uncertain.

A broken copper-alloy *pressblech* die (T2124) from Torksey would have been used as a patrix for producing embossed decorative metal foils in copper-alloy, silver, or gold.[61] The surviving face is decorated with two-strand interlace ornament and a roundel containing a contorted beast, both characteristic of the Trewhiddle style, indicating an English origin.[62] In England the floruit of the *pressblech* process appears to have been in the early Anglo-Saxon period, with the majority of foils and dies dated stylistically to the seventh century and earlier.[63] However, later examples of *pressblech* foils have been noted on material which appears to have originated in Northumbria, suggesting that the technique was preserved there up to the ninth century.[64] Ninth- and tenth-century copper-alloy and stone *pressblech* dies are known from Scandinavia, including Kaupang, Birka, and Hedeby, but used either to make small foils for decorative nail-heads or to shape brooch blanks.[65] A collection of later tenth- and eleventh-century die matrices from Hedeby and the Baltic were used to form brooch and pendant blanks to which filigree and granulation were added.[66] This evidence shows a very different form of production to the English manufacture of larger sheets. It is possible that larger foils were manufactured on organic formers in Scandinavia, as they may have been in Ireland, but again, this difference of technique re-enforces the attribution of the Torksey die to an English style of metalworking.[67] As Coatsworth and Pinder note, the production of multi-use copper-alloy dies required considerable time and expense, suggesting an association with large-scale, highly organised production.[68] The majority of Northumbrian *pressblech* work is found on ecclesiastical objects, such as the side panels on the Rupertus Cross. Whilst clearly not a direct link, the Cross does demonstrate that pressed foils were sometimes used on metal objects in conjunction with the beaded borders that may be represented by the lead casting model (T280) discussed earlier in this chapter. These items show that highly skilled metalworkers were amongst the inhabitants of the camp at

61. Webster and Backhouse 1991, 56–7
62. Wilson and Blunt 1961, 103–5; Thomas 2000a, 71
63. Leahy 2003, 157
64. Laing 1993, 7
65. Pedersen 2016, 78–81
66. Armbruster 2004, 113–22
67. Craddock 1989, 179
68. Coatsworth and Pinder 2002, 110

Torksey, but also suggest that highly specialist metalworking techniques and materials were brought from Northumbria by the Great Army.

Offcuts and fragments

There is a long history of the re-use and recycling of metalwork across post-Roman Europe and Scandinavia.[69] In Chapter 4 we discussed evidence for processing of Anglo-Saxon dress accessories, to which we can add a wide range of material from western Britain and Ireland. This is not surprising since Insular metal ornaments were prized in Scandinavia, but the assemblages from Aldwark and Torksey display the style of fragmentation characteristic of practice in Britain and Ireland, with pieces cut without any apparent consideration for their original form.[70] This suggests that these items were primarily gathered and retained as scrap. Offcuts of metal are typically the preferred source of casting material, as they were convenient for melting in crucibles and reworking into new objects.[71] A secondary economic use as bullion, to make up larger transactions, is another possible use, although Sheehan stresses that the bullion value of Insular metalwork was comparatively small, with the items consisting almost entirely of bronze. Nonetheless, the quality of the design and the casting was typically far higher than in contemporary Scandinavian ornament, which may have rendered fragments a suitable medium for exchange where undecorated metal would not serve.[72] Insular objects were clearly imbued with a prestige value, and the technical quality and exotic nature of the decoration appears to have carried a social significance.[73] Wamers has observed that Insular items found in Scandinavia appear to primarily reflect military activity, and while the fragments from Torksey and Aldwark had been broken for use in metalworking or trading, it may be that they were perceived to imply acquisition through plunder, enhancing their symbolic significance beyond their intrinsic value.[74]

Twenty-seven pieces of copper-alloy Insular metalwork are recorded from Aldwark and seventy from Torksey, most having been removed from original settings or cut. Fragments of ecclesiastical metalwork include the remains of a hinged fitting (A1174), which was probably originally attached to a

69. Fleming 2012, 17; Hårdh 2011b, 59
70. Wamers 1998, 41–2; Heen-Pettersen 2014; 2021, section 4
71. Sindbæk 2001, 51; Pestell 2013, 249
72. Sheehan 2013, 818–19
73. Wamers 1998, 43; Aannestad 2018, 8
74. Wamers 1998, 47; Ashby 2015, 94–6

house-shaped shrine or reliquary. A1141 may be a suspension mount from a hanging bowl, while the geometric cells of T348 are also suggestive of either a hanging-bowl mount or a decorated escutcheon (Figure 5.7).[75] Three formerly-connected strips of openwork sheet (A276, A277, A290) deposited in a pit fill have been interpreted as a possible box mount.[76] However, it was noted that they are very closely paralleled in Ireland by the sheet fittings on the ninth-century Clonard pail (Co. Meath) and similarities can also be identified with a panel of binding recovered from the River Blackwater, dated to the second half of the ninth century or the early tenth century, and so they may have been removed from a bronze-decorated *situla* bucket.[77] Nine of the copper-alloy Insular objects from Aldwark and twenty-seven from Torksey show evidence of gilding, as does a fragment of a Carolingian vessel (T114), pierced with an iron rivet for re-use.

Irish bridle fittings found in England and Scotland have sometimes been seen as indicative of trade or the recycling of metalwork, although Leahy has suggested that some Insular finds, particularly elements of horse harness, may

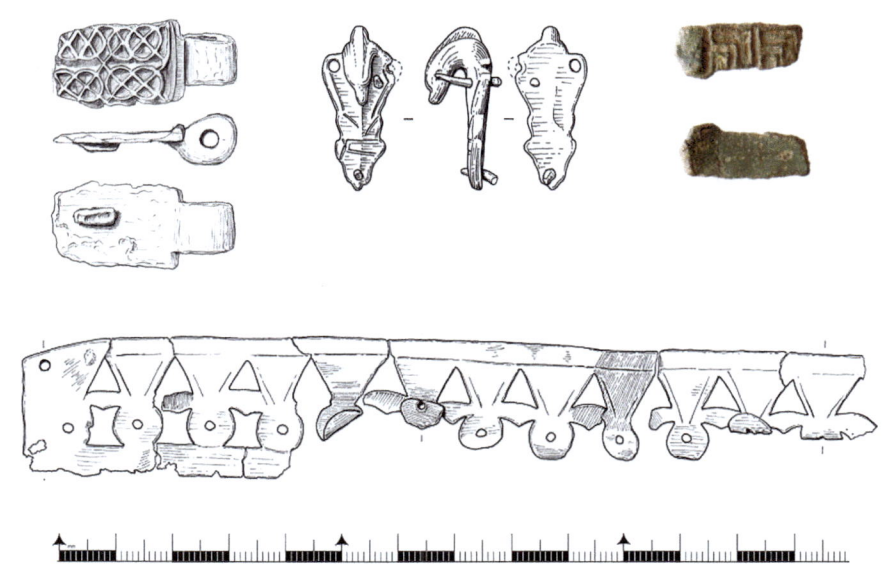

Figure 5.7. Insular metalwork (top row, left to right): A1174, A1141 (YAT), T348 (Fitzwilliam Museum); (bottom row): A276, A290, A277 (YAT)

75. Bruce-Mitford 1987, fig. 4
76. Rogers 2020c, 49, fig. 10
77. Ó Floinn 1989, 121, fig. 119; Bourke 2010, 39, fig. 6:59

have been personal possessions.[78] It is certainly possible that some of the five harness fittings (A1140, A1224, T44, T736, T1137) represent casual losses by members of the Great Army, including some from Ireland, as the only fragmentary example (T1137) appears to have been broken rather than cut (Figure 5.8). However, two seem to have been in the process of being converted into brooches. One Aldwark fitting (A1224) was originally part of a horse bridle, with three perforated lugs on the reverse to connect it to other mounts set along a strap, forming an interlocking, flexible group (Figure 5.9). This was identified as being of eighth- or ninth-century Irish manufacture, and while it lacks a pin, it was interpreted by Graham-Campbell as having been separated from a harness for re-use as a brooch.[79] A fitting from Torksey (T44) may likewise have been in the process of being converted into a brooch, although it was lost before a pin was fitted. It has similarities with two fittings recovered as part of a bridle set from Balladoole (Isle of Man), as those roundels also feature central perforations and a similar 'stepped' profile, although their faces are decorated with rosettes rather than simple crosses.[80] Two small, irregular projecting stubs on the reverse of T44 also have similarities with the remains of filed-down lugs visible on the reverse of an eighth-century harness fitting of Irish type from South Shields fort (Co. Durham), similarly in the process of conversion.[81] The converted harness fittings from Aldwark and Torksey can be

Figure 5.8. Harness fittings (left to right): A1140 (YAT), T44 (Fitzwilliam Museum), T736, T1137 (PAS)

78. Redknap 2013, 188–90; Leahy 2014, 38; Williams 2020f, 45
79. Wamers 1998, 38; Graham-Campbell 2015; 2020
80. Bersu and Wilson 1966, pl. V:F
81. Croom and Youngs 2021, 6

Figure 5.9. Terminal from an eighth-/ninth-century harness mount of Irish manufacture from Aldwark (A1224). Now in the Metropolitan Museum of Art in New York (British Museum)

tentatively added to the evidence for the presence of females on the camps. Reworked Insular fittings have been identified in female graves in Scandinavia, such as three ninth-century burials from the Trøndelag region of central Norway where they appear to have been worn at the waist as an element of female dress, while Wamers has noted that most of the forty Insular harness fittings catalogued from Norway were re-used as brooches.[82]

Several fragments of Irish and Anglo-Saxon metalwork from Aldwark and Torksey may have been earmarked for mounting on lead inset weights, as

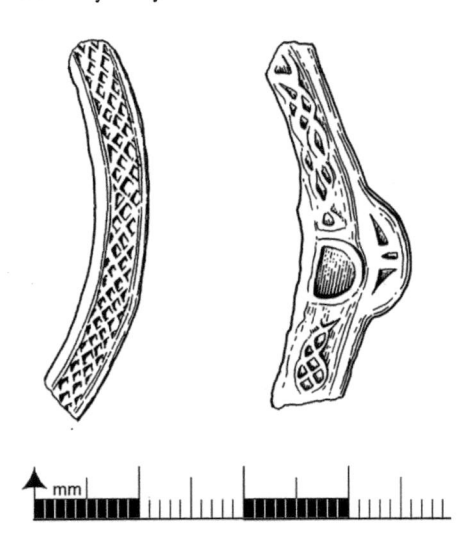

Figure 5.10. Two fragments of annular or penannular brooches from Aldwark: A1099 and A1100 (YAT)

suggested for similar items at Woodstown.[83] They have piercings that do not respect the original design or decoration (A1169, T113, T116, T333, T346) or secondary attachments of rivets (T1123) indicating secondary holes made to fix them to something else. At Aldwark, two fragments of annular or penannular brooches (A1099, A1100) are morphologically similar to a fragment set in one of the weights from the burial at Kiloran Bay (Figure 5.10).[84] Pedersen has noted the preference for inset mounts of animal form, and Ó Floinn proposed that castings of human or zoomorphic heads were deliberately selected for use as insets.[85] A silver three-dimensional bull's-head mount with two rivets (T1637) may have been intended for such use. Two complete inset weights from Torksey (T169, T2127) also have zoomorphic mounts, one of silver, while a silver-gilt human mask is also mounted on a weight recorded from Tadcaster (North Yorkshire).[86]

Over twenty pieces of possible scrap base metals have been recorded from Torksey and Aldwark, but their dating is insecure, and some may derive from

82. Heen-Pettersen 2018, 69–71
83. Ó Floinn 2014, 188–90
84. Rogers 2020c, fig. 16; Grieg 1940, fig. 32
85. Pedersen 2008, 175–7; Ó Floinn 2014, 187
86. SWYOR-EF9E81

post-medieval or modern agricultural activity. Nonetheless, rods of copper-alloy (T277, T278) and lead (T257) have clear parallels from Coppergate, suggesting that they are related to Viking-age metalworking activity. The same may be true of fragments of cast lead sheet recovered from both camps, which are of a type identified as a main source of scrap lead at Coppergate.[87] Elements of disassembled iron swords have been recovered from both sites, and some of these, particularly the pommels, may have been retained as sources of scrap (discussed in Chapter 6). While the nature of the assemblages makes a more detailed comparison challenging, the assemblage nonetheless suggests that individuals at both Aldwark and Torksey appear to have collected rough non-ferrous scrap as another component of metalworking.

Figure 5.11. Lead sheet (T1620) from Torksey pierced top left with runic inscription (authors)

A remarkable lead offcut (T1620) was found at Torksey many years ago. Its current location is uncertain, and it is only known from a low-resolution photograph (Figure 5.11). Nonetheless it shows a rectangular section of lead sheet which appears to have been cut from a larger sheet, with a clean break along its right-hand edge. A hole in the top left corner indicates where it must have been attached to something, and one assumes that originally there was a similar attachment point at top right. The first two letters of three lines survive, which must have continued across the missing section. David Parsons comments that the four characters on lines two and three are Anglo-Saxon not Scandinavian runes. They read:

e a

g e

87. Bayley 1992, 781–8

The e-form is typical of English usage, and the a-form is still more distinctively an Anglo-Saxon innovation. The rather neat-looking arrangement, and the serifs on the ends of all the strokes, are readily paralleled elsewhere and link this to the main run of Christian-period inscriptions of the eighth and ninth centuries. The opening two characters of the top line are, however, more problematic. The first could be a rather strangely proportioned runic **u** or **c**, or possibly an uncial roman letter *h*, as a mixture of scripts is sometimes found, but the second is an unknown character. The fragmentary nature of the inscription makes a reading impossible. A lead plaque from Flixborough, bearing seven personal names, is the closest parallel, with a similar layout and also pierced for attachment.[88] The Flixborough text is uncial roman throughout, not runic, but the general aspect and the forms of serif are similar, and the lettering is also rather idiosyncratically curved in places.[89] It appears likely that the Torksey sheet had been looted from an ecclesiastical site and cut into at least two pieces with the intention of reworking.

Coin production

Direct evidence for coin production has only been recovered from Torksey. This is in the form of two 'trial' coins and two irregularly shaped, angular pieces of lead sheet, one of which (T1697) had been struck with the obverse and reverse dies of an imitative *solidus* of Louis the Pious (Figure 5.12).[90] These are on opposing faces of the sheet, but not accurately aligned, indicating comparatively careless striking. A tear in the sheet has removed roughly a quarter of each die face, and although post-depositional damage is a possibility, it may alternatively indicate a deliberate attempt to deface or destroy the impression. In a discussion of four lead sheets bearing coin die impressions from the later Anglo-Saxon period, that were known by the 1950s, Dolley saw them as being

Figure 5.12. Lead sheet from Torksey with die tests for an imitative Louis the Pious *solidus* (T1697; authors)

88. David Parsons pers. comm.; Brown and Okasha 2009
89. Parsons pers. comm.
90. Blackburn 2007, 71

used to assess the quality of dies during or after production.[91] Whilst he proposed that they can only be associated with die manufacture, rather than minting, the separation of these two activities seems an unlikely proposition for the camp. Arent Pol suggests that such strikings may have served as a method of cleaning coin dies during the minting process, suggesting a use during actual coin manufacture, rather than prior to it.[92] It remains unclear if the dies used to mint imitative *solidi* at Torksey were manufactured in England or were carried by moneyers travelling with the Army from Frisia, where imitations of *solidi* are found in large numbers, and are now regarded as having been minted by Scandinavian settlers.[93] If brought from Frisia it implies an extraordinary level of intentionality and advance planning. The transportation of dies has been identified in other contexts, as Blackburn proposed that just a few years later one side of coins of Guthrum were struck from dies which must have been taken from Quentovic.[94]

The second lead sheet (T84) has a pair of poorly aligned obverse and reverse faces impressed into it; these are retrograde, indicating use of a coin, rather than a die (Figure 5.13). The impressed coin is of the Type A Lunettes series issued by Burgred of Mercia, but the blundered inscription suggests that it was an imitative coin. In the manufacturing process such an impression may have been used in the creation of an imitation die, although the purpose of a negative image in this activity is unknown. Nonetheless, four ninth-century examples of coin-impressed lead are known from the London area, revealing this was an established practice. In this context, the lead sheet may demonstrate the presence of an experienced Anglo-Saxon die-manufacturer at Torksey.[95]

Figure 5.13. Further evidence for coin production at Torksey, not to scale (left to right): trial coin *solidus* (T3577; authors), trial-coin Lunette (T83), and an impression of a Lunette in a lead sheet (T84) (both Fitzwilliam Museum)

Two trial coins are clipped and shaped to form circular flans. One (T3577) is bent double, making it impossible to view the obverse side,

91. Dolley 1954, 177
92. Pol 2011, 186
93. Coupland 2016, 265–6
94. Blackburn 2005, 26–7
95. Archibald 1991, 326–8

and although the visible legend on the reverse is blundered and illiterate, the simplified design is distinct enough that this could be identified by Woods as an imitative Louis the Pious *solidus*. The degraded lead of the second trial coin (T83) makes identification of the ruler difficult, but it is certainly a Lunette. Pirie suggested that eleventh-century trial coins represent final-stage proofs of dies, hammered out before they were used for striking in silver, and so it is possible that these were demonstration pieces, used to confirm that convincing coins could be produced by finished dies.[96] A study of the provenance and mints named on similar lead trial coins dating from the eighth to twelfth centuries, including a concentration of thirty-four from Billingsgate (London), has indicated that such items did not move far from their place of production, as is also proposed for impressed sheet 'trial pieces' and die cleaners.[97] Together, these finds indicate that a minimum of three separate coin dies were present within the Torksey camp, with this workshop detritus suggesting that coins were struck from each die.

The imitative *solidus* die preserved by T1697 is accomplished and literate, indicating a high level of craftsmanship, but the workmanship of the die used for the trial-coin *solidus* T3577 is of a significantly lower grade. *Solidi* were originally minted on a small scale, probably to mark the coronation of Louis the Pious in 816, but do not appear to have been particularly significant within the Carolingian economy. However, imitations continued to be minted into the late ninth century, with single finds concentrated in Frisia. Examples from hoards in the Netherlands indicate a demand for gold coins persisted on the borders of the Carolingian Empire until at least the 880s, with the imitative *solidi* from Torksey and elsewhere in eastern England suggesting a similar requirement in Britain.[98]

A cut fragment of an imitative *solidus* (T38) and a gilded forgery of another (T1695) from Torksey both appear to be Frisian, but one other (T2147) is an English copy of a Frisian imitative coin. The presence of such a volume of *solidi* in one location is unusual, and this reinforces that gold was particularly abundant at Torksey.[99] It seems improbable that such high-value coins would have been useful for local trade in the camp environs. Equally, it is hard to see what

96. Pirie 1986, 38
97. Archibald 1991, 331; Pol 2011, 187
98. Blackburn 2007, 68; Coupland 2016, 264
99. Blackburn 2011, 228

function would be served by minting gold *solidi* for transactions inside the Torksey camp, where a metal-weight economy was clearly practised, and hack-gold was in circulation. The *solidi* may have been minted to apportion loot within the Army, perhaps a symbolic action, undertaken as an expression of the 'display economy' and related to the aspirations of leadership between competing factions of the Army.[100] As such, this relates more to the internal social dynamics of the Great Army.

Although the function of the coin impression T84 is unknown, the presence of trial coin T83 strongly suggests that at least one type of Lunette was struck at Torksey, with a further imitative die of Burgred potentially planned or manufactured. A plated copper-alloy Lunette was also evidently a forgery (T2149).[101] Stephen Merkel observes that the production of coins requires an outlay of labour and materials, with minting holding no economic benefits in economies where hack-silver also circulates.[102] The striking of imitative Lunettes was, therefore, almost certainly to facilitate local trade with the camp.[103] The scale of cupellation at Aldwark indicates a developed, sophisticated economy, with effort put into the management and purity of silver stocks, and while neither coin manufacturing is evidenced at Aldwark, nor silver refining at Torksey, together these activities suggest the presence of centralised control. This is similar to that implied by the comparative popularity of the different lead weight forms reviewed in Chapter 3. The high proportions of blundered and irregular stycas at Aldwark and Torksey have also prompted the suggestion that the Great Army were minting their own stycas.[104] If so, it reinforces the idea that the stycas brought to Torksey by members of the Great Army were being used by them in monetary exchange, not simply as a source of base metal.

Conclusions

The manufacturing assemblages from both camps broadly divide into two main groups: artefacts associated with craft production, such as dress accessories, and items related to economic activities, such as coin production and silver

100. Gaimster 1991, 119; Williams 2007, 178
101. Blackburn 2011, 225
102. Merkel 2013, 77
103. Williams 2020i, 95
104. Kelleher and Williams 2020, 36; Hadley and Richards 2021, 103

refining. The tools recovered suggest a range of fine metalworking on the camps, while the moulds, models, and trial pieces indicate multiple production techniques, including some evidence for mass production. Dress accessories of both Anglo-Saxon and Scandinavian styles were manufactured on both camps, and some of these have added to the evidence for the presence of women travelling with the Army. Insular items were converted to other uses, including jewellery, and as Glørstad and Røstad note, in the unsettled political situations caused by intensive Viking activity, there may have been an increased emphasis on exclusive or symbolic objects as a way of cementing social distinction.[105] Within such an environment at Aldwark and Torksey, Insular decorated metalwork may have carried an additional social or figurative capital which extended to its economic use. As we saw from analysis of flat-headed pins and strip brooches in Chapter 4, the Army had a preference for collecting highly decorated and gilded metalwork.

The assemblages have differing degrees of fragmentation that seem to present a meaningful pattern. For example, Insular metalwork from Torksey displays a higher degree of fragmentation than at Aldwark, similar to the treatment of the ClassA and B strap-ends discussed in Chapter 4, with notably fewer fragmented strap-ends recovered from Aldwark. While it is conceivable that this reflects some difference in economic behaviour, the pattern does not follow that of the fragmented silver and gold discussed in Chapter 3, where the mean weights are similar. An explanation that may make sense of this contrast is differing practices of recording by metal detectorists; those at Torksey are known to have made a point of recovering the smallest fragments of copper-alloy artefacts.

Trade and exchange with the local population may have been common, reflecting some of the documented activities of Viking armies on the Continent. For example, Charles the Bald forbade the sale of military equipment to Scandinavian forces, which implies that such items had previously been commercially available to Viking armies within Francia, while the *Annals of St Bertin* describe a Viking army based on the Seine having 'dispatched about 200 of their number to Paris to get wine' in what has been interpreted as engagement in trade.[106] Its anticipated return into the local economy may have been why Carolingian rulers were willing to pay tribute in coin.[107] If some members of the Great Army were accustomed to purchasing supplies using a

105. Glørstad and Røstad 2021, 101
106. Nelson 1991, 127; Stalsberg 2017, 266–7; Cooijmans 2020, 146, 160
107. Cooijmans 2020, 181; Coupland 2011, 123–6

host nation's currency, and we know that coins continued to be minted in Frisia even after it had passed into Scandinavian overlordship (see Chapter 1), then striking their own coins may have been a logical step. The presence of the two *solidus* dies at Torksey indicates a connection with Frisia, where imitative *solidi* are concentrated, and a region from which some members of the Army had arrived.[108]

Once they had taken control of the Anglo-Saxon kingdoms, Viking rulers such as Guthrum began to mint coins.[109] However, the lead impressions of dies and blundered stycas from Torksey suggest that the minting of coinage emerged during the overwintering phase, even before the Viking leaders had adopted the administrative apparatus of Anglo-Saxon kingship. To a Viking army, coins were not necessarily more logical than bullion, but minting of imitations suggests that they understood something of the political as well as economic value of coinage, and it may have smoothed their path to economic transactions with the locals.[110] The Army may have been minting coinage for a variety of reasons: to use it in economic exchange locally to buy supplies, to display the aspirations of its leaders to establish their authority within the Anglo-Saxon kingdoms, and due to competition between these leaders.

108. McLeod 2014, 133–41; Coupland 2016
109. Blackburn 2005
110. Williams 2007

6

Provisioning the Army

This chapter examines the equipment required for the resupply, repair, and recuperation necessary for any large, long-lasting expedition, and to enable the Great Army to campaign so effectively for so long.[1] Although the sample is limited by the fact that iron objects were not routinely collected by the metal detectorists at either site, it is supplemented by other evidence. At Aldwark the majority come, instead, from the archaeological trial trenches, whilst at Torksey they were only latterly collected by the detectorists. The Torksey dataset is, however, supplemented by a hoard of woodworking tools, including four axe heads, an axe hammer, an adze, and a two-edged blade, and detailed analysis has revealed that these are of Anglo-Saxon type, indicating the use of local equipment, if not labour. In this chapter we have sought to compare the evidence with broadly contemporary finds from urban contexts such as Coppergate in York and the major trading centres in Scandinavia, as well as non-elite rural settlements in England, for which a 2019 study by Hana Lewis of both excavated and metal-detected data provides a valuable survey.[2] Several ironwork hoards of the eighth to tenth centuries provide additional comparative datasets.[3] Throughout the chapter the finds are also contextualised by comparison with similar artefact types from burials and hoards associated with the Great Army. Our analysis has revealed a wide range of activities taking place in the camps, including the processing of timber, textile working in fine and coarse materials, the processing of fleeces, flax, and leather, and the exploitation of natural resources for food with evidence for fishing and birding. The artefacts also provide further insights into the range of craftworkers on the site and the origins of their tools, and illustrate aspects of day-to-day life in the camps.

1. Cooijmans 2020, 141
2. Lewis 2019
3. Thomas and Ottaway 2008; Ottaway *et al.* 2010; Leahy 2013; Thomas *et al.* 2016

Woodworking tools

Woodworking tools recovered from both camps include axes, adzes, chisels, wedges, shaves, and augers, with the majority from Torksey (Figure 6.1). The poor preservation of these iron implements can make identification difficult, and the fact that iron has not been widely collected or retained also has an impact on interpretation. Nonetheless some valuable insights are still possible, with use of X-rays having enhanced interpretation of many of the artefacts discussed here.

Axes and adzes

The classification of axe heads has attracted considerable debate, according to whether they should be regarded as weapons or tools, although it is now generally accepted that most early forms were multi-purpose.[4] There is plentiful evidence for the use of axes as weapons throughout the Viking Age, particularly by Scandinavian forces, but only the Type M broad axe is specifically identified as a weapon, which developed in the later tenth century.[5] Early medieval

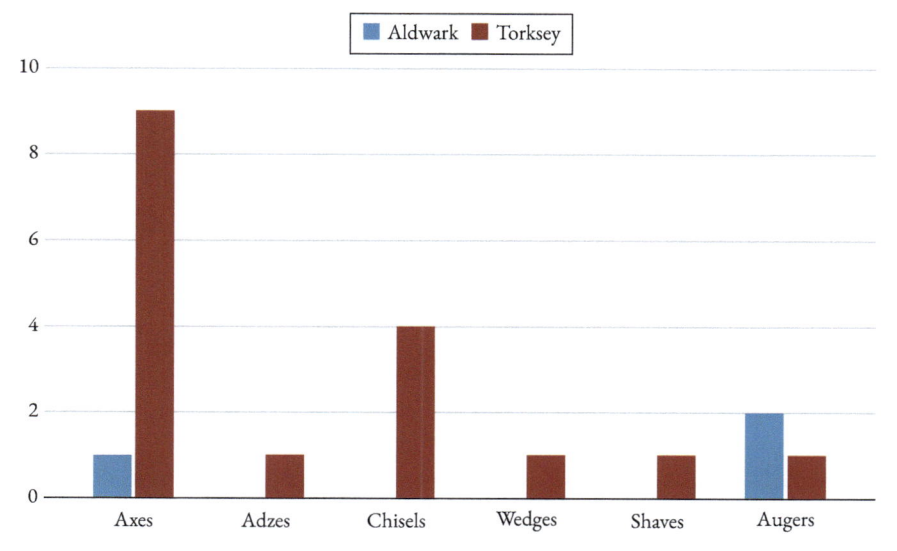

Figure 6.1. Woodworking tools

4. Harrison and Ó Floinn 2014, 114
5. Hjardar and Vike 2016, 162; Pedersen 2012, 205–6

axes took two basic forms, broadly related to their intended functions. Heavy, wedge-shaped axes were a general tool, used for felling, splitting, and rough shaping, while lighter axes with expanded, T-shaped, heads were more special-ised, designed for hewing and dressing converted timbers.[6] The typology for-mulated by Jan Petersen in 1919 remains the standard reference for the evolution of wedge-shaped types, but scarcely considers the T-shaped axe, classed as Type W, and as Type II in a slightly later typology by Mortimer Wheeler.[7] Two complete wedge-shaped axe heads (T1422, T2557) and one fragmentary socket (T2558) were recovered from Torksey, with two more such axe heads in the hoard (T1650, T1660). They all have thick, narrow blades with very little flare and short cutting edges (Figure 6.2).

The narrow wedge-shaped axe heads from Torksey fall somewhere between Types A and G of Petersen's typology, dated to 800–950. They can also be

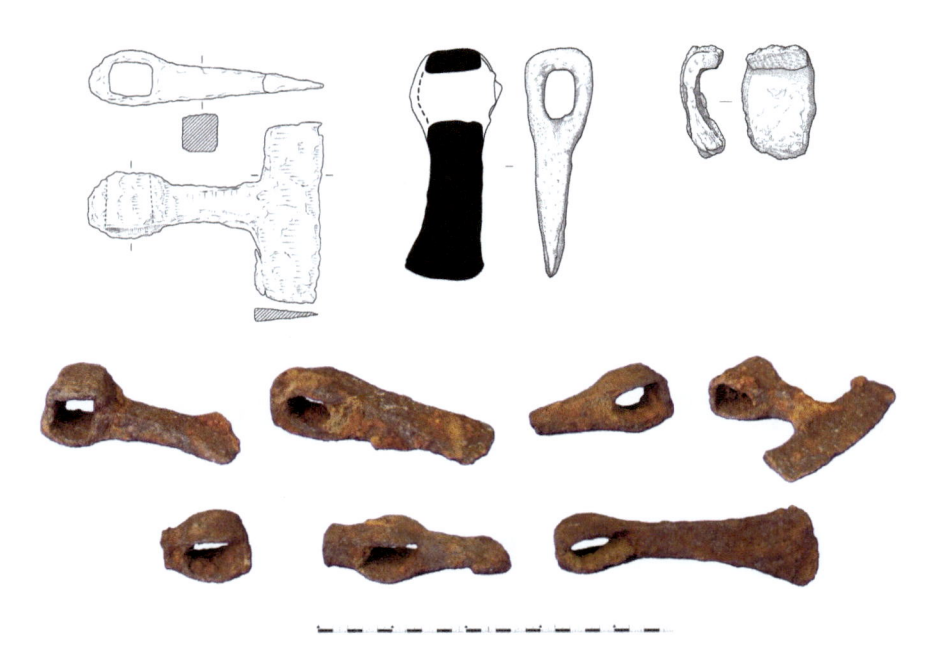

Figure 6.2. Axe heads and adzes: first row: A130 (YAT), T2557, T2558 (Chloe Watson); second row: T1650, T1660, T1649, T1657; third row: T1677, axe hammer T1673, adze T1672 (all Lincoln Museum)

6. Leahy 2003, 17
7. Petersen 1919; Wheeler 1927, 24; Ottaway 2016, 8

accommodated by the more general Wheeler Type I, regarded as a universal cutting axe, little changed from prehistory to the eleventh century.[8] Ottaway considers this narrow form to be principally a felling axe and a carpenter's tool during the early medieval period.[9] Of the four complete axe heads, two (T1650, T2557) have a very strong offset, with the blades aligned onto one side of the socket. This feature indicates that they were shaping tools, with the offset head providing clearance for the user's hand and allowing a cleaving action to cut close to the plane of the timber. The other two complete axe heads have the typical early medieval asymmetrical form, but without any definite offset, suggesting that they were more general hewing axes, used to chop and split timber. A thickened, square poll is visible on the butt of one (T1660), which would have added weight for such work. All four axe heads have a blade length to width ratio of roughly 3:1, with shallowly curved cutting edges, set near to perpendicular with the socket. Tool-mark analysis at Staunch Meadow demonstrates the use of similar narrow-bladed axes to fell large trees in the eighth century.[10] Felling axes need long hafts; a handle of over 0.9m was used for experimental work at West Stow (Suffolk), and two narrow, wedge-shaped axe heads from the early ninth-century Oseberg (Norway) burial were equipped with long hafts, one of which was 0.78m long, set on a head with a blade length of 95mm.[11] If fitted with similar hafts, two from Torksey (T1650, T2557) could easily have served as felling axes.

A T-shaped axe head (T1657), two broken heads of probable T-shaped forms (T1649, T1677), and an axe hammer (T1673) were included in the Torksey iron hoard.[12] A complete T-shaped axe head was also found at Aldwark (A130).[13] Their dimensions are typical of ninth-century forms, corresponding well with the dating of both camps. These are not common excavated finds and are frequently broken. The Aldwark find is very similar to a broken axe head from a ninth-century hoard from Crayke (North Yorkshire), and two broken examples from Coppergate (nos. 2254 and 2256) were thought to have been from a tenement adjacent to a smithy and gathered as scrap for recycling.[14]

8. Wheeler 1927, 23
9. Ottaway 2016, 8
10. Darrah 2014, 136
11. Darrah 1982, fig. 12.7; Grieg 1928, 162
12. Carhart 2014, 17–25
13. Williams and Hall 2020, 84
14. Sheppard 1939, 280; Lewis 2019, Appendix 5.7.5; Leahy 2003, 16; Morris 2000; Ottaway 1992, 527–8; Pritchard 1991, 135

A single adze (T1672) was part of the Torksey iron hoard. Adzes are rare finds from excavated sites, and Lewis recorded only two from a survey of twenty Anglo-Saxon rural settlements, one a re-used Roman implement.[15] Other examples come from an early medieval riverine deposit from Skerne (East Yorkshire), a tenth-century building at Thetford, a Viking grave at Ballinaby (Islay, Scotland), and a hoard of eighth- to tenth-century date at Flixborough, with narrower examples from a ninth- or early tenth-century hoard at Hurbuck (Co. Durham) and a large metal-detected collection of Late Anglo-Saxon tools from Lea Green (North Yorkshire).[16] Like T-shaped axe heads, adzes were used for dressing timber, and shaping hollow areas where axes could not reach. Despite the paucity of comparative finds, they were probably common woodworking tools. An adze from the Mästermyr tool chest hoard has pronounced, triangular lugs projecting from the underside of the neck, and similar pointed lugs can be seen on the Thetford adze. They are characteristic of most Scandinavian socketed tools of this form, including many of the axes recovered from furnished graves of Scandinavian type from Britain and Ireland, including those from Dublin and Repton.[17] In contrast, the socketed tools in the Torksey iron hoard all had either simple, cylindrical sockets or forms with low, rounded lugs, characteristic of most comparative British tool hoards.[18] This suggests that the Great Army may have been using locally-acquired tools, if not craft specialists.[19]

Chisels

Four items from Torksey have been interpreted as chisels (T2511, T2535, T2787, T2800) (Figure 6.3). Chisels are unusual among hoards, where they are typically the tangless type, possibly used as punches or gouges, such as those from the Crayke hoard.[20] As a class, gouges and chisels are more common as excavation finds, with three from Coppergate while Lewis records them on twelve out of twenty surveyed rural sites.[21] The chisel from the Skerne deposit was very similar to one from Coppergate, and a chisel was also recovered from

15. Lewis 2019, Appendix 5
16. Goodall *et al.* 1984, 77–8; Grieg 1940, fig. 15; Dent *et al.* 2000, 230–1; LANCUM-087192
17. Arwidsson and Berg 1983, pl. 26; Waterman 1959, 72; Biddle and Kjølbye-Biddle 2001, 55–6, 66, 68, 70; Harrison and Ó Floinn 2014, 114–17, 551
18. Carhart 2014, 30
19. Grieg 1928, fig. 100
20. Leahy 2013, table 1; Sheppard 1939, 280
21. Lewis 2019, 82, Appendix 5.7.2; Ottaway 1992, 530, 536

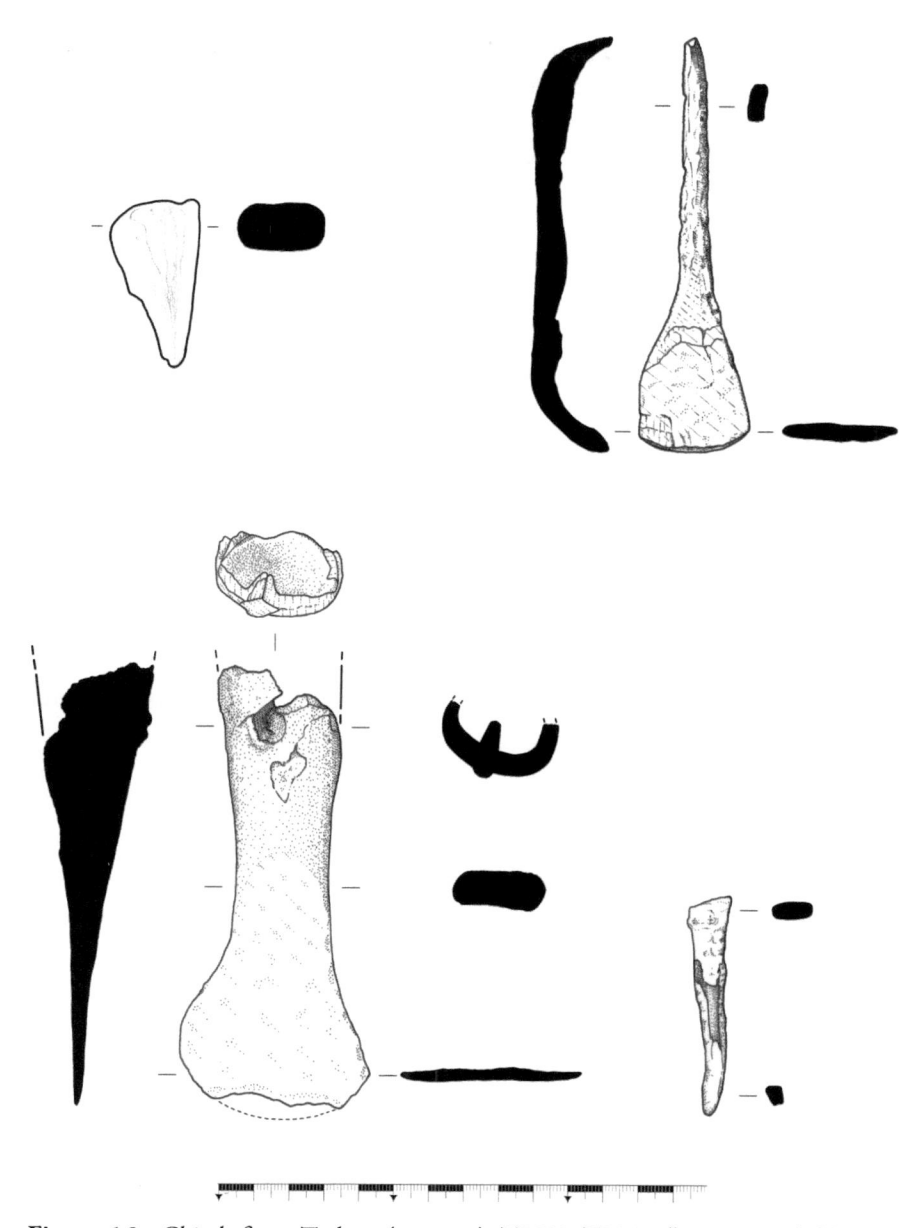

Figure 6.3. Chisels from Torksey (top row): T2511, T2535; (bottom row): T2787, T2800 (Chloe Watson)

the mass grave at Repton.[22] Of the two most clearly identifiable chisels from Torksey one (T2535) is a tanged form, almost identical to one from the Mästermyr hoard (no. 59), but roughly half the size. Although damaged, the other (T2787) is clearly socketed, with a fan-shaped blade. Broadly similar items have been found in the Crayke hoard and at Lea Green, and are interpreted as a socketed gouge and a probable hoe, respectively, although a closer parallel is a ninth-century Coppergate find (no. 2258) tentatively identified as a socketed chisel.[23] While further comparative items are known from Britain, the majority come from Scandinavia, including eleven from Hedeby, two from Aggersborg (Denmark) and one from Gjermundbu (Norway).[24] Implements with blades which are curved widthways are variously described as mattocks, hoes, and adzes, while examples with straight blades are commonly interpreted as bark scrapers or slices. Slices are relatively specialised tools, used for preparing timber and severing wood fibres when splitting logs.[25] It has been suggested that the slice was specifically a boatbuilder's tool, but the near-universal use of riven timber in the early medieval period means that it may have been a more general implement.[26] Goodall notes two later examples from contexts associated with general carpentry rather than shipbuilding, and while Carole Morris describes the Coppergate example as a slice, he suggests it may also have been used as a paring chisel, demonstrating its versatility.[27]

Two other possible chisels from Torksey are incomplete. One is a length of square-section bar (T2800), narrowing towards a point at one end, while the opposite end tapers and widens to a flat, wedge-shaped terminal with the tip missing. The other (T2511) is sub-rectangular with a 'V'-shaped profile, and it tapers to a point along one shorter edge, to form the tip of what may be a shaped chisel. Both are closely paralleled by Coppergate finds (nos. 2269 and 2270) classed as small woodworking gouges, although T2800 also has similarities with a Coppergate implement (no. 2143) identified as a paring chisel.[28] Either way this suggests that fine woodworking was undertaken at Torksey, with such tools used for cutting the rebates or grooves seen on items such as chests and buckets, or to smooth hewn surfaces.

22. Dent *et al.* 2000, 231; Biddle and Kjølbye-Biddle 1992, 45
23. Ottaway 1992, 529–31
24. Schietzel 2014, 92; Roesdahl 2014, 313; Grieg 1947, pl. X, fig. 9
25. Leahy 2003, 18
26. McGrail 1987, 156
27. Goodall 2011, 23; Morris 2000, 2109
28. Ottaway 1992, 536–7; Morris 2000, 2110

Wedges

From Torksey a single iron wedge (135mm long, 39mm wide, and 26mm thick) can be identified as a splitting wedge (T2475) (Figure 6.4). In the early medieval period timber was generally prepared by splitting, and a review of surviving English medieval timbers identified only axe-hewn wood prior to the twelfth century.[29] However, splitting wedges are rare finds. Only four were catalogued by Lewis from twenty rural Anglo-Saxon sites, while at Flixborough, just two of the eighteen iron wedges were interpreted as being used for splitting,

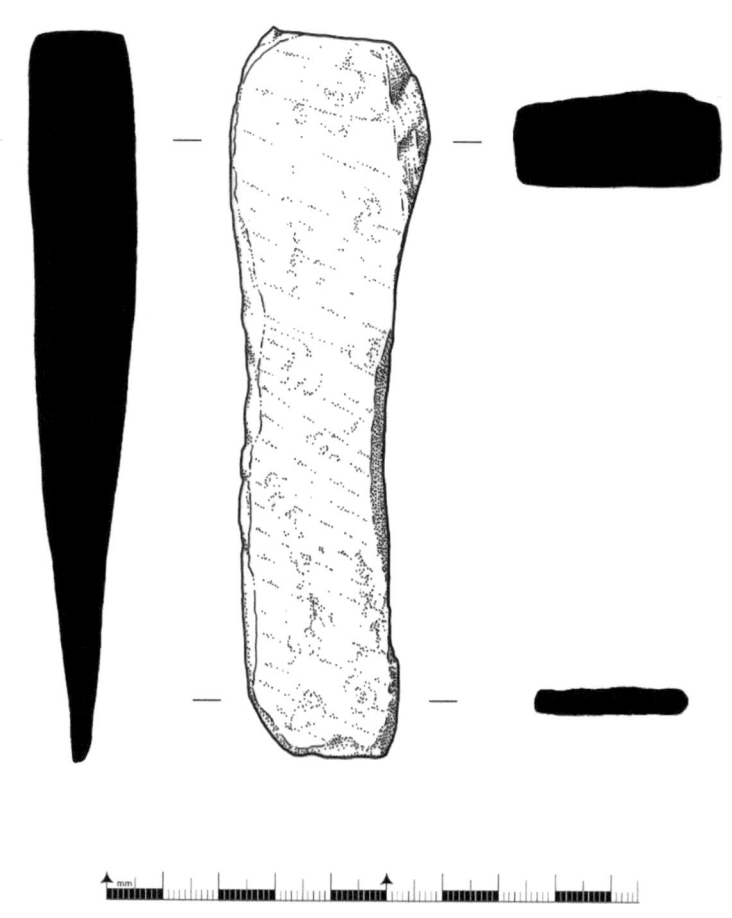

Figure 6.4. Wedge from Torksey (T2475; Chloe Watson)

29. Fleming 2012, 35

on account both of their greater length (60mm and 97mm) than the majority (20–50mm) and the fact that they showed signs of repeated striking.[30] One reason for this apparent paucity of evidence is because many wedges were probably made of materials less likely to survive in the archaeological record. For example, although only a single iron splitting wedge was identified from Anglo-Scandinavian levels in York, good organic preservation meant that fifteen oak wedges were recovered.[31] Wooden wedges between 130 and 300mm long have been used to split trunks in experimental work.[32] The Torksey example sits within this range and is of comparable size to a wooden wedge (no. 8179) from Coppergate. It may represent a specialised but comparatively common tool.[33]

Augers, shaves, and draw knives

There are two augers from Aldwark (A305, A762), and a possible auger and shave blade from Torksey (T2798, T2516) (Figure 6.5). The width of the spoon-shaped bit determines the diameter of the hole each auger creates, whether larger holes for placing wooden treenails into large frames and structural timbers, or smaller ones for starting mortise cuts, establishing pilot holes for nails, or boring into knife or tool handles to insert whittle tangs. A variety of sizes would have been used for woodworking, as reflected in the multiple examples in the Flixborough and Mästermyr hoards.[34] Given this need for different sized augers, they are unsurprisingly a comparatively common find, with Lewis listing them at eight rural sites out of a sample of twenty, while thirteen examples are recorded from Coppergate, and one from Skerne.[35]

The Torksey auger (T2798) comprises a short length of iron bar with a sub-rectangular section, tapering slightly at one end to a spatulate tang with a broken point. The opposite end is flattened, but with a visible curve, suggesting that it represents an abraded spoon bit, asymmetrically worn by repeated sharpening and use, similar to Coppergate examples (nos. 2264 and 2262).[36] It is unlikely that this shape was caused by the metal fracturing, as spoon bits typically break at the tip.[37] Whilst its sub-rectangular central section is unusual,

30. Lewis 2019, 103, 143; Ottaway 2009d, 255
31. MacGregor 1982, 147; Morris 2000, 2106
32. Leahy 2003, 27
33. Morris 2000, 2106
34. Goodall 2011, 23
35. Lewis 2019, 82, Appendix 5.7.5; Morris 2000, 2113; Dent *et al.* 2000, 231–2
36. Ottaway 1992, 543; Morris 2000, 2113
37. Berryman 1998, pl. 2:3

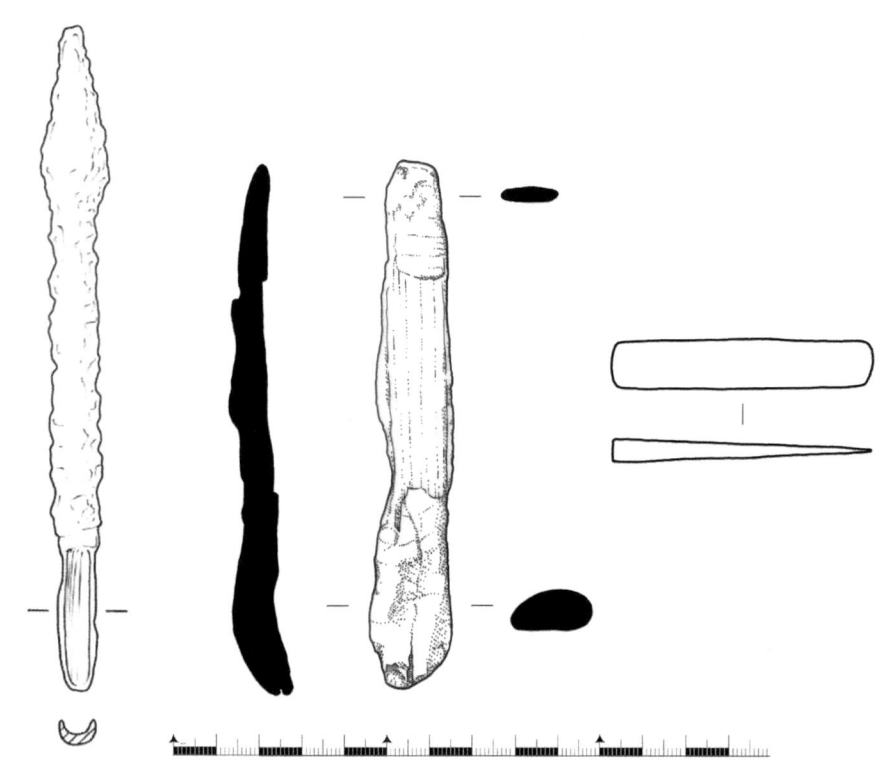

Figure 6.5. Augers A762 (YAT), T2798; shave blade T2516 (Chloe Watson)

augers with flattened sections are known from Thetford and York.[38] The Torksey example could have been used for boring pilot holes and peg holes for large-scale works. Treenails of between 15 and 25mm were routinely used for ship construction, with a standard diameter of 20mm identified on the frames of the Hedeby 3 and Skuldelev 5 wrecks and the Ladby (Denmark) ship burial; the Torksey auger could have been used to bore holes to receive pegs of this diameter.[39] In contrast, the auger from Aldwark with a 9.6mm wide bit (A762) would have been more suited to lighter work, such as to make pilot holes, potentially serving square-section nails with shanks up to 11mm thick. The Hedeby harbour wrecks all had pre-drilled nail holes, used for shanks of all shapes reinforcing the need for augers of differing sizes.[40]

---

38. Goodall *et al.* 1984, 77–8, fig. 117, no. 15; Ottaway 1992, fig. 208: 2266
39. Ravn 2016, figs. 41–2; Sørensen 2001, 223
40. Crumlin-Pedersen 1997, 123

A short, thin length of iron bar from Torksey (T2516), broken at each end, has a triangular section with an edge on one side, forming a blade, with a slight swelling apparent along the cutting edge, similar to early medieval draw knives and shaves. It has some similarities with the shave blades from the hoards at Mästermyr (no. 54) and Flixborough (nos. 2460 and 2461), and one from Coppergate (no. 2259), but these are rounded.[41] Straight-bladed shaves and draw knives are, however, known, often with pierced ends which presumably functioned as fixing points. Ottaway records a similar shave from Coppergate, and unpublished examples from Repton (sfs 3331, 5708).[42] Lewis lists only two draw knives in her survey of rural sites, although four shave blades are also catalogued.[43] Straight-bladed shaves and draw knives would have had a limited range of applications, principally rounding and chamfering pieces of wood, but when mounted the pierced-ended shaves would also have been able to smooth flat timbers, working along the line of the grain. The possible shave from Torksey suggests the conversion of rough timbers before they were worked and smoothed into their final form. This could have been part of the preparation of planks for ship repair, or the first stage of tar production, essential for waterproofing ships. In Scandinavia this would have been made from pine, but here they may have

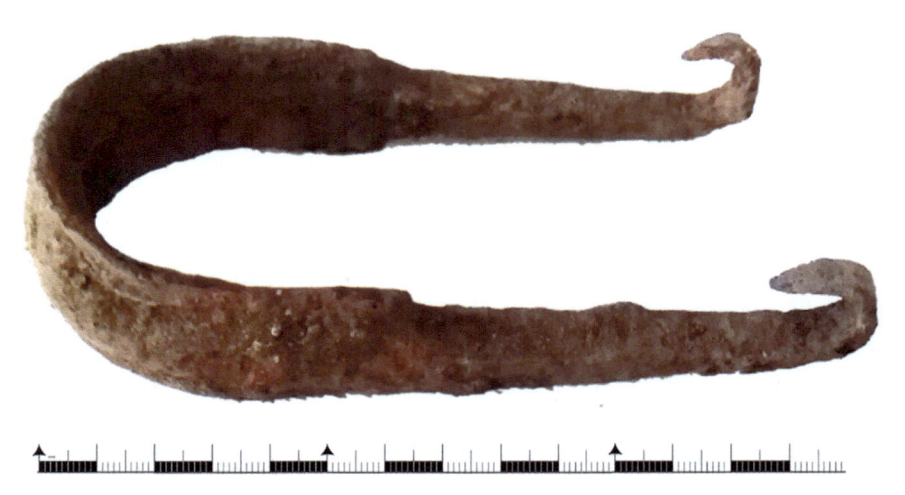

Figure 6.6. Shave blade recovered from land south of the Torksey camp (TORK12 sf180; authors)

41. Arwidsson and Berg 1983, pl. 27; Ottaway 1992, 531; Ottaway and Cowgill 2009, 258
42. Ottaway 1992, 589
43. Lewis 2019, 44, 82, Appendix 5.7.5

used birch, which is common in areas of well-draining sandy environments such as Torksey.[44] One of the few tools recovered from the eleventh-century shipyard at Fribrødre Å (Denmark) was an iron scraper, demonstrating the presence of similar items in other shipbuilding locations.[45] A complete rounded shave (Figure 6.6) and clench nails have also been found in the field to the south of Torksey village, as well as two lead gaming pieces. Given these links with the camp, it seems possible that the floodplain to the south was used as an outlying boat-repair yard by the Great Army.[46]

Nails and chest fittings

Nails from metal-detected assemblages are difficult to assess, especially when they have been largely discarded as undated. The little-changing nature of nail-making technology makes it almost impossible to securely date all but the most modern, machine-made items, but 31 of 49 nails from Torksey can be classified as medieval as all had squared, faceted, or circular-section shanks. The heads were generally flat, as is common for early medieval forms, and they varied between circular and sub-circular, although three had rounded, domed heads. Early medieval nails generally have a square-section shank; for example, this is broadly true of the assemblage of 1300 nails from Coppergate, of which 320 were complete, and two-thirds of the Torksey assemblage similarly have square or sub-rectangular shanks. Ottaway suggests that the Coppergate nails would mainly have been used for furniture, specifically for attaching locks and fittings to chests and boxes, with the nail sizes generally corresponding with the dimensions of those on chests from Oseberg and Mästermyr.[47] At least six probable chest fittings and two hollow-stem keys have been identified at Torksey, including a decorative hinge with niello inlay and a terminal in the form of an animal head (T728), whilst two keys, several box mounts, and two chest handles have been recorded from Aldwark.[48] A flat, wide bar, broken at one end and splayed at the other, from Torksey (T2472) is a possible strap fitting for a chest (Figure 6.7). It is paralleled by unpierced fittings from Coppergate (nos. 3332 and 3398) interpreted as probable hinge strips.[49]

44. Hennius 2018; Stein 2014, 406–8
45. Klassen 2010, 359
46. Richards and Hadley 2020, 18; Hadley *et al.* 2023, 19, 26, fig. 21
47. Ottaway 1992, 608–9, 613
48. Rogers 2020c, 49–50
49. Ottaway 1992, figs. 260, 263

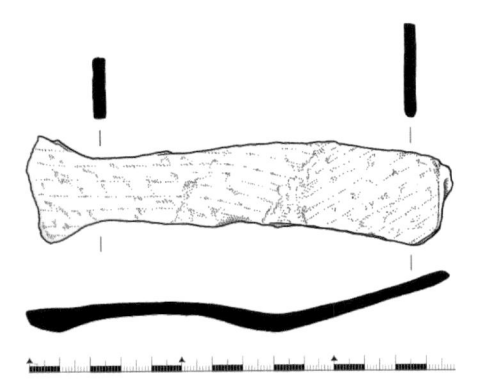

Figure 6.7. Possible strap fitting for a chest from Torksey (T2472; Chloe Watson)

A decorative domed, tinned nail-head (T2284) has clear parallels at Coppergate and with some of those used for securing fittings on chests at Oseberg and Fyrkat (Denmark) (Figure 6.9).[50] Whilst large, fitted chests might seem incongruous with a mobile force such as the Great Army, ninth-century ships did not have thwarts or beams above the decking, and so it is assumed that rowers sat on chests, which would double as containers for their belongings.[51] Furthermore, padlocks and box mounts from the tenth-century 'garrison' hall at Birka have led to the suggestion that each warrior kept their personal possessions in an individual chest.[52] We might also recall here the key placed in Grave 511 at Repton (Chapter 2) as an indication of the symbolic significance of such items in a funerary display created for an important figure within the Army.[53] It was placed separately from the body, and not positioned where it would have been worn in life, hanging from a belt. Deposition of keys in Viking-age burials away from the body has also been identified at Birka, leading Megan von Ackermann to suggest that in such cases keys may have had their own 'additional purpose, perhaps giving the deceased access to a desired place in the afterlife'.[54]

Clench nails have been identified at both Aldwark and Torksey, with both rounded and square-section shanks and differing internal lengths (Figure 6.8). Clench nails were used in the construction of cart bodies and doors, but they probably mainly derive from repair of ships drawn up onto the floodplains adjacent to the camps. With a very short internal width of 15mm, one clench nail (T2367) can only derive from a plank scarf, joining two planks end-to-end to increase their overall length, a procedure unnecessary for the short lengths of timber required for carts or doors (Figure 6.9). Some plank scarfs were secured with clinker nails in the late tenth-century Hedeby Wreck I, and seven of the

50. Ottaway 1992, 614
51. Crumlin-Pedersen 1997, 141
52. Hedenstierna-Jonson 2006, 54
53. Biddle and Kjølbye-Biddle 1992, 50
54. Von Ackermann 2018, 297; see also Berg 2015

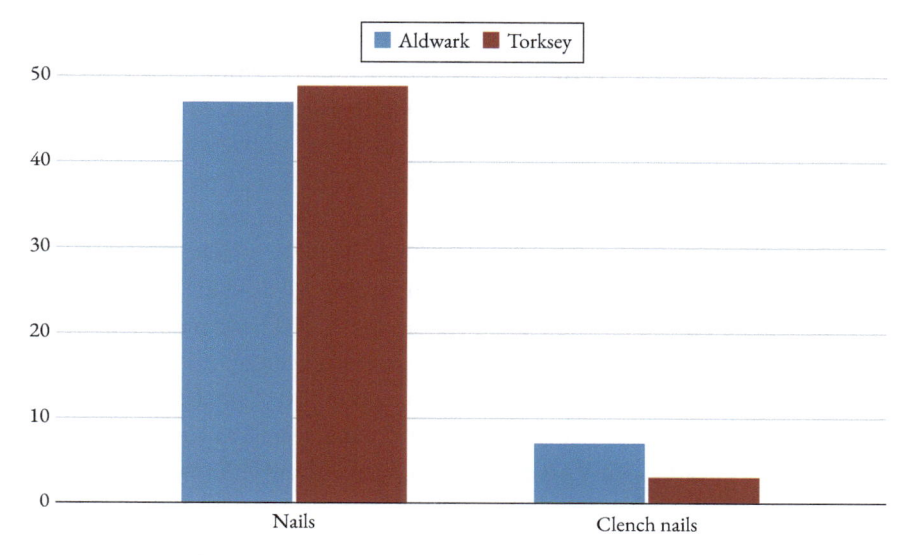

Figure 6.8. Nails and clench nails

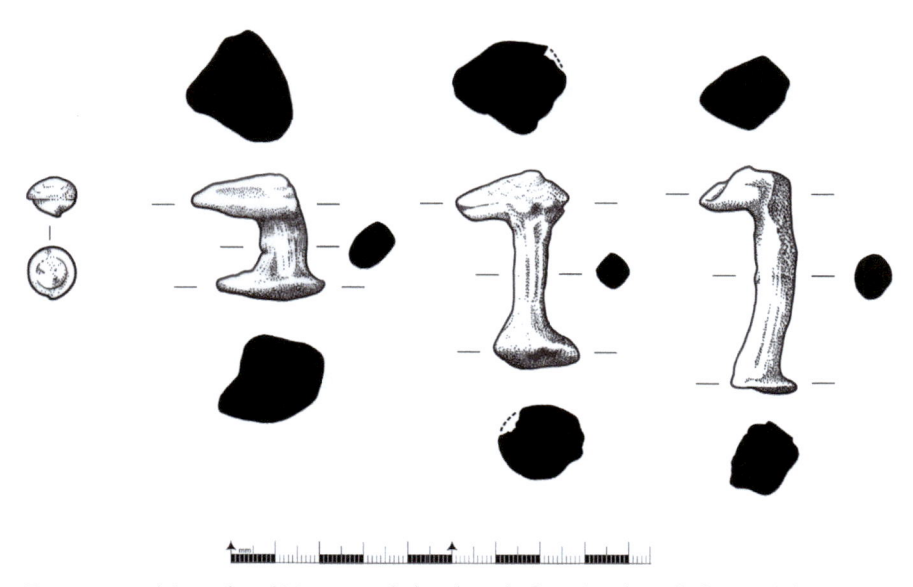

Figure 6.9. Tinned nail T2284 and clench nails from Torksey (left to right): T2367, T2821, T2822 (Chloe Watson)

thirteen measurable strakes had thicknesses under 16mm. Concentrations of nails with internal lengths grouping around 38mm and 25mm from the boat burial from Balladoole both roughly accord with other Torksey clench nails.[55]

Bill proposed that Scandinavian clinker construction overwhelmingly used nails with rounded shanks, with square-section nails representing a Baltic tradition, while Goodburn suggested that small, square-section clench nails were characteristic of later Anglo-Saxon maritime technology.[56] However, square-, round-section, and multi-faceted nails were all used in the same vessel at Hedeby, suggesting a more complex situation.[57] The clench nails from Balladoole were 8mm thick on average, shank thicknesses of 7–10mm were recorded for the Oseberg ship, and the most common diameters among 566 Viking-age clench nails and roves from Woodstown were 8–11mm.[58] Many of these also had heads with diameters of between 14 and 19mm, whilst larger nails with head diameters of up to 20–30mm were found on the late ninth-century Gokstad (Norway) ship.[59] The Torksey clench nails lie comfortably within these distributions. It cannot, however, be assumed from variations in the forms of clench nails that they derived from multiple vessels, since comparative evidence reveals that diverse rove shapes and shank cross-sections were sometimes used on the same vessel.[60] Evidence from Hedeby suggests that similar forms of roves were manufactured from iron strips, and so the considerable variety of roves at Torksey and Aldwark probably originate from differing places of manufacture.[61] The presence of varying types of clench nails has been interpreted as reflecting the construction and repair of ships in zones of technological and cultural contact, which would also have applied to a multi-ethnic and mobile force such as the Great Army.[62]

Textile-working tools

Spindle whorls, needles, and comb teeth have much to reveal about a range of textile-working activities undertaken at both sites (Figure 6.10).

55. Crumlin-Pedersen 1997, 225–6; Bersu and Wilson 1966, 13–14
56. Bill 1994, 58; Goodburn 1994, 102
57. Crumlin-Pedersen 1997, 123
58. Bill 2014; Russell 2023, 143
59. Johnson 2014, 149–53
60. Crumlin-Pedersen 1997, 123
61. Crumlin-Pedersen 1997, 121
62. Ravn 2016, 38

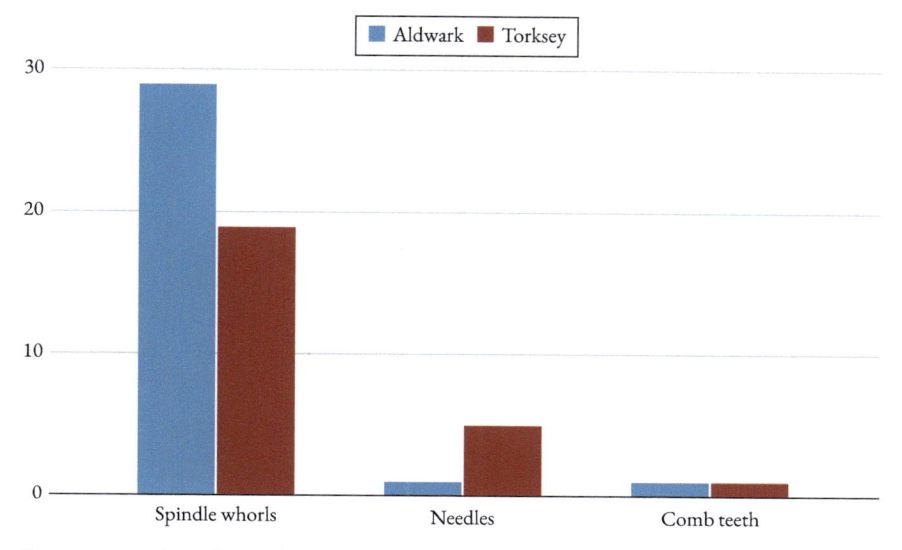

Figure 6.10. Textile-working tools (n=55)

Spindle whorls

All the spindle whorls are made of lead, with three main types represented, broadly distinguished by their form (Figure 6.11). To the 28 lead-alloy spindle whorls from Aldwark available to Walton Rogers we can add an additional Type B whorl, while 19 whorls have been identified from Torksey.[63] The Type A (truncated conical/hemispherical) spindle whorl form was introduced to Britain during the sixth century, and remained in use in East Anglia and Yorkshire until the tenth century.[64] Although Type B (annular/discoidal) whorls are known from the Iron Age and Roman periods, at Coppergate the majority dated to between the later tenth and early twelfth centuries.[65] The Type C biconical forms are generally regarded to be of later medieval date; the late medieval biconical forms from Coppergate, on which the standard typology is based, are made of bone or antler, not lead, but lead examples have been found in late medieval contexts elsewhere. Nonetheless, their occurrence in such large numbers at both Aldwark and Torksey, as well as at continental sites with Viking connections

---

63. Walton Rogers 2020b, 48–9
64. Walton Rogers 2014, 286
65. Walton Rogers 1997, fig. 805

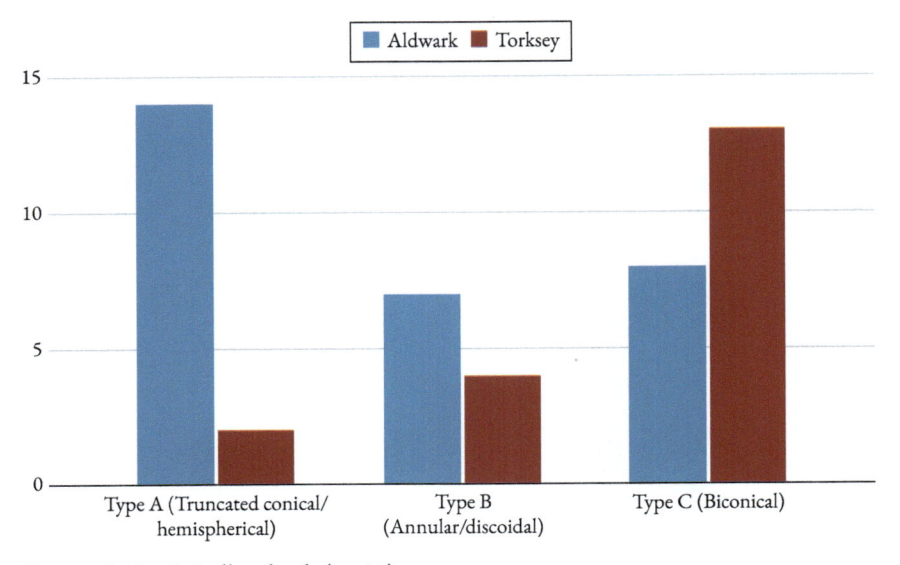

Figure 6.11. Spindle whorls (n=48)

where there is no other indication of late medieval occupation, may indicate that the Type C form originated earlier than has previously been recognised.[66]

The smallest spindle perforations are typically Roman, with Early and Middle Saxon examples having perforation in the 6–9mm range, and diameters larger than 9mm signifying Late Saxon whorls (Figure 6.12).[67] These suggest that both Type A and B whorls are equally present across the Middle and Late Anglo-Saxon periods at Aldwark, while a Type B whorl with a very narrow perforation (A986) probably represents a Roman artefact. Most of the measured whorls from Torksey suggest a later date, with only one Type B whorl (T1448) falling into the 6–9mm range.

The weight of a whorl influences the type of thread produced (Figure 6.13). At 18g the lightest whorl from Torksey (T1448) may have been used to produce a fine thread, while a heavy weight would be preferable for a thicker thread.[68] The weight distribution at Aldwark spans the middle ranges, suggesting production of a variety of threads and yarns, which may partly reflect the earlier activity there. At Torksey, in contrast, three whorls weigh over 50g, half the

66. Walton Rogers 2020b, 49; Standley 2016; Walton Rogers 1997, table 146; they have been found at sites with traces of Viking activity at Elsloo and Wapse (Netherlands): Van den Bossche 2022 and pers. comm.
67. Walton Rogers 2020b, 49
68. Andersson Strand 2011, 5

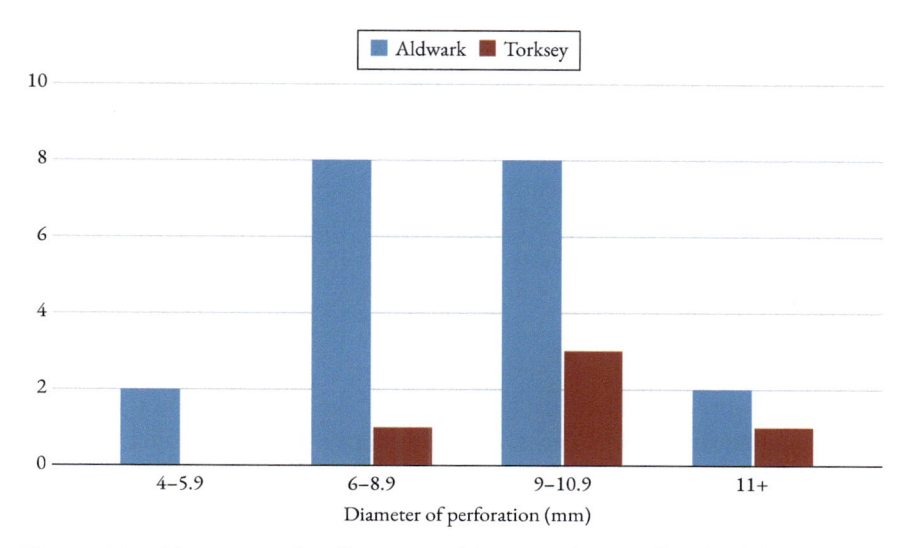

Figure 6.12. Diameters of perforations in Type A and B spindle whorls (n=25)

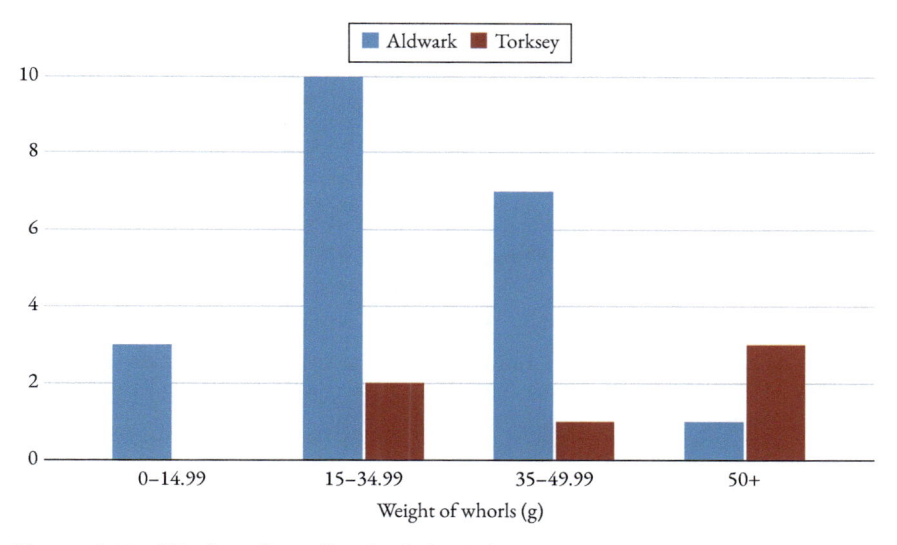

Figure 6.13. Weights of spindle whorls (n=27)

number from the site, which may indicate a focus on producing thick, plied yarns.[69] It is a small dataset, but to set this in context, at Coppergate just two outlying weights of 55g and 63g were noted out of a total of 243 whorls, at Kaupang of the 176 whorls of all materials only six (3.4%) weighed over 50g,

69. Henry 1999, 72; Øye 2015, 43

8% of 309 whorls from Birka where a weight could be measured were over 50g, and just 0.8% of the 755 whorls from Hedeby.[70] The outlying heavier weight groups may imply specialist production, requiring a specific tool, and Andersson has speculated that the very heavy whorls from Birka were used for producing hemp ropes.[71] Similarly, the heavier whorls from Torksey may have been used to produce strong yarns to resupply the Great Army, whether for spinning hemp to make rope or to repair heavy woollen sailcloth.

Needles

Only one copper-alloy needle has been identified amongst the Aldwark material (A1196), and five from Torksey (T139, T140, T2361, T2462, T2966)

(Figure 6.14). The absence of iron needles is almost certainly a recovery bias, given that *c.*97% of the metal needles at Coppergate were made of iron. The copper-alloy needles at Coppergate were 50–80mm in length, with a 2mm maximum width. The lengths of the Torksey needles all fall within this range, although three are thicker. They may have been intended for coarser work than the smaller Aldwark needle, which was probably intended for finer, more delicate stitching. One Torksey needle (T2361) has a regular, even curve, suggesting that

Figure 6.14. Needles (top to bottom): A1196 (YAT), T139, T140, T2462, T2361, T2966 (authors)

this was an intentional feature rather than post-depositional damage. It is possible that this needle was designed for specific tasks, such as sewing sailcloth, as Walton Rogers suggests that the larger needles from Coppergate may have been used to sew canvas.[72]

70. Walton Rogers 1997, 1743; Mainman and Rogers 2000, 2528; Øye 2011, figs. 13.6, 13.12; Andersson 2003, figs. 30, 54
71. Andersson 2003, 142–3
72. Walton Rogers 1997, 1782, 1785

Awls

Awls are typically classed as leatherworking tools, with their diamond-shaped or sub-rectangular cross-section enabling a clean cut through leather. Of the two Aldwark iron finds catalogued as leatherworking awls, one (A766) had a rectangular cross-section, whilst the other (A814) is simply described as being stylistically early medieval.[73] Two artefacts from Torksey (T141, T142) have similar forms to early medieval awls, but are made from copper-alloy for which no parallels have been found.[74] The single iron awl from Torksey (T2505) has a circular section, and is shorter than diamond- or rectangular-sectioned awls (Figure 6.15). Ottaway notes that such awls would have been less effective as leatherworking tools, and they may have been used for piercing materials such as bone, wood, or heavyweight cloth.[75] Rather than a gentle taper, the Torksey awl swells swiftly from the tip and maintains a regular diameter of roughly 5mm along the length, suggesting that it was used for making wide holes in a robust and rela-tively open-weave material, rather than piercing. This accords with the suggestion derived from analysis of the spindle whorls and an unusually large needle that heavy, coarse textiles were worked at Torksey.

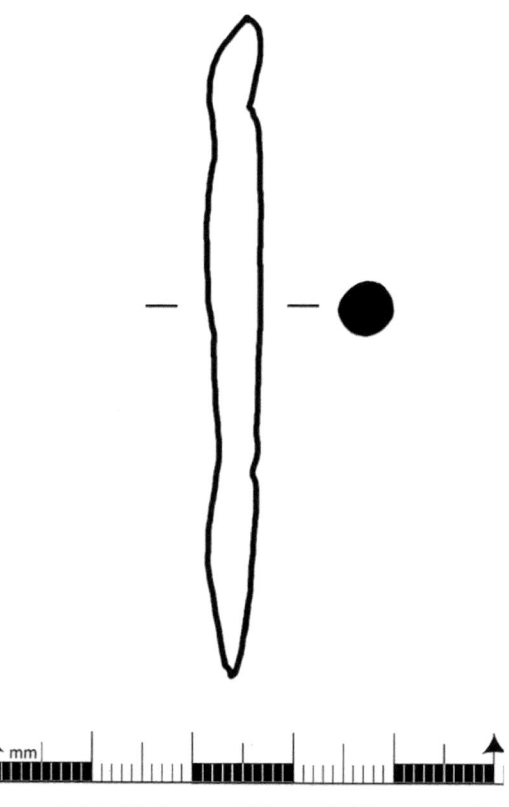

Figure 6.15. Torksey awl T2505 (Chloe Watson)

73. Rogers 2020b, 49
74. Hadley and Richards 2016, fig. 25
75. Ottaway 1992, 552, 554; MacGregor 1982, 80

Iron comb teeth

An iron spike from Torksey (T2851) appears to be a tooth from a wool comb. Although similar in form to many nails from the site, it is longer than the 65mm established as the division between comb teeth and headless nails within the Coppergate assemblage. Furthermore, it has a curving tip and a 'bearded' head, displaying the characteristic lip regarded as being a product of the manufacture of these teeth.[76] Whilst it is shorter than the 90–110mm identified as a standard size for wool comb teeth by Walton Rogers, this can be attributed to the tip of the tooth being broken.[77] A similar spike from Aldwark (A338) has also been identified as either a comb tooth or a flax heckle.[78] This suggests that fleeces were processed at Torksey, as well as potentially flax at Aldwark. Comb teeth and spikes are relatively common settlement finds, with Lewis recording them at 63% of a sample of fourteen ninth- and tenth-century rural sites, including a fragmentary comb set in a wooden card from Cottam.[79]

The production of textiles implies considerable planning and organisation amongst the mobile Army community. Walton Rogers has stressed that textile working would have engaged much of the population throughout the year, and the comparative peace of the camps probably provided the best opportunity to undertake these activities; both sites occupy waterside locations suitable for fleece washing and flax retting.[80] The combs or heckles indicate that fibres were sorted and prepared for spinning, skilled tasks important for determining the quality and type of thread produced.[81] Thread and yarn would have been an essential resource for the Great Army, with particularly substantial yarns implied by the Torksey finds. A spear tip in the Torksey tool hoard (T1675) may have been re-used as a weaving beater, which would have been effective for producing a heavy, tight fabric such as sailcloth.[82]

Textile products have long been viewed as a sign of Scandinavian influence in Insular contexts, with spinning seen as a culturally conservative tradition.[83] While textile tools were not purely associated with women, as whorls and weaving

76. Ottaway 1992, 540
77. Walton Rogers 1997, 1727
78. Walton Rogers 2020b, 48
79. Lewis 2019, 95, Appendix 5.7.1; Ottaway 1999, 74–5
80. Walton Rogers 2007, 248
81. Øye 2022, 37
82. Carhart 2014, 333; Øye 2022, 52
83. Bender Jørgensen 1992, 38–40; Hayeur Smith 2015, 27

tools are occasionally found in Norwegian Viking-age male graves, textile working is thought likely to have been something they controlled.[84] The presence of textile tools and whorls strongly relates to the presence of women, and may have contributed to the role of women as the bearers of cultural tradition in the context of Scandinavian settlement.[85]

Knives

Knives were universal, everyday tools throughout the early medieval period. They occur in several of the graves that appear to date to the period of overwintering at Repton (Graves 511 and 295), Heath Wood (Mound 50), Thetford, and Sonning, where the knife is described as being of northern continental type.[86] Of seven knives from the two camps, three of the Torksey knives were of the 'angle-back' form, Ottaway's Type A, and may provide another example of the Army adopting local material culture.[87] Two were of the A2 sub-type, with the rear part of the blade back angled upwards relative to the cutting edge. This was a late eighth- or early ninth-century development, becoming the most common sub-type from the later ninth century (Figure 6.16). At Coppergate the A2 sub-type comprises roughly 33% of the mid-late ninth- to early tenth-century Period 3 knife blades.[88]

Two further knives appear to be Ottaway's Type C, with straight backs and convex curves towards the tip. Both were possibly of the C1 sub-type, with horizontal backs, although wear on the cutting edges makes it difficult to be certain, and the Torksey example (T2479) was broken near to the angle of the choil, with the tang absent (Figure 6.16). The Type C is a generic knife form, and the most common type in both the Middle and Late Anglo-Saxon periods, comprising 55% of the identifiable assemblage from Coppergate and up to 77% from Flixborough.[89] The Aldwark example (A1050) displays the 'S'-shaped wear pattern along the blade which characterised many of the Coppergate C1 knives, and a similar pattern of wear, although not as pronounced, can also be discerned on the Torksey example.

---

84. Øye 2011, 371–2; Walton Rogers 2020c, 80, 89
85. Kershaw 2013, 173–8
86. Biddle and Kjølbye-Biddle 1992, 50; Richards *et al.* 2004, 62; Evison 1969, 332–3; Rogerson and Dallas 1984, 53, 105–6; McLeod 2014, 141
87. Ottaway 1992
88. Ottaway 1992, 563–4, table 36
89. Ottaway 2013, 114

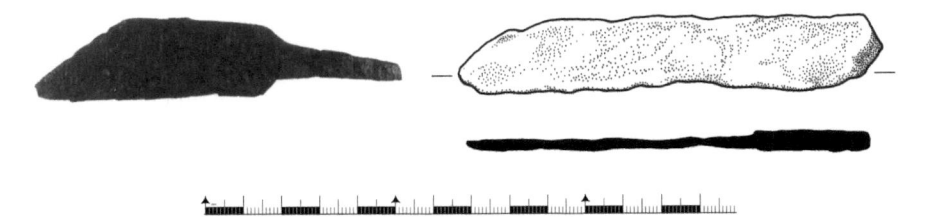

Figure 6.16. Torksey knives. Type A2 (left; T1427) (authors) and Type C (right; T2479) (Chloe Watson)

Other tools

There are also several smaller categories of tools associated with food preparation, heating and lighting, and agricultural equipment. These give us a glimpse of the ongoing daily necessities of life within the camps.

Cauldrons and tripods

The Torksey ironwork hoard may have been scrap collected for reworking, and left when the Army abandoned the camp, but many of its contents were probably part of their food preparation equipment. The hoard included one complete hemispherical bowl (T1671), the base of a second bowl (T1674), and half of a third (T1656), as well as seven fragmentary body sherds, and two rim sherds (Figure 6.17). The complete cauldron (T1671), *c.*230mm in diameter, was made from a single piece of iron, although the X-rays reveal what appears to be a small rectangular plate on the rim, with two rivet holes, one with the remains of a ring or a piece of chain to suspend the vessel. The base (T1674) of a second cauldron of similar size also seems to have been made from a single piece of iron, but a triangular or rectangular plate, maybe a fitting for a handle, stretches from the rim to the base. It was held in place by at least five rivets, some of which extend to the outside of the bowl, while a patch extending from the side to the base was held in place by further rivets. There is also a rim fragment (T1661) from a much larger vessel, *c.*700mm in diameter; the side and base of a fourth large vessel (T1667), comprising two squares of iron and an iron strip, held together with *c.*17 rivets; and a large curved body fragment of a fifth vessel (T1668) with multiple strips of iron which were probably reinforcing seams holding sheets of metal together with at least 18 rivets.[90] The level of repair demonstrates that these vessels were well used before discard.

---

90. The identifications in this section derive from Carhart 2014, 51.

Figure 6.17. Cauldron (T1671) and cauldron base (T1674) from Torksey (Lincoln Museum)

Three looped fittings (T1651, T1652, T1658) had probably been attached to the bowls (Figure 6.18). All are flat with only a single weld line, revealing that they were made from a single piece of iron. Their diameters range from 100–143mm, with a ring width of less than 20mm, and they were large enough to have been used as handles, or for suspending vessels from chains. Similar sized rings were used as vessel handles at Birka, although those rings were rounded, but a similar flat ring was found at Coppergate (no. 3519).[91] Whilst

91. Arbman 1940, I, Taf. 207; Ottaway 1992, 648–9

Figure 6.18. Attachment rings T1651 and T1658 from Torksey (Lincoln Museum)

there was a tradition of hanging iron cauldrons in Scandinavia, the Torksey vessels are the first to be found in England.[92] However, they lack the escutcheons of Scandinavian cauldrons, which also have bases of a separate sheet of metal. Cauldrons may have been more common in England, given the survival of the chains and hooks, such as the suspension chain (no. 1777) found at Flixborough, while several chain loops have been found among the broader metal-detected Torksey assemblage, although they are not closely dated.[93] At Coppergate soapstone bowls were used for cooking, but their weight may have made them less convenient than metal vessels for an army on the move, and none have been found at the camps.[94] There is other comparative evidence for the use of iron cooking vessels from England, including iron pans of the late ninth to early tenth century from Winchester and Coppergate. There are similarities in manufacture to the Torksey bowls, as the Winchester pan has a handle welded to the side and that from York has fittings which would have once riveted a handle in place.[95]

There were remains of at least one tripod (T1665), made from two or three iron rods (Figure 6.19), and potentially a second (T1666). The former would have stood *c*.100mm high, and its sides were 250–300mm in length, sufficient as a stand for the smaller bowls, although it may alternatively have been used as a trivet, to hold vessels off the fire. There are no known parallels of this early date, but its shape is identical to a late medieval example from Northampton.[96]

92. Graham-Cambpell and Kidd 1980, 80–1; Frantzen 2014, 134; Carhart 2014, 58–9
93. Ottaway *et al.* 2009, 174
94. Mainman and Rogers 2000, 2541, 2547
95. Goodall 1990b, 820–1; Ottaway 1992, 604–5
96. Goodall 1981, 59–60; 2011, 306–7

Figure 6.19. Tripod base T1665 from Torksey (Lincoln Museum)

Domestic items

An iron strike-a-light or firesteel (T2837) has a flat, tapering shank, and a curving arm projecting from the wider end with an angled 'lip' at the base (Figure 6.20). The corrosion products suggest a piercing approximately midway along the shank. It conforms to the larger size of an example from Coppergate (no. 3681) with a central piercing, suggested as a suspension point, while another (no. 3682) has a similar 'lip' on the base of the shank.[97]

There is a probable mill pick in the form of a roughly triangular piece of iron, with a lenticular longitudinal section and a sub-rectangular cross-section, and one end coming to a clear, sharp point, and the other forming a curved, wedge-shaped blade (T2794). This would have been used for dressing quern stones, as has been suggested for a similar-sized and shaped object from Coppergate (no. 2271) and an elongated, square-sectioned bar (no. 33) from Goltho.[98] The Torksey pick could have been used for maintaining the corrugated grooves on a quernstone, such as the Mayen lava import at Torksey (T599), or the sandstone rotary quern (A259) from Aldwark.[99]

97. Ottaway 1992, fig. 293
98. Ottaway 1992, fig. 211; Goodall 1987, 181
99. Rogers 2020b, 49

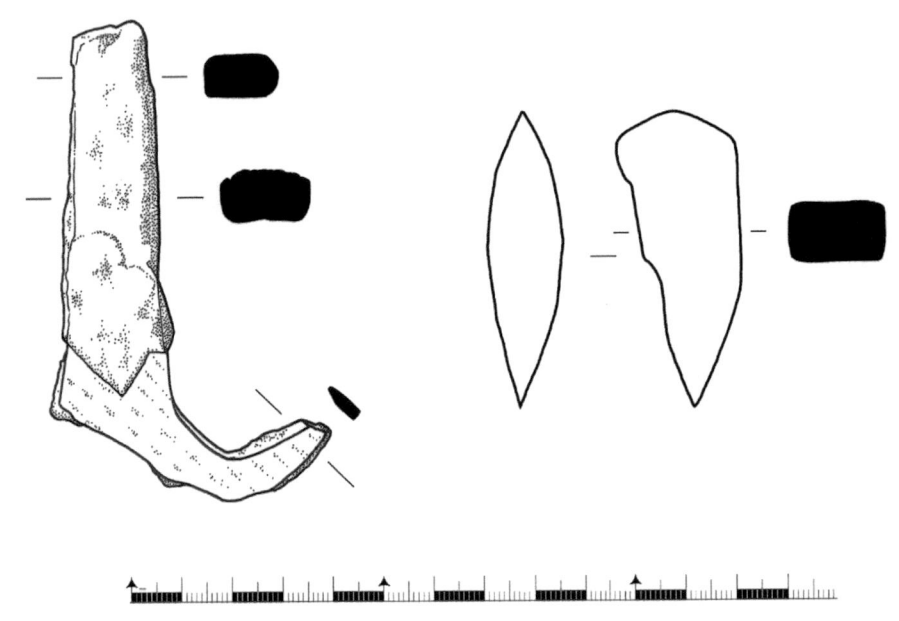

Figure 6.20. Firesteel (T2837) and mill pick from Torksey (T2794; Chloe Watson)

Agricultural equipment

A group of three complete ploughshares was recovered from Torksey (T2330, T2331, T2332), with two of them slotted together (Figure 6.21), and another was found at Aldwark (A160). All four are of a roughly symmetrical, triangular shape, with open flanged sockets where they would have been attached to the plough frame. This form was in use from the Roman period through to at least the tenth century. Comparable ploughshares are known from a ninth-century stratified hoard at Bishopstone (Sussex), the Westley Waterless (Cambridgeshire) and Nazeing (Essex) Late Anglo-Saxon iron hoards, Thetford, Flixborough, Parliament Street in York, and Hedmark (Norway), and the ninth-century boat burial at Westness. Another was found during recent excavations at the Great Army site at Foremark.[100]

The eleventh-century document of estate management known as the *Gerefa*, part of the *Rectitudines Singularum Personarum*, records that

---

100. Thomas and Ottaway 2008, 102; Ottaway *et al.* 2010, 130; Graham-Campbell 1980, 12; Addyman 1973, 94; Goodall *et al.* 1984, 81; Tweddle 1986, 195–6; Ottaway 2009c, 245; Graham-Campbell and Batey 1998, 136–7; Maldonado 2021, 65, fig. 3.23; Hadley and Richards 2021, 115

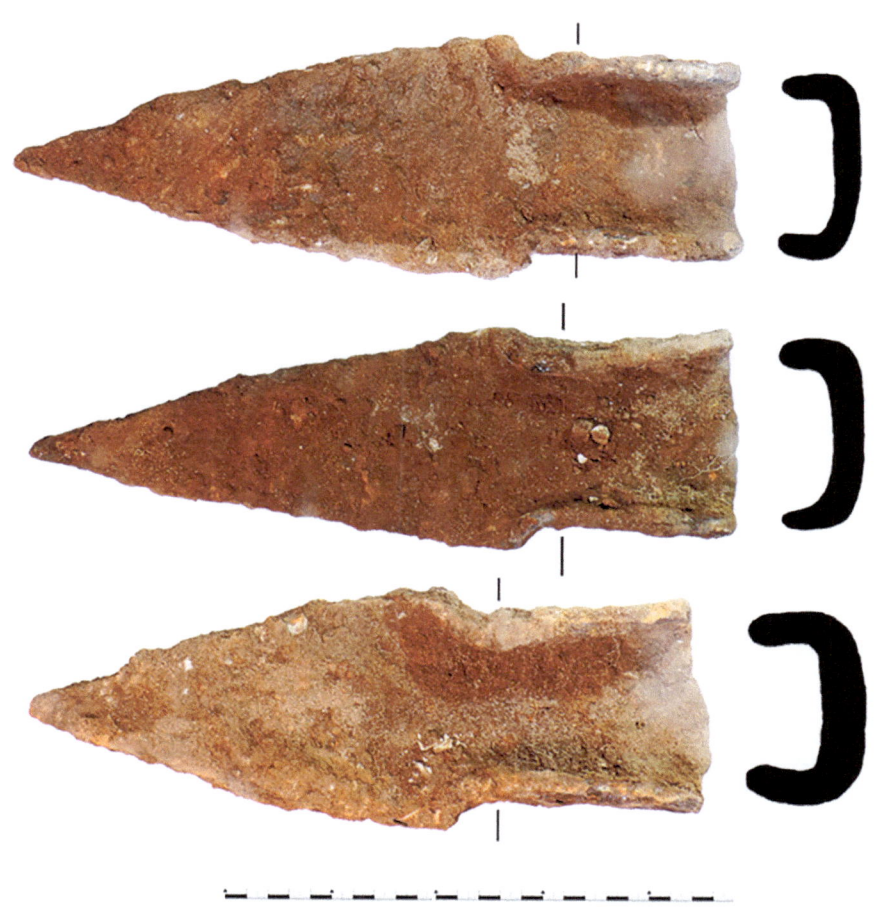

Figure 6.21. Torksey ploughshares T2330–T2332 (PAS)

ploughshares were kept separately from the ploughs themselves, perhaps because of the intrinsic value of the metal.[101] However, other interpretations for the hoarding of tools are possible.[102] The majority of the ploughshares discussed here were in good condition and recovered from contexts suggesting deliberate deposition. For example, the Parliament Street ploughshare had been buried with a coulter in the backfill of the Roman fortress ditch, while the Flixborough example was found in a post-hole, adjacent to a substantial caldron

101. Banham and Faith 2014, 48; Leahy 2003, 171
102. Thomas and Ottaway 2008, 386; Thomas *et al.* 2016, 753–5

suspension chain. The possible symbolism of the Torksey ploughshares is reinforced by their association with fragments of calcined bone, potentially indicating their attachment to a cremation; they certainly were not casual losses.[103] Cooijmans suggests that agricultural tools at Viking camps may indicate that the inhabitants 'adopted agricultural practices in and around the confines of their camps', which seems plausible for the assorted agricultural implements recovered from the longer-lived Scandinavian base at Péran (Brittany), but less likely for the shorter-lived Great Army camps.[104] Even so, this represents only one potential use within early medieval society, with ploughshares featuring in rituals signifying ties to land, fertility, and foundation and closure deposits in domestic settings.[105] Their deposition may therefore potentially represent the expression of a more symbolic relationship with the land by factions of the Great Army.

Fishing and birding equipment

Artefacts from both camps illuminate the exploitation of local resources for food, especially fish and birds, although they are not always easy to identify to precise function and dating can be difficult. For example, fishing weights cannot be dated with certainty; they can be re-used, and many forms are long-lived, with barrel-shaped weights found from the Iron Age to the post-medieval period.[106] Nonetheless, given the riverine location of both camps, it seems probable that fishing weights were used and discarded, and the paucity of evidence for much earlier or later occupation makes it highly likely that these are associated with activities undertaken by the Army. In some cases, the only parallels for the weight forms are from other sites of known Scandinavian settlement.

Fishing weights

Where lead weights have piercings or integral suspension loops, we have generally classified them as fishing weights, with 32 from Aldwark and 22 from Torksey (Figure 6.22). The published typology of the Aldwark weights labels

103. Hadley and Richards 2021, 200
104. Cooijmans 2021, 192; Nicolardot and Guigon 1991, 137–8, fig. 14
105. Thomas et al. 2016, 754–5
106. Redknap 2019, 393

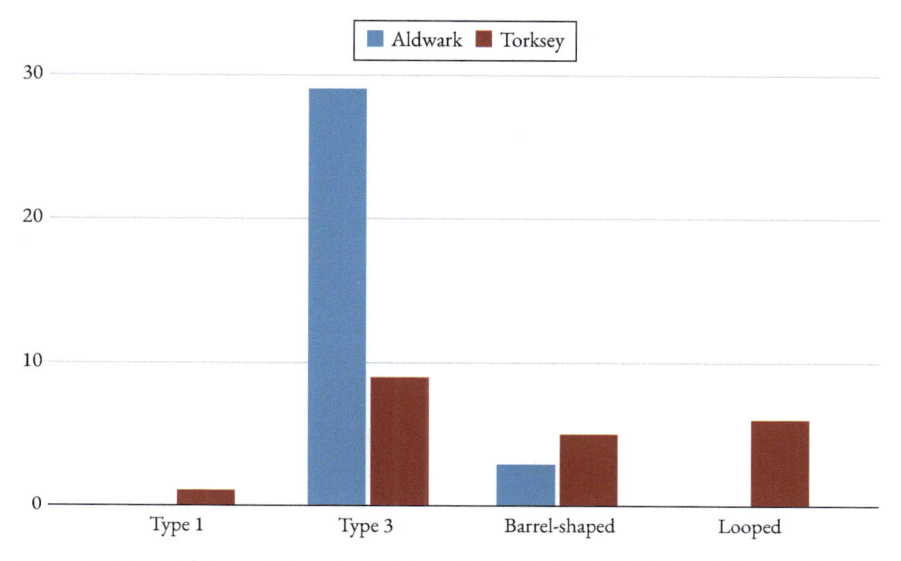

Figure 6.22. Fishing weights, classified on the basis of the Dublin weight types (n=54)

discoidal weights with large central holes (Type L) simply as 'Miscellaneous', but since they are too roughly made to function as spindle whorls it seems more likely that they were fishing weights.[107] Fishing weights are used on either nets or lines, with some morphological differences between them. Wallace defined the pierced Type 1–4 weights with reference to their use in line fishing in Dublin, where no looped weights were identified.[108] However, the integral attachment rings on the looped weights from Torksey suggest that they were designed to be suspended, probably as line sinkers. Whilst line weights serve only a single function, net weights can be employed for two different techniques. For seine netting, Rogers suggests that weights ranging between 80 and 430g would be employed alongside floats to form vertical mesh barriers, whilst cast netting involves the use of thrown nets, with lighter weights from 3–60g, allowing them to fall horizontally.[109] Only a single cylindrical weight (T196) falls into the heavier range (81g), suggesting that hand-casting was the main netting technique employed at both locations.

Eight examples of the Type 1 boat-shaped line weights have been identified in Viking-age tenth- and eleventh-century contexts in Dublin, two of which

107. Williams 2020c, 30
108. Wallace 1998
109. Rogers 1993, 1320

Figure 6.23. Torksey fishing weights (not to scale; left to right): T1781 (authors), T186, T187, T188, T190 (Fitzwilliam Museum)

(DFW 5 and DFW 6) provide close parallels for the single Torksey example (T1781) (Figure 6.23).[110] They all display defined keels and gunwales and closely resemble clinker-built vessels, although both Dublin examples have transverse piercings at each end, whereas that from Torksey is perforated vertically. This characteristic is shared with the less boat-like weights amongst the Dublin finds, a more rounded, boat-like weight from Whithorn, and a vertically-pierced weight from the probable Viking camp near Taillebourg.[111] The Whithorn and Taillebourg weights were probably cast in single-piece moulds, but Wallace suggests that the more defined boat-shaped Dublin examples required two-piece casting, which can also be proposed for the Torksey find. This suggests that, despite sharing the vertical piercings of the less well-modelled examples, the Torksey weight was manufactured with some care.

The Type 1 weights from Torksey and Taillebourg apparently pre-date those from Dublin and may represent an artefact type created amongst the disparate groups which formed the Great Army, later gaining popularity in Dublin. Their forms reflect a maritime theme, and Wallace viewed the Dublin Type 1 weights as depicting specifically Scandinavian vessels.[112] Therefore, it is possible to read the Torksey example as expressing a social grouping, self-consciously invoking a Scandinavian-derived cultural identity which recalls the use of the ship as a cultural symbol.[113]

110. Wallace 1998, figs. 3–4; 2015, 270
111. Mariotti *et al.* 2013, 217; Nicholson 1997, 395; Dumont and Mariotti (eds.) 2013, 137, 186; Deutsch-Dumolin 2023, 174–5
112. Wallace 1998, 4
113. Crumlin-Pedersen 2010, 145

The vertically perforated Type 3 weights are the most common type from Aldwark and Torksey, and incorporate a variety of shapes, including discoidal, cylindrical, and conical. Similar weights have also been identified at Dublin, Flixborough, Fishergate, and Coppergate.[114] Val Fryer suggests that conical or domed weights were attached to nets, based on later medieval examples with an average weight of 46g, while four similarly-shaped finds from Meols have an average weight of 93.9g.[115] The spherical Torksey weights are, however, far lighter, averaging 21g, suggesting a different use, probably as line weights. The single irregularly shaped weight from Torksey (T195) may also have been a net weight, although the narrow aperture of the piercing suggests that it was attached to a thin cord and was probably a line sinker. The conical/domed shape distributes weight unevenly, suggesting that this form was made to be suspended rather than attached to a net.

McDonnell has suggested that ring-shaped weights were used for seine nets, which Rogers argued require weights in excess of 80g.[116] However, the discoidal weights from Aldwark all weigh less than 60g, with over 75% less than 30g, and it is difficult to imagine them successfully securing a seine net, even against a moderate riverine current. The weight range of these discoidal forms is broadly similar to a series of stratified early medieval barrel-shaped weights from Llanbedrgoch, suggesting a similar function.[117] The Aldwark discoidal weights were probably used on hand-cast nets, with their shape reflecting the most commonly produced form of cast lead in the camp. By contrast, net weights are less common at Torksey, where the discoidal shape is almost entirely absent.

Other lead weights from Torksey possibly used in fishing include examples with integrally-cast suspension loops. These are only paralleled by a single unstratified find from Flixborough, although Wallace has illustrated a very similar weight on an historic handline from the Aran Islands (Co. Galway).[118] Other types include barrel-shaped weights, formed from rolled sheets of lead, probably made by bending a lead strip directly around netting cords, and used for hand casting.[119] They have been widely recorded from early medieval sites such as Meols, Llangorse Crannog (Wales), Whithorn, Fishergate, Coppergate,

114. Rogers 1993, 1320; Mainman and Rogers 2000, 2535
115. Fryer 1998, 34–5; Egan 2007, 286
116. McDonnell 1981, 30; Rogers 1993, 1320
117. Redknap 2019, 395
118. Wallace 1998, fig. 2
119. Wastling 2009, 249; McDonnell 1981, 30

and Flixborough, with two partially-unrolled examples recovered from late Anglo-Saxon contexts at Stoke Quay, Ipswich.[120]

The late tenth-century *Colloquy* by Ælfric of Eynsham describes the use of cast nets by wild-fowlers as well as fishermen, and Lisa Wastling suggests that lighter barrel-shaped weights might have been employed for birding.[121] The landscape surrounding the Torksey camp was dominated by wetlands in the early medieval period, including a saturated peat bog to the east. Whilst their vegetation is unknown, both peatlands and floodplain probably formed grassy marshes.[122] This would have been a suitable environment for wading birds and waterfowl, and would have been more extensive than the small alluvial basin identified east of Aldwark.[123] Cast nets were clearly not common at Torksey, and may have been reserved for fowling, but at Aldwark, hand-cast nets appear to have dominated, and were presumably used for fishing in the Ouse. Although there is little to indicate that seine netting was common at either location, it seems possible it was undertaken at Torksey. The low recovery of both seine and cast net weights here may simply be a matter of recovery, but it may also suggest alternative means of fishing, with the strong tidal fluctuations of the Trent creating an ideal environment for fish trapping.[124] Early medieval fish weirs have been documented along the river, including a series excavated in an archaic channel at Hemington Quarry, Castle Donington (Leicestershire) and another at Colwick (Nottinghamshire). Whilst these structures are all upriver from Torksey, similar conditions would have existed in the vicinity of the camp, indicating that wooden weirs and traps may have been a more favoured method of fishing. Such methods would have been particularly useful in the autumn months leading to December, when silver eels would have been migrating downstream *en masse*.[125]

Only a few possible fishhooks were recovered from either camp although no information is available for the single Aldwark example. One from Torksey (T2525) is paralleled by a similarly-sized find from London identified as a fishhook, but it lacks both the pointed barb and looped eye, and so may have had a different function (Figure 6.24).[126] The *Colloquy* notes that baited hooks

120. Egan 2007; Redknap 2019; Nicholson 1997; Rogers 1993; Mainman and Rogers 2000; Wastling 2009; Gaimster *et al.* 2020, 223
121. Swanton 1975, 171–2; Wastling 2009, 250
122. Stein 2014, 247
123. Howard 2020, 5
124. Stein 2014, 161
125. Cooper and Ripper 2017, xii, 4–20; Salisbury 1988; Reynolds 2015, 118–38
126. Pritchard 1991, 138

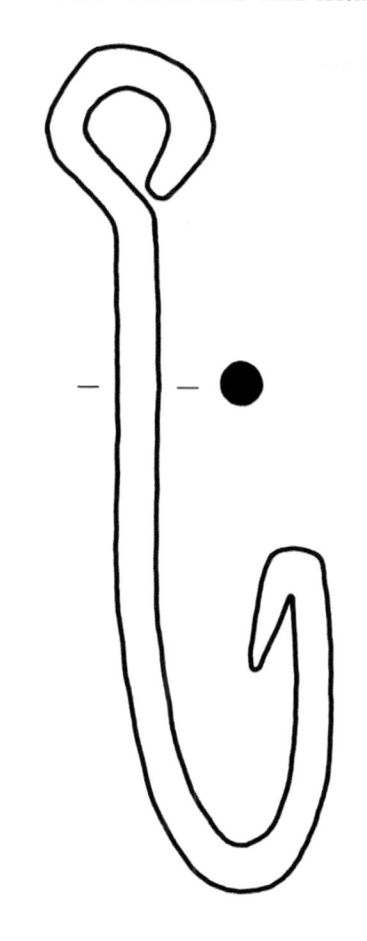

Figure 6.24. Fishhook T2525 from Torksey (Chloe Watson)

were used by fishermen, but they are only occasional individual finds in the archaeological record, with the seven from Coppergate forming the largest single-site assemblage in Britain, or as grave goods, such as an iron hook bound with the mineralised remains of an attached line from the late ninth-century burial at Balnakeil.[127] Despite the paucity of hooks from Aldwark and Torksey, sinkers show that line fishing was undertaken. However, although angling with a rod and line is depicted on a Canterbury manuscript of *c.*1000, fishing was

127. Swanton 1975, 171; Batey and Paterson 2013, 646–7; Ottaway 1992, 600–1

probably normally conducted by using either simple hand lines or with long lines, where multiple hooks are attached to a single main line, as has been suggested for the Coppergate fishhooks.[128] In rivers, both line types are typically deployed from boats, with such fishing known from Anglo-Saxon literary sources.[129] Eels can be caught by hand lines, and the *Colloquy* also lists pike, trout, minnows, and burbot as a typical river catch.[130]

Weapons

Although iron weaponry, including swords, spears, and arrowheads, suffers from the same under-representation as the tools, it was less commonly discarded by the metal detectorists. Nonetheless, the numbers recovered from both sites appear surprisingly low. At Aldwark, there is evidence that some weapons were recovered but not recorded, with an axe and a shield boss allegedly sold prior to archaeological involvement with the site (Figure 6.25).[131]

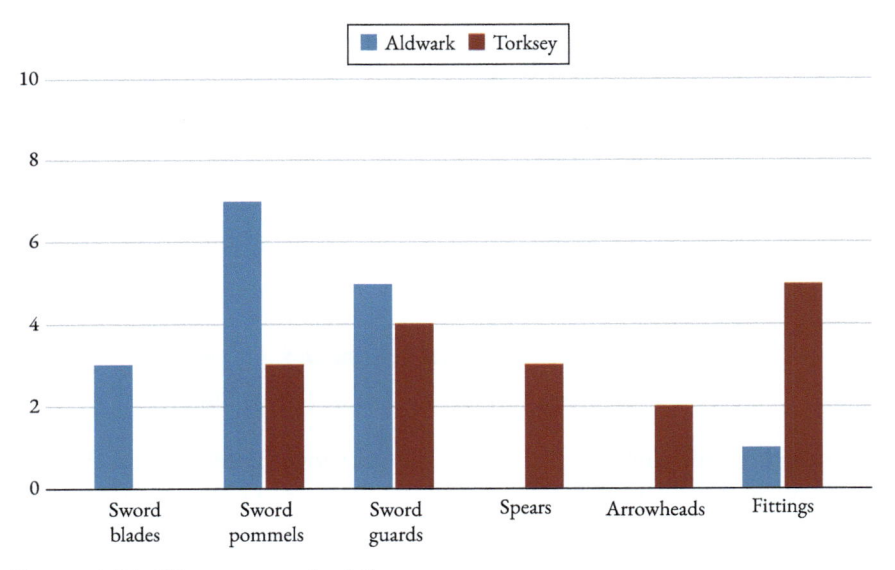

Figure 6.25. Weapon types (n=35)

128. Hagen 2006, 158; Hall 1984, 94
129. Bond 1999, 186
130. Stone Gaines 2007, 8; Swanton 1975, 171
131. Williams and Hall 2020, 84

However, there is nothing to suggest that similar issues affected recovery at Torksey, where the weapons assemblage appears notably small when compared to the amounts of metal- and woodworking tools. This may reflect depositional differences, with weaponry more carefully curated and less readily discarded. The form of the weaponry provides further insight into the cultural origins and experiences of the members of the Army. Some of the same issues of typology that were noted about axes apply to swords and spears. The standard reference remains that of Petersen from 1919, but this focused almost exclusively on Norwegian finds, and the work of Andy Halpin on Dublin swords and Fedir Androshchuk offer important updates.[132] Wheeler produced a basic typology of British spearheads, which is affected by problems with dating, and although Swanton produced a detailed analysis of earlier Anglo-Saxon spearheads, there are no more recent reviews of later Insular sword or spear typologies.[133]

Swords

The blades from Aldwark comprise one complete blade broken into three after deposition (A132.1), and fragments of two others (A911, A1061) (Figure 6.26).

Although A132.1 was found near a pommel (A132.2), this was not attached to the blade, and without a lower guard it seems unlikely that these represent elements of the same weapon. A herringbone/chevron structure is visible on the X-rays of A132.1 and A911, indicating pattern welding, a technique common in England during the fifth to seventh centuries, but which continued into

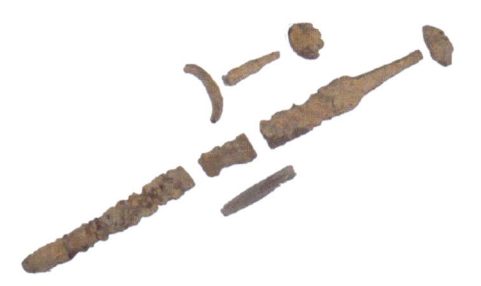

Figure 6.26. Swords from Aldwark: (top) A133.1–3 and (lower) A132.1–2 (PAS)

the tenth century.[134] There has been considerable debate over whether this forging method produced a structurally superior blade, or whether such swords were primarily valued as markers of rank and social hierarchy because of the complexity of their construction.[135] Either way, pattern-welded blades were

132. Androshchuk 2014, 13–27; Halpin 2008, 148–9
133. Wheeler 1927; Swanton 1973
134. Ager 2020, 17–18; Rogers 2020c, 63; Mortimer 2019, 95–6
135. Ellis Davidson 1962, 30; Lang and Ager 1989, 110

highly-valued and valuable items.[136] Since pattern-welded blades required a complex mix of a minimum of four ferrous alloys to forge, when melted down for recycling the resultant iron would only be usable for utilitarian items, as the swords themselves could only be produced from freshly-smelted metal.[137] Thus, it seems probable that both blades were kept for their perceived innate worth, rather than for any potential scrap value. Since it seems unlikely that they would have been easily lost, especially a whole blade, they may represent deliberately hoarded items.

Similar numbers of sword pommels have been identified at Aldwark and Torksey, with six of Type L at Aldwark and three at Torksey, one uncertain at Torksey, and one Type X at Aldwark (Figure 6.27). One pommel (A1053) does not entirely correspond with Type L; although the upper profile displays some of the classic tripartite form, the shoulders are low and lack the concave hollows which typify this type, the base does not have the 'strong curve' characterised by Petersen and it is very thin with pointed, rather than rounded, terminals.[138] Nonetheless,

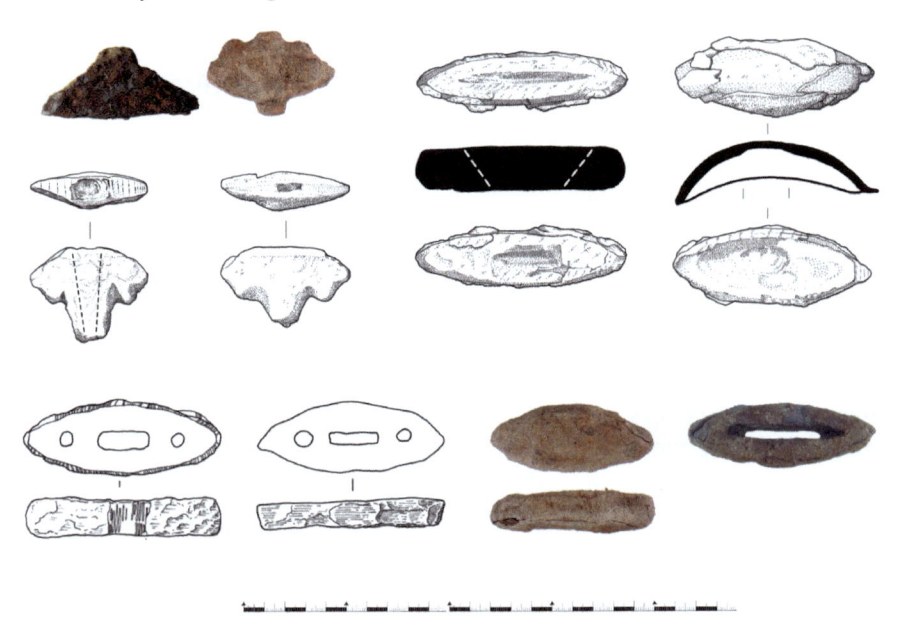

Figure 6.27. Sword guards and pommels (top left) A1053 (YAT), T3483 (authors), (with below) T2312, T2823; (top middle) T2267; (top right) T1428 (all Chloe Watson); (bottom row) A913, A1051 (YAT), T2582, T1424 (authors)

136. Brunning 2019, 86
137. Fleming 2012, 24–7
138. Rogers 2020c, 63, fig. 23

we have included it as a regional variant of Type L, similar to the sub-types from Britain and Ireland identified by Androshchuk.[139] Type L has been classified since the work of Petersen as an 'English' form, and is still seen as originating in either England or Ireland, despite a notable distribution in Scandinavia.[140]

Three definite sword guards are recorded from Aldwark. Both A913, decorated with inlaid wire, and A1051/2, which was found in two pieces, are of Petersen Type H. A strongly curved Petersen Type L (A133.3) was found with a pommel (A133.1) and the remains of a tang (A133.2), indicating a complete hilt, potentially stripped whole from a sword blade. A fragment of iron (A232.1) may be part of another guard, broken across the blade aperture and with only one quillon remaining; the flat, lenticular form suggests it derives from Scandinavian models.[141] One of four sword guards identified at Torksey (T3483) was found within a metre of one of the Type L pommels (T2582), but it is unlikely that they represent elements of the same hilt. The flat guard, with piercings adjacent to the slot to hold the tang, is not a match for a curved Type L pommel; it is more probably part of a Type H sword. Two lower guards certainly are of Type H form (T1424, T2267), with the remains of bands of inlaid wire visible on the former. The guards and pommels of Types H and L can be dated to the later ninth century, and although the single Type X hilt (A241) may be of slightly later date it is as likely that it was brought to Aldwark by a member of the Great Army.[142] One of the two swords from Nottingham, has been identified as a Type X, while a Type X was also found in Repton in 1948.[143]

The curvature of one iron object (T1428) is suggestive of a Type L hilt, and the X-ray shows a sub-rectangular slot in the centre, suggesting it held the tang of a sword guard. Although other upper guards are of copper-alloy, it is possible that this iron fitting was manufactured to house a copper-alloy pommel, and at least one complete hilt of this form survives with mixed iron and copper-alloy guards.[144] Morphological parallels can be drawn with a Type L sword with a 'boat-shaped' upper guard from Vardal, Oppland (Norway), and several cast copper-alloy guards recorded by the PAS, particularly a find from 'near Chichester' (Sussex), with a similar dished recess, although the Torksey example is slightly larger.[145] These

139. Androshchuk 2014, 67–9, 190–1
140. Bone 1989, 66; Dunning and Evison 1961, 129; Androshchuk 2014, 68
141. Rogers 2020c, 62–3
142. Jones 2002, 20; Hjardar and Vike 2016, 169; Androshchuk 2014, 81–2
143. Graham-Campbell 2001, 106; Biddle and Kjølbye-Biddle 2001, 57
144. Vlasatý 2018
145. Androshchuk 2014, 474 and plate 121; SUSS-A6ADE2

guards are associated with a highly standardised form of five-lobed cast copper-alloy pommel, unknown to Petersen. Over 50 of these undecorated cast pommels with peened tangs are now recorded from across England, and 24 baldric components, similar to those in the Cronk Moar (Isle of Man) Viking burial, including distributor hubs, distributor bars, and strap stiffening bars, all decorated with Borre-style animal heads.[146] This wide distribution may best be explained by such weaponry having seen much movement through military action, with the pommels having been weakly attached to the hilt, or deliberately stripped for re-use. The number of individual losses far exceeds that of any other type of Viking or Anglo-Saxon sword pommel. Given this and their uniformity we might conjecture that they were mass produced for swords to equip the Great Army.[147]

The relative abundance of pommels at both Aldwark and Torksey may reflect the use of these fittings as a source of scrap. Type L swords frequently have precious metal foils applied to the hilts, and so these pommels may have been collected for their valuable metalwork and discarded after this was removed.[148] For example, both faces of a Type L pommel from Coppergate have a circular central indentation from where decorative mounts have been removed, while a unique gold-embellished Type L pommel in the Bedale hoard of *c.*900 was presumably retained for this decorative material rather than any inherent value in the iron.[149] The straight Type H guards also had their fittings removed, which in the cases of the two decorated examples (A913 and T1424), may have been to facilitate removal and recycling of the inlaid metals. Guards with similar inlays were found at Coppergate (no. 3941) and Wharram Percy (North Yorkshire) (no. 257), and other inlaid Type H guards are recorded from Staunch Meadow, all contexts with metalworking activity, where the fittings have been interpreted as probable sources of scrap.[150] However, the plain Type H guards at both camps may indicate stripping of swords for more functional reasons of refitting and repair. The Great Army certainly appears to have changed fittings on usable blades, as illustrated by a straight lower guard and a curved, Type L-style upper guard used on the same sword in Mound 1 at Heath Wood.[151] A comparison can be found in a sword from Hegge (Norway), which has a decorated Type L pommel and grip but a plain lower guard, which is also

146. Bersu and Wilson 1966
147. Haldenby *et al.* 2022, 98–9
148. Ellis Davidson 1962, 69
149. Ottaway 1992, 716 and fig. 312; Brunning 2019, 11
150. Ottaway 1992, 716–18; Webster 2000, 138–9; Rogers and Ottaway 2014, 265–6
151. Richards *et al.* 2004, 29

believed to have been altered in antiquity.[152] Pommels and hilt fittings were especially prone to wear; separate hilt furniture, particularly pommels, have been identified at multiple sites across Europe, including Dorestad, suggesting that the refurbishment of sword blades was commonplace.[153] There are also examples of highly prized Frankish sword blades—which Charles the Bald had to prohibit from being sold to Viking raiders—acquiring regional forms of hilt furniture as they were refitted.[154]

Aside from the removal of pommels for recycling or the refitting of blades, the presence of disassociated pommels in Scandinavian funerary contexts suggests a potential ritual dimension to the practice. For example, the Woodstown burial contained a Petersen Type N sword, deliberately broken in three places with the pommel removed; two other sword pommels, of Types O and X, were also recovered from the site.[155] Two detached Type H pommels were recovered from the Kilmainham-Islandbridge cemetery.[156] Charlotte Fabech has suggested that swords were sometimes closely associated with individuals in Scandinavia, and therefore were sometimes disposed of in such a way to prevent recovery when the owners could no longer use them; a similar motivation has been proposed for the re-emergence the practice of depositing swords in 'watery' contexts in Viking-age England.[157] Sue Brunning has argued that similar notions of 'personality' could lead to the destruction of swords of vanquished warriors as a means of bestowing an enduring, symbolic defeat onto their former owners.[158] These concepts intersect with the 'ritual killings' of early medieval weaponry, and could account for the burial of dismembered swords; Hedenstierna-Jonson suggests a similar motivation behind the deliberate burial of a scabbard chape in the main hall building of the Birka garrison.[159] Such actions would not seem out of character in an encampment of a militarised force, establishing itself in hostile territory. A similarly symbolic action may have lain behind the deliberate deposition of other items, ploughshares in particular.

The dominance of Type L pommels in both assemblages conforms with the local character of many of the tools at Torksey, and one interpretation might be that they reflect the conglomerate nature of the Great Army. However, this

152. Wilson 1965, 36–7
153. Brunning 2019, 84; Willemsen 2021, 103–7
154. Owen-Crocker 2011, 211; Kleingärtner and Williams 2014, 64–5
155. Harrison 2014a, 92; 2014b, 156–7
156. Harrison and Ó Floinn 2014, 378, 399
157. Fabech 2006, 29; Lund 2010, 55; Reynolds and Semple 2011, 46; Raffield 2014, 644
158. Brunning 2019, 87–8
159. Hedenstierna-Jonson 2006, 66

may not be so clear cut when taken alongside other items of locally-acquired material culture, such as dress accessories and jewellery, in the process of being cut up and repurposed rather than worn. Swords are one of the few Viking-age artefacts to which concepts of ethnicity still attach, with certain hilt forms persistently seen as representing national origins.[160] However, given the personal nature of early medieval military obligation, with service in a retinue or warband essentially formed as a contract between individuals, concepts of nationality or ethnic origin would have been of little relevance.[161] Furthermore, the histories of swords, as manifestations of plunder or war trophies, may have been more significant than any perceptions of ethnic affiliations.

Some of the swords deposited in burials that can be associated with the Great Army are consistent with the sword fittings from the camps, including Type H swords from the burial at Sonning, and Mound 7 at Heath Wood, a sword with a Type L pommel from Mound 1 at Heath Wood, and a Type L sword was found at Repton in 1839 'in the midst of a large quantity of human bones' 150m north-west of the church.[162] Others, however, have a different profile. For example, Grave 511 at Repton contained a Type M sword, which has dense concentrations in Norway but is widely found.[163] In contrast, the burial at Reading contained a Scandinavian sword with gripping beast decoration dated to c.800, similar to one recovered from near the Houses of Parliament in 1948.[164] Other burials, in contrast, included swords of Anglo-Saxon manufacture, such as a 'Late Saxon sword' of uncertain type from a burial at Thetford, while Mound 50 at Heath Wood contained a hilt with Trewhiddle-style decoration.[165] These examples serve as a reminder of the selectivity inherent to the creation of funerary tableaux, which are not simple reflections of the available material culture.

Spearheads

An intact spearhead, damaged at both the tip and the end of the socket (T25), was described by Blackburn as a Petersen Type A, with a leaf-shaped blade, usually regarded as a late eighth- and early ninth-century form (Figure 6.28).[166]

160. Halsall 2000, 269
161. Innes 2000, 81; Ystgaard 2021, 285
162. Evison 1969, 330–1; Richards *et al.* 2004, 30; Biddle and Kjølbye-Biddle 2001, 57
163. Biddle and Kjølbye-Biddle 1992, 41
164. East 1986
165. Rogerson and Dallas 1984, 53
166. Blackburn 2011, 243; Halpin 2008, 143

Figure 6.28. Torksey spearheads: (top) T1423 (authors), (middle) T25 (Fitzwilliam Museum), and (bottom) T1675 (Lincoln Museum)

However, the sharply-angled shoulders at the base of the blade suggest it is a type of angled spearhead common in Scandinavia from 850–1100.[167] Its form is echoed by a second spearhead (T1423), of slightly smaller dimensions, although retaining a pointed tip. Both appear to have split sockets, and display central ribs along the blade, producing a diamond-shaped section. The blades are, however, short by comparison with ninth-century Scandinavian types, and the split sockets and shorter heads are more typical of English types from the seventh century onwards.[168] A potential parallel can be seen in a ninth- to tenth-century spearhead with a split socket and pattern-welded blade core recovered from the River Thames at Cookham (Berkshire), although it is more ornate.[169] There is a possible depositional bias, similar to that suggested for Dublin where small, more easily lost, spearheads dominate the settlement contexts, in contrast to graves where larger examples are more common.[170]

167. Hjardar and Vike 2016, 176
168. Bersu and Wilson 1966, 57, 76; Grieg 1940, 50; Wheeler 1927, 27; Swanton 1973, 81–3
169. Williams 2014, 108, fig. 52; British Museum no. 1868,0128.2
170. Halpin 2010, 128, fig. 12.4; Harrison and Ó Floinn 2014, 93 and chart 1

However, if both Torksey spearheads were looted English types, regarded as a source of iron scrap, this may be why they were discarded.

A third Torksey spearhead (T1675) was recovered from the iron hoard, having been included after its re-use as a weaving beater. Its blade tip is consistent with an Anglo-Saxon spearhead of Swanton Type E3, with regular curves towards the point, dating to the mid- to later Anglo-Saxon period.[171] Two spearheads of this type were found in the late tenth-century tool hoard from Westley Waterless, and another, albeit with a diamond section, in the Late Anglo-Saxon iron hoard from Nazeing. These hoards have other similarities to Torksey with respect to their hafted tools.[172] The small number of spearheads is not unusual as they are rare finds from settlements, with only one complete example and a stratified fragment from Coppergate, one each from Goltho and Cottam, and twenty-nine from the whole Hiberno-Norse period in Dublin.[173] Scandinavian forms are, however, occasionally found as grave goods in Viking burials, such as those at Woodstown, and Nottingham.[174]

Arrowheads

The best-preserved arrowhead from Torksey (T287) has the point missing, but the tanged, leaf-shaped form corresponds with Jessop's Type T1 and Halpin's Type 1, a typically Scandinavian form (Figure 6.29). These are broadly dated to the ninth to eleventh centuries, although the majority of Halpin's Type 1 from Ireland are found in contexts pre-dating c.950.[175] The Torksey arrowhead is 22mm wide, and this is generally seen as a hunting rather than military type, which tend to be much smaller with blades under 14mm wide, although acknowledged as being multi-purpose.[176]

Another arrowhead (T2569) may be represented by the top of a broken socket, extending into a square-section rod which begins to swell before it terminates in another break. The socket is malformed, making the profile difficult to determine; two roughly parallel sides remain, suggesting a square section, although the socket is cracked and has been crushed. If this is an arrowhead, the square-section rod, representing the base of the blade, indicates that it is of 'bodkin' type, classically seen as a military form, with a long, narrow head

171. Swanton 1973, 55–9, 83–7, figs. 13 and 27e
172. Swanton 1973, 85; Morris 1983, 30, fig. 2g
173. Ottaway 1992, 715; Goodall 1987, 186; Halpin 2008, 132; Haldenby 1992, 39
174. Harrison 2014b, 161; Graham-Campbell 2001, 106
175. Jessop 1996, 195; Halpin 2008, 91
176. Halpin 2008, 35, 79–80, 93; 2010, 129

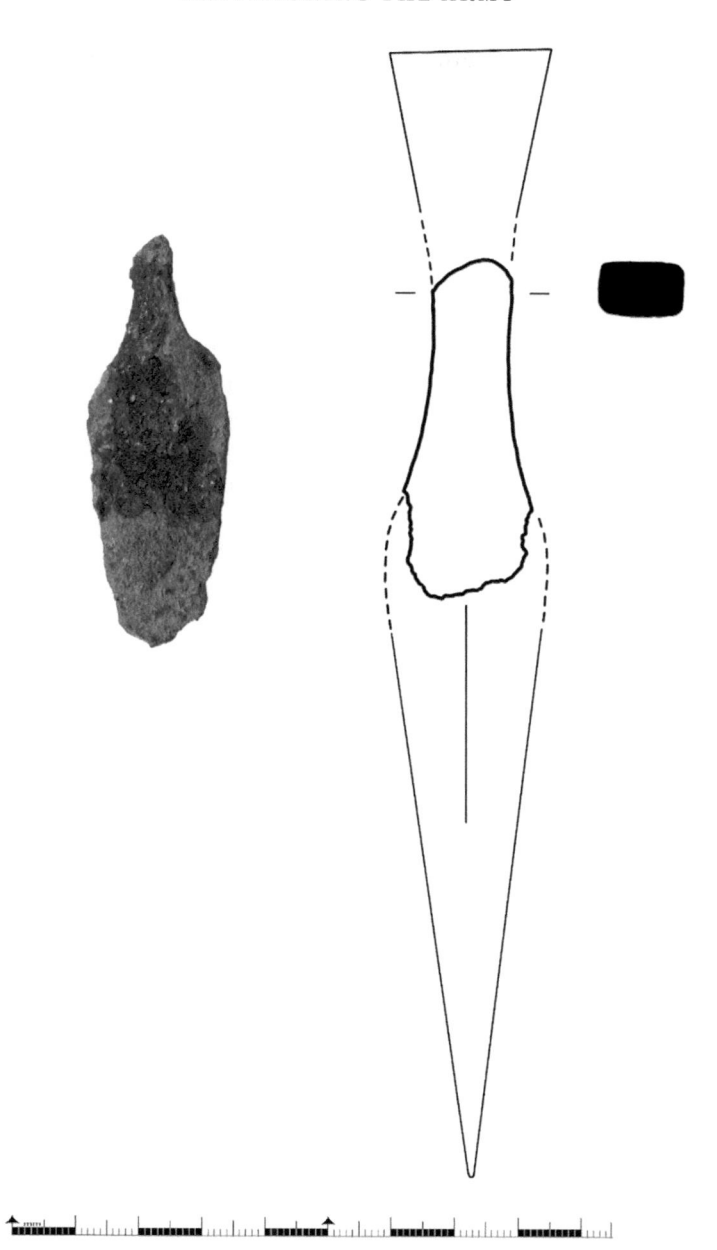

Figure 6.29. Torksey arrowheads: (left) T287 (Fitzwilliam Museum) and (right) T2569 (Chloe Watson)

designed to penetrate mail armour (a Jessop M7 or M8). These have generally been dated to the eleventh to fifteenth centuries, but examples have been recovered from a tenth-century context at Coppergate (nos. 3918 and 3916) and a ninth-century burial at Kaupang, while one is catalogued amongst the artefacts from the Dublin Kilmainham-Islandbridge burial complex but without secure context.[177] Arrowheads are considerably more common in Hiberno-Norse levels in Dublin, where over 500 have been recovered, far more than among burials, and on Coppergate, which has produced 25 stratified examples.[178] However, arrowheads are somewhat rarer finds from rural sites; eight were recorded from Flixborough, only one from Cottam, and merely a single iron socket of a possible arrowhead at Staunch Meadow.[179] Given that these three locations were all extensively metal-detected, these finds may provide us with a more accurate comparison for the assemblages from the camps. Arrowheads are not common in Viking-age burials, but six of varying types were found with the probable Viking Great Army burial at Sonning.[180]

Weapon fittings

Several ferrules, scabbard and shield fittings were also recovered from Torksey. A decorative copper-alloy sword-grip ferrule (T130), featuring a zoomorphic interlace, forming a series of stylised beast heads, is similar to a Type H sword fitting from Swandro, Rousay with more naturalistic animal masks (Figure 6.30).[181] Another fitting (T804) of heavily gilded copper-alloy has the same dagged shape, but with a more abstract interlace design, and is similar to the lower ferrule of a Petersen Type D sword from Kilmainham. The Torksey ferrule is so similar to two gilded copper-alloy ferrules on the hilt of a

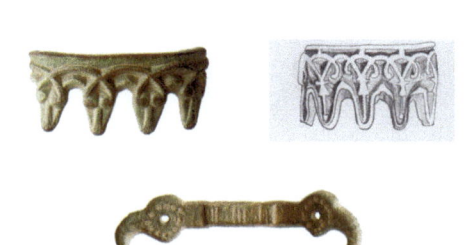

Figure 6.30. Torksey fittings (not to scale): (top) sword-grip ferrules T130 (Fitzwilliam Museum) and T804 (PAS); (bottom) scabbard fitting T131 (Fitzwilliam Museum)

177. Goodall 1987, 186; Jessop 1996, 198; Ottaway 1992, 711–13, fig. 309; Harrison and Ó Floinn 2014, 131, 416: arrowhead Wk18; Halpin 2008, 125
178. Halpin 2008, 75; 2010, 129, table 12.2; Ottaway 1992, 710
179. Ottaway 2009b, 123; Haldenby and Richards 2016; Rogers and Ottaway 2014, 266
180. Evison 1969, 333
181. Grieg 1940, 89, fig. 51

sword in the Hedeby boat burial that they may have been produced in the same workshop. The Hedeby sword has been tentatively identified by Wamers as the one presented to Harald Klak by Louis the Pious following his baptism in 826; irrespective of that association, it is a reminder that the Torksey ferrule would have been significantly older than its date of deposition.[182] The Hedeby sword is a Type K and a comparative rarity in Denmark, but the type has a significant distribution in southern Norway and Ireland.[183]

A scabbard fitting (T131) formed of a thin, flat copper-alloy bar with a raised central section is decorated with transverse grooves and has pierced zoomorphic bird's-head terminals. It has strong parallels in a series of Merovingian scabbard fittings of late sixth- to early seventh-century date mainly from north-eastern France and the Ardennes.[184] Given that this is of a type otherwise unknown in Britain, it may be another example of comparatively ancient objects acquired and transported considerable distances by the Army. Two Carolingian belt or baldric mounts from Torksey (T580, T1633) are of a type widely found on the PAS in eastern England (Figure 6.31).[185] Both are of the so-called Marsum-type of hollowed mount with one or two thickened, 'rolled' ends. Noting their rarity in

Figure 6.31. Carolingian scabbard/strap mounts from Torksey: T580 (PAS), T1633 (authors)

the Carolingian realm, Wolfram Giertz has suggested that since those found in England frequently lack their rear frame, they had been deliberately clipped from the belts of the elite, perhaps providing a means of meeting tribute payments to Viking groups.[186]

Grips were sometimes attached to the rear of Viking-age shields by means of a pair of Y-shaped cast copper-alloy fittings, used as terminals on either end of a wooden bar. These terminals had two short, flat arms which lay flush to the shield board and a third, curved extension which formed the means of attachment to the rounded grip. While incomplete, a decorative item from Torksey (T115) may

182. Wamers 2005b; Wolfram Giertz pers. comm.
183. Harrison and Ó Floinn 2014, 78, 334, fig. 33; Müller-Wille 1976, 67–9, Abb. 23, 31–2
184. Menghin 1983
185. Blackburn 2011, 232; Thomas 2012, 498; e.g. NMS-B0FF45, 559F25, -F7F6BE, -ADCA16, -636BF3, -638554; YORYM-EAF943; LIN-2D80AB; ESS-2B2E50, -109B16; FAHG-123AB4
186. Wolfram Giertz pers. comm.

Figure 6.32. A possible shield fitting from Torksey (T115; Fitzwilliam Museum)

be such a grip, as the two surviving arms, each pierced by an iron rivet, would easily serve to attach it to a flat surface (Figure 6.32). Similar examples from other sites associated with the Army are discussed in Chapter 7. A break is clear roughly at the point where the third terminal would typically start to curve; whilst this change in shape would obviously form a weak spot in any such casting, the absence of the characteristic curve means that the identification of this item is not secure. However, the decoration has parallels with several finds of shield-grip fittings from Birka (e.g. Graves 942 and 1151).[187] Such origins are not implausible, given the presence of silver-wire embroidery of a type found at Birka and on Gotland in Mound 11 at Heath Wood, and the iron shield clamps from Mound 50 which also have parallels at Birka.[188]

Conclusions

The assemblages recovered from each camp are remarkably similar, with differences generally accounted for by recovery practices. In essence, they demonstrate concern with the practicalities of provision and repair, but a more nuanced picture emerges from a detailed analysis of the artefacts. The woodworking equipment of Anglo-Saxon type suggests that after years of campaigning, the Army must have needed to replace worn-out or lost tools with locally available types, although the presence of local craftworkers is also a possibility. In contrast, the Scandinavian-influenced textile tools, such as the Type B spindle whorls, suggest the continuation of deep-seated Scandinavian cultural traditions, with the heavy lead whorls potentially showing a link to methods of yarn production also seen at Kaupang. Many of the sword pommels were of English type, and other fittings were of Carolingian manufacture, but this seems to reflect the stripping of swords for recycling rather than having any specific ethnic associations with members of the Army.

The material culture associated with textile working, fishing, and birding, along with the metalworking discussed in Chapter 5, reveals some of the ways

---

187. Arbman 1940, II, Taf. 19, 3 and 4
188. Richards *et al.* 2004, 44, 68

in which the Army was provisioning itself, but also encourages us to think about the organisation of the camps. They must have had designated areas for undertaking some tasks and as the Trent and the Ure would have been the main water sources, regulation of areas to be used as latrines would have been required, to avoid the risk of spreading dysentery or cholera, as well as the polluting impact of manufacturing and processing activities. Settlements of this scale, even temporary ones, would have required a high degree of organisation. Yet we cannot readily find evidence for distinct zoning of activities, even where metal-detected finds have been plotted with GPS or excavation undertaken, suggesting similar activities being undertaken at several locations. This may reflect the fact that the Army comprised multiple sub-groups, factions aligned with one or other of the Army's various leaders, the 'brotherhoods' into which Viking armies are described as dividing in continental sources, and ships' companies, which may have formed the basic unit of organisation, whether fighting, foraging, or feasting.[189]

The woodworking tools recovered from Torksey, in particular, provide insights into how the local landscape was exploited. The trimming axes (T1650, T255), slice (T2787), and wedge (T2475) suggest that timber was processed, with large pieces riven and converted, while the T-shaped axe heads indicate that timber was shaped into planks for ship repair, a deduction reinforced by the recovery of clench nails and spoon augers.[190] In shipbuilding, it was usual practice to fell trees in winter, when low sap limits the amount of potential warping of converted timbers, and the splitting of tree trunks was also a winter task; the *Gerefa* states that timber should be cleaved when there is a frost.[191] Clinker construction requires the use of unseasoned planks, which can be easily bent and which resist splitting.[192] Although timber can be kept in a workable 'green' condition for up to two years, with careful storage, often with the timbers submerged, the Great Army would almost certainly have worked recently-felled trees, with planks riven from fresh timber.[193] Oak would have been the preferred wood for shipbuilding and, whilst frame components could be produced from the natural curves found on field trees or those grown in open-canopy woodlands, planks and stringers would require large trunks with

189. Ravn 2016
190. Goodall 2011, 23
191. Ravn 2016, 26; Swanton 1975, 32
192. McGrail 1987, 108
193. Darrah 1982, 219; Ravn 2016, 29

straight growth.[194] These trees would require dense, closed-canopy environments, with the undergrowth cleared and grazing or browsing animals excluded.[195] Well-managed woodlands produced high-quality timber in early medieval England, with woodland management specifically mentioned in land charters.[196] At Torksey, charcoal samples recovered from pottery kilns to the south of the modern village show the use of large-diameter oak branches or trunks as fuel, and although this evidence post-dates the camp it clearly shows the existence of mature oaks in the area.[197] The Domesday survey also records large acreages of woodland near to Torksey, at Lea, Bole, Knaith, and Brampton all within easy reach of the camp, and tree clearance is suggested by the build-up of sand, up to 4.5 m in depth, to the east of the camp in the years after the overwintering.[198]

Exploitation of this woodland would, however, have seen the Army reliant on local knowledge about where resources could be obtained. Gathering of suitable timber would take time and a significant degree of organisation, implying ready access to the surrounding countryside, and considerable interaction with the local population.[199] Once felled and lopped, transportation of trunks back to the camp would be difficult and slow, and so it seems probable that the timbers would have been split and partially dressed before moving them, suggesting work parties outside of the main encampment. The final shaping and fitting of timber would presumably occur within the camp, close to the vessels, and where specialised craftworkers would have conducted the repairs.[200] Procuring and processing suitable timber for ship repairs, as well as acquiring fleece or flax for textile production, or clay for the manufacture of moulds and hearths necessary for metal casting and smithing, may have required the establishment of satellite camps or workstations, as Cooijmans has argued for Viking forces in Francia, where a diverse range of locations are recorded as Viking bases.[201] As such, the assemblages indicate the central position of both Aldwark and Torksey for dispersed activities.

The fishing and birding weights suggest exploitation of the Trent and the Ouse and their floodplains. This evidence also reminds us that repair of fishing nets would have been required. The needles used for this may have been a type

194. Ravn 2016, 56; Crumlin-Pedersen 2010, 43
195. Ravn 2016, 88
196. Berryman 1998, 7; Hooke 2010, 156–9
197. Hadley et al. 2023, 26
198. Stein 2014, 200–2, 313
199. Baker 2013, 97
200. Ravn 2016, 26–7
201. Cooijmans 2020, 125–7; 2021, 197

not recovered from either site, such as the bone and antler needles found near a causeway at Skerne in the valley of the River Hull which were interpreted as netting needles.[202] This reinforces how much associated material culture is represented by the metal-detected discoveries, which are proxies for a much wider material record.

The exploitation of the wider landscape and riverine resources could sometimes have been achieved by plunder, as Asser tells us occurred when the Army overwintered at Reading. Some of the population near Chippenham reportedly fled in 877, partly as a result of famine, which can probably be linked to the plundering of local resources by the Great Army.[203] However, many of the resources required would not have lent themselves to acquisition through raiding, and their gathering must reflect engagement with local communities, who would have had the knowledge of where to access resources. They could also have presented a threat to any successful acquisition of resources, and ensuring this did not happen may have been one of the consequences of the peace that is recorded as being made whenever the Army set up camp. While the contemporary English sources are not forthcoming about the resources the Army acquired as part of peace making, aside from payments of silver and the giving and taking of hostages, it is entirely possible that they also included food renders, as is recorded in the more detailed continental sources. For example, in 869 the Vikings on the Loire subjected the locals to payment of tribute in wine, flour, and livestock.[204] After his victory at Edington, Alfred pursued the raiders to their camp at Chippenham where Asser notes the capture of their cattle which were outside; these must have been acquired locally.[205] The late tenth-century account of the martyrdom of St Edmund by Abbo of Fleury reported that the Great Army leader Ivar had demanded a share of the wealth of the kingdom, which McLeod has suggested may have included the royal *feorm*, or food renders.[206]

The Army probably also exploited local tribute networks, typically collected at the royal and ecclesiastical estates centres near where it camped. McLeod suggests that the Burghal Hidage provides an indication of the food available, and given that the people living near Wareham were expected to provision a force of 1600 in the early tenth century, similar resources may have

202. Dent *et al.* 2000, 233–4
203. Keynes and Lapidge 1983, 83; McLeod 2006, 145; Deutsch-Dumolin 2023, 179
204. Nelson 1991, 112; Deutsch-Dumolin 2023, 179–80
205. Keynes and Lapidge 1983, 85
206. McLeod 2006, 151; 2023, 208

been available to the Great Army when they wintered there in 875–6.[207] The potential of accessing the food renders owed to major estate centres, including churches, may have been another key factor in choosing where to overwinter. Torksey was located close to at least two churches of likely early origins, at Stow, just 4km to the north-east, and South Leverton (Nottinghamshire), on the opposite banks of the Trent.[208] While there is no such clear evidence from the vicinity of Aldwark, it was located close to York and available supplies by road and river.

The presence of clench nails suggests ship repair, but the woodworking tools from the camps could also have been used to construct temporary dwellings. There is no direct evidence for that at Aldwark or Torksey, and it is often assumed that tents were employed, but the possibility is opened up by excavations at Woodstown, which uncovered a rectangular building, while GPR survey identified traces of up to six more. Whether these were for domestic use or craftworking is, however, less clear, and the assemblage associated with the excavated building suggested that 'the structure was not residential in nature but more likely served an industrial/craftworking purpose'.[209] Woodstown also seems to have been occupied for much longer than were Torksey and Aldwark, and this may have been a factor in the presence of these structures. We might also recall the Viking army that overwintered on an island in western France 'in something like a permanent settlement'.[210]

Finally, we have shown that both assemblages contain items preserved through deliberate deposition, such as the tool hoard from Torksey, the sword blades from Aldwark, and the ploughshares from both locations. While a functional interpretation of concealment for later recovery is possible, it seems a little implausible that the members of the Great Army would have been intending to return to collect scrap metal. Accordingly, these deposits may have been more symbolic actions, related to conquest and the acquisition of land at a time when the Army was clearly making plans to keep control over the regions through which it moved.

207. Keynes and Lapidge 1983, 193; McLeod 2006, 148–9; 2023, 208
208. Hadley and Richards 2016, 60–1; 2018, 11; McLeod 2006; 2023, 209
209. Russell 2023, 138–9
210. Nelson 1991, 56

PART III

Impact and legacy

In Part III we examine the wider impact of the Viking Great Army in the countryside and on the development of urban industry. Chapter 7 considers the broader activities of members of the Army beyond their main camps whilst Chapter 8 provides a comprehensive review of the development of late ninth- and early tenth-century pottery industries which we argue developed in those regions where the Army was active, and sometimes near the camps themselves. Finally, in Chapter 9 we consider the longer-term legacy of members of the Army, both those who settled and those who departed, as well as reflecting on future directions for research.

The Aldwark and Torksey assemblages are so similar, but so different from those from other settlements of the period, that they have allowed us to identify an artefactual 'signature' of the Viking Great Army. In Chapter 2 we discussed how this has the potential to identify the location of other camps, both those documented in historical sources, and those previously unrecorded. In Chapter 7 we will demonstrate how the signature enables us to trace the activities of members of the Army and its followers beyond their camps.

In 2018, when we first published the evidence for the Great Army 'signature', we defined it as comprising six main elements, which we have subsequently refined:[1]

(1) Hack-metal, including complete and fragmentary silver and gold ingots, although copper-alloy examples also occur. Fragmentary Islamic dirhams are also a key indicator of Viking activity, and generally cut into such small pieces that they must have been used for very low value transactions.

(2) Lead and copper-alloy weights, which also indicate the operation of a bullion economy. Lead inset weights appear to be a distinctive late ninth-century

---

1. Hadley and Richards 2018

phenomenon, possibly appearing first at Woodstown but widely adopted in England, with the distinctive insets, often coins or fragments of Irish or English metalwork, used to signal identity.

(3) Stycas, although common at ninth-century Northumbrian sites, are a distinctive part of the Great Army signature when found outside their normal monetary circulation area. Those deposited at Torksey were probably acquired while the Army was in Northumbria and were then used for small-scale transactions. As we have seen over a quarter of the stycas at both Aldwark and Torksey are 'blundered', or derivative, suggesting an attempt to mint them in the camps.

(4) Anglo-Saxon silver pennies, outside their primary area of circulation, or where pierced or cut, such as coins of Mercia and Wessex at Aldwark.[2] Things 'out of place' are often an indication of members of the Army having moved them. In the light of the examples of much earlier precious metalwork turning up in Great Army hoards, in inset weights, and at Aldwark and Torksey despite limited other evidence for Early or Middle Saxon activity, then we should also add things 'out of time' to the signature.

(5) Anglo-Saxon and Irish dress accessories and mounts, deliberately pierced or cut for re-use (e.g. as decorative insets in lead weights). The fact that there are many Anglo-Saxon strap-ends but very few dress pins at Aldwark and Torksey reinforces that these are not typical ninth-century settlement assemblages, in which pins and strap-ends tend to be found in roughly equal numbers.[3]

(6) Lead gaming pieces, comprising hollow or solid domed cones, sometimes with raised protuberances or knobs, and often crudely made. They are known in large numbers from Torksey, and subsequently also identified at Foremark and Aldwark. They are a key element of the Great Army signature and may provide a highly important *terminus post quem* of 872–3 given that none have yet been reported from sites known to have been visited by the Army prior to Torksey. They are crudely manufactured objects, easily made and readily discarded, which enhances their value as dating indicators since they were not treasured, and they do not occur in tenth-century Anglo-Scandinavian deposits, such as those at Coppergate in York, for example.

2. Ager and Williams 2004
3. Richards and Haldenby 2018

Subsequent refinements to artefact chronologies and evidence for manufacture on the camps have allowed us to further nuance this set of criteria.[4] As we have seen in Part II, several categories of dress accessory can be linked to the Army, including Class F double-sided strap-ends and buckles which arrived from Dublin as sword-belt fittings, alongside five-lobed hollow and cast sword pommels. This was closely followed by the introduction of new forms of strap-end, with casting used to manufacture them in large numbers, including the A1avii and B5 types as well as plate-headed pins. B4a, E3, and E4 strap-ends were also introduced in the late ninth century, although these continued in use into the tenth century. Their numbers are too low to demonstrate that they were lost during the movements of the Great Army, and they were adopted more widely, but their presence at Aldwark and Torksey indicates a link, and they are often found alongside other elements of the Great Army signature.

We have already mentioned that the arrival of the Great Army in Northumbria led to the introduction of A1avii or 'Wooperton-type' strap-ends, as an outlier was found at Torksey (see Chapter 4). We have identified forty-four examples, mainly from Yorkshire, with a handful from Lincolnshire and just one from East Anglia. Given their highly homogeneous form, we believe that they were cast, as Bailey and Thomas tentatively suggested, possibly in a York workshop given their distribution, from the late ninth century.[5]

The B5 strap-ends have been classified into three sub-types according to the decorative details: the B5–1 features 'free-rings', the B5–2 has 'ring-chain', and B5–3 is decorated with simple braid (Figure III.1). The ring device employed within the interlace of the B5–1 and B5–2 sub-types was a Scandinavian introduction. All three interlace types also occur among the Class F group of strap-ends introduced to Northumbria from Ireland, which provided the inspiration for the B5–1 sub-type.[6] The distinctive interlace on the B5–1 strap-ends is almost identical on each example, and while there are none from Aldwark or Torksey several of the twelve examples of this type known from England are from sites with a Great Army link, including Fishergate, Cottam, and other northern sites.[7] James Graham-Campbell concluded that the B5–1 must have been made in a northern English milieu under Scandinavian influence.[8] We

4. Haldenby *et al.* 2022
5. Haldenby *et al.* 2022, 104–6; Bailey 1993; Thomas 2000a, 149
6. Bailey 1980, 71–2
7. Haldenby *et al.* 2022, 100–3; since this paper was published a new example has been reported from Cave (East Yorkshire)
8. Graham-Campbell 1980, 52–3, no. 187

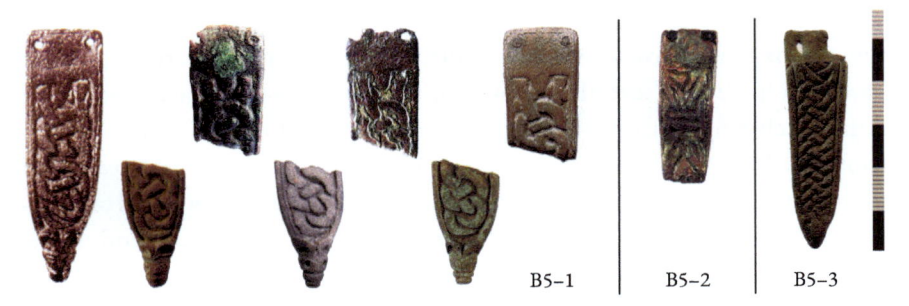

Figure III.1. Examples of Type B5 strap-ends. Sub-type B5–1 (left to right, top): Aggersborg (Graham-Campbell 1980); YORYM-04F067; NCL-190500; YORYM-635EE3; (bottom): YORYM-4F55E0; LIN-DDEA45; YORYM-0219E8; sub-type B5–2: YORYM-482EE5; B5–3: YORYM-B001D5

have seen that casting of E3 strap-ends was undertaken at Aldwark, and the B5–1 sub-types may have been made a few years later in York.

Remarkably, eleven of the twelve B5–1 strap-ends are broken diagonally along the same deep transverse groove in the interlace, strongly suggesting a design weakness in an early casting experiment, leading to a very limited period of usage. The only complete B5–1 strap-end known was found in a late ninth- or tenth-century context during excavations of the Viking fortress at Aggersborg, in northern Jutland in 1945–54, where it may have been taken as part of the military belt fittings of a returning member of the Great Army.[9]

Plate-headed pins also emerged during the transition to Scandinavian settlement, a decade or a little more beyond the arrival of the Great Army in Northumbria in 866. Evidence for this comes from Cottam where more plate-headed pins have been found than anywhere else, including York which has produced twelve.[10] They were in contemporary usage with A1avii and B5–1 strap-ends and have a clear northern focus. All three categories belong to a suite of distinctive dress accessories produced in large numbers in workshops under new Viking control, following the capture and occupation of York. We also suggest that, in common with the strap-ends, these pins were cast, their two-dimensional shape facilitating speedy pouring into simple one-piece moulds and finishing by filing and decorative drilling.

When we look at the wider metal-detected assemblages recovered from sites with elements of the Great Army signature this reveals several which are not abandoned when the Army departs but where we have evidence for tenth-century

9. Roesdahl *et al.* 2014, 285–6
10. Haldenby and Richards 2016, section 4.3; Haldenby *et al.* 2022, 106–8

finds associated with permanent settlement.[11] These also include some distinctive Scandinavian or Anglo-Scandinavian artefact types which are not found on the camps and denote later activity. These include copper-alloy hexagonal bells, often stamped with ring-and-dot decoration, as well as lead- and copper-alloy disc brooches decorated according to Scandinavian tastes.

Cottam is one of a small number of these sites which was originally discovered by metal-detecting but has subsequently been subjected to archaeological excavation and survey (Figure III.2).[12] It has been extensively discussed elsewhere, but it is important to what follows in Chapter 7 to rehearse a few key aspects of its development as it provides an example of settlement trajectory. Over 850 Anglo-Saxon and Viking artefacts have now been recovered from Cottam; they have all been geospatially located meaning that the horizontal stratigraphy of the site is well understood, charting its development across the landscape. The settlement originates in the south of the site where a subrectangular 'Butterwick'-type enclosure indicates the location of an eighth-century estate centre which had acquired a market function by the ninth century. This was abandoned in the late ninth century followed by two phases of Viking activity to the north: an initial period with traces of looting, probably linked to activity by a group derived from the Great Army, followed by the establishment of a settlement with evidence of later Scandinavian influences.[13]

This captures the moment of a critical transition in Viking behaviour in England, from raiding to settlement, and was the first time that the activity of a Viking raiding party has been identified at a rural site. The initial phase of looting was characterised by a wide distribution of artefacts, beyond the later settlement area. The assemblage associated with this phase comprises many of the categories of object identified at Aldwark and Torksey: bullion and metal processing related finds, including melts of silver, a pecked sceat of Eadberht (737–58), a broken silver penny of Æthelberht of Wessex (c.858–65), lead weights, two balance beam fragments, crudely broken fragments of Anglo-Saxon metalwork, two spearheads, and a sword guard.[14] The case for this representing looting and processing rather than settlement rests upon several factors. Firstly, the assemblage mirrors those found at the camps, albeit in microcosm. It has a military character, but also reflects the melting down of objects, including non-local items. Trade may also have been involved, and those items which

11. Richards and Haldenby 2018
12. Richards 1999; 2013; Haldenby and Richards 2016
13. Haldenby and Richards 2016
14. Haldenby and Richards 2016, section 4.4.1; the sword guard was found after the publication of this paper.

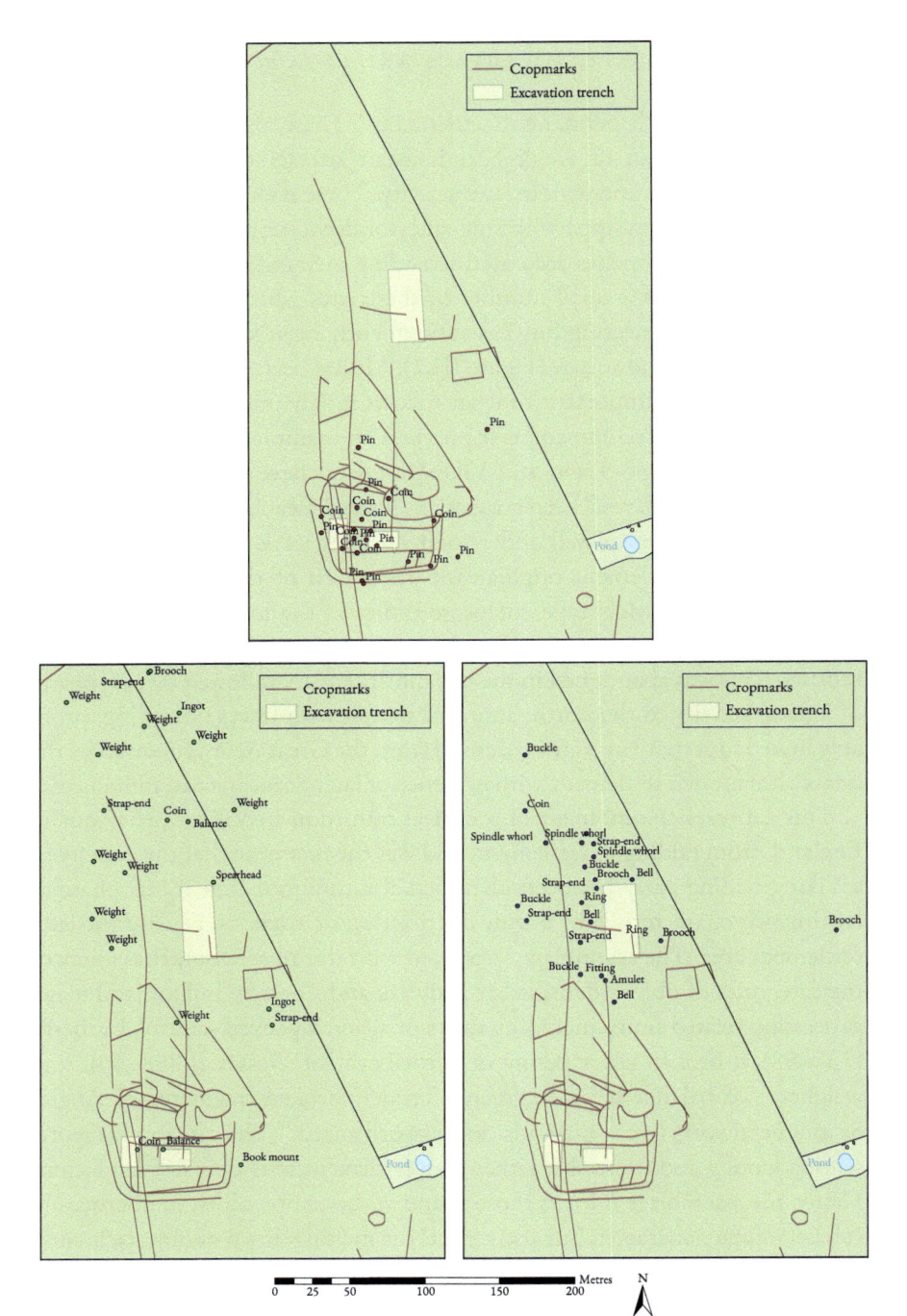

Figure III.2. Plans of Cottam showing crop-marks of Butterwick-type enclosure in the south and distribution of metal-detected finds: (top) eighth-century coins and artefacts; (bottom left) Great Army signature finds; (bottom right) early tenth-century settlement (authors)

reflect bullion transactions may indicate exchange in archaeologically intangible goods, such as slaves, as well as precious metals, as in the camps. Secondly, the lack of any settlement traces within the wide area from which the metalwork has been recovered, despite extensive geophysical survey and fieldwalking, is itself significant. It indicates temporary occupation, again as seen in the camps, rather than permanent settlement. Thirdly, the fact that the abandonment of the Anglo-Saxon site can be dated to the same moment confirms that this was not peaceful coexistence. By contrast, in the subsequent phase a new settlement was established, with a more compact distribution of finds focused on the settlement area, as reflected in the geophysics and a concentration of sherds of Torksey ware recovered during fieldwalking. The metalwork was of a domestic nature, including buckles, brooches, and rings in Anglo-Scandinavian style, copper-alloy bells, and lead spindle whorls, reflecting that they belong to a second phase of activity.[15] This can be seen to correspond to what the *Anglo-Saxon Chronicle* describes as one of the great land partitions between members of the Great Army when that group under Healfdene returned north and 'seized the land of the Northumbrians and proceeded to plough and to support themselves'.[16]

Cottam therefore provides an example of a Great Army signature in microcosm, but also has traces of an artefact signature for what happened next, when elements of the Army settled. It is possible to apply these signatures to areas of the country known to have been visited by the Army in order to identify its archaeological traces and the places it, and its offshoots, may have visited. There are relatively small numbers of relevant excavated sites, but for England the PAS provides an invaluable resource in the search for artefact assemblages, despite the database being subject to a number of limitations and biases.[17] These include the lack of evidence from urban areas (which includes many of the known camps), as well as the relative paucity of detected finds in north-east England, including the Northumbrian sub-kingdom of Bernicia.[18] Other difficulties in using PAS data include the fact that some of the categories of finds have hitherto been unrecognised by both the detectorists and the Finds Liaison Officers. These include the lead gaming pieces, which are also often unassigned to a period. Other artefact types, such as weaponry, including iron axes, spears, and swords, were no doubt common possessions amongst members of the Great Army, and have been recovered from the camps, but they are underrepresented on the PAS given that metal detectorists generally ignore the iron

15. Haldenby and Richards 2016, section 4.4.2
16. Whitelock 1961, 48
17. Richards *et al.* 2009, section 2.6
18. Richards and Naylor 2012, 135–9

finds. Yet, while there are some notable limitations with PAS data, many areas of eastern Yorkshire, Lincolnshire, and East Anglia, which were later subject to longer-term Scandinavian settlement, are ploughed agricultural land today and are well served by the PAS.

The analysis in Chapter 7 is therefore based in part on the artefacts recorded on the PAS, but incorporating recording by Dave Haldenby of material from East Yorkshire accessioned by Hull Museum, and re-categorisation of some previously misidentified material. For East Anglia, the impact of the Great Army has received less attention in part because metal-detected data reported prior to the advent of the PAS has not routinely been subsequently added to that database, unlike practice in regions further north. Relevant information therefore has been acquired from reports to the county-based Historic Environment Records, and annual reports on archaeological finds to local journals such as *Norfolk Archaeology* and the Proceedings of the *Suffolk Institute of Archaeology and History*.

Although the numbers of finds may be small in comparison to the camps, these sites have been subject to variable levels of survey, lacking the sustained level of metal-detecting to which Aldwark and Torksey have been subjected. The assemblages reflect a range of settlement histories: some Anglo-Saxon sites yield a few Viking finds, and were then apparently abandoned; others have evidence for longer-term Scandinavian settlement; and in some cases there is no clear evidence for pre-existing settlement where Viking finds are recovered, although they may neighbour Anglo-Saxon sites. It should also be noted that many of the finds have been recovered from a broad area, and may reflect several concentrations of activity, relating to repeated visits by members of the Army to the locality.

In Chapter 8 we turn from the countryside to the towns and to explore the impact of the Great Army on the development of industry. The diversity of activities at Torksey and Aldwark combined with the immense scale of these camps, larger than most contemporary urban centres, suggest that the Army was virtually a town on the move.[19] It is hardly surprising, then, that it should have a major impact on the socio-economic development of ninth-century England. The Army was a major catalyst for urban growth, especially through the introduction of continental craftworkers, including metalworkers, moneyers, and potters. While urban growth continued across the tenth and eleventh

19. Williams 2015, 116

centuries, the earliest evidence for urban development in northern and eastern England is largely in the areas of activity of the Army. Torksey has provided an opportunity to explore this issue in detail for the first time, as both the Army's camp and a large part of the town of the ensuing decades are unencumbered by later development. The urban status of Torksey by the tenth century is reflected in evidence for five cemeteries and at least thirty-five pottery kilns. The pottery industry emerged in the immediate wake of the overwintering, evidently involving the arrival of potters from the Continent. Chapter 8 extends our analysis of the Torksey industry to the other wheel-thrown wares introduced in eastern England in the late ninth and early tenth centuries, proposing that the Army provided the catalyst for this. It has been more than a decade since such a review was undertaken, but many of the industries discussed in Chapter 8 were not included, and new dating evidence has since emerged, along with new analyses of the products of the industries. As with Chapter 7 we have undertaken new research using online digital resources, in particular the unpublished fieldwork reports and archives which have now been made available for several of the towns where the new industries emerged. For example, for Ipswich we have made extensive use of the 1974–90 excavation archive covering thirty-four sites, and for Lincoln we have drawn upon reports from the Alan Vince Archive.[20] We have also extended our analysis of Torksey ware and its daughter industries to study the manufacturing methods employed for other wares.[21]

20. Suffolk County Council Archaeological Service (SCCAS) 2020; Medieval Pottery Research Group 2010
21. Perry 2016; 2019

7

Beyond the camps

This chapter explores the impact of the Great Army on the countryside, setting the evidence from the camps in its wider context. The artefactual signature identified at Torksey and Aldwark can be used to trace the presence of the Army and its offshoots at many rural settlements in eastern and northern England. In the light of our analysis, we can now go beyond those items previously assigned to the agency of the Great Army—including hack-metal, dirhams, lead and copper-alloy weights, and lead gaming pieces—to include a wider range of material culture that we have now identified as characteristic of the Army, including dress accessories that were produced in the camps and items with a short-lived circulation (discussed in the Part III Introduction). The chapter also considers other items 'out of place' or 'out of time' which, when found in combination with more characteristic signature material culture, are likely to have been introduced by the Army. We can also use metal-detected evidence to identify settlements with plentiful Middle Saxon activity that seem to be abandoned in the later ninth century, which may also relate to the disruptions created by the Army and the ensuing Scandinavian settlement. As we will see, the sites discussed are overwhelmingly in those regions where the *Anglo-Saxon Chronicle* records that the Great Army was active, albeit that they are not named. Some of these are concentrated in areas where overwintering is documented but the precise location of the camp has not previously been identified. This archaeological evidence therefore enables us to explore the impact of the Great Army far beyond the reaches of the written sources. It must reflect a range of activities, including looting and foraging, and since the Army routinely made 'peace' when it camped, this would have also created opportunities for trade.[1]

---

1. McLeod 2006; 2023; Williams 2023, 50–1

Some sites visited by the Army, or its offshoots, were subsequently abandoned or restructured, while others show continuity of occupation, but there is variation in whether there are further traces of Scandinavian influence. We can also go beyond the discussion of the evidence as simply assemblages of artefacts, because in some cases the metal-detected finds have been closely plotted, such that we can relate their distribution to other settlement activity. The chapter also looks at what these settlements reveal about the routes travelled by the Great Army, by considering where they were located with respect to transport networks. In the camps we saw extensive evidence for the fragmentation of objects and in this chapter we will see how parts of the same object have been recovered many kilometres apart, demonstrating how much some items carried meaning and were highly valued, as well as how members of the Army became dispersed across large areas of England.

North of the Humber

There are numerous sites in northern England, especially in Yorkshire, where metal-detecting has yielded traces of the activities of the Great Army, many of which are along major routeways or river crossing points, and in the vicinity of Anglo-Saxon estate centres (Figure 7.1). For example, a collection of objects from Spofforth (West Yorkshire) is indicative of an Army presence. Spofforth lies on the primary land corridor (the modern A661) which runs from Wetherby to Harrogate, and onwards to Skipton. This route provides access westwards across the Pennines for those who had taken the Great North Road, or Roman Ermine Street, towards York, and would have been a major routeway for those travelling between York and Dublin. A modern causeway carries the A661 across the floodplain of the River Crimple, a minor tributary of the River Nidd. Today the Crimple is narrower and deeper, and closer to Spofforth, following modern drainage improvements, but in the ninth and tenth centuries it would have been wider, spreading out across the low-lying floodplain, and forded, as indicated by the place-name of Spofforth ('a small piece [of land] at the ford'). Spofforth was an important place in the ninth century. Excavations on the south bank of the River Crimple revealed an eighth- and ninth-century cemetery, with 141 inhumations *in situ* in graves, plus commingled remains representing as many as another 300 individuals. There were at least seventeen burials in wooden chests, with iron fittings, including locks, keys, straps, hinges, and hasps; mineralised wood revealed that the chests were made of elm.

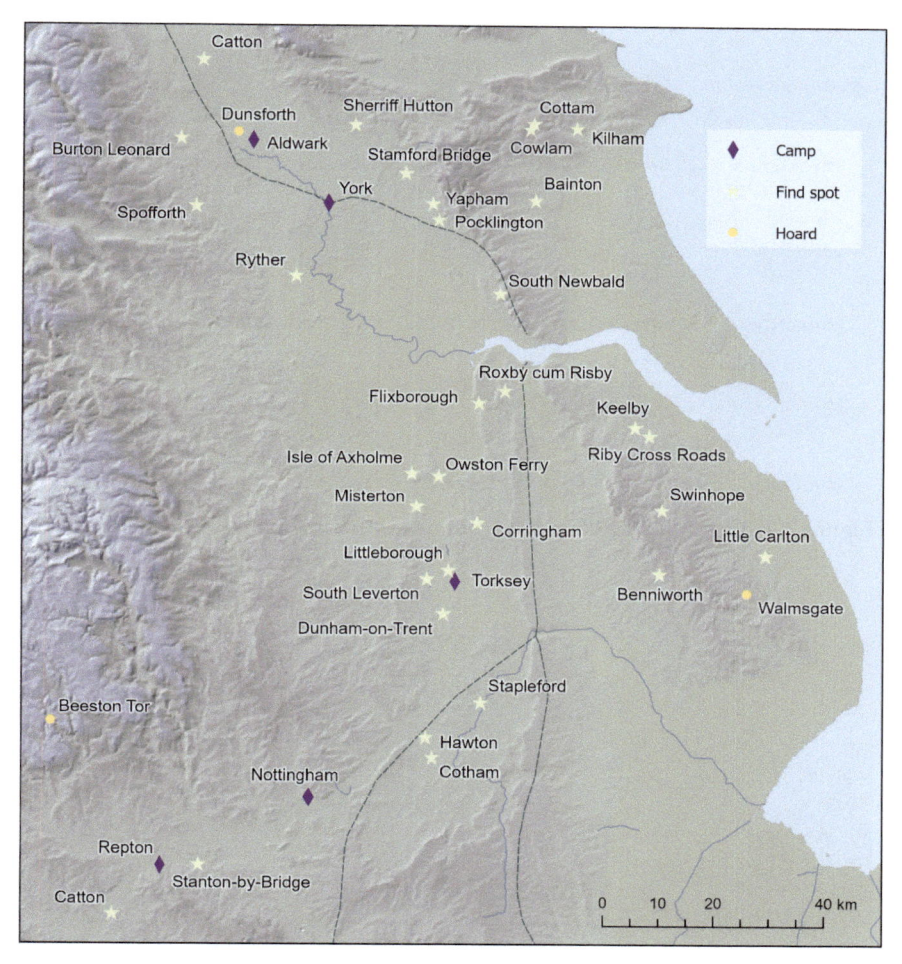

Figure 7.1. Map showing location of key sites in eastern England mentioned in the text with major rivers and Roman roads (Helen Goodchild). (Base map contains public sector information licensed under the Open Government Licence v3.0, elevation data from NASA JPL 2013, and Roman roads from McCormick *et al.* 2013)

Such grave types are typically associated with high-status churches, and traces of two stone walls and a fragment of an eighth-century stone sculpture may have come from a church.[2]

The metal-detected assemblage was found on higher ground on the opposite bank of the Crimple (Figures 7.2 and 7.3). It includes signature items that

---

2. Johnson 2002; Hadley and Richards 2020, 127

SWYOR-0D5863   SWYOR-4243E2   SWYOR-7D9846   SWYOR-3A1135   SWYOR-1FC7A8   SWYOR-1F9435

SWYOR-24F666   SWYOR-55BBB2   SWYOR-7DE7F4   SWYOR-7E3651   SWYOR-39D257   SWYOR-598651

SWYOR-515FA5   SWYOR-516A58   SWYOR-396A20   SWYOR-58AFB4   SWYOR-651B01   YORYM-A662C6

Figure 7.2. Selection of Viking finds (not to scale) from Spofforth (PAS)

Figure 7.3. View from Spofforth churchyard looking north across the Crimple valley to the finds area (authors)

can clearly be linked to the Army, including hack-silver in the form of cut fragments of both a dirham and a denier of Charles the Bald, a fragmentary strip decorated with triangular punches, probably from a bracelet, an unidentified object made from cast gilt silver, and part of a Permian-type arm-ring, suggesting a connection to southern Scandinavia.[3] Other finds include ninth-century dress accessories that reflect the range found on the camps. Some display Scandinavian influences, such as a fragment of either a Class E strap-end or the end of a trefoil brooch, a Borre-style B5–3 strap-end, and a B4a strap-end, while a fragment of an eighth- or ninth-century ansate brooch may also have arrived under Scandinavian agency. Items of typical ninth-century Anglo-Saxon types recovered include a B1 and seven Class A strap-ends, at least four polyhedral pins with ring-and-dot decoration and six biconical forms with a medial band. Over 25 stycas have also been recovered from Spofforth, and although not unusual in Northumbria around a quarter of them are late issues including derivative types.[4]

Research at Cottam has shown the importance of horizontal stratigraphy when analysing the significance of such assemblages of finds.[5] This can only be attempted where accurate plotting was undertaken and, fortunately, the metal detectorists at Spofforth plotted their finds using GPS, locating them to within a metre accuracy, which enables a detailed insight into their distribution. This reveals that the hack-silver was concentrated to the south-west of the Middle Saxon finds, where the B4a strap-end was found. At Torksey and Aldwark, the Great Army had collected together a wide range of dress accessories, particularly strap-ends and pins, that were in widespread use in the regions where they had been raiding, and so it is conceivable that some of the material arrived at Spofforth through Army agency; the pins, in particular, show the same selectivity as the assemblages from the camps, with a focus on the more decorative types. However, in the light of the distribution pattern, and taking account of the presence of earlier coins, including two seventh-century gold thrymsas, possibly from a hoard, and four eighth-century silver sceattas, it seems likely that this was an area of long-standing Middle Saxon settlement that experienced a visit by an offshoot of the Great Army. There is also some evidence for

3. SWYOR-58AFB4, -55BBB2, -651B01, -598651; EMC 2012.0049; Horne 2022, 186
4. YORYM-E555D1, -FAB89C, -868EC4, -CCCB09, -2DB58D, -C215DD, -C1F24B, -AF561F, -EA9B13, -2767A3, -26E8A4, -C63C81, -22EABC, -22F8D5, -252389; SWYOR-396A20, -D2BB11, -D2B28A, -7E3651, -7DE7F4, -7D9846, -3A1135, -39D257, -92B7D1, -929EF1, -BBC816, -1FC7A8, -697FF9; -69735C, -690BBB, -5141D8, -24F666
5. Haldenby and Richards 2016

later Scandinavian influences on material culture, including a D-shaped Borre-style buckle with animal heads similar to examples from Cottam, a silver ring with a bezel decorated with plain and twisted pairs of wires and with overlapping tapered ends to the hoop, typical of Viking-age Scandinavian types, and a tenth-century copper-alloy convex disc brooch decorated with Borre-style knotwork, and a loop on the reverse distinctive of Scandinavian origins.[6] A kite-headed pin of Irish type is also likely to be a Scandinavian introduction of the tenth century.[7] Furthermore, a fragment of a tenth-century cross-shaft from the medieval parish church of Spofforth is decorated with interlace pattern that 'shows clear Hiberno-Norse influence', also found on Scandinavian sculptures from the Isle of Man.[8] This case study suggests that activity consistent with the presence of members of the Great Army can be found in a clustered area at the edges of an existing Middle Saxon settlement focus, and that subsequent Scandinavian influences can be found over the following decades.

In the area around the Army's camp at Aldwark, there are a few other indicators of its impact, including the hoard of the mid-870s from Lower Dunsforth mentioned in Chapter 2. A further 14km to the west beyond the Roman road now represented by the A1 is a concentration of signature finds from Burton Leonard, including three gaming pieces, a dirham fragment, and a silver-plated copper-alloy finger-ring with a knotted band, and decorated with triangles containing dots.[9] Some 20km north-west of Aldwark, near Catton, another group of signature finds has been recovered, including a cubo-octahedral weight, several lead gaming pieces or conical weights, a piece of hack-gold, and an Irish penannular brooch, with a Type N sword pommel (dated 850–900) found nearby.[10] A lead Class E strap-end may have been a casting model as the single pierced hole does not go all the way through the butt, suggesting it was not a wearable fitting.[11] Other assemblages suggest places visited by the Army as it reconnoitred south of York. For example, from Ryther, at a bend on the River Wharfe close to where it joins the Ouse, there are at least four gaming pieces, and a fragment of eighth-century chip-carved and openwork gilded copper-alloy jewellery (Figure 7.4).[12] The location may have had a strategic importance;

6. SWYOR-4243E2; YORYM-A662C6; Ager 2006b; Kershaw 2013, 24–5, 162–70
7. SWYOR-0D5863
8. Coatsworth 2008, 49, 250–1
9. SWYOR-4BBF91, -4BAE58, -8B5D84, -E07258, -380021
10. SWYOR-D4E270, 2023 T85, SWYOR-5F58DD; Amy Downes pers. comm.
11. SWYOR-ACB11D
12. NLM-889AE0 and other gaming pieces recorded by Leahy; jewellery reported by Haldenby; Hadley and Richards 2018, 14

Figure 7.4. Ryther, with All Saints' church, and River Wharfe behind the tree line (authors)

at that point the Wharfe is tidal and Ryther is also close to the crossing point of the Ouse at Cawood. John Naylor has suggested that the number of Middle Saxon coins recovered makes it likely that Ryther was a stopping place for ships moving up the Humber and which acted as a periodic market or toll stop.[13] A broad range of Anglo-Scandinavian brooches and strap-ends, an early tenth-century dirham, a copper-alloy bell, and a spindle whorl indicate longer term settlement and by the eleventh century Ryther had acquired a church.[14]

In contrast, most Middle Saxon sites identified by metal-detecting in East Yorkshire appear to have been abandoned in the late ninth century. Many of these sites have yielded a small proportion of finds similar to those from the camps which suggest visits by elements of the Great Army, either as part of raiding or trading activity, or possibly as reconnaissance, and then nothing of later date.[15] Several are located on the Yorkshire Wolds in the vicinity of the Anglo-Saxon royal estate centre at Driffield: Bainton, a recently discovered site 9km south-west of Driffield, with three weights, a gold ingot fragment, two gaming pieces, two A1avii strap-ends, and two plate-headed pins;[16] Cowlam,

---

13. Naylor 2001, 86
14. NLM-587C1B, -47636B, -468AF9, SWYOR-148082; other items recorded by Haldenby
15. Richards and Haldenby 2018
16. YORYM-E7CE31, -944777, -AB5949, -72A2EB, -33E477, -66698A; NLM-E33865; weights recorded by Haldenby; Loveluck 1996

1km west of Cottam, with two gaming pieces, one weight, a fragment of a silver ingot, and one B4a, one A1avii, and three E3 strap-ends;[17] and Kilham, with three gaming pieces.[18] Other sites follow the line of the Roman road from the Humber crossing up to York. They include South Newbald, with four gaming pieces, two weights, one of which was inset with a styca, a bun-shaped silver ingot, seven plate-headed pins, and both an A1avii and B4a strap-end.[19] A newly recorded site known as 'near Pocklington' has produced seven gaming pieces, seventeen lead weights (one inset with a Roman potsherd), a fragment of a beam and an arm from two different balances, three A1avii and at least three E3 strap-ends and one B5 form, although the sub-type could not be identified (Figure 7.5). The 'near Pocklington' site also has evidence for the processing of

NLM-5EBDCC   NLM-70A894   NLM-72B9D3   NLM-718F51   NLM-82E21D   NLM-859A8D

NLM-198B34   NLM-19B714   NLM-1A544B   NLM-1B0F96   NLM-B1DBCD   NLM-03547D

Figure 7.5. Selection of finds (not to scale) from the site known as 'near Pocklington' (PAS)

17. Richards 2013; two gaming pieces recorded by Haldenby; YORYM-9A0961 (but with incorrect spatial information on PAS); FAKL-284426; Thomas 2000a, 398
18. FAKL-CED235, -CEFD68, -CEE182
19. Hull Museum KINCM 2000.86.282, 1991.74.782.1, 1991.74.782.2; two gaming pieces recorded by Haldenby; Williams 1999, 26; Haldenby *et al.* 2022, 114–15

decorative metalwork, including a cut piece of an eighth-century chip-carved pin, the terminal of a penannular brooch which had been refashioned into the head of a pin, half of an Irish cross-shaped mount, a roughly torn copper-alloy mount, and a Carolingian strap-slide.[20] Taken as a whole, the evidence suggests disruption to settlement patterns and reorganisation when the Great Army was active in the region. We listed some of these sites in two papers published in 2018, and new material reported to the PAS since then has continued to reinforce the picture of late ninth-century settlement disruption.[21]

Elsewhere in East Yorkshire, there is evidence for settlement continuity but with a shift in focus in the late ninth century, with the associated material culture suggesting that the impact of the Great Army was a key factor. Two examples from Stamford Bridge and Yapham serve to demonstrate this process. Stamford Bridge is located at the point where the east–west Roman road from York to Bridlington crosses the River Derwent and intersects with a second Roman road running north-west from the Humber crossing at Brough, before continuing north-east to Malton. Nearby, there are two metal-detected sites c.2km apart that reveal contrasting late ninth-century trajectories. Helpfully the same metal detectorist has surveyed both areas, plotting the finds closely, and this enables detailed and reliable comparisons to be generated. Over eighty Middle Saxon artefacts have been recovered from Stamford Bridge 1, with just six that may reflect Scandinavian activity, including part of a chain from a balance and two silver ingots.[22]

To the north-east, in contrast, there is a very different artefactual signature at the site known both as Stamford Bridge 2 and 'Skirpenbeck'. Here just two Middle Saxon items have been recovered, but there are over sixty objects of later date, some of which can be associated with the Great Army, while others indicate Scandinavian influence extending into the tenth century (Figure 7.6). The finds include silver ingots and hack-silver, part of a balance chain, fragments of a Louis the Pious denier and a dirham, seventeen lead weights, one inset with a styca and another with a fragment of glass, and a copper-alloy and iron oblate-spheroid weight, while a silver Thor's hammer was found across

20. Pers. comm. Haldenby and NLM-8637A7, -859A8D, -852DC2, -84CB51, -8469C2, -842F7A, -82E21D, 832199, -829093, -73FEB5, -73C9B2, -7379C1, -72B9D3, -727EDD, -71D29D, -718F51, -70A894, -5EF567, -5EBDCC, -5E922F, -5CA734, -5C5EC1, -5B8397, -5B691E, -03547D, -E06618, -B1DBCD, -19B714, -34452F, -01FF5A, -DF6ED2, -1B0F96, -19B714, -198B34, -DCBC8C, -34D829, -3479F7, -1A544B
21. Hadley and Richards 2018; Richards and Haldenby 2018
22. Richards and Haldenby 2018, 330, 332; Hadley and Richards 2018, 13

LVPL-5E4310   YORYM-6AD518   YORYM-6AE013   YORYM-6AC476   YORYM-01F154   YORYM-01F580

YORYM-6BA7B5   YORYM-6B45F7   YORYM-37FD30   YORYM-01C134   YORYM-FD78D5   YORYM-81FB8D   YORYM-9526A2

Figure 7.6. Selection of Viking finds (not to scale) from Stamford Bridge 2 (LVPL-5E4310 Gary Johnson; all others PAS)

the Derwent in Buttercrambe.[23] There is a wide range of strap-ends, including a notable concentration of types we now know to have been present on the camps, and in some cases introduced in the wake of the arrival of the Great Army. These comprise four B5 strap-ends, including one of the B5–1 forms with a characteristic diagonal break, four B4a styles and an E4.[24] The landscape of Stamford Bridge 2 would have been distinctive, with Bronze Age barrow burials strung along the south banks of the Derwent and its tributary the Skirpen Beck. While many of these have been ploughed out and are only identifiable from aerial photography, recent survey of a surviving mound in woodland on a cliff above the Derwent revealed that the barrow had been constructed in two phases.[25] The date of this re-use is conjectural without excavation, and while this could have been in the seventh century, the paucity of material culture of this date from the immediate vicinity, may make Scandinavian re-use for mound burial more likely. There are well-known instances of Scandinavian re-use of prehistoric burial mounds elsewhere, such as at Claughton Hall (Lancashire), while there were Bronze Age barrows reported in the area of the Scandinavian mound burial at Hesket-in-the-Forest (Cumbria).[26] The evidence

23. LVPL-4AA178, -5E4310; YORYM-FD78D5, -9526A2, -FAE529, -3BAF25, -6B45F7, -6AD518, -6AE013, -6B0A11, -37FD30, -6AC476, -37F393, -6B45F7, -83BB55, -37DC91, -6BA7B5, -01C134, -01F580, -01F154; -81FB8D (EMC 2020.0137)
24. YORYM-4855E8, -0219E8, -0210C2, -482EE5, -14F920, -4FD9F3, -4872F1 -4846D6, -484DA8, -4877E3, -485AA7
25. Jamieson and Pearson 2021, 31–2
26. Redmond 2007, 102–4, Appendix 6

Figure 7.7. The landscape of Yapham 2 in an area not perpetuated by subsequent settlement (authors)

from the two Stamford Bridge sites indicates that there was settlement disruption, but that the new site to the north-east of the river crossing continued into the eleventh century, with ongoing Scandinavian influences.

Yapham is located 4km to the north of the major estate centre of Pocklington, and was within its extensive late medieval parish, suggesting a long-standing connection (Figure 7.7).[27] A Middle Saxon settlement at Yapham 1 came to an end in the later ninth century with the two latest artefacts comprising half a silver penny of Burgred of Mercia, and a gold strip.[28] However, around 1km to the north-east is a second metal-detected site known as Yapham 2, where the material recovered is very different, with proportionately more Scandinavian influences. These include twelve lead weights, at least one of which had previously been inset, two gaming pieces, a terminal from an eighth- or ninth-century Irish penannular brooch, and at least three pieces of bullion, including a fragment of a silver ingot, a gold finger-ring, decorated with two rows of punched triangles each containing a single pellet, and a fragment of a silver one, decorated with small, punched triangles. Other finds include ten lead spindle whorls and a range of Anglo-Scandinavian jewellery, including single examples of E4, B4a, and A1avii strap-ends, and an Irish kite-headed pin (Figure 7.8).[29]

27. Pickle 2018, 150–1, 155
28. YORYM-90AE41, -9133BA
29. YORYM-29D955, -C2F885, -C2F130, -06B5C2, -6056B7, -F0F231, -1B2DA6, -AF4626, -669BF4, -1C9562; Haldenby *et al.* 2022, 114, n. 5

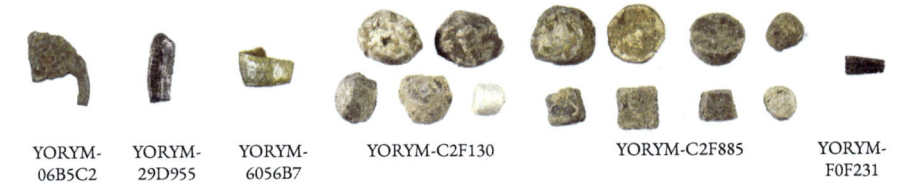

| YORYM-06B5C2 | YORYM-29D955 | YORYM-6056B7 | YORYM-C2F130 | YORYM-C2F885 | YORYM-F0F231 |

Figure 7.8. Selection of finds (not to scale) from Yapham 2 (PAS)

Yapham 2 is located at the convergence of the boundaries of three parishes, and seems to reflect activity at a newly occupied site that may have persisted into the early tenth century but not beyond. The contrast with the site known as 'near Pocklington' is striking, and it shows that even within the single estate of Pocklington the Army had differing impacts.

Lincolnshire Wolds

In the Lincolnshire Wolds there is a range of evidence to demonstrate the impact of the Great Army, which rather like the picture from East Yorkshire, is varied. The neighbouring parishes of Swinhope and Binbrook have yielded more than 120 eighth- to tenth-century metal artefacts, among which are over thirty that are characteristic of material associated with the Great Army (Figure 7.9). These include a gold finger-ring, a silver ingot, ten lead weights, including one of the inset variety, and an offcut from a copper-alloy strap-end with iron spots on the reverse suggesting that it had been used as an inset, six gaming pieces, and two dirham fragments, dated 786–809 and 788–807, respectively.[30] Three continental ansate brooches, nine E3, an E4 and a Class F strap-end, a Borre-style mount and three stycas may also be linked to the Army.[31] Two mid-ninth-century West Saxon coins, one of Ecgberht (c. 828–39) and another of Æthelwulf (839–58), are outside of the areas where they are mainly found.[32] The majority of finds have been recovered from sloping ground looking across the valley to Swinhope, where a Neolithic long barrow

30. NLM-1A2DAC, -066A5C, -EB13E1, -67EA51, -973C42, -736B77, -FAFB63, -FB2018, -81457A, -59445A, -5BA62D, -C17F91, -CE80A5, -1E65F2, -B35042, -7AD374, -7ABE36, -17F496, -1802C4, -D59E66, -7127, -1F77A8, -E3F860, -E3890A, -8B46D9, -8B32B0, -FC835D, -76B7C9, -878FB7
31. NLM-2063B4, -83A75F, -76B7C9, -D16E7E, -16D3F5, -22DA08, -A30415, -DED022, -DD1F31; SUR-7EA696; EMC 1999.0053
32. NLM-FAF1BF, -668B5B

NLM-CE80A5 NLM-FB2018 NLM-81457A NLM-973C42 NLM-5BA62D NLM-736B77

NLM-7ABE36 NLM-7AD374 NLM-B35042 NLM-C17F91 NLM-FAFB63 NLM-59445A

NLM-2D13CF NLM-33E8D7 NLM-C52D45 NLM-6309B5 NLM-1802C4 NLM-17F496

NLM-67EA51 NLM-1F77A8 NLM-16D3F5 NLM-07B302 NLM-66E8F9 NLM-22CFC7

NLM-DE19D1 NLM-AD60CD NLM-76B7C9 NLM-4DAF0B NLM-06A882 NLM-BBCAC5

Figure 7.9. Selection of finds (not to scale) from Swinhope and Binbrook (PAS)

was re-used for the burial of an adult female and a juvenile in the later Anglo-Saxon period. There were no accompanying artefacts, and the radiocarbon date range (published as AD 885–1010 at the 68% confidence level) is very broad, but it is intriguing that these irregular burials occur in a locale with a concentration of Viking finds.[33] We can also trace later Scandinavian influence, in the form of a swordless St Peter's coin minted in York under Scandinavian agency after 905, a St Edmund coin, and a Scandinavian copy of a coin of Edward the Elder, perhaps minted in Lincoln. There is also a die for producing filigree pendants, of the tenth-century Hiddensee-Rügen type, similar to examples from Hedeby and Trelleborg (Denmark), and ninth- and tenth-century jewellery,

33. Phillips 1989, 32–4; Hadley and Richards 2020, 122–3

bridle fittings, and dress accessories displaying Scandinavian influence.[34] There seems to have been widespread Middle Saxon activity that saw the influence of the Great Army in the same broad areas and continuity of activity into the tenth century, with some ongoing Scandinavian influences through material culture arriving from other areas of Scandinavian settlement.

At the north end of the Wolds on the prehistoric routeway now known as Barton Street is Riby Cross Roads, where excavation of a pipeline in the early 1990s revealed a settlement occupied from the seventh to mid-ninth centuries, at which point both pottery and metalwork petered out.[35] Metal-detecting has since recovered several signature finds, including three gaming pieces, three fragmentary ninth-century strap-ends, a deliberately cut brooch or mount, an Irish mount, a ringed pin, and a solitary Northumbrian styca, out of place south of the Humber.[36] A fragment of a tri-lobed mount is identical to one from Torksey, some 50km to the south-west.[37] The PAS database also reveals a site that seems to have been abandoned at the same time, around a kilometre to the north 'near Keelby', where metal-detecting has recovered over 100 mainly Middle Saxon artefacts, and very little that could be securely dated to the late ninth or tenth century, although a gaming piece stands out.[38] Similarly, six lead gaming pieces have been recovered from the Middle Saxon site at Benniworth, on the western edge of the Wolds, which has otherwise produced nothing of later date.[39] Thus, once again the demise of a settlement corresponds with the appearance of artefacts associated with the Great Army.

In the coastal marshes to the east of the southern end of the Wolds, the high-status site of Little Carlton seems to have been abandoned at the end of the ninth century. It has produced over 700 late seventh- to late ninth-century metal artefacts, and whilst there is nothing that clearly indicates a visit from the Great Army there are very few traces of any activity after the late ninth century, with the latest coin being one of Burgred from the early 870s.[40] As noted in Chapter 2, the only hoard dating to the early 870s known from Lincolnshire was found at Walmsgate on the Wolds close to Barton Street, providing another probable indication of disturbances in this period. In the Lincolnshire Wolds,

34. NLM-08D897, -0A69E7, -74E2E4, -07B302, -690F57; Kershaw 2013, 113
35. Steedman 1994
36. NLM-948453, -94576D, -944778, -8E45DA, -8E3969, -8E22A7; LIN-B8FA61, -4997F4, -134231, -68709F
37. LIN-939104; T115
38. NLM-1C5EE7
39. LIN-A61F45, -A6173D, -0EA63B, -5C189A, -5AC4F3, -5A4C35
40. Daubney 2016, 249–68; Willmott and Daubney 2019

therefore, there are a range of settlement trajectories. Like Yorkshire, some sites were apparently abandoned in the late ninth century, which may be the result of wider disruption caused by the Great Army, particularly to high-status sites where Anglo-Saxon lords may have been deposed, but other sites continued in use with evidence for Scandinavian influence in the tenth century.

The Trent valley

Excavations at Flixborough between 1989 and 1991 revealed a settlement occupied from the seventh to the eleventh centuries, but with late ninth-century disruption. This enables us to put metal-detected data from the vicinity in context. In the ninth century the settlement was characterised by extensive craftworking, including production of fine textiles at a scale that has been interpreted as being intended for trade, with the preponderance of mature sheep bones reflecting a focus on wool production. Lead-working emerges at this time, suggesting import of raw materials, probably from the ores of the Derbyshire Peak District, and in the first half of the century pottery was arriving from long distances, principally Ipswich. Together this suggested 'increasing integration within regional and inter-regional exchange networks, between the early and middle decades of the ninth century', in a period when the settlement was also characterised by a literate element. However, at the end of the ninth century the buildings were reorganised, there was reduction in the range of craftworking activity, and disappearance of evidence for inter-regional links, suggesting that 'the inhabitants of the settlement were not able to manage domesticated animal resources on the level of earlier decades of the century...the scale of production was much diminished'. The site report suggested that this reflected estate reorganisation, but the impact of Viking raiders was little discussed given limited evidence for any Scandinavian influence on the material culture from Flixborough.[41]

By contrast, the PAS reveals a concentration of material culture indicative of the Great Army in the neighbouring parish of Roxby cum Risby, which has been a focus of intensive metal-detecting activity, with good GPS geospatial data. This reveals that signature finds were largely found close to the Flixborough parish boundary, including two cubo-octahedral weights, three discoid weights,

41. Loveluck 2007, 154–7

NLM-EBA6E3   NLM-A27134   NLM-296817   NLM-588554   NLM-602494   NLM-683755

NLM-C995EB   NLM-C7BB75   NLM-CF5995   NLM-92AFEC   NLM-C6EB24   NLM-124D04

Figure 7.10. Selection of finds (not to scale) from Roxby cum Risby (PAS)

a lead weight with a copper-alloy inset, a silver ingot, a gaming piece, a ninth-century Irish mount, a Thor's hammer, a B5–3 strap-end, and a range of metal-working debris (Figure 7.10).[42] Related finds have been recovered more widely across the parish including five more lead weights, one inset with a fragment of gilt eighth-century metalwork.[43] A single Cross-and-Lozenge coin of Alfred is of a type now known to have been in the hands of the Army from 186 examples in the Watlington hoard.[44] Continuing Scandinavian presence in the area is reflected in Scandinavian place-names, including both Roxby and Risby, and an array of artefacts with Scandinavian stylistic influences, including brooches, rings, bridle fittings, buckles, and a copper-alloy bell.[45] The Great Army's activity in the Roxby area seems to have paved the way for long-lasting Scandinavian settlement. Yet at Flixborough, there are no such tenth-century Scandinavian artefacts, and following the evident late ninth-century disruption the settlement continued uninterrupted into the tenth century, when the largest buildings were constructed; this reveals how diverse the impact of the Great Army was, even within the space of a little over a kilometre.[46]

Many other sites along the Trent have elements of the Great Army signature, reflecting the use of the river as a major routeway. Most of these have seen only limited metal-detecting and therefore the assemblages of relevant material are small, largely restricted to weights, gaming pieces, and occasional pieces of

42. NLM-A27134, -EBA6E3, -602494, -296817, -683755, -CF5995, -92AFEC, -DA7151, -C6EB24, -4F524A, -E2D945, -572335, -ADFA0B
43. NLM-588554, -C995EB, -C7BB75, -605A12, -4F524A, -572335
44. NLM-124D04; Williams and Naylor 2016
45. Leonard 2015, 104–79; Schoenfelder and Richards 2011
46. Loveluck 2007, 155; Loveluck and Atkinson 2007, 97–107

hack-metal and ingots. We surveyed these sites in a recent paper and there is little more to be added to what was reported there, but it is notable that the strap-end types that we have since identified as being innovations in the wake of the Great Army's arrival have also been found at these places. Examples include a concentration at Haxey on the Isle of Axholme, including four lead and one oblate-spheroid weights, a gaming piece, and a mid-ninth-century East Anglian penny, and from where B5–3, E3, and E4 strap-ends have been recovered. Other notable assemblages include: two gaming pieces and a weight from Laughton, which is close to a crossing point from the Isle of Axholme over the Trent at Owston Ferry; an inset weight, a copper-alloy oblate-spheroid weight, over twenty gaming pieces, two fragmentary copper-alloy ingots, and both copper-alloy and silver metalworking debris from the neighbouring parishes of Corringham and Blyton; and a cubo-octahedral weight from Misterton (Nottinghamshire). At South Leverton, across the Trent from Torksey, where there was an important early church, a gold ingot was found.[47]

Around 8km south of the camp at Torksey the toll bridge at Dunham-on-Trent may mark the location of another ancient crossing point. Four lead weights, including two insets, one of which appears to have contained a coin, and a gaming piece have been found near here.[48] On the eastern bank, near Newton-on-Trent, finds include a Carolingian Temple type denier, or possibly a Viking imitation, as well as a silver hooked tag fashioned from a dirham fragment.[49] The finds come from a similar type of site to the camp, albeit smaller in size, surrounded by wetlands to the east and the Trent to the west.[50] In Chapter 3 we already noted the concentration of stycas at Littleborough, the nearest crossing point north of the camp, and it should be no surprise that these strategic points should have also been occupied and controlled.

Around 15km south-west of Repton on the banks of the Trent at a second Catton, close to more ancient crossing points over the river, fifteen gaming pieces, two weights, one inset with an Anglo-Saxon coin, a silver ingot, a copper-alloy Thor's hammer pendant, and a mid-eighth-century dirham have been recovered.[51] At Stanton-by-Bridge, 8km east of Repton, and at another crossing point over the Trent, a gaming piece and weight have been retrieved. The weight was inset with the head of an Anglo-Saxon globular pin, a common type of Middle

47. DENO-938F3D
48. Hadley and Richards 2018, 11; NLM-CCC93C, -70EE23, -84D5E1
49. SWYOR-2D8B67, DENO-708753
50. Stein 2014, 332
51. PUBLIC-0058FD, -14F64D, -E6DC4E, -1A6EE8, -071C0B, -E2A64A, -E27AD8, -30461B, -55B858, -559762, -557681, -9B1DD8, -E5574E, -A5304F, -740CEE, -8790D1, -B8D647, -458D27, -DEDO73, -D21AF9

Saxon dress accessory that was collected for reprocessing at both Aldwark and Torksey.[52] A handful of sites have also been identified close to the Fosse Way, including Cotham and Hawton (Nottinghamshire), where hack-silver, lead weights, hack-gold, gaming pieces, and a B5–3 strap-end have been recovered.[53] At Stapleford (Lincolnshire) twenty-one gaming pieces, a silver ingot, and a Type L five-lobed sword pommel, of a form we have seen in concentrations at the camps, were found close to a crossing point over the River Witham, reflected in its place-name (OE *stapol, ford*, 'post/pillar, ford'). The place-name Stapleford has been identified as being associated with Anglo-Saxon royal or urban centres, with the element 'stapol' perhaps reflecting a feature, a post, at which announcements were made. The finds are from the opposite banks of the Witham to Brant Broughton, which has a place-name (*burh, tūn*, 'farmstead of the fortified place') often associated with Mercian royal centres or minsters.[54]

East Anglia

Previous analyses of the Scandinavian impact on East Anglia have mainly focused on the extensive evidence for tenth-century settlement, in the form of large numbers of highly standardised disc brooches. Decorated with Borre-style knotwork and backwards facing beasts, these have been identified as having been manufactured in East Anglia.[55] In contrast, the impact of the Great Army has received little attention. There is currently no concentration of archaeological evidence from East Anglia consistent with the presence of an overwintering camp, despite the fact that we know that the Great Army spent its first winter on English soil in this region and returned to Thetford in late 869 to spend the winter in East Anglia a second time (Figure 7.11). The Army divided in two after overwintering at Repton in 873–4, and that part of the Army under the authority of Guthrum, Oscetel, and Anwend subsequently returned to East Anglia, spending a year in Cambridge, close to the boundary of Mercia and East Anglia, before Guthrum was granted East Anglia in 880. As we saw in Chapter 2, archaeological investigations at both Thetford and

52. DENO-650DB1, -646EE0
53. NLM-1B0476, -1B89B2; DENO-FC3487, -7E724A, -489F9E, -9236D3, -918343, -912387, -7E724A, -7C8272, -174A55, -475FD2
54. LIN-CB2640, -AC716B, -C552C3; Blair 2013, 188
55. Kershaw 2013, 49–65

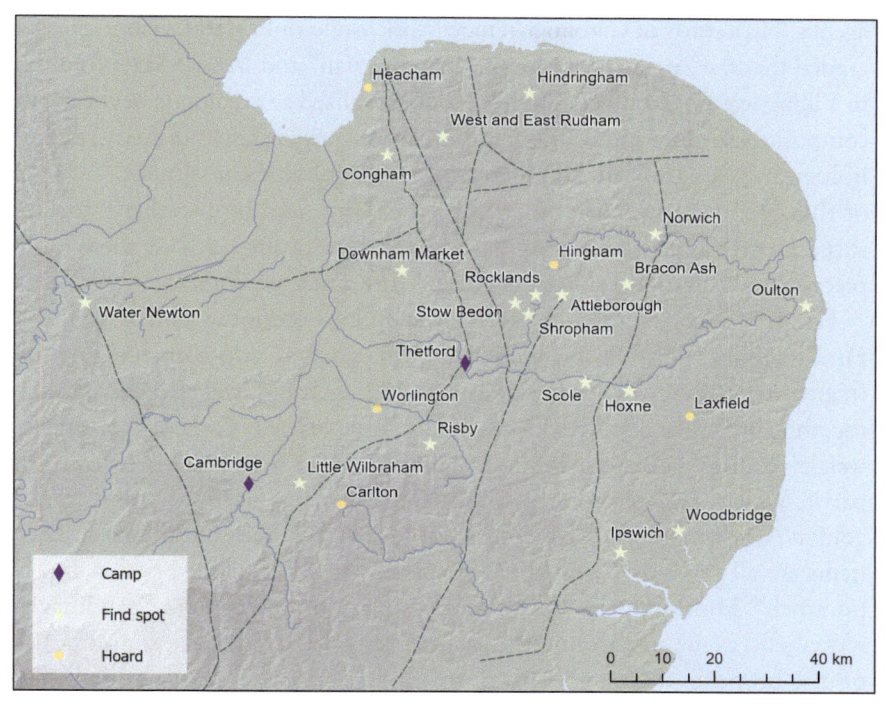

Figure 7.11. Map showing location of key sites in East Anglia mentioned in the text, with major rivers and Roman roads (Helen Goodchild; base map copyright as Figure 7.1)

Cambridge have revealed little evidence of the presence of the Army, but traces can be found across the East Anglian landscape. While the evidence is disparate, there are concentrations in the vicinity of Thetford and Norwich, on the north-west coast of Norfolk and the east coast of Suffolk and around the River Deben, as well as at crossing points of long-distance routeways over major rivers or fenland, in common with distributions further north. However, East Anglia differs in providing evidence for continuity in minting from the 860s to the end of the century and beyond, under Scandinavian overlordship. While in most cases we do not know where the coins were minted, as they rarely contain mint names, there is evidence for minting at sites with other traces of the presence of members of the Great Army. There are also more finds of Carolingian coins and metalwork from East Anglia than the other regions discussed in this chapter. While Carolingian coins were coming into England earlier in the ninth century, it is notable that those post-dating the coinage reform of 864 are concentrated in eastern England, suggesting their arrival through Viking agency.[56] In a study of Carolingian metalwork found in England, Gabor Thomas argued that the 'encounter between "Scandinavian" and "Anglo-Saxon" culture in Viking-age England needs to be reconceptualized as a dialogue between two composite identities united in their melding of Carolingian/Northern Frankish influences as a significant and increasingly recognizable constituent'.[57] Not all of this needs to have been brought by the Army, and both earlier trade and subsequent Viking raiders may have played a part, but many of these exotic pieces have been found alongside Great Army signature finds.

Familiar traces of the operation of a bullion economy can be found at Hindringham (Norfolk) on the River Stiffkey where two complete and two fragmentary silver ingots (weighing 94.08g in total) were recovered close together, perhaps a disturbed hoard as Pestell has argued. Two cubo-octahedral weights and two oblate-spheroid weights have also been recovered from this parish, while a gold-plated copper-alloy forgery of an imitative Louis the Pious gold *solidus*, which may have been made locally, had been cut in half.[58] These items are all consistent with the Great Army, as is a five-lobed sword Type L pommel.[59] Hindringham was evidently a place of longer term Scandinavian settlement, as the area around the parish church has produced a concentration of disc brooches decorated with Borre- and Jelling-style motifs made locally, and a fragment of a trefoil brooch of Scandinavian manufacture.[60] Similar types of material from the wider area around Hindringham include a silver ingot from Langham, two silver Thor's hammers from Holt, and a weight inset with a fragment of a silver denier of Louis the Pious from Walsingham.[61]

There is another concentration of signature finds within 5km of both banks of the River Waveney near Scole (Norfolk). This is the crossing point of the Roman road from London and Colchester to Caistor St Edmund, known as the Pye Road, which passes close to Ipswich; the river is also the ancient boundary between Norfolk and Suffolk. Finds include five silver ingots, a gold and a copper-alloy ingot, a denier of Charles the Bald, and an inset weight.[62] Scole is also one of the few locations in East Anglia where a B4a strap-end has been

56. Story 2003, 253–4
57. Thomas 2012, 511
58. NMS796, NMS-2157; NHER 24909, 25071; Blackburn 2007, 82; Blackburn and Rogerson 1993; Pestell 2013, 247–8
59. NMS-1A4452
60. NMS-E8EA91, -1A2FF6, -56E967, -E324E1; Gurney 1994, 112; Pestell 2013, 233–4; Kershaw 2013, 86–7
61. NMS-118FE5, -2FAA5E, -8E57D8, -16C428
62. BM-893E52; NMS-8FBB21; SF-9203D5, -3F0F52, -FB31F3, -144CA2, -18EDA7; Martin *et al.* 1999, 363; NHER 22538; Pestell 2013, 249

recovered.[63] From the nearby parish of Hoxne (Suffolk) is an unusual lead striking of dies for a coin modelled on Frankish designs and featuring a temple. Members of the Great Army would have been familiar with such coins before they came to England, and all seven Carolingian coins in the Croydon hoard deposited *c.*872 were of the Temple type. This design had previously been employed by two English-named kings in East Anglia, Oswald and Æthelred, who succeeded Edmund after his death at the hands of the Great Army in 869; as noted in Chapter 2, they may have been Scandinavian appointees. The Hoxne coin die was made for minting coins of Guthrum in his baptismal name of Æthelstan, and the continuing use of the Temple type has suggested to Blackburn that it is the earliest coin type minted for this king. He dates it to shortly after Guthrum took control in East Anglia, *c.*880, and before he adopted Alfred's coin designs, which followed the reform of the West Saxon coinage in the early 880s, when the Horizontal Two-Line and London Monogram coins were introduced. It has been suggested that examples of Temple type coins with blundered inscriptions from the Cuerdale hoard may also have been for Guthrum, using official reverse dies from the royal mint at Quentovic.[64] There seems, then, to have been a focal point of Great Army activity near to the crossing over the River Waveney, including not only bullion exchange but also one of the means by which royal authority was established under Guthrum. When mentioned in the will of Bishop Theodred of London (942x951) Hoxne was episcopal property, with an early church dedicated to St Æthelberht, a martyred late eighth-century East Anglian king; Pestell suggests that this 'implies some measure of continuity with an East Anglian past'.[65] By the early twelfth century, Hoxne had come to be associated with the place of the martyrdom of St Edmund, although there is nothing to suggest that this was anything other than a later invention.[66]

Another area with signature finds is close to the prehistoric trackway the Icknield Way in north-west Norfolk. There is a concentration at Congham, which has also been subject to fieldwalking, excavation, and geophysical survey (Figure 7.12). The results were synthesised by Gareth Davies, and it permits at least some of the metal-detected finds, including those recovered since his 2010 study, to be put into a more localised context. Congham was a polyfocal settlement, with continuous activity evident from the sixth to eleventh century and beyond. There were two distinct Middle Saxon settlement foci: the

63. NMS-0E78A4
64. Blackburn 2005, 26–7, 30; Williams 2014, 23; Porter 2021, 51–8
65. Pestell 2004, 81–3, 94; Whitelock 1979, 552–4
66. Pestell 2004, 94

Figure 7.12. Congham showing areas from which Middle and Late Saxon finds have been recovered (authors)

northernmost was characterised by high-status metalwork and two-thirds of the coin losses and has been interpreted as a marketing centre; while the southern focus has produced more functional metalwork, and is regarded as having been the estate centre, where traces of buildings have been excavated. This echoes the situation at Cottam, where a marketing area emerged to the north of the Middle Saxon estate centre.[67] The two settlement foci at Congham continued into the late Anglo-Saxon period, and metalwork indicative of Scandinavian influences can be found at both (Figure 7.13). At the southern site these items include a copper-alloy ingot, an E4 strap-end repurposed as a brooch with catch plate and lug on the reverse, a ringed pin, a trefoil brooch, a silver Thor's hammer, two disc brooches, a Scandinavian imitation of an Alfred Two-Line coin, and four St Edmund pennies, possibly from a disturbed hoard. A now lost church with associated, but undated, burials has been

67. Haldenby and Richards 2016

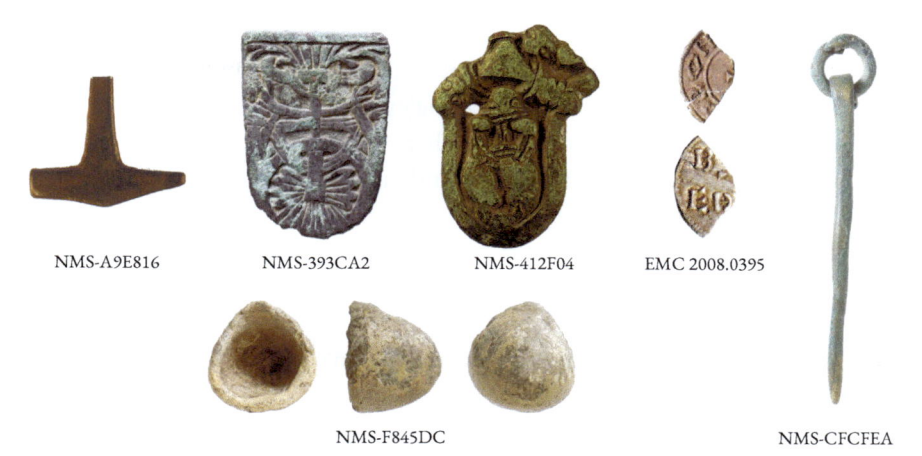

NMS-A9E816   NMS-393CA2   NMS-412F04   EMC 2008.0395

NMS-F845DC   NMS-CFCFEA

Figure 7.13. Selection of finds (not to scale) from Congham (PAS)

excavated in this area.[68] A silver ingot, a rare instance of a gaming piece from East Anglia, and several lead weights were found in the northern settlement focus.[69] This is also where a unique gold coin was recovered, which incorporates an obverse with a copy of a bust from a Roman coin of Constantine I or II, with a reverse struck from an official, if rusty, die for a Carolingian silver denier from Chartres (France) c.870–5. Mark Blackburn argued that it was probably minted locally, given that gold was available to Scandinavian settlers in England. Its form mirrors the imitations of the Quentovic Temple types minted for Guthrum using his baptismal name of Æthelstan, and the blundered spelling of this name is typical of coins minted for Scandinavian kings.[70] The evidence from Congham reveals activity of the earliest phases of Scandinavian settlement, some of it clearly of high status, with ongoing Scandinavian influence into the tenth century, including a recently discovered St Edmund penny which had been pierced and folded for use as a pendant.[71] There was continuity of two settlement foci through this period, although there seems to have been a change of types of activity with more coin loss in the southern settlement in the late ninth and early tenth century, although a short-lived economic focus in the northern settlement seems to have briefly continued the high-status nature of the Middle Saxon site.

68. Davies 2010, 168–95; NMS-CFCFEA, -412F04, -393CA2, -A9E816, -8882ED; EMC 2008.0395; NHER 25765, 25928, 3562, 3565, 11743
69. NMS-F845DC; NHER 25765; Davies 2010, 177–8
70. Blackburn 2005, 27; NHER 25765
71. https://www.bbc.co.uk/news/uk-england-norfolk-62325754 (last accessed 17 October 2023)

There is a concentration of other signature finds in the vicinity of Congham, including another copper-alloy ingot from Flitcham with Appleton, lead Thor's hammers from each of Gayton, Babingley, and Sandringham, and cubo-octahedral weights from both Sandringham and Babingley. A local imitation of an Alfred Two-Line coin has been found in Heacham, as well as seven stycas, which may be from a dispersed hoard.[72] Stycas are rare finds in East Anglia and such an assemblage seems likely to have been in Viking hands. Strap-ends of types found at Aldwark and Torksey have also been found in this region, including E3 strap-ends at Bawsey and Snettisham, while strap-ends recovered from Grimston include a Class F and also the only B5–3 from East Anglia.[73] An unusual burial at nearby Sedgeford of an adult female with a horse has been interpreted as a Viking presence, but a radiocarbon date from the horse of AD 670–820 at the 95% confidence level suggests it was much earlier.[74]

Around 14km to the east of Congham, at West and East Rudham, plotting of metal-detected finds enables them to be set in a local context. Concentrations of Middle Saxon and later Saxon activity have been found in the same places, indicating continuity of settlement organisation from the eighth century onwards, although the later material is more widely distributed.[75] Subtle differences can, however, be identified. In East Rudham two copper-alloy ingots have been recovered with weights suggestive of adherence to fractions of a Scandinavian weight standard of 26g. A Carolingian mount has been identified as a Middle Saxon find, but it is possible that it arrived under Scandinavian agency in the late ninth century.[76] At West Rudham Davies has identified two distinct areas of Late Saxon activity: one to the north was deemed 'indicative of a settlement focus', and the other, to the south, 'a slightly more enigmatic focus of trade and exchange', with a range of higher-status items.[77] The southern-most settlement focus, close to the medieval church of St Peter, has produced three silver-inlaid Trewhiddle-style strap-ends, suggestive of pre-existing high-status activity. Like the pattern at East Rudham, there are evident Scandinavian influences on material culture in this southern settlement that could date to either the late ninth or early tenth century, including a trefoil brooch and a convex disc brooch, and a copper-alloy ingot. The rare find of a swordless

72. NHER 3257; Gurney 2000, 520; Bonser 1998, 229; Pestell 2013, 240–2; EMC 2001.0463–9; NMS-998885
73. Thomas 2000a, cat. 1237; NMS-DA971B, -246FD4, -2CE528, -CBEC83
74. Graham-Campbell 2001, 112; Cross 2011, 202
75. Davies 2010, 203–24
76. Davies 2010, 207, 210; NHER 40787
77. Davies 2010, 211

St Peter's coin from York indicates a connection with other areas of Scandinavian rule.[78] In the northernmost settlement area of West Rudham, a ninth-century Carolingian strap distributor has been attributed to Middle Saxon activity, but it may, again, have been a Scandinavian introduction.[79] The presence of a metalwork hoard in this northern focus, containing two lead vessels, one of which had an iron handle, a lead handle, a lead ingot, and an iron ploughshare is intriguing. Davies suggests that 'we are perhaps observing the contrasting acts of different contemporary social groups—hoarding versus conspicuous consumption—at the same activity focus', noting that this hoarding was broadly contemporary with the introduction of new Scandinavian influences.[80] Settlement continuity at West and East Rudham is accompanied by the adoption of material culture showing Scandinavian influences, such as a bird brooch of Viking type and Borre-style brooches, while a tenth-century dirham must have arrived under Scandinavian agency.[81]

Whilst the location of the camp at Thetford has proved elusive, there is plentiful evidence from the vicinity that is indicative of its presence. In 2004 three coins of King Edmund were found at Worlington (Suffolk), on the River Lark c.22km south-west of Thetford. The suggestion that these were from a disturbed hoard has been reinforced by the discovery of another twelve such coins in the immediate area, which seem likely to have been deposited together in the wake of the arrival of the Army in East Anglia.[82] A scattering of other finds may also be linked to the activity of the Great Army. These include a gaming piece and silver ingot fragment from Icklingham close to the Icknield Way, while a second silver ingot was found at Hockwold-cum-Wilton, c.10km west of Thetford on the edge of the fens.[83] Other notable finds include an oblate-spheroid weight from Lackford, a gaming piece and a weight inset with a copper-alloy mount featuring rosette pattern, triquetra knots, and animals from Mildenhall, and a weight inset with a cut fragment of chip-carved Insular metalwork from Risby, where an E4 strap-end and a decorative mount, possibly from a Type L sword pommel, have also been found.[84] Early in 2024 a new example of a Temple-type coin of Guthrum was found 'near Thetford'.[85]

78. NHER 30441, 28130, 28131, 30611; Davies 2010, 211–14; EMC 1996.0195
79. Gurney 1999, 366; Davies 2010, 213; Thomas 2012, 495–6; NHER 32133
80. NHER 32133; Davies 2010, 213, 319
81. Davies 2010, 203–10; NHER 40787; Blackburn and Rogerson 1993, 222–4
82. Newman et al. 2004; SF-077A54, -076841, -D99E44, -E1C3B5, -AAFFB2, -C21281, -D872A7, -002DD1; described as from 'near Mildenhall' in some entries.
83. SF-735931, -5BA9C9; Gurney 1996
84. SF-042327, -DA4DC6, -20A507, -1AA037; Kruse 1992, 81
85. EMC 2024.0080

Figure 7.14. Selection of artefacts and coins from the Hingham hoard (Norfolk County Council)

Between Thetford and Norwich, a concentration of signature finds has been found close to a routeway running north-east from a crossing point over the River Little Ouse. In 2012 a hoard was found at Hingham, which comprised twenty-three silver pennies of Edmund, a silver disc brooch, incomplete silver cross-shaped brooch, and two silver strap-ends, all with Trewhiddle-style ornamentation, and fragments of two other silver brooches (Figure 7.14).[86] The composition of the hoard, with both coins and jewellery, may suggest Great Army ownership, but all of the items are of Anglo-Saxon manufacture, making it at least as likely to have been hidden by a local inhabitant, either when the Great Army first arrived in East Anglia or when it overwintered at Thetford. At Attleborough finds include a lead Thor's hammer, a copper-alloy weight with incised curvilinear pattern, fragments of a trefoil brooch, a Carolingian belt or harness, and a Scandinavian lozengiform brooch decorated with filigree wire and Borre-style animal heads, an equal-arm cross brooch, and a Borre-Jelling-style composite brooch.[87] From Shropham there is a rare example from East Anglia of an A1avii strap-end, which as we saw in Chapter 4 is a type overwhelmingly found north of the Humber. Two E4 strap-ends, a trefoil brooch, and a ringed pin also came from an area of long-lived Middle to Late Saxon occupation, along with a folded lead plaque bearing an inscription

86. NMS-972E58
87. Pestell 2004, 70–1; Rogerson and Ashley 2013, 565; NMS-AC3743, -A388C5

in Old English runes, reminiscent of the example from Torksey. While this may have been disturbed from an area of ecclesiastical activity there is no evidence for an early church at Shropham, and another possibility is that it had been acquired as scrap, perhaps by Viking raiders.[88] A silver ingot and a weight inset with silver have been found at Stow Bedon, from where there is also a base silver copy of a late seventh- or an early eighth-century dirham which had been transformed into a brooch with the addition of lug attachments.[89] Two small silver ingots with transverse hammering have been recovered from Old Buckenham.[90] A silver and a copper-alloy ingot and a cubo-octahedral weight were found at Bracon Ash, as well as a denier of Charlemagne, in an area with a concentration of Scandinavian-style jewellery and dress accessories, including an E3 strap-end.[91] A mount from Rocklands is very similar to examples from both Torksey (T115) and Swinhope, while a cubo-octahedral and an oblate-spheroid weight have also been recovered from this parish.[92]

There is also a cluster of finds indicative of the activities of the Great Army in the vicinity of Norwich. These include a fragment of a silver ingot from Witton, copper-alloy ingots from both Keswick and Costessey, where a Carolingian belt mount has also been found.[93] A weight inset with a copper-alloy disc has been recovered from Bawburgh, and an Irish circular convex harness stud decorated with geometric red enamelling. This is of a type known from Viking graves containing bridles, revealing that they had been adopted by Scandinavians as harness fittings, with an exact parallel known from Aggersborg.[94] At Postwick, c.4km to the east of Norwich in a bend in the River Yare, items recovered include a crowned gaming piece, two fragments of trefoil brooches and a complete example, and at least four Borre-style brooches. There is also the copper-alloy handle from an iron strike-a-light, which would originally have been decorated with a pair of horses and riders in profile but is now broken in half. This is an exceptionally rare find, dated to the late ninth or early tenth century, with most parallels coming from Russia and Finland.[95] Within c.10km to the west of Norwich a silver and gold filigree Thor's hammer has been found at Great Witchingham, while a weight inset with a styca was recovered from Barnham Broom.[96]

88. NMS-B8801E, -6ACE19, -B63E39, -D439A3, -FD4FFA; Pestell 2013, 157–60
89. NMS-3CA557, -9E85DE; HAMP-9A67D4
90. NMS-23FFF2; SF-DACA35
91. NMS-0D94E5, -DCA8F5, -8B9C16, -6E6202, -A41963, -D1F1E4; EMC 2017.0365
92. NMS-ACE0BD, -A599E8, -C87D47
93. Gurney 2000, 520; 2005, 744; Thomas 2012, 497; NMS-C270D6
94. NMS-C8B931, -875; Roesdahl *et al.* 2014, 285–6
95. NMS-2F649A, -6A8BA7, -E08641, -DCC275, -A342C6, -DC7AC8, -5A0BE4, -9535A5; Geake 2000
96. Pestell 2013, 242

Norwich has rarely featured in discussions of the Great Army as it is not mentioned in contemporary accounts of its activities. Nonetheless, there are a few excavated finds that suggest Viking activity in the late ninth century. In particular, excavations at the Greyfriars site recovered a lead weight bearing the imprint of a Scandinavian imitation of a coin of Alfred, which has given rise to speculation that there was a mint under Scandinavian control in Norwich in the early 880s. Lead weights of this type, struck between coin dies, are of Anglo-Saxon form, and their weights are typically multiples of the coin depicted, with the Anglo-Saxon coinage standard being c.1.60g. However, this example weighs 12.1g, roughly half of the well-known Scandinavian weight standard of c.24–6g (the *eyrir*). As Marion Archibald has noted, when the Scandinavian rulers began to mint coins, they also adopted the local practice of producing official die-struck weights, which they adapted to their own weight system. Such weights were used for weighing bullion, using coins to demonstrate their official status. Anglo-Saxon equivalents are found near to mints, which implies that a mint was nearby. There is damage to the weight which Archibald deems deliberate, and commensurate with how similar weights for Anglo-Saxon mints were treated once the coinage changed.[97] Another find from Norwich that may belong to this period is a gold ingot, unfortunately from an unstratified context although the transverse hammering suggests a Viking-age date, while a Charles the Bald denier minted in Rouen is another possible trace of the Army.[98]

Ingots, lead weights, and gaming pieces are widely found across East Anglia, and while few of these have been found alongside many other items indicative of the activities of the Great Army, they tend to be found along major routeways. For example, close to the Fen Causeway Roman road, at a site known as 'near Downham Market' (Norfolk), a silver ingot was recovered; it is stamped with triangular motifs containing a single pellet, of a type found on Viking-age arm-rings. From the same area two cut fragments of dirhams have also been recovered, dating to 737–46 and 813–14 respectively.[99] To the north-east a silver and a copper-alloy ingot were found in the parishes of Shouldham and Shouldham Thorpe, respectively, near a concentration of Carolingian metalwork including a strap fitting or mount, and two strap-ends, and while not closely datable the juxtaposition is notable.[100] Another silver ingot has been

97. Archibald 2007, 148–9
98. Blackburn 2007, 89; EMC 2020.0342
99. NMS-730A92; Naismith 2005, 215–16; Rogerson and Ashley 2013, 565
100. NMS-5661BF, -3C9A72, -6F341C, -E7DB27, -C53D81

recovered from Ditchingham (Norfolk), where the Roman Pye Road from Caistor St Edmund crosses the River Waveney.[101] There is also a clustering along the River Deben up to Woodbridge (Suffolk). These include two lead weights, one inset with a cut copper-alloy strip, and a copper-alloy weight with rune-like scratchings on one surface, an oblate-spheroid weight, a cubo-octahedral weight, a gaming piece, and four silver ingots with transverse hammering visible.[102] The area had ongoing Scandinavian influences on its jewellery, and there is a rare example from East Anglia of a York swordless St Peter's coin.[103]

A hoard found in the early nineteenth century at Laxfield (Suffolk) has been dated to the late 870s, and comprised at least nine Carolingian deniers, an unknown number of Anglo-Saxon coins, perhaps some pennies of East Anglian manufacture, a silver arm-ring, and finger-ring. Three apparently illegible 'Temple coins' suggested to Blackburn that these may have been local copies of Carolingian coins.[104] The parish has also produced an oblate-spheroid weight, while a gaming piece was found in the neighbouring parish of Badingham.[105] In the vicinity of Lowestoft a weight inset with a styca was found in 1998.[106] This seemed an isolated find in this part of Suffolk, but developer-funded excavations at Oulton in 2015 led to the discovery of eleven weights, four inset with coins (Figure 7.15). The weights were found in a post-hole, where they appear to have been hidden, with iron fragments the probable

Figure 7.15. Assemblage of Viking weights from Oulton (not to scale; Mustchin and Walker 2016)

101. Blackburn and Rogerson 1993
102. SF-E2E16C, -E2C7C2, -9421, -580AC2, -49AA4A, -57B6A3, -68708B, -68844D, -EE6A37, -68A246
103. SF-735C71
104. Brooks and Graham-Campbell 1986, 89; Blackburn 1989, 22; 2005, 30; Graham-Campbell 2011, 106; Pagan 2020
105. SF-334CE5; ESS-B06B18
106. Williams 1999, 25

remains of scale pans. Three were plain lead weights, and one was inset with a 'black glassy material with a crazed surface'. There were also three iron weights with copper-alloy casing of the oblate-spheroid variety, one of which was decorated on the top with a ring of punch marks around a central three-armed motif, while another was decorated with triangles of punch marks with a cluster of three ovid shapes at each corner. The other four weights were inset with coins, and they present a highly unusual combination. Two of them were Carolingian coins that post-date 864; they are thought likely to have been coins of Charles the Bald of the Gratia D[e]i rex ('king by the grace of God') type. In both cases the reverse was chosen to be visible, incorporating a cross, suggesting that those making these weights were drawing on a symbol of royal and Christian authority, and perhaps also reflecting the regions in which they had previously travelled. The other two weights contained very worn second- or third-century Roman coins, probably either a *sestertius* or a *dupondius*. One of these displays the reverse of a coin depicting a seated female figure, holding a cornucopia in the cruck of her left arm and with her right arm outstretched; although the coin is worn, similar examples depict scales at this point. This suggests a very deliberate selection to add legitimacy to the use of the weights during exchange. This may have been reinforced by the presence of an inscription ('TRP'); even if it is unlikely that it would have been understood that this denoted Tribunician Power it may have been seen as a means of conveying authority. Excavation revealed five sunken-featured buildings and twenty-three pits dating to the Early to Middle Saxon period, and a rectilinear enclosure of *c*.3200m^2 delineated by ditched trackways broadly dated to the Middle to Late Saxon period. The pit containing the weights was associated with this phase, as were two gullies 3.8m apart, which were tentatively interpreted as structural, perhaps a building with beam slots, although no floor surface was identified.[107] It was difficult to characterise the ninth-century activity on the site, but the weights were clearly being used within a settlement context.

Dispersal of objects

Throughout this chapter we have seen examples of the widespread distribution of material culture like that found in the camps, reflecting the movements of the Army and its offshoots. Another aspect of this can be seen when pieces of

107. Mustchin and Walker 2016, 35–9, 46–53

the same object are discovered many kilometres apart. This applies in particular to objects selected for use in inset weights, reinforcing that they were chosen for their specific qualities and associations, split into several parts, and then transported to different parts of England as members of the Army moved on. For example, two weights from Water Newton (Cambridgeshire)

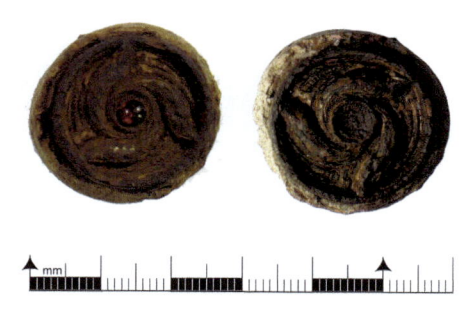

Figure 7.16. Inset weights from (left) Water Newton and (right) Sheriff Hutton (PAS)

and Sheriff Hutton (North Yorkshire) are each inset with identical circular mounts suggesting that they had been removed from the same original object (Figure 7.16). The weights have matching projections on their rear, and are both *c.*72g, suggesting that they were made together; as Heen-Pettersen has observed, they 'illustrate the potentially complex itineraries of such objects' found almost 200km apart.[108] While there is little else indicative of Viking activity near to Water Newton, the weight was found close to Ermine Street, around 10km south of Stamford, while a lead weight or gaming piece was found close to the inset weight from Sheriff Hutton.[109]

Weights from three sites in Cheshire (Saighton, Mere, and 'near Chester') and one in Lancashire (Newton) also seem to have been inset with items of similar origin, in the form of gilt copper-alloy sheet decorated with spirals, of Irish origin (Figure 7.17). They are of different shapes and weights—*c.*22g, *c.*33g,

Figure 7.17. Weight assemblage from Cheshire and Lancashire (left to right): LANCUM-45FF34 (Newton), LVPL 9C24B6 ('near Chester'), LVPL1684 (Saighton), and LVPL1745 (Mere) (PAS)

108. DUR-8BA064; SWYOR-4F2B32; Hiett 2020, 27; Heen-Pettersen 2021, section 5
109. SWYOR-F4C504

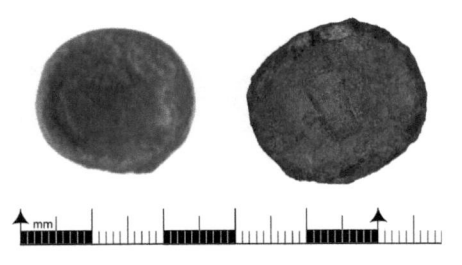

Figure 7.18. Inset weights from (left) Campsea Ashe and (right) near Beccles (PAS)

and two of *c.*40g—but despite this variability the insets seem to derive from the same object, or very closely related types.[110] It appears that the weights were created as a set but then split between different members of the Army. There are no other finds likely to have been associated with the Great Army from the immediate areas, but capacity to check is hampered by the fact that the find spots of two of them are unknown. Nonetheless, there are some traces of the Great Army in the region, including gaming pieces and hack-silver.[111] Two weights from Campsea Ashe and near Beccles (both Suffolk) inset with broadly rectangular offcuts of copper-alloy are sufficiently similar as to believe that they were produced at the same time, yet were found over 40km apart (Figure 7.18).[112]

In addition to pieces of the same object being re-used in weights there are rare examples of other items of loot being divided between members of the Army and then carried by their new owners to different parts of the country. One half of a cross-shaped Irish mount of eighth- or ninth-century date was found at Melton Ross (Lincolnshire), while the second half was found by a different metal detectorist *c.*40km to the north on the opposite side of the Humber, at the site known as 'near Pocklington' (Figure 7.19). There are other traces of Great Army activity here, as discussed earlier in the chapter, and these two finds provide evidence of a piece of ecclesiastical loot being divided between two members of a Viking warband.[113] It is standard archaeological practice to search for conjoining fragments of artefacts and sherds of pottery within a site, in order to understand the movement and disturbance of deposits within a small area. In Chapter 3 we observed that at Torksey two weights were inset with fragments of the same decorative

110. LVPL-1684, -9C24B6, -1745; LANCUM-45FF34; Hiett 2020, 27–8; another weight from Alvanley is described by the PAS as being similar although no photograph is available (LVPL-1778)
111. LVPL-2274, -2071, -2104
112. SF-F1F814, -9421
113. Leahy 2007, 130–5; the more recent discovery was recorded by Haldenby (NLM-34452F)

Figure 7.19. Two halves of a cross-shaped Irish mount from (left) 'near Pocklington' (authors) and (right) Melton Ross (Kevin Leahy)

metalwork, which must have been loot processed in the camp. However, it is remarkable to be able to identify parts of the same artefact from different counties. These provide a very visual representation of the impact of the Army. They reflect the spoils of war literally being divided between the victors, and then carried by former comrades as elements of the Army fragmented and split into separate groups and continued their journeys.

Conclusions

From the evidence discussed in this chapter we have been able to trace the impact of the Great Army beyond the documented camps and into the wider landscape. Many of the sites that have produced signature material of the Great Army are in locations that reflect those of the known camps, often on regional transport routes. Some are clustered along the major river networks of the Trent, Ouse, Derwent, Waveney, and the Deben, and often at crossing points over them. In the Yorkshire Wolds the sites we have discussed are found on the major Iron Age trackways which continued in use into the early medieval period, and in the Lincolnshire Wolds many lie adjacent to the prehistoric Barton Street. Elsewhere sites are close to major Roman roads, including the Fosse Way, Ermine Street, the Pye Road, and the Fen Causeway, as well as minor roads such as those connecting York to the Humber and the Wolds and the trans Pennine routes heading west, including one running through Spofforth.[114]

The types of sites at which material indicative of Great Army activity has been found vary. Some were major settlements or estate centres in the ninth

114. Hadley and Richards 2018, 15; McLeod 2023

century, but others were located at the edge of estates, as we have seen with discussion of the sites near Driffield, in the vicinity of Pocklington and close to Flixborough. Different settlement trajectories can also be traced. In some cases, there is evidence of only a short-lived period of Scandinavian activity that can be linked to the Great Army, but in others Scandinavian influences continue into the tenth century. In many cases, irrespective of whether there is later Scandinavian influence, there is continuity of settlement activity, albeit that we need to be careful on the basis only of metal-detected evidence of assuming that there were no changes in settlement status. As Loveluck has observed from the excavations at Flixborough, if the site had been investigated as a ploughed-out scatter of artefacts, characteristic of metal-detected evidence, then the impression would have been gained that the tenth century saw the settlement's decline, yet this is the period when the most substantial buildings have been excavated.[115] Nonetheless, in East Yorkshire, where there has been extensive metal-detecting, many of the Middle Saxon sites have no tenth-century arte-facts, suggesting abandonment at the end of the ninth century.

In East Anglia, which has benefited from extensive programmes of field-walking and survey, as well as metal-detecting, there is a lot of evidence to suggest continuity of settlement activity in the wake of the activities of the Great Army. That is not to deny that there was any disruption, but the settlement trajectories seem more continuous. As we have seen, East Anglia has evidence for continuity of minting activity under the aegis of the Great Army, with coins copying Carolingian forms minted for two English-named successors to Edmund and for Guthrum. Imitations of the coins of Alfred were also minted in East Anglia. Although many copy the names of Alfred's moneyers, two or three of the seventeen moneyers recorded on the imitations of Alfred's Horizontal Two-Line type had continental names, providing another insight into the influence of continental moneyers in East Anglia. At the same time, the traditional East Anglia weight standard was employed for these various issues.[116] The coin die from Norwich and a lead striking of dies at Hoxne may indicate that minting occurred nearby, but other minting sites are uncertain. Imitations of Alfred coins simply copy his mint names, but two coins minted by a moneyer with a continental name for an otherwise unrecorded Earl Sihtric give the mint name as Shelford, c.6km south of Cambridge, and a St Edmund penny incorporates the mint name 'NORDVICO' which has been interpreted

115. Loveluck 2007, 158–9
116. Blackburn 2001, 127–33; 2005; Porter 2021, 55–6

as Norwich. In the years after Guthrum died in 890 coins were minted widely across East Anglia and in the East Midlands to commemorate King Edmund. This overtly Christian coinage, treating Edmund as a saint, mirrored the coins minted during Guthrum's reign adhering to the traditional East Anglian weight standard, and continental moneyers were in the majority among this issue.[117] The arrival of continental moneyers in East Anglia may have been connected with disruptions to mint organisation in Francia; the Edict of Pîtres in 864 sought to limit the numbers of official mints, but they proliferated anyway to around 100 before declining rapidly over the last decades of the ninth century.[118] Given this evidence and the fact that the Army is known to have initially arrived in East Anglia, before returning in 869 and 874, leads to consideration of whether the Army was more widely and continuously based in East Anglia than the written sources suggest. In the light of this, one wonders whether the death of Edmund was less an unprovoked attack and more a result of a falling out between former allies.

By looking in detail at these sites, it is possible to trace a wider range of places where the Great Army's impact was felt, and it also provides insights into the spread of objects from the camps. These include examples of similar inset weights found at different sites, and the highly unusual example of two cut halves of the same Irish mount turning up on opposite sides of the Humber. Humble items such as the gaming pieces are all of forms found at Torksey, which reinforces the argument we have made previously that these items were initially manufactured at Torksey from where they were transported as members of the Army moved on. Had that not been the case it seems implausible that identical forms would have been manufactured independently at multiple, widely spread sites, not least because they are not all simply skeuomorphs of existing types from Scandinavia in other materials. These include a set of four pinnacled gaming pieces identical to types from Torksey from Canewdon (Essex).[119]

The activities represented by the evidence discussed in this chapter must have varied. Sometimes, it may reflect the movement of the Army through a region as it travelled between camps or other strategic sites. In some cases the evidence may derive from raids, while McLeod has suggested the need to consider the possibility that there were 'overnight camps' for short stays

---

117. Blackburn 2001, 132–4; Porter 2021, 317–19, 349
118. Armstrong 1998, 151–2; Porter 2021, 321
119. ESS-22C296

away from the main camp while forces were engaged in campaigns.[120] However, in other cases the Army may have been taking advantage of the peace forged each year when it overwintered in a new kingdom to engage in trade.[121] As McLeod has pointed out, the Army was not always moving through hostile territory; for example, the journey undertaken in 872 from London to York over 300km to the north was through Mercian territory and the lack of any recorded battles may reflect easy movement facilitated following the peace made with the Mercians at the end of 871.[122] Cooijmans has noted that Viking armies on the Continent routinely divided and acted independently as 'self-contained, self-centred politico-military entities' with their own leaders, before combining forces again, and such practices may have continued among the Great Army.[123]

In some areas, the evidence may reflect the broader landscape of the camps. As we saw in Chapter 2, we now know that the overwintering at Repton saw the Army based close to the church of St Wystan but also at Foremark, while a cemetery was located at Heath Wood some 4km away. Concentrations of finds such as those from the Derbyshire Catton and Stanton-by-Bridge may also reflect activity undertaken during the overwintering of 873–4. In this chapter we discussed evidence from the vicinity of Torksey, at Dunham-on-Trent, Newton-on-Trent, and Littleborough, suggesting control over crossing points of the Trent. In the light of this, the distribution of finds between Thetford and Norwich may reflect the area where the Army was based when it over-wintered in 869–70. In sum, the influence of the Great Army can be found both at its camps and more widely spread across the landscape, and we have also been able to nuance the accounts in the contemporary written sources to show that it was not just at the sites recorded by the scribes where the Army made its presence felt.

120. McLeod 2023, 213–19
121. McLeod 2006; 2023, 208
122. McLeod 2023, 210
123. Cooijmans 2020, 125

8

The Great Army and
the ceramic revolution

In Chapters 4 to 6 we examined the extensive evidence for manufacturing on the camps of the Great Army, provisioning daily needs and underpinning trade and exchange. We revealed innovation in metalworking techniques, new decorative forms, and mass production, facilitated by technological changes including the introduction of the casting of new styles of jewellery and dress accessories. In this chapter we discuss another dimension of innovative manufacturing and trade that emerged in the wake of the Great Army's political conquest of eastern England and ensuing settlement. This provides the first detailed comparative analysis of the transformation in pottery production that we propose was sparked by the activities of the Great Army and was closely linked to urban origins.

The ceramic revolution in eastern England

There was a revolution in ceramic production in eastern England in the ninth and tenth centuries, with the introduction of a new technological package, including the first use of the fast potter's wheel since the Roman period, innovative kiln technologies, and mass-production of new ceramic forms.[1] It is generally accepted that the techniques were imported by highly experienced potters from the Continent, but there has been disagreement about when and under what circumstances this occurred. Most interpretations have proposed

---

1. Hurst 1956; 1958; 1976, 314–34; Hurst and West 1957; Dunning 1959; Kilmurry 1980; Vince 1993; Young *et al.* 2005, 41–2; Blinkhorn 2013; McLeod 2014, 132–58; Perry 2016; Hadley and Richards 2021, 249–65; Hadley *et al.* 2023

that the industries emerged following Scandinavian settlement although there has been debate about whether there was any direct connection. A few commentators have, however, argued that some of the industries already existed.[2] This chapter provides a much-needed review of the chronology of the new industries, returning to primary sources and bringing in evidence that has become available in recent years, or was not considered in previous reviews.

To understand the ceramic revolution of the ninth and tenth centuries we need to set it in the context of existing pottery production. In the eighth and ninth centuries this was regionally varied, while many areas appear not to have used pottery at all.[3] In south-eastern England, the Thames Valley, and around York, handmade pottery was produced, often tempered with vegetal matter, and formed from coil-building or pulled from lumps of clay. In the Southwest and the East Midlands, vessels were made by coil building from a flat base, with vertical or slightly bulging walls. They were typically shell tempered, and some are known as Maxey wares, after the Northamptonshire site where the fabric was first identified but produced at multiple sites in the East Midlands. In Cornwall, similar grass-tempered pottery was produced, and the vessels often had lugged suspension loops, and are known as Bar-lugged wares. These handmade wares were fired in bonfires and had much in common with pottery production of the fifth to seventh centuries. At the *wic* of Ipswich, in contrast, from at least the early eighth century pottery was coil-built but finished using a tournette, or turntable, and fired in an updraught kiln. While the influence of continental practices on the kilns and some of the forms and decoration of vessels has been noted, other aspects, including the spouts and burnishing on the lower bodies of the vessel, derive from earlier pottery traditions in England. Ipswich ware has been found widely across East Anglia, where very little handmade pottery seems to have been in use, and in Kent, Hampshire, and as far north as Yorkshire. Ipswich ware vessels found beyond East Anglia are dominated by forms thought to have filled a gap in those produced by other industries and probably used for the transport of goods, including large storage jars, perhaps for salt, and pitchers for wine.[4] Elsewhere in early medieval England pottery seems not to have been used. The ceramic revolution in eastern England saw the Middle Saxon coil-built traditions largely replaced by new

---

2. Blinkhorn 2013; Blinkhorn and Griffiths 2023
3. Hurst 1959; 1976, 299–311; Vince 1993, 151–4; Blinkhorn 2012; Sudds 2020, 183–9; Perry forthcoming
4. Blinkhorn 2012, 34; Sudds 2020, 183; Frantzen 2014, 118; Pestell 2017, 215–17

wheel-thrown fabrics. These were fired to high temperatures in up-draught kilns, and sometimes glazed.[5] The standardised vessels produced included bowls, jars, and pitchers, decorated with roller stamping, applied strips, and thumbed impressions. These changes in craft practice suggest an influx of skilled craftworkers into eastern England, producing pottery for which there were no direct antecedents in the region. Elsewhere coil-built wares persisted, with wheel-throwing not introduced until the late tenth century, and aceramic regions remained so until after the Norman Conquest, a conservatism that is in sharp contrast to eastern England.[6]

In the 1950s the inception of the wheel-thrown industries was dated broadly by John Hurst to 'c.850', partly informed by a general tendency to assign the end of the Middle Saxon period to this date.[7] Hurst's view continues to be repeated in site reports, despite his acknowledgement that 'the dating of 850 is...rather vague', while he described the evidence that the wheel-thrown industries emerged before the Scandinavian settlement as 'ambiguous' given the challenges of fine dating of deposits of 850 to 875, or 875 to 900.[8] Radiocarbon and archaeomagnetic dating evidence for the industries has since become available but is typically rather broad. For archaeomagnetic dating there remain problems with the calibration curve, and it has been deemed to have 'poor potential' for the early medieval period when changes in the earth's magnetic field were relatively slow. Earlier studies were also typically based on far fewer samples than is recognised as good practice today, while samples taken from disturbed contexts of kiln fabric may have reduced reliability.[9] Therefore, we are largely reliant on the contexts in which the products of the kilns are found for dating evidence. There is broad consensus that the ceramic revolution occurred in the ninth century, but precisely when and under what circumstances are disputed (Figure 8.1).

5. Dunning 1959, 34–44; Kilmurry 1980; Perry 2016
6. Brown 2003. Recent claims (e.g. Blair 2018, 268) that wheel-throwing was introduced in Wessex in the ninth century are mistaken; the examples cited all date to the tenth century or are not wheel-thrown: Hurst 1976, 338; Blinkhorn 2013, 167; Mepham and Brown 2007.
7. E.g. Hurst 1958, 38; 1976, 284–6, 314–18
8. Hurst 1958, 41; 1976, 318; Blinkhorn 1993, 19; 2013; Blinkhorn and Griffiths 2023, 116; Spoerry 2016, 27–9
9. Linford 2006, 12; Batt et al. 2017; Wilkinson and Batt 2022, 11–13

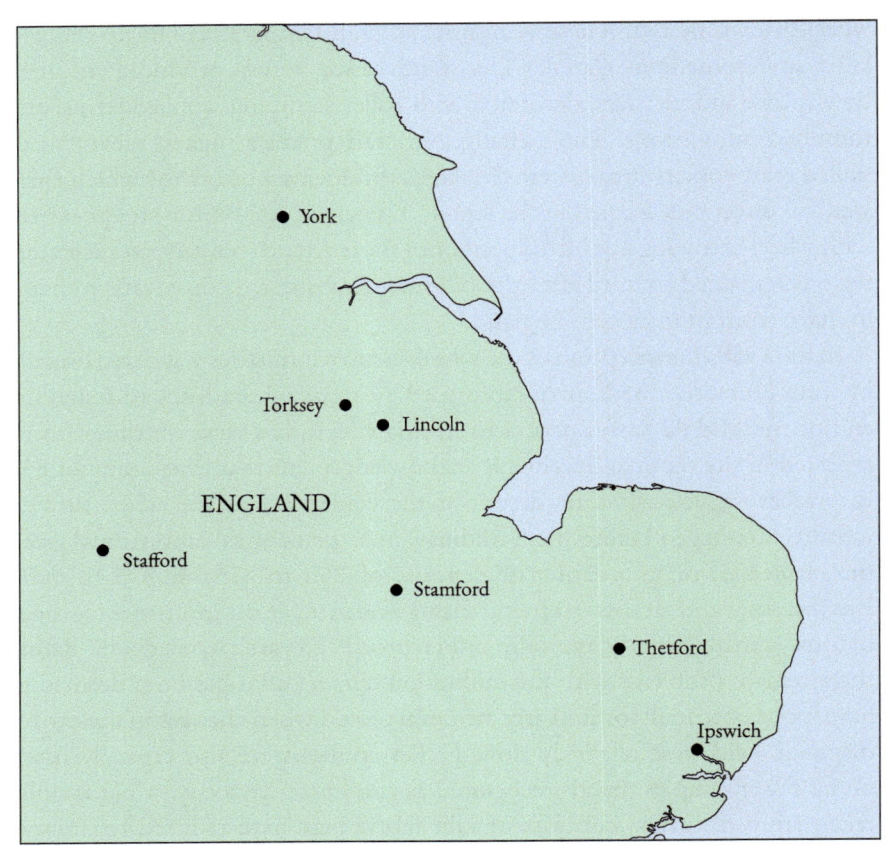

Figures 8.1. Centres of Late Saxon pottery production and consumption discussed in this chapter (authors)

The chronology, practices, and settlement contexts of the new industries

This review focuses on those industries believed to have been in operation by the start of the tenth century at the latest. It examines the dating evidence and the *chaîne opératoire* of each industry, that is the series of operations that turn raw materials into finished products, from acquisition of those raw materials, to the forming, firing, and finishing of the vessels. This is important for understanding the likely ancestry of the industries and the connections, and distinctions, between the different potting traditions. The new industries are largely found in the regions where the Great Army campaigned, in some cases where it overwintered. So, determining whether any of the industries were already in existence and survived through the period of disruption and political conquest, or were established soon after its arrival, or, alternatively, emerged much later is critical to understanding the impact of the Army. We begin with the industry from Torksey, where, as we have seen, there is extensive evidence for the camp of 872–3.

Torksey

The first reference to Torksey occurs with the overwintering of the Great Army, but this does not reveal anything of the nature of any pre-existing settlement. The pottery industry provides most of the earliest archaeological evidence within the area of the medieval town, alongside some broadly contemporary unfurnished inhumation cemeteries.[10] A kiln was first excavated in 1949 but Torksey ware only became widely known after it was mentioned in Gerald Dunning's 1959 review of the pottery of the late Anglo-Saxon period.[11] In the early 1960s, Maurice Barley led new excavations, which re-exposed the previously excavated kiln (now known as Kiln 1) and a second example. In the following years he excavated the complete or partial remains of another five kilns at the southern edges of the village, and between the 1990s and 2008 another eight kilns were identified in developer-funded excavations.[12] Our excavations south of the village revealed a sixteenth kiln in 2020, while fieldwalking and geophysical survey suggest the presence of at least another twenty. This represents the largest concentration of pottery kilns anywhere in Anglo-Saxon England.[13] The Torksey industry produced a range of cooking pots, bowls, dishes, storage jars, and pitchers, and decoration includes roller-stamping, and thumbed bands of applied clay, while our fieldwork has identified early but short-lived experiments in glazing (Figure 8.2).[14] The excavated kilns were circular, and their diameters vary, from $c.$1m (Kilns 2, 4, and 16) to the majority at $c.$2m. Most had a central pedestal from which firebars radiated, although Kiln 4 had only firebars and Kiln 2 lacked both features. Our analysis of the clay sources used for the pottery suggested that clays with naturally occurring sand inclusions had been selected from a band of Rhaetic clay around 1.5km to the east of the kiln sites; it was essentially a 'ready-made' potting clay. In contrast,

10. Hadley *et al.* 2023
11. Dunning 1959, 44
12. Barley 1964; 1981; Hadley *et al.* 2023, 7
13. Richards and Hadley 2020; Hadley *et al.* 2023
14. Barley 1964, 175–87; 1981, 270–87; Perry 2016

Figure 8.2. Torksey ware sherds splashed with glaze; an early experiment that was not continued into the tenth century. The rouletting on some of the sherds is typical of the earliest products of the Torksey kilns (authors)

the kilns were made from the silty clay of the Mercia mudstone on which they were located, close to the banks of the Trent.[15]

The distinctive Kiln 2 is believed to be the earliest, and it differs in several other ways (Figure 8.3). Microstructural analysis of the pottery suggests that it was fired to higher temperatures (in the *c*.800–950°C range) than other Torksey kilns (generally below *c*.800–850°C). Kiln 2 pottery was almost entirely reduced grey/black throughout the vessel wall, which indicates a distinctive firing regime. In contrast, the other kilns produced pottery with a characteristic 'sandwich firing'—with grey/black surfaces, red margins, and reduced grey/black cores—which indicates initial firing in an oxidising atmosphere, but which was insufficient for the oxygen in the kiln to fully penetrate and oxidise the whole body of the vessel, with the atmosphere switched to reducing (oxygen poor) in the latter stages to produce the grey/black surfaces.[16] The flat bases of the pottery from Kiln 2 had been cut from the wheel with wire; the vessels from other kilns have sagging bases, where they had been pushed outwards after removal from the wheel, obscuring the means of removing them.[17]

When first commented upon by Dunning a date in the eleventh or twelfth century was suggested for Torksey ware. In a paper published in 1964 Barley sug-

15. Perry 2016, 85–90
16. Barley 1964, 179; Perry 2016, 87–90; Hadley *et al.* 2023, 8–9
17. Barley 1964, 178–9; Perry 2016, 92

Figure 8.3. Torksey Kiln 2 during excavation in 1962, after half the fill of the firing chamber and stoke-hole had been removed; unlike other kilns from Torksey it lacked both fire bars and a central pedestal (University of Nottingham Museum)

gested an early eleventh-century date for Kiln 1 based on archaeomagnetic dating (AD 1050–1150) and Kiln 1 pottery from the late Saxon defences at Nottingham. Kiln 2 was deemed to be 'working a generation or two' earlier due to the differing forms of its products, and an archaeomagnetic date of AD 900–1000.[18] In a second paper published in 1981 he reported on two new archaeomagnetic dates from Kilns 4 (AD 900–1000) and 5 (AD 1050–1150). Nonetheless, despite these late dates, Barley claimed that the industry had originated in 'the first half of the ninth century', citing the discovery of Torksey ware in what were believed to be contexts of this date at the rural settlement of Goltho.[19]

The 1987 publication of the Goltho excavations of the 1970s seemed to reinforce this interpretation.[20] However, the dating of the early medieval phases was questioned by David Stocker; he observed that Guy Beresford was more dogmatic than Glyn Coppack, who described the dating of the pottery as 'somewhat speculative'.[21] Wheel-thrown wares from Torksey, Lincoln, and Stamford occur first in post-holes of the settlement boundary, and in a spread

18. Dunning 1959, 44; Barley 1964, 180–1; Aitken and Weaver 1962, 11, 15, 21, 25–6
19. Barley 1981, 287; Aitken and Hawley 1966, 190–1
20. Beresford 1987, 22–8; Coppack 1987, 136–7, 167
21. Stocker 1989; Coppack 1987, 167

adjacent to one of the post-built structures (House 2).[22] The assemblage also included handmade fabrics known as Early Lincolnshire Fine-Shelled ware (ELFS), which is found at sites spanning the ninth and tenth centuries, and a few sherds of Middle Saxon Northern Maxey-type ware, probably manufactured near Lincoln given the nature of the temper.[23] However, the claims in the site report about the contemporaneity of these wares are problematic. They were influenced by the recovery of a similar combination of material from three ditches excavated at Barrow-upon-Humber (Lincolnshire) in the 1970s.[24] Yet Colin Hayfield had already argued that those findings were compromised by the intercutting of two Middle Saxon ditches by a later ditch, which was undercut during excavation, and material was trampled into the ditch fills meaning that the assemblage lacked secure context.[25] New radiocarbon dates from animal bones now place the earliest phase at Goltho in the early tenth century.[26] In sum, the Goltho excavations did not demonstrate an early ninth-century date for the appearance of wheel-thrown wares.

Our recently excavated Kiln 16 was extensively sampled for archaeomagnetic dating, but only provided a very broad date range of AD 823–1203, which does not help to refine the chronology of the industry.[27] Instead, we must rely on dating from consumer sites. The earliest contexts in which Torksey ware can confidently be identified date to no earlier than the late ninth century. These include Coppergate in York, where Torksey ware first appears in Period 3, dated broadly to the second half of the ninth century, and pre-dating the laying out of the tenements c.900. While the nature of the pre-tenth-century settlement activity at Coppergate has been difficult to characterise, there is evidence for craftworking including blacksmithing, copper-alloy, bone, antler, and amber working taking place in the vicinity. There were also three isolated and disorderly burials in pits, and while it has been suggested that these were individuals of Scandinavian origins the results of stable isotope analysis are equivocal.[28] Torksey ware was not, in contrast, found at Fishergate, the Middle Saxon trading focus.[29] Torksey ware has also been recovered from Lincoln in phases dated to the turn of the tenth century on the Flaxengate site in the lower city of the former Roman *colonia*.[30] At Flixborough, it is first found in phases dated to the

22. Beresford 1987, 22, 25
23. Young *et al.* 2005, 37
24. Coppack 1987, 136–7
25. Hayfield 1982, 257–60, 282; Miles *et al.* 1989, 211–12
26. Aleks McClain pers. comm.
27. Wilkinson and Batt 2022
28. Hall *et al.* 2014, 543–62; Buckberry *et al.* 2014
29. Mainman 1990, 426–7; Vince 1993, 156
30. Adams Gilmour 1988, 120–3; Young *et al.* 2005, 90, 275

mid-to-late ninth century, and is mainly of the uniform grey fabric typical of Kiln 2, the earliest in the Torksey sequence (Figure 8.4).[31] This coincided with a major settlement reorganisation and construction of a series of smaller buildings, and the ceramic profile contrasts with that of earlier phases of occupation and refuse deposits, characterised by Ipswich ware, Maxey-type wares, and ELFS, from which wheel-thrown wares were absent.[32] Fieldwork at Cottam provides important horizontal stratigraphy for the introduction of Torksey ware; it was absent from the Middle Saxon settlement, which had been abandoned by the late ninth century, but present in the new settlement to the north where traces of members of the Great Army have been identified.[33] The evidence from these

Figure 8.4. Fresh breaks of sherds from a selection of the industries discussed in this chapter, to show their characteristics: (top left) Torksey ware from Kiln 2, which is the earliest known kiln from Torksey, producing a reduced grey fabric; (top right) Torksey ware from Kiln 1, displaying the characteristic 'sandwich firing' produced by most kilns at Torksey, with grey/black surfaces, red margins, and reduced grey/black cores; (bottom left) Stamford ware from the Flaxengate excavations in Lincoln, with characteristic white fabric; (bottom right) Lincoln Kiln-Type ware from Flaxengate, with a narrow red oxidation surface layer (authors)

31. Young *et al.* 2005, 90
32. Loveluck and Atkinson 2007, 82–91; Young and Vince 2009, 368–73
33. Richards 2013, 208

very different sites is consistent in suggesting that the industry originated no earlier than the last quarter of the ninth century and was already distributing its wares before *c.*900.

Lincoln

Little Middle Saxon activity has been traced in the former Roman town of Lincoln (Figure 8.5). In the Upper City there was an ecclesiastical enclave

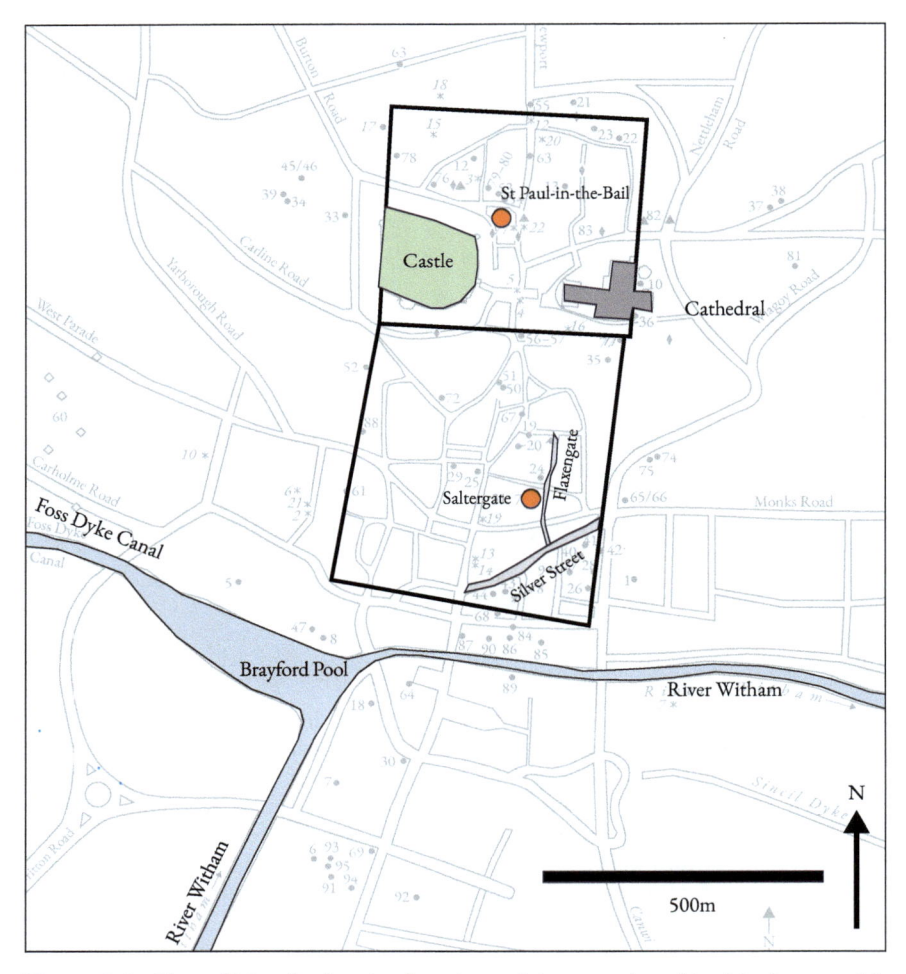

Figure 8.5. Plan of Lincoln showing locations of sites mentioned in this chapter with walls of the Roman city and rivers (authors after Stocker 2003, fig. 1.1)

around the church of St Paul-in-the-Bail, while the Lower City has produced limited evidence for eighth- to ninth-century occupation, mainly in the form of burials on Saltergate thought to have been associated with the possible double foundation of St Peter-at-Pleas and St Peter-at-Arches. There is some slight evidence of occupation across the River Witham to the south in the Wigford ('ford by/to the *wic*') area, but it appears to have been abandoned in the ninth century.[34] Several potting communities were, however, working in Lincoln by the end of the ninth century at the point when urban life, in the form of trade and manufacture, emerges for the first time since the Roman period. The industries used differing methods of forming and firing, diverse raw materials and distinctive decorative features, suggesting the arrival of several different manufacturing traditions. Wasters for the quartz-tempered Lincoln Late Saxon Sandy ware (LSLS) have been found at Flaxengate, although no kiln has yet been identified. Vessels are wheel-thrown and fired in a reducing atmosphere, with ceramic petrography indicating that the clays used had been obtained locally in and around Lincoln. The survival of traces of organic content suggests either 'reduced firing conditions or a short duration for the firing'.[35] Products of this industry are almost exclusively found in Lincoln; there is just a single sherd from tenth-century contexts at Flixborough. Vessel forms are mainly small- to medium-sized jars.[36] A similar ware found during the Flaxengate excavations, known as Lincoln Late Saxon Pale-bodied Sandy (LSPLS) ware, was manufactured from a lighter firing local clay source; no wasters have been recovered and so its place of manufacture is unknown.[37] Another industry produced a quartz-tempered fabric now known as Lincoln Gritty ware (LG) (Figure 8.6). The kilns are believed to have been located near Flaxengate where wasters were found. Around 500 sherds have been recovered within Lincoln and it is thought to have been a short-lived industry, with few finds beyond the immediate vicinity of Lincoln, but including both Flixborough and Goltho.[38] The sources of its raw materials are not known, but it evidently used a different sand temper from the other Lincoln industries. Ceramic petrography suggests firing in a reducing atmosphere. It was generally thought not to be fully wheel-thrown, but that some vessels were coil-built and

---

34. Vince 2003, 147–56; Steane 2016b, 217–23; Vince and Jones 2016, 483; Blair 2018, 259
35. Young *et al.* 2005, 46
36. Adams Gilmour 1988, 100–2; Young *et al.* 2005, 44–6; Young and Vince 2009, 392
37. Young *et al.* 2005, 44–7
38. Adams Gilmour 1988, 98; Vince 2001, 160–1; Young *et al.* 2005, 42–4; Young and Vince 2009, 369–70, 398

Figure 8.6. Lincoln Gritty ware sherd from Flaxengate with roller-stamped decoration (left; Reb Ellis-Hakon) and a sherd of this fabric in fresh break revealing the reduced firing regime of this industry (right; authors)

finished on a turntable.[39] However, new analysis of LG sherds has revealed that even vessels previously visually identified as fully or partially coil-built were, in fact, wheel-thrown, with X-rays revealing that the voids and inclusions are orientated diagonally throughout vessel walls, a feature typical of wheel-thrown pottery.[40] The vessel rims were shaped with a tool, while the lower bodies were often knife-trimmed, leaving surface burnishing.[41]

Three kilns that produced a shell-tempered ware known as Lincoln Kiln-type Shelly ware (LKT) were excavated on Silver Street, to the south-east of Flaxengate. LKT vessels were produced to a standard form, with even the handles and spouts thrown on the wheel. They represent *c*.30% of the pottery from the earliest post-Roman contexts across Lincoln, and over 80% of tenth-century ceramic assemblages.[42] Both the clay and the shell-sand temper may have derived from outcrops of Cornbrash near Potterhanworth to the south of Lincoln, although Lincolnshire limestone to the west is another possibility.[43] The most completely excavated kiln (Kiln 200) probably dates to the early tenth century and was rectangular in form and unusually large (1.5m × 5.9m internally). The destruction of its east end may have obscured any evidence for a stoke-hole, flue, or raised floors. The Silver Street kilns probably operated as

39. Adams Gilmour 1988, 98; Young *et al.* 2005, 42
40. Pourmomeni 2022, 49–76
41. Young *et al.* 2005, 42–3
42. Miles *et al.* 1989; Adams Gilmour 1988, 83–93; Young *et al.* 2005, 47–56
43. Young *et al.* 2005, 8, 54

clamps, rather than true kilns, with the fuel and the vessels placed together in the firing. When viewed in cross-section LKT sherds often have a narrow, crisply defined oxidation surface layer, indicative of the rapid cooling characteristic of a clamp, in contrast to the slower cooling in a true kiln, which typically shows up as a broader and more diffuse zone of oxidation.[44]

Wasters from a quartz-tempered and externally glazed fabric known as Early Lincoln Glazed ware (ELSW) suggest it was also being made near Flaxengate and the same clay source was used as for many of the products of the LG ware industry. The potters of ELSW had, however, made different decisions about temper, such as adding shell, and the firing regimes employed. They mainly produced jars and pitchers, although an unusual crucible for glass working was found at Flaxengate. There was a connection between the ELSW and LKT industries, which had very similar vessel and rim shapes. In addition, LKT vessels were used as stands during firing of ELSW pottery, while the lead carbonate found in some LKT jars may have been used in the glazing of ELSW.[45]

These various Lincoln wheel-thrown industries produced a standardised range of wares, mainly jars and bowls, but occasionally pitchers, lamps, and crucibles; decoration included roller stamping of lines of squares or diamonds on the shoulders of vessels, and to a lesser extent incised wavy decoration, thumb-pressed applied strips, bosses and lattice burnished lines. There was also use of glaze, most notably on ELSW, but some glazed sherds of LKT are also known. Most of the wares circulated only or mainly within Lincoln, but LKT has been found at over 130 sites in Lincolnshire and further afield in the East Midlands, and in Staffordshire and Yorkshire, although these assemblages mainly date to the tenth century.[46]

Important dating evidence for the inception of these industries comes from excavations at Flaxengate in the 1970s. In Dominic Perring's report the features were grouped into phases of activity divided into broad periods, with the pottery analysed in another report by Lauren Adams Gilmour.[47] Jane Young and Alan Vince later established a series of ceramic horizons in the city, 'using overall patterns that, within a broad range, repeated themselves from group to group across the sites in the city'.[48] At Flaxengate the earliest post-Roman activity is represented by a levelling layer—referred to as 'pre-Period I'—of

44. Miles *et al.* 1989, 200
45. Adams Gilmour 1988, 102; Young *et al.* 2005, 62–4, 238
46. Adams Gilmour 1988, 102; Young *et al.* 2005, 56; Young and Vince 2009, 368–70; Symonds 2013, 98–108
47. Perring 1981, 33–5; Adams Gilmour 1988
48. Young *et al.* 2005, 10

largely Roman material but incorporating over 750 sherds and wasters of the Lincoln wheel-thrown wares, including LSLS, LG, LKT, and ELSW, as well as Torksey ware (ceramic horizon ASH7).[49] A street running north–south was subsequently laid out over this (Period I and ceramic horizon ASH8).[50] This road was resurfaced with a large dump of material containing the same wheel-thrown fabrics and kiln wasters.[51] Buildings began to be constructed facing onto the street at this time; one of these contained a hearth which yielded an archaeomagnetic date of AD 850+/−50, although it has never been properly published and no archive report survives.[52] The same range of wheel-thrown pottery was recovered from associated contexts, including a levelling deposit to the west of the street and pits to the west of another building.[53] One of these pits also contained a St Edmund penny minted under Scandinavian authority probably somewhere in East Anglia, which was assigned a date of no earlier than 905.[54] A hearth post-dating two of the Period I buildings had an archaeo-magnetic date of AD 960+/−60.[55] The Period I buildings were sealed beneath another dump deposit (Period II and ceramic horizon ASH9) containing large amounts of Roman building material and almost 7000 sherds of wheel-thrown pottery, as well as some residual Middle Saxon material.[56] This deposit also included a Scandinavian imitation of a silver penny of Alfred's Two-Line type. While residual, Blackburn believed its freshness 'makes it unlikely to have been lost much later than the 890s' and it is therefore indicative of activity of broadly this date, a deduction reinforced by other late ninth- or early tenth-century finds, including a spearhead, ansate brooch, and polyhedral pin.[57] This dump sealing the Period I buildings has been deemed in a recent review by Steane to be 'consistent with deposition in the early/mid to mid 10th century'.[58]

The phases of dumping and construction, and the associated coins, other artefacts, and archaeomagnetic dates suggest that the street frontage was the focus of densely-spaced buildings by the early tenth century.[59] Since there are

49. Perring 1981, 5–6; Adams Gilmour 1988, 77–102; Young *et al.* 2005, 41–64, 88–90, 238; Steane 2016a, 21–2
50. Perring 1981, 6; Young *et al.* 2005, 12; Steane 2016a, 21–3, 486
51. Perring 1981, 8; Young *et al.* 2005, 62, 237–9; Steane 2016a, 23
52. Perring 1981, 7–8, 33, 36; Mark Noel pers. comm.
53. Perring 1981, 36; Young *et al.* 2005, 12–13; Steane 2016a, 20–5, 55–7
54. Young *et al.* 2005, 13; Steane 2016a, 25; Porter 2021, 125–6
55. Perring 1981, 7–8, 33, 36
56. Steane 2016a, 25
57. Blackburn *et al.* 1983, 11–12; Steane 2016a, 56–7
58. Steane 2016a, 25
59. Perring 1981, 6, 36; Vince and Jones 2016, 486–8; Blair 2018, 266–7

kiln wasters and wheel-thrown sherds in the dump layer preceding this occupation (pre-Period I), it seems clear that pottery production had commenced in the late ninth or early tenth century at the latest. This deduction is reinforced by the fact that LG and LKT sherds are found alongside Torksey ware in mid-to-late ninth- and early tenth-century phases at Flixborough.[60] Wheel-thrown wares are also notably absent from the few post-Roman contexts in Lincoln where mid-ninth century or earlier activity has been identified. As Young and Vince have argued, this counters any argument that 'the correlation of Viking activity with the introduction of wheel-thrown, kiln-fired pottery is assumed rather than tested on many sites in Eastern and Northern England'.[61] From this they conclude that in Lincoln wheel-thrown pottery production emerged no earlier than the end of the ninth century.

Stamford

The most distinctive of the new wheel-thrown wares was manufactured at Stamford (Lincolnshire), a strategically important location where Ermine Street and the prehistoric Jurassic Way crossed the River Welland.[62] Stamford ware was mainly made of a white firing clay with a low iron content, identified as an Upper Estuarine Clay.[63] Other distinctive aspects of Stamford ware include occasional, red-painted decoration in the earliest phases and glazing. The industry produced a wide range of vessels including bowls, pitchers, storage jars, and lamps, as well as crucibles for use in metalworking (Figures 8.7 and 8.8).[64] Remains of at least six kilns have been excavated, and pottery and wasters found across the town suggest the locations of others, mostly dating to the tenth century or later.[65]

The Stamford ware industry was the subject of a doctoral thesis by Kathy Kilmurry, published in 1980. She reported on the archaeological context of the earliest kilns excavated at the site of the later medieval castle, and subsequent studies have relied heavily on this.[66] However, the unpublished site report by the excavator, the late Christine Mahany, with input from David Roffe and

60. Young and Vince 2009, 368–73
61. Young *et al.* 2005, 238
62. Hall 1989, 193–6; EMC 1986.8717, 1996.0095
63. Kilmurry 1980, 63–7; Perry 2016, 99; Mahany forthcoming
64. Kilmurry 1980, 25–9
65. Kilmurry 1980, 31–61; Mahany and Roffe 1983, fig. 4; Bradley-Lovekin 2003; Morris and Walsh 2008
66. Kilmurry 1980, 31–4; Blinkhorn 2013, 162; Blinkhorn and Griffiths 2023, 108–11

Figure 8.7. Wasters from the Stamford Castle kilns (YAT)

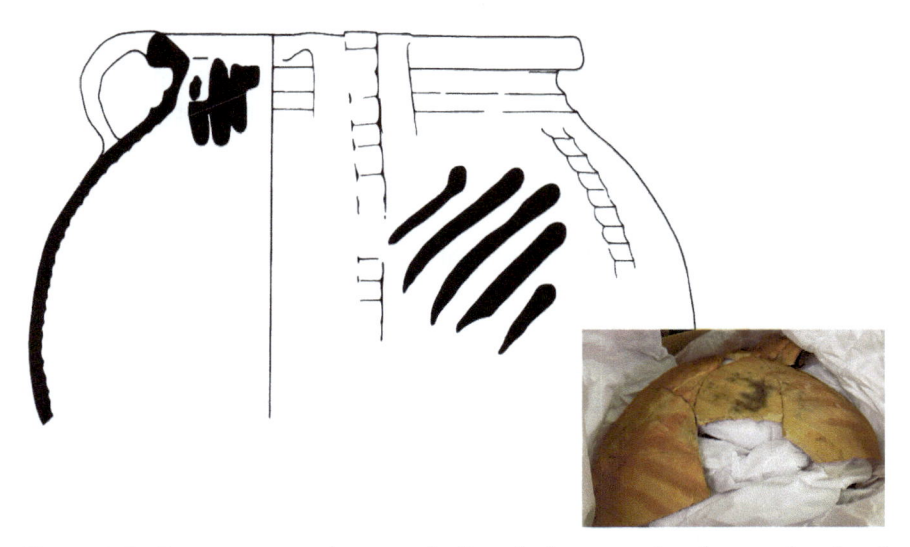

Figure 8.8. Reconstruction drawing of a Stamford ware pitcher decorated with red paint (authors after Kilmurry 1980, 37) with inset photograph of sherds from the same vessel (Samantha Parker, Lincolnshire County Council)

Paul Garwood, has revised key aspects of this account.[67] Therefore, here we present the updated phasing, which establishes the chronology of the industry and its relationship to a pre-existing defensive, probably royal, site. There has been much debate about the date of the start of the pottery industry at Stamford, but despite problems with the dating evidence it combines to indicate late ninth-century origins.

The earliest feature on the castle site was an enclosure, defined by two substantial ditches; the inner one was V-shaped, $c.3$–4m wide and up to 2.5m deep, with the outer one more irregularly-shaped, up to 2.5m wide and 1.5m deep. On the inside of these ditches was a smaller gully up to 1m deep and 1m wide interpreted as a palisade trench supporting an interior rampart comprising limestone rubble and clay. The defensive capacities of this enclosure were enhanced by the marshy floodplain of the Welland to the south and a stream valley to the east. A pit $c.$2m deep at the northern end of the excavated palisade coincides with a narrowing of the ditches suggesting the location of an entranceway. Extrapolation of the line of the ditches suggests that they may have enclosed the higher ground to the north-west including the church of St Peter. This has yielded no early medieval dating evidence, but several aspects of its history suggest early origins, including the fact that the smaller parishes of other churches in Stamford seem to have been carved from its parish. St Peter's was a holding of Hambleton (Rutland) in 1066, one of Queen Edith's manors, and Mahany and Roffe argued that it was the nucleus of the seventy properties ('messuages') she held in Stamford that were noted as having 'belonged to *Roteland*'.[68] Lack of clear evidence for recutting of the ditches indicates that the enclosure was short-lived, and the consistency of the fills of the palisade gulley and inner ditch suggest deliberate dismantlement and backfilling.

Two kilns were excavated adjacent to the east side of the enclosure. These were similar in size to Torksey Kiln 2, but more elongated in shape and with narrow straight-sided walls; no flue arches survived, there was no indication of any internal structure, and the lack of structural fragments suggested a temporary roof removed after firing (Figure 8.9). Kiln 1 was relined several times, and associated pits may have been for fuel storage and stoking, while a limestone

---

67. The revised dating is based on Mahany forthcoming; Garwood forthcoming; Roffe and Garwood forthcoming.
68. Mahany and Roffe 1983, 203; Haslam 2017, 24–5

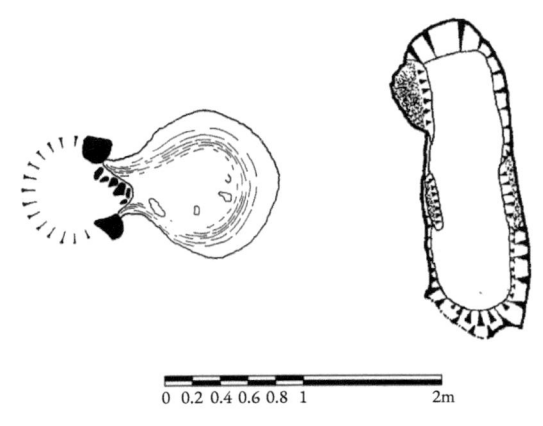

0 0.2 0.4 0.6 0.8 1   2m

Figure 8.9. Kiln 2 Torksey (left; after Barley 1964, fig. 5) and Kiln 1, the earliest kiln at the site of Stamford Castle (right; after Kilmurry and Mahany 1977, fig. 66)

rubble surface was perhaps part of an associated workshop area. Kiln 2 was constructed further east and turned through 180 degrees from the orientation of Kiln 1, and it destroyed the eastern side of Kiln 1. Kiln 2 was rebuilt multiple times. A large pit to the south may have been a puddling pit for clay preparation.[69] Two radiocarbon dates were acquired from charcoal in the 'badly disturbed' stoking areas; these cannot easily be linked to any particular phase of kiln operation and certainly not to the 'final firing' that has been claimed.[70] These were originally published as AD 678 +/− 83 and AD 837 +/− 77, but the most recent calibration curves render them as AD 600–894 and AD 692–1027 at the 95% confidence level.[71] These are very broad dates and it is, in any case, possible that old sources of wood had been used as fuel, further limiting their usefulness for establishing the start of the industry other than providing a *terminus post quem*.[72] An archaeomagnetic date of AD 850 +/− 50 was reported from a floor surface associated with Kiln 1, but re-use and disturbance may reduce its reliability.[73]

Supposed stratigraphic relationships between the ditched enclosure and the kilns have been offered as additional dating evidence, but published accounts are contradicted by the unpublished site report. Kilmurry thought that the excavated kilns were in operation while the enclosure ditches were still open, but she was apparently unaware of the evidence for an entranceway into the enclosure. As the site report notes, it is 'impossible to envisage' the presence of a kiln or the dumping of kiln waste 'in the entrance of a substantial defended site which is in use'. The excavation report also rules out the possibility that the

69. Kilmurry 1980, 32; Mahany forthcoming
70. Kilmurry 1980, 32; Roffe and Garwood forthcoming; contra Blinkhorn and Griffiths 2023, 108
71. Perry 2016, 104
72. Kilmurry 1980, 32; Hall 1989, 196, n. 236
73. Kilmurry 1980, 32; Clark *et al.* 1988, 653

kilns preceded the enclosure in date, noting that the low level of pottery in the ditch fills is 'irreconcilable with the idea of a post-kiln establishment of the defensive circuit'.[74]

These excavated kilns are not, however, the earliest evidence for pottery production at Stamford. After the construction of the ditched enclosure, pits were dug to the east of it, associated with pottery production beyond the excavated area. They may have been dug to acquire clay, and the primary fill of the pits was yellow sand, perhaps also raw material for use in pottery production. They were later used for waste disposal, with the upper fills including Stamford ware, some decorated with red paint, firing debris and pottery wasters. The pits were sealed by a substantial deposit of firing waste and a layer of loam, and this phase of production clearly preceded that of the excavated kilns which cut through it. Kilmurry also claimed that the outer enclosure ditch cut this layer, but the excavation report does not support this. Indeed, 'the earlier kiln debris horizon…was not found to the west of the kiln', which is where the enclosure ditch was located.[75]

Much has also been made for dating purposes of a Scandinavian imitation of a Two-Line Alfred coin of the 880s reportedly retrieved from the fill of the inner enclosure ditch.[76] However, the excavation report contradicts this, stating that the coin was recovered from 'a disturbed and ill-defined context' associated with the building of the hall of the medieval castle, and 'is not therefore a useful precise chronological indicator'. Although the coin does not then precisely date the infilling of the ditch it does suggest Scandinavian activity in this area of the 880s or a little later as such coins continued in circulation to c.900.[77] It seems highly unlikely that a defensive, perhaps royal, enclosure would have been infilled during the period of Viking raids, when it would have been useful, and it seems more plausible that it was levelled after proving insufficiently large for the Great Army once eastern Mercia came under its control in 877; a larger defensive circuit of c.6ha was subsequently constructed to the east. In sum, the evidence suggests the foundation of a pottery industry towards the end of the ninth century after Stamford came under Scandinavian control. It has been important to outline this revised phasing because it has been claimed that the industry was founded earlier in the ninth century, but this rests on the Kilmurry

74. Kilmurry 1980, 32; Roffe and Garwood forthcoming; Garwood forthcoming
75. Kilmurry 1980, 32; Roffe and Garwood forthcoming; Garwood forthcoming
76. Kilmurry and Mahany 1977, 185; Blackburn 2005, 42
77. Kilmurry 1980, 32; Blackburn 2005, 20; Roffe and Garwood forthcoming

account of phasing which is not accepted by those bringing the excavations to publication.[78]

Ipswich

The term 'Thetford wares' has been widely applied to a range of ceramic forms produced in East Anglia, that were wheel-thrown and fired in a reducing atmosphere. Despite the name, they were manufactured not only at Thetford, but also Norwich and Ipswich, and by the late tenth century at Grimston, Langhale, and Bircham (Norfolk).[79] 'Thetford ware' and 'Thetford-type wares' have become catch-all terms for dark grey, gritty, reduced pottery, and the interchangeability of the terms, and lack of specificity about production centres in many reports make it difficult to refine dating. Therefore, in what follows we have selected the best studied sites and assemblages.

A Thetford ware industry was in operation at Ipswich and is hereafter referred to as Ipswich-Thetford ware. It emerged at the same place as the Middle Saxon Ipswich ware industry, encouraging a direct comparison between the two types of manufacture.[80] Seven of the eight excavated Ipswich-Thetford ware kilns are in the same Cox Lane/Carr Street area as some of the earliest Ipswich ware kilns, with another in the centre of the town at the Turret Lane site. The recovery of over-fired sherds of Ipswich-Thetford ware in the Stoke Quay area suggests production south of the River Orwell, where another Ipswich ware kiln has recently been discovered.[81] Berni Sudds has recently commented on some of the similarities between the industries, including both rim forms and 'a chemical link' between the clays used to make both Ipswich and Ipswich-Thetford ware, suggesting the possibility of a 'direct connection and some shared local knowledge between the industries'.[82] Yet there are also differences, as the Ipswich ware potters used a wider range of raw materials from variable clay beds, while the Ipswich-Thetford ware potters seem to have selected finer clays.[83] Both wares have a reduced grey fabric, but are otherwise distinctive. For example, Ipswich-Thetford ware vessels are typically flat-based,

---

78. Blinkhorn 2013, 162; Blinkhorn and Griffiths 2023, 108–11, which also states that Stamford ware (p. 124) was found in a Middle Saxon phase at Staunch Meadow, Brandon, but the site report says it is unstratified and 'typical of the products of the industry during the late 10th–12th centuries' (Blinkhorn 2014, 159).

79. Hurst 1976, 314

80. Wade 1988; 1993

81. Smedley and Owles 1963; Wade 2013b and pers. comm.; Sudds 2020, 147, 185–6, 188; Poole 2020

82. Sudds 2020, 155

83. Badreshany 2020; Sudds 2020, 147–9

high-shouldered, with thin walls, uniform profile, and restricted necks, whereas Ipswich ware vessels have sagging bases and thick, uneven walls, and are wide-mouthed with a baggy uneven profile (Figure 8.10).[84] The kilns are also very different. The Stoke Quay Ipswich ware kiln is circular with a central pedestal, while that at Buttermarket is elongated with a central spine from which sprung arches form a suspended floor. In contrast, none of the known Ipswich-Thetford ware kilns appear to have had any form of pedestal or spine and are all roughly circular to ovoid in plan.[85] Furthermore, while Ipswich ware

Figure 8.10. Ipswich-Thetford ware jar from the kiln excavated near St Helen's Street, Ipswich (Suffolk County Council Archaeological Service)

vessels are decorated with stamped designs, such as circular grids and 'hot cross bun' designs, the decoration used in the later industries is very different, and includes rouletting, thumbed impressions, and applied strips. While Ipswich ware is widely distributed across eastern England, very little of the later Ipswich-Thetford ware was transported beyond Ipswich before the eleventh century.[86]

The differences between the two industries indicate a transformation in craft production, in the *chaîne opératoire*, from selection of raw materials through to decoration and finishing, and in how the vessels were then circulated and used. Importantly, there is no evidence for gradual application of the wheel-throwing technique from small open forms to increasingly larger closed vessels, a development that would be expected if the potters' wheel had been an indigenous innovation.[87] Instead, a range of forms, from small bowls to large storage jars, appear simultaneously, indicating the arrival of highly skilled potters. In sum, there is little to suggest continuity of craft practice from Ipswich ware to Ipswich-Thetford ware.[88]

84. Hurst and West 1957, fig.1; Hurst 1976, 314; Blinkhorn 2014, 162; Sudds 2020, 147
85. Hurst and West 1957; Smedley and Owles 1963; Blinkhorn 1989; Wade 2013b; Poole 2020
86. Smedley and Owles 1963; Sudds 2020, 147
87. Berg 2007, 247–8; Sudds 2016, 83
88. Sudds 2020, 154–5

Over fifty excavations in the historic core of Ipswich have yielded assemblages of Ipswich-Thetford ware, but its dating has been recently deemed to be 'as vague and problematic as in the late 1950s when Hurst first defined the type'.[89] Archaeomagnetic dating of Kiln I at Cox Lane suggested that it was in operation between c.950 and 1000, but this was clearly not the earliest kiln.[90] Ipswich-Thetford ware often occurs alongside Ipswich ware but issues of residuality and intrusive finds in complex urban stratigraphy make it difficult to use this evidence to date the end of the Ipswich ware tradition and the start of the Ipswich-Thetford ware industry. Indeed, even in later medieval contexts around 20% of the pottery is residual Ipswich ware.[91] A few pits containing only Ipswich ware and imported Badorf ware dating to no later than the mid-ninth century, but no Ipswich-Thetford ware, may provide evidence for its later origins.[92] Hurst noted the occurrence of both Ipswich and Ipswich-Thetford ware in contexts pre-dating the arrival of continental Pingsdorf ware, which he believed replaced Badorf ware in the late ninth century, leading him to deduce that Ipswich-Thetford ware emerged in the mid-ninth century.[93] However, Pingsdorf ware is rare in England, and its absence is therefore not a very convincing indicator.[94]

Dating for both the end of the Ipswich ware production sequence and the commencement of the new wheel-thrown production mainly depends on contexts with associated coins. The latest coin found in a stratified context in Ipswich containing only Ipswich ware is a penny of Coenwulf of Mercia, minted in Canterbury c.805–10; such coins are known to have circulated into the 830s, suggesting a deposition date of c.805–40.[95] At Flixborough, Ipswich ware occurs in stratified contexts that provide 'a substantial increase in the corpus of known associations of Ipswich ware with mid 9th-century material culture' as Paul Blinkhorn has observed. These include two separate ditch fills which each also contained pennies of Æthelberht of Wessex, minted 858–64, and in another ditch fill Ipswich ware is found alongside two mid-to-late ninth-century Class A strap-ends of sub-types A1ax and A1axii.[96] Sherds from a later phase at Flixborough indicate that 'Ipswich ware may have come from vessels in

89. Sudds 2020, 154
90. Hurst and West 1957, 234, 247; Smedley and Owles 1963, 318; Sudds 2020, 154
91. Blinkhorn 1993; 2012; 2014, 162; Wade 2013a, 4–7
92. Sudds 2020, 155
93. Hurst 1976, 319
94. Sudds 2020, 155
95. Blinkhorn 1993, 19; 2012, 6; Archibald 2011, 2; Wade 2013a, 5
96. Blinkhorn 2009, 359; 2012, 6; Thomas 2000a, Appendix 3; Thomas et al. 2009, 13

contemporary use in the late ninth or early tenth centuries'.[97] At North Elmham (Norfolk) an almost complete Ipswich ware vessel was recovered from a cesspit associated with an early tenth-century building.[98] In summary, outputs of the Ipswich ware industry, especially storage jars, continued to be in use, even if not being made, well beyond 850.[99]

The earliest contexts in Ipswich in which Ipswich-Thetford ware can be coin-dated belong to the late ninth century.[100] For example, at St Stephen's Lane an area of copper-alloy working has produced over 1800 Ipswich-Thetford ware sherds and three coins, each from distinct layers of burning and metalworking. They comprise a Scandinavian imitation of an Alfred penny of the 880s or 890s and a denier of Charles the Bald of a type minted after 864, neither of which is likely to have been in circulation beyond c. 900, and a St Edmund penny probably deposited in the early tenth century.[101] Two pits dominated by Ipswich-Thetford ware and containing St Edmund pennies were also excavated at this site, and another at Franciscan Way was associated with a road and buildings that clearly post-dated the Middle Saxon period represented by Ipswich ware.[102] At School Street, there were fifteen pits containing Ipswich-Thetford ware sealed under the early tenth-century town bank, including one with 600 sherds and a denier of c. 864–900.[103] Two St Edmund pennies were recovered from the defensive bank at School Street, in contexts dominated by over 3000 sherds of Ipswich-Thetford ware.[104]

Excavations at Stoke Quay have reinforced this conclusion that the Ipswich-Thetford ware industry was already in existence in the last quarter of the ninth century. Ipswich-Thetford ware was recovered from features that preceded a cemetery of over 300 burials, which originated in the late ninth to early tenth century. The earliest radiocarbon dates from skeletal remains are AD 888–996 and 860–1040 (at the 94% confidence level). Earlier features included 25 pits, which mainly contained Ipswich ware, but some Ipswich-Thetford ware. There were also three cellared buildings, the fills of two of which contained

97. Loveluck and Atkinson 2007, 95–6; Pestell 2017, 215; this evidence was not considered in Blinkhorn and Griffiths 2023.
98. Wade 1980, 424
99. Sudds 2020, 155
100. Wade 2013a
101. Archibald 2011, 5–6; Wade 2014a, 17–18; Thomas 1997, 3–4; 2000a, 433; SCCAS 2015b
102. Wade 2014c, 5; SCCAS 2015b; Wade 2014a, 21; Archibald 2011, 6–7; Sudds 2020, 156
103. Wade 1988, 97; 2014b, 2, 5–6; SCCAS 2015a; West 1963, 237–46; Blinkhorn 1993, 19; 2013, 162; Sudds 2020, 154
104. Archibald 2011, 31–2; Blinkhorn 1993, 19, 30; 2013, 162; West 1963, 237–46; Wade 1988, 97; 2014b, 6; Sudds 2020, 154

largely Ipswich-Thetford ware, while the third contained a mixture of Ipswich and Ipswich-Thetford wares. This evidence suggests that the buildings were constructed late in the period when Ipswich ware was in use and fell out of use after Ipswich-Thetford ware was being manufactured, all of which occurred before the cemetery was founded by the late ninth or early tenth century.[105]

Thetford

The area of the tenth-century town of Thetford, delineated by a ditched enclosure, was largely abandoned after the Norman Conquest and so has been subject to numerous excavations that have revealed much about its pottery industry. These have also shown that Middle Saxon activity was only found at the western edges of the town, and further west. The majority of the excavated features in the town date to the tenth century, or are not closely datable, but there are some indications of late ninth-century activity in the form of coins and at least two furnished Scandinavian graves, as noted in Chapter 2.[106] Eleven kilns have been excavated in Thetford and concentrations of wasters suggest the locations of others, largely located on the edges of the tenth- and eleventh-century town. Unlike the other industries discussed here, the kilns were horse-shoe shaped.[107] There is no clear dating evidence for the origins of the industry from the kiln excavations, and this needs to be pursued through analysis of findings of its products from consumer sites (Figure 8.11).

Thetford ware has long been regarded as emerging in at least the early tenth century, since a hoard of coins dated to *c.*925 from Morley St Peter (Norfolk) was contained within a Thetford-ware vessel.[108] There have been recent claims that Thetford ware was first produced in the 840s or 850s, but this seems to be informed by the dating offered by Hurst decades ago.[109] Certainly, Thetford ware has been recovered in small quantities at sites that were otherwise dominated by Middle Saxon wares, but in most cases these sites can be shown from other evidence to have continued in use into at least the later ninth century. For example, Thetford ware is found in small amounts at Brandon Road, west of Thetford, a site broadly thought to have been abandoned following the arrival

---

105. Brown and Popescu 2020, 73–7, 426
106. Andrews 1995, 24–7; Atkins and Connor 2010, 31–4, 115–17
107. Musty 1993, 70
108. Clarke and Dolley 1958; Blinkhorn 2013, 165
109. E.g. Spoerry 2016, 27, 105

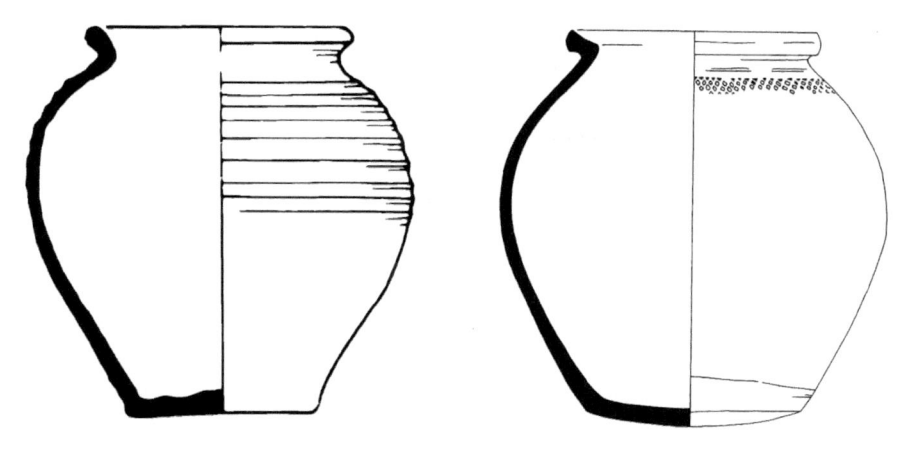

Figure 8.11. Ipswich-Thetford ware (left) and Thetford ware (right) jars (authors after McCarthy and Brooks 1988, fig. 87; Rogerson and Dallas 1984, fig. 156)

of the Great Army in 869.[110] However, some of the metalwork may be of later ninth- or early tenth-century date, including an A2 strap-end and a hooked tag, while metal-detecting has retrieved items of similar date, including strap-ends, hooked tags, and iron knives, to the west of the site near the Thetford Bypass.[111]

Thetford-type ware appears at Chesterton Lane in Cambridge in a layer above a series of Middle Saxon execution burials, and in the area where Everson and Stocker believe the Army established their winter camp in 874–5.[112] The report is unclear if the pottery is from Thetford itself, but this is the closest site of manufacture. Other than some abraded Roman sherds, no pottery was directly associated with the burials, which have been radiocarbon dated to between the early seventh and early ninth centuries, with Bayesian modelling of the dates suggesting that the cemetery came into use AD 640–830.[113] These burials were sealed by a 0.1m thick gravel surface, which had been repaired at least once, and incorporated three sherds of Thetford-type ware, two of Ipswich ware, and one sherd of Maxey ware. Cut through this layer was another burial, radiocarbon dated to 750–940 at the 95% confidence level; when combined with the other radiocarbon dates, this suggests that the first phase of burial ended 720–880 at the 95% confidence level.[114] This suggests that

110. Blinkhorn 2010, 70–9, table 14; Atkins and Connor 2010, 117
111. Crummy 2010, 42–59; Atkins and Connor 2010, Appendix 5
112. Cessford *et al.* 2007, 215–16; Everson and Stocker 2022, 58
113. Cessford and Dickens 2005b, 78; Cessford *et al.* 2007, table 3
114. Cessford *et al.* 2007, 212, 216

Thetford-type ware was introduced here in the later ninth century. On top of the gravel surface a make-up layer and a compacted white clay floor was laid down and a building constructed, with associated pottery now dominated by Thetford-type ware and St Neots ware, another East Anglian wheel-thrown product.[115]

In Chapter 7 we discussed metal-detected and fieldwork evidence for settlement disruption and abandonment in the late ninth century, and in some cases, this can help to refine the dating of the inception of the wheel-thrown industries. For example, the eighth- and ninth-century elite site at Staunch Meadow, Brandon appears to have come to an end in the late ninth century, with occupation moving closer to the later medieval village.[116] Analysis by Blinkhorn shows that wheel-thrown pottery was mainly from unphased contexts, or clearly intrusive in earlier contexts.[117] Thetford ware appears in a phased context only at the end of occupation, represented by a ditch flanking a pathway leading from a causeway and a timber bridge replacing a stake-lined causeway over the River Little Ouse, and it represents just 8.6% of the ceramic assemblage of that phase. Thetford ware was also recovered from a pit close to the waterfront which cut through Middle Saxon rubbish deposits, but which had seemingly been open for some time, and incorporated a range of finds, some residual, including Ipswich ware, as well as nails, bone combs, and a late ninth-century A5 strap-end with silver wire inlay.[118] There is little material culture securely datable to the tenth century, by which time the site seems to have gone out of use, and taken together this suggests that Thetford ware arrived before the end of the ninth century. Around 120m to the south of Staunch Meadow, excavations at the site of Brandon Leisure Centre produced a more extensive Late Saxon assemblage, suggesting that settlement continued there after that at Staunch Meadow came to an end. Some of the late ninth- to tenth-century dress accessories and jewellery are of types not found at Staunch Meadow, while the pottery assemblage is dominated by Thetford ware, and other wheel-thrown wares from Stamford and St Neots.[119]

Excavations of Cambridgeshire rural settlements indicate reorganisation in the later ninth century, with Middle Saxon activity associated with Ipswich

115. Cessford and Dickens 2005b, 81; Cessford *et al.* 2007, 216–17; this does not support the claim in Blinkhorn and Griffiths 2023, 115 that Thetford ware was introduced between 840 and 875.
116. Tester *et al.* 2014, 356–93
117. Blinkhorn 2014, 159–62; overlooked in Blinkhorn and Griffiths 2023, 114
118. Tester *et al.* 2014, 22–5, 128–32, 159–66, 227, 383–93; Riddler 2014, 354; Thomas 2000a, 435
119. Tester *et al.* 2014, 341–9; Blinkhorn 2014, 343–4; Riddler 2014, 354–5

ware and the later occupation associated with Thetford ware and other wheel-thrown wares. The excavators of both Lordship Lane, Cottenham, and West Fen Road, Ely, concluded that there is nothing to suggest that the two wares were in simultaneous use.[120] Similarly the settlement at Church End, Cherry Hinton, is associated only with Thetford, St Neots, and Stamford wares, and while there is little dating evidence, a single A1 silver strap-end inlaid with niello is a ninth-century form not thought to have been in circulation beyond *c.*900 (see Chapter 4).[121] A recent survey of rural settlement in west Norfolk by Davies also revealed ninth-century settlement reorganisation that helps refine the dating of Thetford ware pottery. At Wormegay, for example, a Middle Saxon settlement focus, including a ploughed-out cemetery, was succeeded by a more restricted area of activity to the west, where geophysical survey identified a sub-circular enclosure ditch, *c.*3m wide and with a projected diameter of *c.*80m, in 'an Ipswich Ware free area towards the church'. This enclosed area yielded a 'handful' of Thetford ware sherds, a Borre-style brooch, and a gold ingot, while two fragments of an oval brooch from the cemetery area may indicate the location of a furnished Scandinavian burial. This settlement focus has been described as 'a short-lived and potentially greatly transformed phase of settlement activity'.[122] It provides a valuable example of the chronology of the introduction of Thetford ware at a settlement previously using Ipswich ware.

York

Like Ipswich, York was a major trading centre, or *wic*, in the eighth and ninth centuries, and an ecclesiastical centre where the archbishops were based. Excavations at Fishergate have suggested that the *wic* was, however, in decline by the middle of the ninth century.[123] Wheel-thrown pottery in a gritty and often oxidised fabric dominates assemblages in York in the late ninth and early tenth centuries. There are two variants known as York A ware and York D ware. Vessels in York A ware mainly comprise cooking pots (over 80% of the assemblage) and bowls, the former typically had everted rims, with flat wire-cut bases, and there is very little decoration, limited to rouletting on the shoulders of just six sherds from Coppergate. York D ware is less coarse than A ware and vessels have simple everted rims, although roulette decoration is more common

120. Mortimer and Hall 2000, 24–5; Mortimer *et al.* 2005, 148
121. Cessford and Dickens 2005a, 58–61
122. Davies 2010, 147–63, 308–9; NMS-156, -DE2312
123. Rogers 1993; Mainman 2019, 83–4

Figure 8.12. York A ware vessel excavated from the pre-tenement phase (Period 3) at Coppergate (YAT)

than on A ware. Much D ware is in the form of cooking vessels with flat or sagging bases, with occasional lamps. There is very little York A ware at Fishergate, but it accounts for around 70% of the non-Roman pottery in Period 3 at Coppergate in the mid-late ninth to early tenth century (Figure 8.12). Despite the name, no kilns producing this ware have been excavated in York and where it was made is uncertain.[124] Ceramic petrography has revealed the inclusion of baryte in York A ware and also in the late medieval pottery produced at Thorner (North Yorkshire) c.30km to the south-west of York, suggesting that this may have been the clay source for York A ware.[125] York seems to be unusual among the towns in the regions of Scandinavian settlement in apparently importing all of its pottery in the late ninth and tenth centuries.

York D ware comprised only c.3% of non-Roman pottery in Period 3 at Coppergate. More York D ware was found in the Lurk Lane excavations in Beverley (East Yorkshire), in roughly equal proportions to the A ware, suggesting the production centre for D ware may have been somewhere to the east of York.[126] Sherds of both A and D ware were found in the latest fill of one of the ditches defining the Lurk Lane site; in the top of the adjacent bank was a hoard of stycas dated to no earlier than 851. The ditch was infilled after this date and so the pottery was dated to the late ninth or early tenth century.[127]

Stafford

Whilst Stafford is an outlier to the other wheel-thrown industries described in this chapter it is important to address recent suggestions that it provides

124. Mainman 1990, 400–15; 2020, 68–71
125. Vince 2004
126. Mainman 1990, 411–15
127. Armstrong *et al.* 1991, 10–15, 62, 72–4

evidence for the inception of the wheel-thrown revolution by the mid-ninth century. Stafford's potters produced vessels in a sandy oxidised fabric, in a range of forms, from small to large bowls and jars, pitchers, and lamps. Vessels were decorated with incised horizontal lines below jar necks, roller stamping, and thumb-applied strips on large storage jars. A handful of sherds from Tipping Street were also glazed.[128] The wares from this industry are largely found only in Stafford and other *burhs* founded in the early tenth century, including Chester.[129] Seven pottery kilns have been excavated in the east part of the town centre and the locations of others have been inferred from the recovery of wasters.[130]

Radiocarbon dates were acquired from fuel in the first three excavated kilns, of AD 670–1020, AD 820–960, and AD 780–990, respectively, at the 95% confidence level, which led to the conclusion that they 'were perfectly compatible with occupation after AD 913 and before AD 1066'.[131] Excavations in 2009 of three more kilns recovered large amounts of charred plant remains, probably used as fuel, which produced six more calibrated radiocarbon dates of AD 680–890, two of AD 770–980, one of AD 780–990, and two of AD 880–1020, all at the 95% confidence level.[132] An archaeomagnetic date of AD 866–1089 (95% confidence level) was derived from fired clay samples from one of these kilns. Together these dates were interpreted as representing related activity and application of Bayesian statistics led to the claim that the industry commenced between AD 800 and 880 at the 68.2% confidence level, interpreted in the site report as showing that 'Stafford-type ware came into production some time around the middle of the 9th century'.[133] This has been described by John Blair as evidence 'that this critical innovation was getting underway as the Mercian regime faced its final disaster' from Viking attacks.[134] However, a recent reassessment of the earlier radiocarbon dates to allow for an old wood effect on the dates derived from charcoal samples, and the acquisition of new radiocarbon dates, has modified this interpretation. This most recent analysis suggests that the pottery industry origins should be dated later, to the late ninth or early tenth century, but it agreed that 'significant activity, including pottery production and crop processing, took place at Stafford before the historically attested establishment of the burh in AD 913'.[135]

128. Ford 1998–9, 27–8
129. Ford 1998–9, 32–3
130. Carver 2010, 77–9; Ford 1998–9; Dodd *et al.* 2014
131. Carver 2010, 77, 92, 149–50
132. Dodd *et al.* 2014, 46, 79–82
133. Dodd *et al.* 2014, 101
134. Blair 2018, 267
135. Hamerow *et al.* 2020, 5; Blinkhorn and Griffiths 2023, 115–16, 131–6

Figure 8.13. Stafford ware jar in a sandy oxidised fabric; a waster from the 1982 Tipping Street excavations, Kiln S1 (photo by Reb Ellis-Haken; courtesy of The Potteries Museum & Art Gallery, Stoke-on-Trent City Council)

It has also been debated whether Stafford ware really was a wheel-thrown industry. Initial analysis concluded that vessels were 'hand-formed from coils of clay and then wheel-finished', with bases having been made from flat clay slabs that were then joined to the body, although it was also suggested that some of the vessels were so well finished that they may have been 'entirely wheel-thrown'.[136] However, more recent analysis suggested that

136. Ford 1998–9, 20; Carver 2010, 79

'the majority of vessels could have been wheel-made, with some degree of hand-forming, principally on the bases'.[137] Visual inspection of a range of vessels from Tipping Street indicates a range of possibilities, as some vessels have thick, uneven lower walls indicative of hand forming methods but thin, rilled upper walls suggestive of wheel-throwing (Figure 8.13). To resolve this matter, we undertook X-ray analysis of sherds from the 1977 (ST17), 1982 (ST32), and 2009 (STTIP09) excavations at Tipping Street. This revealed that Stafford ware is entirely wheel-thrown and that the uneven lower walls are a consequence of potters using a tool to scrape clay away from the thickly thrown walls and bases to make them thinner. This secondary forming technique obscured evidence of the primary wheel-throwing and created a very uneven wall thickness, giving the impression that the lower walls had been handmade. The bases were wheel-thrown, with their sagging uneven profile resulting from potters using their fingers to push out the freshly scraped base from the inside, the same technique used at Torksey.[138] In conclusion, it seems likely that the Stafford ware industry did come about as the result of continental influences, but as a secondary development; this probably saw potters relocating from eastern Mercia, and there are similarities with kiln forms at Torksey, although the tongue-shaped pedestal of one kiln (4287) is of a type not found anywhere else in England at this time.[139]

Continental influences

The ceramic revolution was not the result of importing technology from Scandinavia, where the fast wheel and updraught kilns were unknown. Rather the influences came from the northern part of the Continent, in particular northern France and the Low Countries, where the distinctive elements of the various wheel-thrown industries in England can be found in the ninth century.[140] A selection of the most recently excavated or studied industries are discussed here (Figure 8.14).

While the fast potter's wheel had ceased to be used in Britain after the end of the Roman period, it continued to be used alongside kiln-firing in the

137. Dodd *et al.* 2014, 45
138. Perry 2016
139. Dodd *et al.* 2014, 23, 98
140. Perry forthcoming

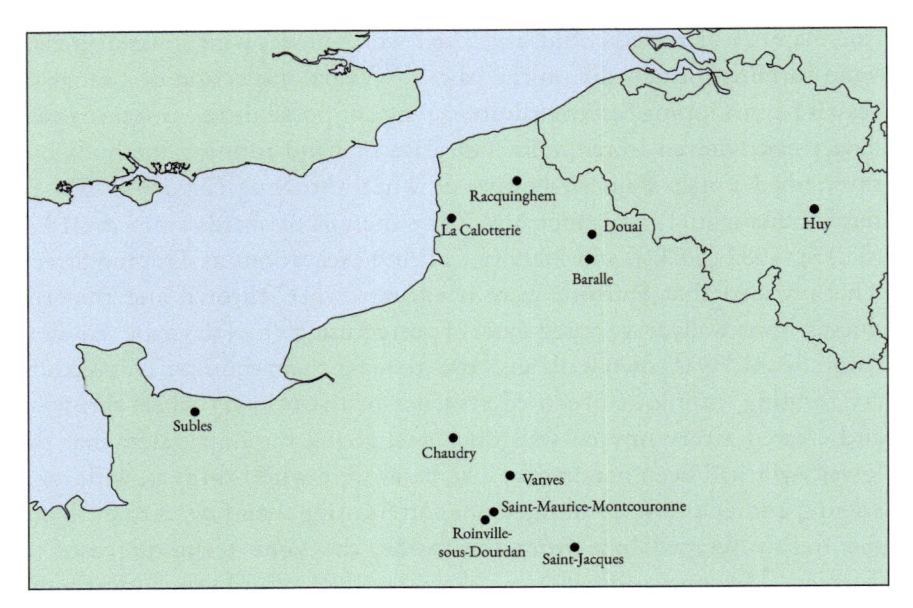

Figure 8.14. Map of location of selected northern continental kilns (authors)

northern part of the Continent.[141] In the ninth century there were numerous pottery industries operating between Paris and Dorestadt, producing bowls, jars, pitchers, socketed bowls, lamps, and costrels. However, despite producing wheel-thrown and kiln-fired wares, there were differences in the manufacturing processes, especially with respect to clay choice, forming and decoration, firing regimes, and kiln structures. For example, many of the northern French industries fired sandy ferruginous clays in either oxidising or reducing atmospheres, or a combination of the two, which produced a diverse range of fabrics. In the Île-de-France these include reduced fabrics at Saint-Maurice-Montcouronne, oxidised fabrics at both Vanves and Saint-Jacques, and fabrics with oxidised cores and reduced surfaces at Roinville-sous-Dourdan.[142] In the northern part of the Île-de-France region the sandy fabric was light in colour, typically beige, pink, or orange (e.g. Vanves, Saint-Jacques, and Chaudry), whilst to the south grey wares were the norm, for example at Saint-Maurice-Montcouronne and Roinville-sous-Dourdan.[143] Elsewhere, fine low iron white clays were fired in an oxidising atmosphere by potters working at Huy (Belgium)

141. Kilmurry 1980, 182–7; Piton 1993; Hincker and Husi 2006; Thuillier and Louis 2015; Perry forthcoming
142. Goustard 2015; Lefèvre and Peixoto 2015; Lefèvre *et al.* 2015
143. Lefèvre *et al.* 2015

and Baralle (Pas-de-Calais), while other potters using similar clays fired them in a reducing atmosphere, as at Douai (Nord).[144] All of these practices can be found in eastern England. For example, sandy clays, fired in reducing atmospheres, were manufactured at Torksey (Kiln 2), Thetford, and Ipswich, and pottery with reduced cores, oxidised margins, and oxidised surfaces are typical of most of the other Torksey kilns. Beige to buff pottery is paralleled in York ware, orange pinks at Stafford and white firing clays used by potters at Huy are paralleled at Stamford.

The northern continental industries each produced a broadly similar range of vessels, but with distinctive qualities (Figure 8.15). For example, jars were

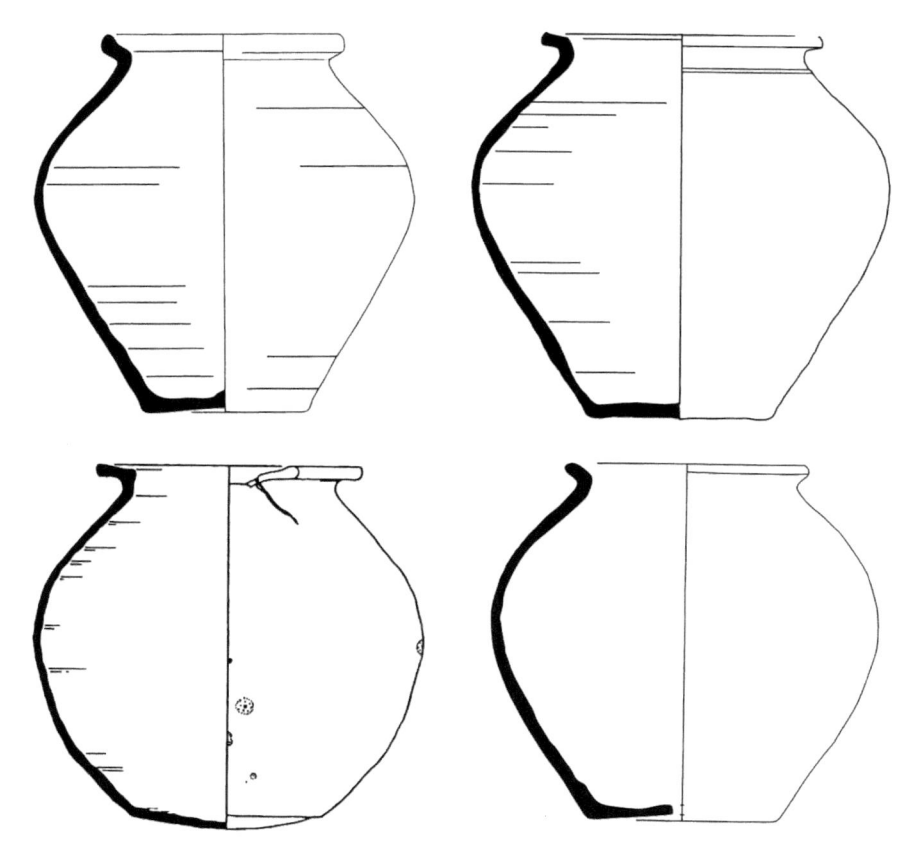

Figure 8.15. Vessels from selected continental industries: (top left) Vanves; (top right) Chaudry; (bottom left) Huy; (bottom right) Subles B (authors after Giertz 1996, fig. 5; Hincker *et al.* 2006, fig. 10; Lefèvre and Peixoto 2015, fig. 10; Lefèvre *et al.* 2015, fig. 2)

144. Louis 2015; Jacques 1976, 78; Giertz 1996, 40–2

typically high shouldered with restricted necks, but their bases differed. Some have a sagging form, such as those from Chaudry, but flat bases are more common, with wire marks showing how the vessels were removed from the wheel-head. Flat bases were characteristic of northern France and the Low Countries, unlike the Rhineland where they had given way to 'trimmed convex bases' by the mid-ninth century.[145] Rims varied, with simple everted forms common at Subles (Normandy) and Saint Maurice-Montcouronne, but lid-seated forms known at Vanves.[146] Decoration included the use of paint at La Calotterie (Pas-de-Calais), burnishing at Douai, rouletting at Baralle, Douai, and Roinville-sous-Dourdan, and wavy lines on vessel shoulders at Saint-Maurice-Montcouronne. Vessels with prominent grooved ridges on their upper shoulders, similar to those found on Ipswich-Thetford ware jars, were produced at Barralle.[147] Painted decoration was common in the Seine valley and north towards Normandy as well as at Huy in the Meuse valley where glazed wares were also produced in the mid-/late ninth century.[148] Parallels for these features can be found among the early wheel-thrown industries in England. For example, Ipswich-Thetford and Torksey Kiln 2 vessels had flat bases with wire marks from where they had been cut from the wheel, while sagging bases are characteristic of the products of other Torksey kilns. Simple everted rims are typical of York D ware, LKT, and Torksey Kiln 2 products, while lid-seated rims characterise vessels made at Stamford and Ipswich. Roulette decoration is found on most of the early wheel-thrown industries in England, while wavy lines occur on LSLS ware. Glazed pottery was produced at Stamford, Torksey, Stafford, and Lincoln, although it is only at Stamford where glazed wares were produced over a long period and widely traded. Stamford is the only industry where paint is known to have been used. Kilmurry drew parallels between the products of the Castle site kilns and those from the region spanning Normandy to the Pas-de-Calais, but the products of the middle Meuse valley, especially at Huy, seem more likely influences.[149]

The continental kilns comprise three main features: a stoke-hole, single flue, and circular/slightly ovoid firing chambers, generally less than c.1.5m in diameter, but their construction varied. Some had stone-lined firing chambers, such as those at Vanves; others were clay-built, as at Racquinghem (Pas-de-Calais),

---

145. Lefèvre *et al.* 2015; Jacques 1976, 78–81; Kilmurry 1980, 190
146. Hincker *et al.* 2006; Goustard 2015; Lefèvre *et al.* 2015; Lefèvre and Peixoto 2015
147. Thuillier *et al.* 2015; Jacques 1976, 81–5; Louis 2015; Lefèvre *et al.* 2015; Hincker *et al.* 2006; Goustard 2015
148. Adrian 2006; Giertz 1996; Husi 2010
149. Kilmurry 1980, 195; Giertz 1996, 51

while at Subles the internal kiln walls were lined with broken fragments of pottery.[150] Some kilns, such as those at La Calotterie and Racquinghem, had inclined or horizontal firing chamber floors without internal structures, suggesting that vessels were placed directly on the chamber floor.[151] Others had a tongue extending from the rear wall, such as at Subles and Vanves, or vessels were placed on the base to produce a raised floor, as at Saint-Maurice-Montcouronne.[152] There is some evidence for regional practices: in north-eastern France and Belgium, kilns rarely had internal structures, whilst kilns with a central tongue were more common further west.[153] This variation is characteristic of the kilns in eastern England. Torksey Kiln 2 and the Ipswich-Thetford Cox Lane kiln are both clay-lined with no internal structure, while kilns with central tongues are known from Stafford.[154]

The diversity of the wheel-thrown pottery industries in late ninth-century England suggests that the technological revolution was not the product of the influence of a single continental potting community.[155] Rather, it seems that the movement of potters from more than one region was involved. Some of the industries of the Rhineland may also have been influences, with the decorative strips typical of vessels produced in the Vorgebirge region on so-called relief-band amphorae similar to decorative elements on vessels from Thetford and Stafford, with the means of attaching the rims at Thetford identical, but at present the dating evidence places these innovations into the tenth century.[156] Some of the choices made in the *chaine opératoire* of the new industries were driven by the local availability of raw materials, but the others were deliberate choices derived from communities of craft practice.

Pottery production centres and the Great Army

At least some members of the Great Army arrived from northern France and the Low Countries where Viking armies had been active in the ninth century, and some of the new pottery industries emerged where the Army overwintered. At Torksey, the first kilns were constructed on open ground less than 0.5km from the

---

150. Lefèvre and Peixoto 2015; Thuillier 2015; Hincker *et al.* 2006
151. Thuillier *et al.* 2015
152. Hincker *et al.* 2006; Lefèvre and Peixoto 2015; Goustard 2015
153. Thuillier 2006; Lefèvre and Peixoto 2015
154. Thuillier 2015
155. Giertz 1996, 52; Perry forthcoming
156. Giertz 2000, 262–5

southern edge of the camp, where gaming pieces, clench nails, and woodworking tools led us to suggest that this may have been used as a secondary shipyard by the Great Army before becoming a focal point of pottery production. We undertook stable isotope analysis on eight individuals buried in an enclosed cemetery contemporaneous with the kilns and the results indicated that at least four were non-local. The combined oxygen and strontium values are equally compatible with them growing up in western Britain, central France, southern Scandinavia, or the Low Countries, and whilst we obviously cannot say that these were continental potters the results at least reflect the diversity of the population living and dying in Torksey after the overwintering of the Army.[157] Other centres of pottery production discussed in this chapter were not documented in association with the Army but all, except Stafford, have evidence of Scandinavian activity in the late ninth century, some of which is characteristic of the material culture associated with the Army. Here we provide a brief survey, as this evidence has been overlooked in previous reviews of the emergence of wheel-thrown wares.[158]

Lincoln is only 20km from Torksey, less than a day's travel, and almost the same distance as York is from Aldwark. It is inconceivable that members of the Army would not have visited, and various finds provide supporting evidence. For example, items from near the church of St Paul-in-the-Bail in the Upper City are characteristic of material found at Great Army sites, including four silver Lunette pennies from Wessex and Mercia dating to the early 870s, at least one of which was cut, a Carolingian belt buckle and strap slide, and a Trewhiddle-style strap-end and belt buckle. These items have been interpreted as a disturbed hoard, and the Trewhiddle-style strap-end and buckle seem likely to have been closely associated given that 'they are of the same metal, have similar niello-inlaid Trewhiddle-style decoration and dimensions'.[159] While it has been noted that there is otherwise little archaeological evidence from Lincoln that can certainly be dated to the earliest period of Scandinavian activity (c.873–80), the evidence is more complex.[160] Traces of bullion exchange associated with the Great Army are rare in towns, where, as Kershaw has argued, there may have been an early requirement to use coins; at the same time coins of this period are rare single finds, beyond metal-detected contexts.[161] Even so, there is, in fact, quite a lot of material from Lincoln, if mostly residual, likely to

157. Hadley *et al.* 2023, 25, 29
158. Blinkhorn 2013; Blinkhorn and Griffiths 2023, 113–14, 119–21
159. Blackburn *et al.* 1983, 10–11; Vince 2001, 159–60; 2003, 151
160. Vince and Jones 2016, 486; Blinkhorn and Griffiths 2023, 119–20
161. Kershaw 2017, 184

date to the last quarter of the ninth century that can be associated with Viking activity, even where such items are not of Scandinavian manufacture. Letty Ten Harkel has recently reviewed this evidence, much previously unpublished, which includes an iron spearhead from Flaxengate, ringed pins, a Borre-style buckle, and a B4 Borre-style strap-end similar to types from both Aldwark and Torksey.[162] Ansate brooches span the Middle and Late Saxon periods, but one of the three Lincoln examples is similar to a type from Domburg and another is a rare outlier of a Frisian-influenced type produced in East Anglia; taken together this suggests their arrival in Lincoln through Scandinavian agency. Globular and biconical pins are common Middle Saxon items but, as we have seen, they also continue into later periods; three of the five from Lincoln are polyhedral-headed with ring-and-dot decoration, like types from Torksey. Other items of either late ninth- or early tenth-century date include a Borre-style disc brooch, two lead-alloy flat disc brooches with a stylised cross design, and a copper-alloy buckle with a triangular plate.[163] There was also a mint in Lincoln operating under Scandinavian control before the end of the ninth century. This produced copies of Alfred's coins in which the monogram representing the name of London was modified to represent Lincoln; Blackburn argues that these imitative coins were minted soon after Alfred's original issue dated to the early 880s.[164] St Edmund coins minted under Scandinavian control in East Anglia and a St Peter's coin from York have also been recovered from the town.[165]

There is no record of a Great Army presence in Stamford, but some of its former members were clearly based there. Evidence includes the Scandinavian imitation of an Alfred coin of a type being manufactured during the reign of Guthrum in East Anglia discussed earlier, and the finds from the Castle excavation include a ringed pin, and bone pins, of a type Arthur MacGregor has identified as being characteristic of Viking-age contexts in Scandinavia, Britain, and Ireland.[166] A poorly recorded hoard discovered in 1902 dated to c.890 contained Scandinavian imitations of Alfred's Two-Line and London Monogram types, similar types bearing the monograms of Lincoln and Leicester, and a Carolingian denier of Charles the Bald. Some of these coins had been pecked to test for silver content in a characteristically Scandinavian practice.[167] This is

162. Ten Harkel 2018, 2
163. Ten Harkel 2018; see also Vince 2003, 153; Weetch 2014, 153–5, 158–63, 169–72; Steane 2016a, 56; Haldenby *et al.* 2022, 17
164. Blackburn 2005, 21
165. Blackburn *et al.* 1983, 12–13; Vince 2006, 528–32; Porter 2021, 125–6
166. Mahany forthcoming; MacGregor 1985, 120–1
167. Grueber 1903; Blackburn 1989, 22, 25; 2001, 130–1; Porter 2021, 70–1

unequivocal evidence for Scandinavian activity in Stamford in the 880s and 890s. Æthelweard's late tenth-century chronicle mentions land to the west of Stamford being under Scandinavian control in the early 890s, and Stamford has been suggested as the location of one of the mints that struck St Edmund pennies.[168] At Great Casterton, 4km to the north-west on Ermine Street, another indicator of Scandinavian activity comes from possible remains of a hoard containing two coins of Burgred of the 870s from the ruins of a Roman bath-house.[169] Stamford was evidently occupied by the earliest generations of Scandinavian settlers following the Great Army's settlement of eastern Mercia in 877, remaining under Scandinavian control until 918 when it was seized by Edward the Elder and a second *burh* was built south of the Welland.[170]

The Ipswich-Thetford ware industry clearly emerged during the period that followed the establishment of Scandinavian kingship of East Anglia under Guthrum. Ipswich is not documented in this period and so has largely escaped discussion of the Scandinavian impact in the late ninth and early tenth century, but the archive from excavations in Ipswich reveals numerous traces of Scandinavian activity. In particular, coins that were minted under Scandinavian control have been recovered in significant numbers, and this is clear evidence for Ipswich having been a centre of Scandinavian settlement in the immediate wake of the Great Army taking control of East Anglia. Five Viking imitations of the coins of Alfred were recovered from St Stephen's Lane, one of which was a plated forgery (Figure 8.16), and another imitative coin of Alfred was recovered from a pit at Tacket Street.[171] Three imitative halfpennies of Alfred were recovered from a burned building at St Stephen's Lane dating to the early tenth century and may have been the remains of a hoard.[172] Alongside the St Edmund pennies from this site was a lead striking from dies for the St Edmund issues.[173] One of two

Figure 8.16. Plated forgery of a coin of King Alfred from St Stephen's Lane, Ipswich (Suffolk County Council Archaeological Service)

168. Campbell 1962, 51; Blackburn 2001, 130–1; Porter 2021, 340–1
169. Corder 1961, 74, 88
170. Mahany and Roffe 1983, 209–11
171. Archibald 2011, 3, 13, 19, 25; Wade 2014a; 2014d
172. Blackburn 2005, 20; Archibald 2011, 19
173. Archibald 2011, 7, 9–10, 13

St Edmund pennies found at Foundation Street had a peck mark.[174] Two coins of Charles the Bald, recovered at School Street and St Peter's Street, may also reflect late ninth-century Scandinavian activity, especially since the former shows pecking.[175] While these coins were all recovered from later contexts they nonetheless combine to reflect late ninth- and early tenth-century Viking activity. Blackburn has argued that Ipswich is likely to have been where both Alfred imitations and St Edmund coins were minted.[176]

Other artefacts found in the same contexts are also indicative of Scandinavian influence. At the St Stephen's Lane site these include an A2 strap-end, a ninth-century form well represented at Torksey and Cottam, fragments of moulds for manufacturing strap-ends, including a tongue-shaped Class E, of a type that we have discussed as having been adopted by the Scandinavians from continental forms, and an antler brooch mould for producing disc brooches with concentric decoration of broadly tenth-century date. A Borre-style disc brooch with a flat profile is indicative of Anglo-Saxon forms of manufacturing and so it is a hybrid product.[177] The site has also produced fragments of nine balances, used either by merchants or craftworkers, and three plain lead weights, although none typical of types from the camps.[178] A B5–3 strap-end, a short-lived type associated with the Great Army, was found in a late ninth- or early tenth-century ditch at Franciscan Way.[179] A recent study of bone and antler objects has identified a hitherto unrecognised Scandinavian influence in Ipswich 'something not seen on the same scale anywhere else in England, even at York'.[180] The evidence for Scandinavian activity in Ipswich during the period when East Anglia was under the control of Guthrum and his Scandinavian successors is, in sum, stronger than has previously been widely recognised.

Wheel-thrown pottery industries are known from other centres in the tenth century, such as Norwich, Northampton, and Leicester. There is currently no clear evidence that they emerged any earlier; 'Leicester-type' ware was found in pre-Period I at Flaxengate, but the only excavated kiln in Leicester is of much later date.[181] On current evidence these seem to belong to a later generation of industries, although it is worth noting that both Leicester and Norwich have evidence

174. Archibald 2011, 45; Wade 2014c, 5
175. Wade 2014b, 6; Archibald 2011, 31, 39
176. Blackburn 2009, 54; Porter 2021, 347–8
177. Archibald 2011, 5–6; Wade 2014a, 17–18; Thomas 1997, 3–4; 2000a, 145–6, 242, fig. 5.1, 433; SCCAS 2015a; 2015b; 2015c; Newman 1993; Weetch 2014, 312
178. Kruse 1992
179. Thomas 1997, 6; Wade 2014c
180. Riddler *et al.* 2023, 390
181. Young *et al.* 2005, 72–3

for minting under the agency of the Great Army and its rulers, and so seem to have been key places in the early generation of Scandinavian settlement in Mercia and East Anglia, respectively. Both were also under Scandinavian control into the early tenth century, as was Northampton, and all three are thought likely to have minted St Edmund coins.[182] These industries have much in common with those discussed in this chapter with origins in the late ninth century. In Norwich a Thetford-type ware was manufactured, the pottery produced at Northampton was the only other industry besides Stamford to use fine white, low iron clays, while the Leicester industry has similarities with other East Midlands industries using sandy clays.[183] Unless new evidence should emerge to place their origins any earlier, these, like Stafford, were among the second generation of industries.

Conclusion

This chapter has demonstrated that wheel-thrown pottery began to be produced in England in the late ninth century, during the period of Scandinavian control. It is also clear that the earliest wheel-thrown industries occur in regions where the Great Army had been active, and most of them have evidence for the presence of the Army in the immediate vicinity. East Anglia remained under direct control of Guthrum until his death in 890, and the coinage shows it was under ongoing Scandinavian control until the second decade of the tenth century.[184] Eastern Mercia similarly remained under Scandinavian control at least until the second decade of the tenth century, while Northumbria saw a succession of Scandinavian kings into the mid-tenth century.[185] We propose that the ceramic revolution was initiated by potters who arrived from northern France and the Low Countries, under the patronage of the Great Army's leaders and their successors. It seems unlikely that the transformation was driven by potters operating independently, since they would have required support and protected access to raw materials as well as to markets. Therefore, the new Scandinavian rulers must have permitted industries to be set up in the major centres through which their authority was exercised, and where coins were being minted under their economic and political influence, sometimes also involving continental craftworkers.

---

182. Blackburn 2001, 126–7, 130–1; Williams *et al.* 2021, 45; Porter 2021, 338–40, 355–7
183. Lentowicz 2007, 165
184. Whitelock 1961, 50–60; Blackburn 2005
185. Blackburn 2001; 2004; Whitelock 1961, 63

Ipswich is the only place discussed in this chapter that had seen earlier pottery production on any scale, and it does seem a remarkable coincidence that a wheel-thrown industry should emerge here. Given the issues of residuality, it is impossible to be sure when Ipswich ware ceased to be produced, but if still in production or at least in use this may have provided an impetus to replace existing craft practices.[186] Perhaps, alternatively, Ipswich was a centre of authority that was perpetuated by the new regime, mirroring the continuity of minting from the Middle to Late Saxon periods that Blackburn noted, and another indication of Guthrum and his followers adopting aspects of the existing administrative infrastructure.[187] Even so, we cannot account for the new pottery industry merely by appealing to 'continuity' as the practices inherent to each of these industries were very different, from raw materials selection to forming and firing techniques.[188] Potters could not simply have copied production practices from elsewhere by looking at finished products; there is no evidence of transitional 'practice' products, and in any case craft practices need to be learned, not in the abstract but through guidance and training, and embedded within a community of craft culture.[189] This renders entirely unconvincing a recent claim by Blinkhorn and Griffiths that 'it is hard to believe that the incumbent potters would have been unable to quickly grasp how to make pots on a continuously-rotating wheel'.[190] Wheel-throwing is 'a radically different technique' from coil-building requiring 'the acquisition of entirely new and unfamiliar motor skills as well as continuous and directed exercise', as Ina Berg has shown.[191]

The industries each had a very different *chaîne opératoire*, suggesting the arrival of potters from multiple different industries, each bringing their distinctive skillset, rather than gradual diffusion of technological change from a single point of innovation.[192] It is even possible that potters from more than one tradition were involved in setting up new industries at a single location. For example, at Torksey we see two distinct potting traditions, in terms of forming, firing, vessel types, and kiln structure, and there were evidently several different potting traditions in operation in Lincoln.[193] While the new industries were mainly found in regions where pottery was already widely used,

186. Blinkhorn 2014, 162
187. Blackburn 2009, 54
188. Blinkhorn 2013; Blinkhorn and Griffiths 2023
189. Kilmurry 1980, 177; Hadley 2020, 186–7
190. Blinkhorn and Griffiths 2023, 117
191. Berg 2007, 247
192. Vince 1993, 161
193. Perry 2016

distribution networks were transformed. For example, the wares of the new East Anglian industries largely only circulated within that region, unlike the preceding Ipswich ware which was widely distributed. Middle Saxon Maxey ware was produced on a commercial scale at multiple sites and widely distributed in eastern England, whereas wheel-thrown industries served distinctive regions, with Torksey ware, for example, mainly found in Lindsey and Yorkshire. The Lincoln products were largely distributed locally until well into the tenth century, perhaps principally provisioning a new mercantile group from the Continent and some elite rural settlements, although the presence of competing industries may have simply meant that some failed to take off any further.[194] Stamford ware was more widely distributed, but its primary zone of usage was the southern parts of Lincolnshire and East Anglia.[195] The new industries also imply changes in consumer demand, with new types of vessels produced, although recent lipid analysis of wheel-thrown and earlier handmade pottery has suggested no notable changes in diet.[196] We should also note that some handmade pottery production continued in the areas where new wheel-thrown wares began to be manufactured, and wheel-thrown production was less extensively taken up in Northumbria, a region with a more limited pre-existing tradition of pottery production and use, and also with a more centralised political regime.[197] In contrast, the more dispersed distribution of the wheel-thrown industries in eastern England reflects what we know of the different political structure of those regions. In the East Midlands and East Anglia there were multiple centres of Scandinavian control in the late ninth and early tenth centuries, reflected in the distribution of early tenth-century *burhs* which were also typically minting coins under Scandinavian overlordship from the 880s, including the St Edmund coins.[198] Many of these are precisely the same places that the wheel-thrown industries emerged, and the link with regions under Scandinavian control seems clear.

To understand the ceramic revolution, we need to do more than just prove that it pre- or post-dates the Scandinavian settlement; it needs to be seen as a complex set of variables relating to political and economic circumstances, pre-existing ceramic traditions, and the subtleties of the *chaîne opératoire*.[199] Scandinavia was not aceramic, as handmade pottery was used, and while wheel-

194. Blair 2018, 268
195. Symonds 2003, 108–13; Young *et al.* 2005, 44, 56, 64; Perry 2016, 101–8; Blair 2018, 268
196. Ashby *et al.* forthcoming
197. Young *et al.* 2005, 37, 81–8; Hall *et al.* 2014, 568; Sudds 2016
198. Blair 2018, 276–9; Porter 2021, 192, 314–61
199. Perry 2016, 105; Sudds 2020, 154

thrown pottery production was unknown some was imported, especially from the Rhineland via Frisia.[200] Furthermore, any members of the Great Army who had visited major settlements in northern Francia or Frisia, would have been familiar with wheel-thrown pottery. The wine they received as tribute in Francia may have come in wheel-thrown vessels, and both ninth-century Viking hoards on Wieringen were buried in Badorf ware vessels from the Rhineland.[201] Richard Hodges has recently highlighted that the precise dating provided by the new excavations in Ribe now places the main import of Tating ware within the period 820–60, and argues that it was linked to adoption of a 'package of Frankish cultural practices', including wine drinking, as well as dress accessories and swords. He also notes that whilst much of this pottery originated in the Rhineland, it arrived in Scandinavia via Frisian traders, and was being used in domestic contexts rather than for the liturgical functions once supposed.[202] Scandinavians clearly had access to wheel-thrown pottery in the ninth century and this may, then, have been a factor prompting the ceramic revolution in eastern England.[203] Connections between Frisia and eastern England were already well established, although as we have seen the ceramic influences also came from a wider area of northern Francia, after imports directly from the Rhineland dried up, showing that it was not simply continuity of contacts that underpinned the emergence of the new industries.[204]

While potters may have followed in the wake of the Great Army settlement in England, seeking new opportunities in the ways that some moneyers and metalworkers had, there may have been other factors. There were renewed Viking attacks in the 870s and 880s in the Meuse and Scheldt valleys, into the eastern Netherlands and the Rhineland and the region around Paris, with patronage networks for craftworkers and protection of trade undoubtedly disrupted.[205] Ecclesiastical communities were major landowners and key consumers in these regions and some fled from Viking raids, as occurred on the Scheldt in 880 when according to the *Annals of St Vaast* 'all monks, canons, and nuns of all ages and conditions fled with the remains of the saints'.[206]

200. Deckers 2022b; Hodges 2023
201. Kilmurry 1980, 182–3, 188; Besteman 2004; McLeod 2014, 155–6
202. Deckers 2022b; Hodges 2023
203. Hurst 1976, 311–12; Giertz 1996, 38–41; Young and Vince 2009, 364–8; Pestell 2017, 215–17; Mainman 2020, 62–6
204. Pestell 2017, 212
205. Giertz 1996, 52; Capelle 2006; Cooijmans 2020, 130, 139, 144, 146–9, 151; Van den Bossche 2022
206. Cooijmans 2020, 160

Disruptions to trading activity in late ninth-century Frisia have been suggested by Coupland on the basis of reductions in the supply of silver coins, while archaeological evidence of burning and destruction that can be dated to the late ninth century at Zutphen, Deventer, Liège, Huy, Aachen, and Duisburg has been linked to recorded Viking raids of the period.[207] If these circumstances combined to prompt potters to relocate then it also betokens a knowledge of available opportunities and access to necessary raw materials and patronage. There is evidence for continuing connections with the northern part of the Continent, including the arrival of an army in 879 that departed for Ghent, while an army that arrived in 892 had previously been in eastern Francia, which included parts of Frisia, before embarking from Boulogne in the Pas-de-Calais.[208] There may, then, have been several factors that combined to encourage the movement of experienced potters from the Continent to eastern England in the late ninth century, with decades of contact and influence playing their part.

That the leaders of the Great Army would foster pottery production is entirely consistent with the considerable innovations in production of dress accessories, jewellery, gaming pieces, and coins characteristic of its camps. As we have seen, these combined influences from Scandinavia, England, Ireland, and the Continent; some were short-lived introductions, and may have been restricted to the members of the Army, but others were long-lived and widely adopted. The minting of coinage copied the economic and political apparatus of western European kingship, drawing on the skillset of both English and continental moneyers who sometimes brought with them the dies with which they had worked on the Continent. We know that members of the Great Army were engaged in trading networks that spanned England, Ireland, the northern part of the Continent, Scandinavia and beyond, adopting new forms of exchange and manufacture to facilitate this.[209] Guthrum also engaged in written diplomacy with Alfred, an innovation for a Scandinavian king.[210] In this wider context the transformation of pottery production is readily explicable, as part of the socio-economic package adopted by Viking leaders who became kings of their new territories.

207. Giertz 1996, 62; Coupland 2006, 253–4, 261–2; Groothedde 2004, 116; Cooijmans 2020, 138; Neuray 2020; Krause 2020; see also Chapter 9
208. McLeod 2014, 139–40, 156
209. Williams 2007; Hadley and Richards 2016; Kershaw 2017; Woods 2020; Heen-Pettersen 2021; Horne 2022
210. Kershaw 2000; McLeod 2014, 209–13

9

The legacy of the Great Army

In this final chapter we examine what happens next, both in terms of the Viking Great Army and future research on it. In Chapter 7 we demonstrated that we can now see traces of the Army beyond its camps, and at places where its former members chose to settle in England. Now we extend our investigation of the artefactual signature of the Army to look for traces of its members who may have returned to Ireland, the Continent, or Scandinavia. Finally, we consider the wider implications of our findings, both for Viking armies in general, as well as for archaeological research more broadly, including the importance of data re-use.

The Viking Great Army moves on

In Chapter 2 we saw that the success of the Viking Great Army led to partitions of three Anglo-Saxon kingdoms: Northumbria in 876, Mercia in 877, and East Anglia in 880. Many members of the Great Army took over the land they had been gifted or seized, and established a new life in England, eventually adopting local customs and religions. Some of the weapon burials that date to the end of the ninth or early tenth century may be of warriors who had arrived decades earlier with the Great Army. However, it is difficult to distinguish these from the burials of subsequent arrivals, and it is likely that the cluster of accompanied burials in north-west England, including those discovered at Cumwhitton, relate to a later settlement phase.[1] Nonetheless, a Great Army association is a reasonable interpretation in the case of those buried with signature items, such as a grave discovered at Kildale (North Yorkshire) in the nineteenth century which contained a set of scales and two lead weights.[2]

1. Paterson *et al.* 2014
2. Redmond 2007, 110, xlii–xliv

Other former members of the Great Army appear to have settled further afield. This is suggested by some of the finds associated with a male burial at Kiloran Bay on the island of Colonsay in the Inner Hebrides. He was buried in a stone enclosure over which a small boat was placed, and two slabs at either end were marked with crosses, either Christian emblems added to a pagan burial, or re-used grave-markers from nearby. A horse was buried outside the enclosure, with its metatarsal severed by a massive blow, and weapons in the grave included a sword with inlaid silver wire decoration, a spear, axe, and shield with an Irish type of boss. There was also an Insular bridle mount, a set of bronze scales, comprising a balance beam, both pans, and six decorated lead weights, inset with Insular metalwork (Figure 9.1). Three stycas had also been included amongst the grave goods, two of which had been perforated, perhaps for use as insets on lead weights, while a lead object, originally interpreted as a weight, resembles crowned gaming pieces from Torksey.[3] This assemblage, reflecting a cosmopolitan lived experience, may reveal the burial of a former

Figure 9.1. Kiloran Bay grave goods (National Museums Scotland)

---

3. Graham-Campbell and Batey 1998, 118–22

member of the Great Army whose journey north had ultimately led him to settle on this distant Hebridean island.

Documentary sources reveal movement between England and Ireland by some of the leaders of the Great Army and there are some archaeological traces of members of the Army returning to Ireland in the late 870s. For example, among the lead weights dredged from the River Blackwater was one inset with a coin of Alfred of the Lunettes series, and a hoard of at least seven West Saxon and Mercian coins from Leinster dates to c.875.[4]

Some members of the Great Army clearly left the British Isles completely and may have resumed raiding in northern Europe, or headed to the trading centres of Scandinavia, northern Francia, and the Baltic. Viking raids documented in the eastern Netherlands and along the River Rhine in 881–2 must have involved former members of the Great Army. Some of them may have left along with an army that had briefly been in England over the winter of 878–9, based at Fulham. It made contact with the Great Army, before leaving for Ghent, subsequently spending several years raiding in Flanders and the Low Countries. In Nijmegen, destruction layers dated to the late Carolingian period have been tentatively linked to a documented camp set alight over the winter of 880–1.[5] In 882 the *Annals of Fulda* record that 'The Northmen burned the port called in the Frisian tongue Deventer…with great loss of life', and this raid has been traced in archaeological evidence of large areas of burning and destroyed buildings beneath the later town rampart.[6] At Zutphen, c.18km south of Deventer, archaeological evidence for another Viking raid was identified when building the new Town Hall in 1997. A burnt layer containing late ninth-century pottery sealed the destroyed remains of two houses and five sunken huts. They were filled with large amounts of tuff, thought to be from an ecclesiastical building and implying an attack on the church of Zutphen. On the floors of two of the huts were the skeletons of a c.12-year-old child and a woman aged 30–40, with sword wounds on her leg (Figure 9.2). Amongst the debris in these huts were many lower limbs and skulls of cattle, suggesting the meat-bearing portions had been taken away, perhaps by Viking raiders acquiring food supplies. Among charred grain next to the skull of the child, was a styca of Æthelred II, reflecting the involvement of a Great Army veteran. Lead gaming pieces have been found more recently on the opposite bank of the River Ijssel among metal-detected finds from Wapse, an island of c.5ha in the

4. Bourke 2010, 26, 74–5
5. Cooijmans 2023, 148; MacLean 2009, 184
6. Reuter 1992, 93–4; Groothedde 2004, 116

Figure 9.2. Female skeleton lying on the floor of burnt-out and collapsed hut, Zutphen; believed to be a victim of a late ninth-century Viking raid (Collection Stedelijk Museum, Zutphen; photo Bert Fermin)

floodplain, in a location not dissimilar to that of Torksey, albeit rather smaller. Other finds include a Borre-style mount, Irish cross-shaped brooch, and a Carolingian mount and Trewhiddle-style strap-end which had both been deliberately cut.[7] Together this is compelling evidence for the activities of former members of the Great Army finding new places to plunder after they had departed England.

The growth of metal-detecting in the Low Countries and Germany, and the availability of formal reporting mechanisms and online databases, has increased evidence for Viking activity, in the form of dirhams, cubo-octahedral weights, weaponry, and jewellery, some of which indicate individuals who had previously been in England. Other indicative finds include an Alfred penny of the 890s that had been pierced for suspension from Tiel (Netherlands), and a styca from Druten.[8] Late ninth-century hoards containing Anglo-Saxon coins

7. Hadley *et al.* 2020, 3
8. E.g. Portable Antiquities of the Netherlands (https://portable-antiquities.nl); PAN-00023023, -00039972; Capelle 2006

suggest an element of the Army that had been in England returned to raiding on the Continent; maybe after their defeat at Edington when some promised Alfred 'that they would leave his kingdom'.[9] For example, a hoard including silver ingots and deniers uncovered at Saint-Pierre-des-Fleurs (Eure) may have been partly assembled in England since it also contained Scandinavian imitations of Alfred's Two-Line coins. It is thought to have been buried or lost around 895 by Vikings encamped along the nearby River Seine.[10]

Other former members of the Great Army returned to Scandinavia. We have already noted the B5–1 strap-end manufactured in Northumbria recovered from the high-status settlement that pre-dated the tenth-century fortress at Aggersborg, in northern Jutland (Chapter 4), and other components of the Viking Great Army signature are identifiable elsewhere in Scandinavia. For example, four lead gaming pieces were found in a mid-to-late ninth-century hut at the Viking-age settlement at Füsing in southern Jutland, on the northern shores of the Schlei Fjord (Figure 9.3). Within sight of Hedeby, and with a direct road connection to the Danevirke fortification, Füsing may therefore have had a military role, reflected in the recovery of arrowheads and axes, and may even have been the home of a royal representative connected to the *emporium* at Hedeby. Three more gaming pieces have now been identified from Hedeby itself, and it seems highly likely that these were brought to southern Denmark by former members of the Army.[11]

Northumbrian stycas have been found in several Scandinavian, Frisian, and Slavic trading centres, including Hedeby, Birka, Dorestad, Schouwen (Netherlands), Mainz, Menzlin, Schuby (Germany), and Staraya Ladoga (Russia), and may provide other traces of the onward journeys of members of the Great Army. Stycas would have had no monetary value in these regions, so they are best seen as trophies or souvenirs. The two examples from Birka are

Figure 9.3. Two of the Viking lead gaming pieces from Füsing (Andres Dobat)

9. Whitelock 1961, 49
10. Cardon *et al.* 2008; Cooijmans 2023, 148
11. Dobat 2017, 602–3; 2022

from graves, one of which also contained a ringed pin of Irish type, providing further evidence of connections with areas of Viking raiding. Two stycas have been found at Janów Pomorski on the Baltic coast in Poland, near the town of Elbląg. The site has been identified as the ninth-century trading place of Truso and excavations have retrieved not only Slavic material culture, but also numerous finds of Scandinavian origin including weapons, jewellery, Valkyrie figures, and extensive evidence for production of amber, metal, bone, and horn artefacts. There are over 1000 coins, mainly dirhams, as well as more than 1200 weights, including cubo-octahedral types, but also lead weights, some inset following the practice adopted by the Great Army. Some thirteen non-Islamic coins have been found, from Frisia, Francia, Denmark, and England, including one of Æthelwulf of Wessex, most of which had been pierced to enable them to be suspended, showing that they were no longer of monetary use.[12] While these were minted no later than the 850s, taking into account the form of the coins and the presence of the later weights, there are grounds for suggesting that the stycas, and perhaps some of the other coins, reflect the arrival of former members of the Army.

There is also evidence that suggests some members of the Army returned to Scandinavia. A burial in the Aust-Agder county of south-east Norway at Vig, Fjære, contains two lead weights inset with stycas of Eanred (Figure 9.4).[13] In both cases the reverse side of the coin is face up, featuring the name of the moneyer, rather than the king, but most significantly, perhaps, a cross. The burial was placed under a mound c.20m diameter, and also contained a plain lead weight, a sword, and axe. There were also items used in smithing including an iron anvil, a hammer and pliers, an ingot mould, and a piece of soapstone with a hole in it which would have been used in the forge to direct the current of air from the bellows onto the fire.[14] These items would have been used in the transformation of precious metals into ingots. The individual buried at Vig

Figure 9.4. Two lead weights inset with Northumbrian stycas from the male burial at Vik, Fjære (CC-BY-SA, Kulturhistorisk Museum, Oslo)

12. Pirie 2000, 90; Bogucki 2009; Gardeła 2015, 219–20; Jagodziński 2010, 140
13. Williams 1999, 24
14. Nicolaysen 1877

was being commemorated as a warrior, a silversmith, and a trader, exhibiting the skillset typical of veterans of the Great Army.

Heen-Pettersen has catalogued thirty-three inset lead weights from Norway, the highest concentration in Scandinavia. Eight were recovered from Kaupang, 11 are either stray or metal-detecting finds, and 14 were found in graves, of both males and females.[15] The weights probably originated in England and came to Norway with returning members of the Great Army. Their occurrence in graves demonstrates the high personal value attached to them, almost as 'campaign badges', signifying involvement in successful overseas expeditions and the status accrued by this. Most of the Scandinavian examples appear to have been selected for their distinctive and exotic qualities; weights with plain insets were only rarely taken to the Viking homelands. As well as the coin inset weights, two with glass insets from Kaupang and Heimdalsjordet are similar to examples from Torksey, Woodstown, and other metal-detected finds from England.[16] A weight inset with decorative metalwork from Aalgaard has close parallels at Torksey and from a burial at Islandbridge, while another from Håland, Sandeid, Vindafjord is almost identical to one from Gisburn (Lancashire).[17] Heen-Pettersen notes that the influx of inset lead weights to Norway coincides with the arrival of Anglo-Saxon swords.[18] There are twenty-six examples of Type L, generally found in late ninth- or early tenth-century burials. This is especially noticeable in south-eastern Norway, where a marked concentration of decorated lead weights and Anglo-Saxon swords are found in association with, or relatively close to, Kaupang. Maybe this was an area from where many of those who joined the Great Army were drawn, and to where they returned.

Lead weights inset with Insular metalwork and coins have also been found elsewhere in Scandinavia. There is a stray find from Lund (Sweden), and examples from graves at Birka include one inset with gold inlay and another similar to a weight from Steyning (Sussex).[19] There are also six published examples from Denmark, discovered as stray or metal-detected finds, some of which are associated with settlements, and two more found by metal-detecting in Hedeby.[20] The greater number of stray finds from Denmark may

---

15. Heen-Pettersen 2021
16. Pedersen 2008, fig. 6.36; Pedersen and Rødsrud 2013, fig. 4
17. Harrison and Ó Floinn 2014, fig. Ill. 269; T2127; LANCUM-107126; Hiett 2020, 28
18. Heen Pettersen 2021
19. Wamers 1985, 107; Gustin 2004, 21; Sperber 2004, 71; SUR-4094E0; Hiett 2020, 26
20. Baastrup 2013a, 12–15; 2013b, 172–82; Heen Pettersen 2021

be explained by metal-detecting being more common there, with a national recording scheme (DIME).[21]

Viking armies: new and old data sources

This book could not have been written twenty years ago. Much of our new knowledge about the Viking Great Army and this critical decade of English history has been the result of hobbyist metal-detecting, a form of what is now often termed Citizen Science. Metal-detecting led directly to the discovery of what have become the best understood camps of the Great Army at Aldwark and Torksey, and it is metal-detecting that has now updated the previous model for a Viking camp, at Repton, having indicated its wider landscape context. Furthermore, it is the national database of metal-detected finds catalogued by the Portable Antiquities Scheme that is now revealing many more sites that were visited by members of the Viking Great Army, across eastern and northern England, as we saw in Chapter 7. This also suggests varying impacts, sometimes disrupting the local population, and causing settlement abandonment or reorganisation, other times leading directly to ongoing Scandinavian settlement, while elsewhere providing a brief interlude in otherwise continuous occupation.

As we have seen, these datasets are vital for understanding the composition, scale, and activities of the Great Army, and help illuminate the nature of Viking armies of the ninth and tenth centuries more broadly, especially when even small-scale archaeological excavation and survey can provide additional context for the finds. But of the countries in which Viking armies were active, a study of this nature is only possible in England, given the ban on metal-detecting in Ireland and France, other than as part of professional archaeological investigation. This English evidence helps to demonstrate what we are missing in Ireland and many regions of the Continent, and therefore broadens our perspective of Viking activity there too. However, we should not assume that the camps in those regions were identical to those in England, in terms of scale, landscape setting, or material remains. The camp at Woodstown, which is often cited as the best parallel for the English camps, is no more than a tenth of the size of Aldwark or Torksey. The *Annals of St Bertin* also indicate that the Viking forces on the Seine split into individual 'brotherhoods' when they

21. Dobat *et al.* 2019

overwintered, which would have created a distributed series of widely dispersed smaller camps.[22]

But metal-detected finds, like any other form of evidence for past activity, from documentary sources to place-names, only provide a partial picture. For one thing there is a strong element of serendipity in the discovery of sites. It was pure chance that led to the discovery of Aldwark and Torksey, and a decline in deep ploughing at Torksey now means that very few artefacts are being brought within detector range.[23] A detectorist visiting the site afresh would likely give up before finding anything of significance. The importance of proper recording of finds is essential to being able to interpret them, and the challenges presented when this does not occur have been emphasised. The focus of metal-detecting is also on non-ferrous metals, which for an age obsessed with the working and reworking of gold, silver, copper-alloy, and lead is invaluable, yet our controlled detecting for ironwork at Torksey, and the small-scale excavations at Aldwark, have also indicated the importance of the blacksmith and weapon smith. Furthermore, while excavation and fieldwalking have recovered some animal and human bones, we otherwise lack the organic remains, in bone, antler, ivory, leather, and wood, for which we only have to look at the special anaerobic preservation encountered in the excavations at Viking-age Coppergate for a glimpse of what more there is to be known. Beyond that are the intangible aspects of Viking culture, most notably the people: the warriors, craftworkers, and slaves, and the multi-cultural groups that travelled with the armies. For that our selective sample of material culture must stand surrogate.

Nonetheless, our detailed analysis of the assemblages from Aldwark and Torksey indicates that in another sense nothing is missing, despite metal-detecting bias. The two assemblages, collected by different combinations of people, and recorded under very different circumstances are remarkably similar, demonstrating that they provide representative samples of the assemblages. There are some differences between the sites, and we have indicated where we believe these are a product of differential recording and where they reflect real differences between Viking activities and material culture in camps just a few years apart. Ten more years of detecting at either site, and larger numbers of finds, would not change the picture. Where limited excavations have been conducted at both sites, they have confirmed the picture from metal-detecting,

22. Cooijmans 2020, 141–51; 2023; Raffield 2016
23. Hadley and Richards 2021, 88–9, 208

and the same range of finds has been recovered, albeit in proportion to the area examined compared with the massive scale of the camps. What has become apparent, however, is that in both cases the objects which reflect the occupation of the camps are now in the plough zone, and the subsequent land use has truncated or destroyed most structural features relating to the occupation, if there were any. However, we now know what a Viking camp looks like, and a priority for future research must be to target any such camp where there might be an expectation of buried land surfaces, particularly if waterlogged.

The precise dating resolution provided by documentary sources for metal-detected assemblages is also incredibly important, and unique in archaeology. We have demonstrated that over 1800 artefacts from Torksey were discarded within a twelve-month window, and even if the 800 from Aldwark were gathered over a few years such precise dating is still exceptional. In general, archaeologists should be reluctant to ascribe specific identities to material culture assemblages, particularly as material culture fashions are actively used to create identities, which are adopted by wider populations. However, in the case of the Great Army camps, we can be confident that the assemblages are a direct reflection of the cultural groups occupying them and that many of the categories, including the gaming pieces, were short-lived. Furthermore, as we move beyond the camps we can see that the Great Army signature had a very limited currency, no more than a generation, before new hybrid cultural artefact forms emerged, and which were more widely adopted across northern and eastern England over coming decades.[24] Again this degree of dating precision is unusual and allows us to develop some nuanced site histories, and our research has also helped to refine the chronologies of many late ninth- and early tenth-century artefact classes. Through detailed analysis of how the material culture from the camps had been treated, including evidence for re-use and repurposing, we have also been able to distinguish items that had been gathered for such purposes from those that were being worn and were recovered as casual losses.

Another objective for future research should be those metal-detected sites which have revealed an undocumented Great Army presence. We have demonstrated that they have a very varied settlement history. At Swinhope and Binbrook there were what appear to be two high-status Middle Saxon estate centres, both of which had Great Army visitors, followed by a more enduring Scandinavian presence and connections with other areas of Scandinavian influence into the tenth century. A similar pattern emerges from some of the East

24. Hall 2000; Thomas 2000b; Kershaw 2013; Haldenby *et al.* 2022, 108–14

Anglian sites such as Congham, and West and East Rudham. By contrast, most of the Anglo-Saxon sites in southern Northumbria ended abruptly in the late ninth century, apparently abandoned. Only a handful of sites investigated, including Yapham 2, Stamford Bridge 2, and Cottam have tenth-century activity. Where metal-detecting has been undertaken using GPS survey allowing detailed spatial recording we can see the importance of horizontal stratigraphy in understanding settlement evolution, but when we only have distributions of non-ferrous artefacts this can be difficult to interpret. Our work at Cottam and Torksey has demonstrated the value of deploying a barrage of archaeological approaches alongside metal-detector survey, including fieldwalking, geophysics, aerial photography transcription, and targeted excavation. The work of Gareth Davies on settlement sites in west Norfolk has similarly shown the benefits of integrating metal-detected data with survey, fieldwalking, and excavation.[25] Geomorphological examination of the landscape of the Torksey camp and its environs, including use of LiDAR, surface geology, coring and pollen analysis demonstrates how these techniques can help us understand the choices made by Viking armies in deciding where to camp, and how they might be used as tools for predictive modelling of site location.[26] To these we might add the detailed historical geography study of parish boundaries in conjunction with place-names employed by Stuart Wrathmell in North Yorkshire as a means of studying longer-term Scandinavian settlement.[27]

A key feature of our research has been the importance of data re-use. Most of the metal-detected evidence we have drawn upon to understand life in the Viking camps was not collected for our research. At the national level, none of it was. Yet it has been an invaluable resource, and we have been able to make use of it, as an open access resource, publicly available to all, and we have not had to undertake large-scale expensive archaeological fieldwork, nor intervene in extant sites via new excavation; as we have seen, such interventions on ploughed sites would have been unlikely to have been any more insightful. Similarly, our research into the pottery industries which followed as part of the legacy of the Army has largely been a desk-based study, drawing upon open data archives recording decades of rescue archaeology in advance of development in towns such as Ipswich and Lincoln. The increasing availability of grey literature reports in open access formats via the ADS has also been invaluable to this study. None of this was recorded or made available with our research in

25. Davies 2010
26. Stein 2014
27. Wrathmell 2020

mind, but it again demonstrates the importance of a culture of data sharing and re-use. The potential to undertake comparative analysis with the growing body of similar datasets from parts of the Continent and Scandinavia should be a future research priority.

Our work has also demonstrated the potential of using physical archives and museum stores of pottery recovered from development-led excavations in English towns from the 1970s onwards to undertake new research on the transformation in pottery production. We have shown that X-ray imaging is effective in identifying production methods, obviating the need for the more expensive techniques of ceramic petrography. We have also identified the similarities with continental industries, and the influences of the new industries on later generations of industries in England. Further priorities for future research would be to undertake a programme of analysis of all the ninth- and tenth-century industries, using ceramic petrography and X-ray imaging, to establish more closely their links and to establish the longer-term impact of the ceramic revolution. Our pottery study has also emphasised the importance of consistency of recording, to enable comparative analyses. Reference collections of pottery fabrics and forms are essential tools in encouraging the use of standard terminologies.

The Viking Great Army, and its longer-term impact, is an extremely fruitful area of current archaeological investigation. In writing this book we have demonstrated the possibilities and having made our datasets available for others to use we also hope to have inspired research projects yet to come.

Bibliography

Aagård, G.-B. 1984. Gleicharmige Spangen. In Arwidsson (ed.), *Birka II*, 95–110.

Aannestad, H.L. 2018. The allure of the foreign: the social and cultural dimension of imports in Scandinavia in the Viking Age. *Viking and Medieval Scandinavia* 14: 1–19.

Abels, R. 2003. Alfred the Great, the *micel hæðen here* and the Viking threat. In T. Reuter (ed.), *Alfred the Great: papers from the eleventh-centenary conferences*. London: Routledge, 265–79.

Abramson, T. 2018. *Coinage in the Northumbrian Landscape and Economy, c.575–c.867.* BAR British Series 641. Oxford: Archaeopress.

Adams Gilmour, L. 1988. *Early Medieval Pottery from Flaxengate, Lincoln.* Archaeology of Lincoln 17:2. London: Council for British Archaeology.

Addyman, P.V. 1973. Late Saxon settlements in the St Neots area. III: the village or township of St Neots. *Proceedings of the Cambridge Antiquarian Society* 64: 45–100.

Adrian, Y.-M. 2006. Répertoires et approvisionnements sur le plateau de Saint-André-de-l'Eure durant le Haut Moyen Âge: principaux caractères de la céramique mérovingienne et carolingienne au sud d'Evreux (Eure). In Hincker and Husi (eds.), *La céramique du haut Moyen Âge*, 339–63.

Ager, B. 2006a. A lead model for a late 5th- or early 6th-century sword-pommel. *Medieval Archaeology* 50: 243–9.

Ager, B. 2006b. Spofforth, North Yorkshire: Viking silver ring (2006 T312). *Treasure Annual Report 2005/6.* London: Department for Culture, Media and Sport, 77.

Ager, B. 2020. Artefacts. In Williams (ed.), *A Riverine Site Near York*, 13–15.

Ager, B. and Williams, G. 2004. North Yorkshire area: closely associated group of Viking-period and Late Saxon objects and coins (2004 T13). *Treasure Annual Report 2004.* London: Department for Culture, Media and Sport, 91–3.

Ager, B. and Williams, G. 2020. Gold and silver. In Williams (ed.), *A Riverine Site Near York*, 33–6.

Aitken, M.J. and Hawley, H.N. 1966. Magnetic dating. III. Further archaeomagnetic measurements in Britain. *Archaeometry* 9: 187–97.

Aitken, M.J. and Weaver, G.H. 1962. Magnetic dating: some archaeomagnetic measurements in Britain. *Archaeometry* 5: 4–18.

Akerman, J.Y. 1867. Thursday, March 28th. *Proceedings of the Society of Antiquaries of London* 3: 460–3.

Alcock, L. 1976. A multi-disciplinary chronology for Alt Clut, Castle Rock, Dumbarton. *Proceedings of the Society of Antiquaries of Scotland* 107: 103–13.

Alcock, L. and Alcock, E. 1990. Reconnaissance excavations on early historic fortifications and other royal sites in Scotland, 1974–84: 4, excavations at Alt Clut, Clyde Rock, Strathclyde, 1974–75. *Proceedings of the Society of Antiquaries of Scotland* 120: 95–149.

Alcock, L., Alcock, E., and Driscoll, S.T. 1989. Reconnaissance excavations on Early Historic fortifications and other royal sites in Scotland, 1974–84: 3, excavations at Dundurn, Strathearn, Perthshire, 1976–77. *Proceedings of the Society of Antiquaries of Scotland* 119: 189–226.

Ambrosiani, B. (ed.) 2004. *Excavations in the Black Earth 1990–1995. Eastern connections. Part two: numismatics and metrology.* Birka Studies 6. Stockholm: The Birka Project, Riksantikvarieämbetet.

Ambrosiani, B. 2008. Birka. In Brink and Price (eds.), *Viking World*, 94–100.

Ambrosiani, B. 2013. *Excavations in the Black Earth 1990–5. Stratigraphy Vol. 1. Part one: the site and the shore. Part two: the bronze caster's workshop.* Birka Studies 9. Stockholm: The Birka Project, Riksantikvarieämbetet.

Andersson, E. 2003. *Excavations in the Black Earth 1990–1995. Tools for textile production from Birka and Hedeby.* Birka Studies 8. Stockholm: The Birka Project, Riksantikvarieämbetet.

Andersson Strand, E. 2011. Tools and textiles: production and organisation in Birka and Hedeby. In Sigmundsson (ed.), *Viking Settlements and Society*, 1–17.

Andrews, P. 1995. *Excavations at Redcastle Furze, Thetford.* East Anglian Archaeology 72. Gressenhall: Norfolk Museums Service.

Andrews, P. and Penn, K. 1999. *Excavations in Thetford, North of the River, 1989–90.* East Anglian Archaeology 87. Gressenhall: Norfolk Museums Service.

Androshchuk, F. 2014. *Viking Swords: swords and social aspects of weaponry in Viking societies.* The Swedish History Museum, Studies 23. Stockholm: Historiska.

Anon. 1851. Antiquities and works of art exhibited. *Archaeological Journal* 8: 421–7.

Anon. 2023. Early medieval settlement discovered in Coquet Valley. *Current Archaeology* 395: 9.

Arbman, H. 1940. *Birka I. Die Gräber*, 2 vols. Uppsala: Almqvist & Wiksells Boktryckeri-aktiebolag.

Archibald, M. 1991. Anglo-Saxon and Norman lead objects with official coin types. In A. Vince (ed.), *Aspects of Saxo-Norman London II: finds and environmental evidence.* London: London and Middlesex Archaeological Society, 326–46.

Archibald, M. 1998. Two ninth-century lead weights found near Kingston, Dorset. *British Numismatic Journal* 68: 11–20.

Archibald, M. 2007. Half eyrir lead weight. In Emery (ed.), *Norwich Greyfriars*, 148–9.

Archibald, M. 2011. *Specialist Report: coins from the Ipswich excavations.* York: Archaeology Data Service. https://doi.org/10.5284/1034376

Armbruster, B. 2004. Goldsmiths' tools at Hedeby. In Hines *et al.* (eds.), *Land, Sea and Home*, 109–23.

Armstrong, P., Tomlinson, D., and Evans, D.H. 1991. *Excavations at Lurk Lane Beverley, 1979–82.* Sheffield: University of Sheffield.

Armstrong, S. 1998. Carolingian coin hoards and the impact of the Viking raids in the ninth century. *The Numismatic Chronicle* 158: 131–64.

Arwidsson, G. (ed.) 1984. *Birka II:1. Systematische Analysen der Gräberfunde.* Stockholm: Almqvist and Wiksell International.

Arwidsson, G. and Berg, G. 1983. *The Mästermyr Find: a Viking Age tool chest from Gotland.* Lompoc: Larson Publishing Company.

Ashby, S.P. 2015. What really caused the Viking Age? The social content of raiding and exploration. *Archaeological Dialogues* 22: 89–106.

Ashby, S.P., Radini, A., Perry, G., and Craig, O.E. forthcoming. Cuisine and culture-contact: lipid residue analysis reveals an absence of fish in pottery from Viking-Age England.

Ashby, S.P. and Sindbaek, S.M. (eds.) 2020. *Crafts and Social Networks in Viking Towns.* Oxford: Oxbow Books.

Astill, G. 1984. The towns of Berkshire. In J. Haslam (ed.), *Anglo-Saxon Towns in Southern England.* Chichester: Phillimore, 53–86.

Atkins, R. and Connor, A. 2010. *Farmers and Ironsmiths: prehistoric, Roman and Anglo-Saxon settlement beside Brandon Road, Thetford, Norfolk.* East Anglian Archaeology 134. Gressenhall: Norfolk Museums Service.

Axworthy Rutter, J.A. 1985. Glass, other metal, industrial and organic artefacts. In D.J.P. Mason (ed.), *Excavations at Chester 26–42 Lower Bridge Street 1974–6: the Dark Age and Saxon periods*. Chester: Chester City Council Grosvenor Museum, 62–5.

Baastrup, M.P. 2013a. Irske lodder. *Skalk* 4: 12–15.

Baastrup, M.P. 2013b. Continental and insular imports in Viking Age Denmark: distribution and circulation. *Zeitschrift für Archäologie Mittelalters* 41: 85–208.

Baastrup, M.P. 2014. Continental and insular imports in Viking Age Denmark: on transcultural competences, actor networks and high-cultural differentiation. In H.C. Gulløv (ed.), *Northern Worlds: landscapes, interactions and dynamics. Proceedings of the Northern Worlds Conference Copenhagen 28–30 November 2013*. Publications from the National Museum Studies in Archaeology and History 22. Copenhagen: University Press of Southern Denmark, 353–67.

Badreshany, K. 2020. ICP–AES analysis of Middle Saxon to medieval pottery. In Brown *et al.* (eds.), *Stoke Quay*, Appendix 4, 459–64.

Bailey, R.N. 1970. An Anglo-Saxon pin-head from Pontefract. *Yorkshire Archaeological Journal* 42: 405–6.

Bailey, R.N. 1980. *Viking Age Sculpture in Northern England*. London: William Collins.

Bailey, R.N. 1993. An Anglo-Saxon strap-end from Wooperton. *Archaeologia Aeliana* (series 5) 21: 87–91.

Baker, J. 2013. References to timber building materials in Old English place-names. In Bintley and Shapland (eds.), *Trees and Timber*, 78–103.

Baker, J. and Brookes, S. 2013. *Beyond the Burghal Hidage: Anglo-Saxon civil defence in the Viking Age*. Leiden: Brill.

Bakka, E. 1963. *Some English Decorated Metal Objects found in Norwegian Viking Graves: contributions to the art history of the eighth century A.D.* Årbok for Universitetet i Bergen Humanistisk Serie No 1. Bergen: Norwegian Universities Press.

Banham, D. and Faith, R. 2014. *Anglo-Saxon Farms and Farming*. Oxford: Oxford University Press.

Barley, M.W. 1964. The medieval borough of Torksey: excavations 1960–2. *Antiquaries Journal* 44: 165–87.

Barley, M.W. 1981. The medieval borough of Torksey: excavations 1963–8. *Antiquaries Journal* 61: 264–91.

Batey, C.E., Jesch, J., and Morris, C.D. (eds.) 1993. *The Viking Age in Caithness, Orkney and the North Atlantic: select papers from the proceedings of the eleventh Viking Congress*. Edinburgh: Edinburgh University Press.

Batey, C.E. and Paterson, C. 2013. A Viking burial at Balnakeil, Sutherland. In Reynolds and Webster (eds.), *Early Medieval Art and Archaeology*, 631–59.

Batt, C.M., Brown, M.C., Clelland, S.-J., Korte, M., Linford, P., and Outram, Z. 2017. Advances in archaeomagnetic dating in Britain: new data, new approaches and a new calibration curve. *Journal of Archaeological Science* 85: 66–82.

Bayley, J. 1992. *Non-Ferrous Metalworking from Coppergate*. The Archaeology of York: The Small Finds 17/7. London: Council for British Archaeology.

Bayley, J. 2008. *Lincoln: evidence for metalworking on Flaxengate and other sites in the city*. English Heritage Research Department Report Series no. 67. Portsmouth: English Heritage.

Bayley, J. and Barclay, K. 1990. The crucibles, heating trays, parting sherds, and related material. In Biddle (ed.), *Medieval Winchester*, 175–97.

Bayley, J., Cotton, J., Rehren, T., and Pernicka, E. 2014. A Saxon brass bar ingot cache from Kingsway, London. In J. Cotton, J. Hall, J. Keily, R. Sherris, and R. Stephenson (eds.),

'*Hidden Histories and Records of Antiquity': essays on Saxon and Medieval London for John Clarke, Curator Emeritus, Museum of London.* LAMAS Special Paper 17. London: Museum of London, 121–8.

Bender Jørgensen, L. 1992. *North European Textiles until AD 1000.* Århus: Århus University Press.

Beresford, G. 1987. *Goltho: the development of an early medieval manor c 850–1150.* English Heritage Archaeological Report 4. Dorchester: Historic Buildings and Monuments Commission for England.

Berg, H.L. 2015. 'Truth' and reproduction of knowledge. Critical thoughts on the interpretation and understanding of Iron-Age keys. In Eriksen *et al.* (eds.), *Viking Worlds*, 124–42.

Berg, I. 2007. Meaning in the making; the potter's wheel at Phylakopi, Melos (Greece). *Journal of Anthropological Archaeology* 26: 234–52.

Berryman, R.D. 1998. *Use of Woodlands in the Late Anglo-Saxon Period.* BAR British Series 271. Oxford: John and Erica Hedges.

Bersu, G. and Wilson, D.M. 1966. *Three Viking Graves in the Isle of Man.* Society for Medieval Archaeology Monograph Series 1. London: Society for Medieval Archaeology.

Besteman, J. 2004. Two Viking hoards from the former island of Wieringen (The Netherlands). In Hines *et al.* (eds.), *Land, Sea and Home*, 93–108.

Besteman, J. 2006–7. A second Viking silver hoard from Wieringen: Westerklief II. *Jaarboek voor Munt- en Penningkunde* 93–4: 5–80.

Biddle, M. (ed.) 1990. *Object and Economy in Medieval Winchester.* Winchester Studies 7.ii.i. Oxford: Oxford University Press.

Biddle, M. 2023. The Vikings at Repton: *Wintersetl og mindesmærke*—winter camp and place of memory. In Hedenstierna-Jonson and García Losquiño (eds.), *Viking Camps*, 66–77.

Biddle, M., Blunt, C., Kjølbye-Biddle, B., Metcalf, M., and Pagan, H. 1986. Coins of the Anglo-Saxon period from Repton, Derbyshire: II. *British Numismatic Journal* 56: 16–34.

Biddle, M. and Kjølbye-Biddle, B. 1988. *Repton 1987: interim report.* Oxford: unpublished.

Biddle, M. and Kjølbye-Biddle, B. 1992. Repton and the Vikings. *Antiquity* 66: 36–51.

Biddle, M. and Kjølbye-Biddle, B. 2001. Repton and the 'great heathen army', 873–4. In Graham-Campbell *et al.* (eds.), *Vikings and the Danelaw*, 45–96.

Biddle, M., Kjølbye-Biddle, B., Northover, J.P., and Pagan, H. 1986. A parcel of pennies from a mass-burial associated with the Viking overwintering at Repton in 873–4. In Blackburn (ed.), *Anglo-Saxon Monetary History*, 111–23.

Bill, J. 1994. Iron nails in Iron Age and medieval shipbuilding. In C. Westerdahl (ed.), *Crossroads in Ancient Shipbuilding: Proceedings of the Sixth International Symposium on Boat and Ship Archaeology, Roskilde 1991.* ISBSA 6. Oxford: Oxbow Books, 55–63.

Bill, J. 2014. Nails. In Russell and Hurley (eds.), *Woodstown*, 141–55.

Bintley, M.D.J. and Shapland, M.G. (eds.) 2013. *Trees and Timber in the Anglo-Saxon World.* Oxford: Oxford University Press.

Blackburn, M.A.S. (ed.) 1986. *Anglo-Saxon Monetary History: essays in memory of Michael Dolley.* Leicester: Leicester University Press.

Blackburn, M.A.S. 1989. The Ashdon (Essex) hoard and the currency of the southern Danelaw in the late ninth century. *British Numismatic Journal* 59: 13–38.

Blackburn, M.A.S. 1998. The London mint in the reign of Alfred. In Blackburn and Dumville (eds.), *Kings, Currency and Alliances*, 105–23.

Blackburn, M.A.S. 2001. Expansion and control: aspects of Anglo-Scandinavian minting south of the Humber. In Graham-Campbell *et al.* (eds.), *Vikings and the Danelaw*, 125–55.

Blackburn, M.A.S. 2002. Finds from the Anglo-Scandinavian site of Torksey, Lincolnshire. In B. Paszkiewicz (ed.), *Moneta Mediaevalis: Studia numizmatyczne i historyczne ofiarowane*

Profesorowi Stanislawowi Suchodolskiemu w 65. rocznice urodzin. Warsaw: Wydawnictwo DiG, 89–101, 526–7.

Blackburn, M.A.S. 2004. The coinage of Scandinavian York. In Hall (ed.), *Aspects of Anglo-Scandinavian York*, 325–49.

Blackburn, M.A.S. 2005. Presidential address 2004. Currency under the Vikings. Part 1: Guthrum and the earliest Danelaw coinages. *British Numismatic Journal* 75: 18–43.

Blackburn, M.A.S. 2007. Gold in England during the 'Age of silver' (eighth–eleventh centuries). In Graham-Campbell and Williams (eds.), *Silver Economy in the Viking Age*, 55–98.

Blackburn, M.A.S. 2008. The coin finds. In Skre (ed.), *Means of Exchange*, 29–74.

Blackburn, M.A.S. 2009. Currency under the Vikings. Part 5: the Scandinavian achievement and legacy. *British Numismatic Journal* 79: 43–71.

Blackburn, M.A.S. 2011. The Viking winter camp at Torksey, 872–3. In M.A.S. Blackburn, *Viking Coinage and Currency in the British Isles.* British Numismatic Society Special Publications 7. London: Spink/British Numismatic Society, 221–64.

Blackburn, M.A.S., Colyer, C., and Dolley, M. 1983. *Early Medieval Coins from Lincoln and its Shire c.770–1100.* The Archaeology of Lincoln, 6.1. Lincoln: Council for British Archaeology.

Blackburn, M.A.S. and Dumville, D.N. (eds.) 1998. *Kings, Currency and Alliances: history and coinage of southern England in the ninth century.* Studies in Anglo-Saxon History. Woodbridge: The Boydell Press.

Blackburn, M.A.S. and Keynes, S.D. 1998. A corpus of the *Cross-and-Lozenge* and related coinages of Alfred, Ceowulf II and Archbishop Æthelred. In Blackburn and Dumville (eds.), *Kings, Currency and Alliances*, 125–50.

Blackburn, M.A.S. and Rogerson, A. 1993. Two Viking-age silver ingots from Ditchingham and Hindringham, Norfolk. *Medieval Archaeology* 37: 222–4.

Blackmore, L. and Dennis, M. 2003. Non-ferrous metalworking. In G. Malcolm, D. Bowsher, and R. Cowie (eds.), *Middle Saxon London: Excavations at the Royal Opera House 1989–99.* MoLAS Monograph 16. London: Museum of London, 271–8.

Blair, J. 2013. Holy beams: Anglo-Saxon cult sites and the place-name element *bēam.* In Bintley and Shapland (eds.), *Trees and Timber*, 186–210.

Blair, J. 2018. *Building Anglo-Saxon England.* Princeton and Oxford: Princeton University Press.

Blindheim, C. 1963. Smedgraven fra Bygland i Morgedal. *Viking* 26: 25–80.

Blindheim, C. 1976. A collection of Celtic (?) bronze objects found at Kaupang (Skiringssal), Vestfold, Norway. In B. Almqvist and D. Greene (eds.), *Proceedings of the Seventh Viking Congress, Dublin 15–21 August 1973.* London: Viking Society for Northern Research, 9–19.

Blinkhorn, P. 1989. Middle Saxon pottery from the Buttermarket kiln. *Medieval Ceramics* 13: 12–16.

Blinkhorn, P. 1993. *Specialist Report: the pottery from excavations in Ipswich 1974–1990.* York: Archaeology Data Service. https://doi.org/10.5284/1034376

Blinkhorn, P. 2009. Ipswich ware. In Evans and Loveluck (eds.), *Life and Economy at Early Medieval Flixborough*, 357–63.

Blinkhorn, P. 2010. Anglo-Saxon and later pottery. In Atkins and Connor, *Farmers and Ironsmiths*, 70–8.

Blinkhorn, P. 2012. *The Ipswich Ware Project: ceramics, trade and society in Middle Saxon England.* Medieval Pottery Research Group Occasional Paper 7. London: MPRG.

Blinkhorn, P. 2013. No pots please, we're Vikings: pottery in the southern Danelaw, 850–1000. In Hadley and Ten Harkel (eds.), *Everyday Life in Viking Towns*, 157–71.

Blinkhorn, P. 2014. Pottery. In Tester *et al., Staunch Meadow, Brandon*, 149–66.

Blinkhorn, P. and Griffiths, S. 2023. The Vikings and the origins of wheel-thrown pottery production in ninth century England. *The Archaeological Journal* 180: 104–36.

Blunt, C.E. and Dolley, R.H.M. 1959. The hoard evidence for the coins of Alfred. *British Numismatic Journal* 29: 220–47.

Bogucki, M. 2009. Two Northumbrian stycas of Eanred and Æthelred II from early medieval Truso in Poland. *British Numismatic Journal* 79: 34–42.

Bond, C.J. 1999. Fishing. In M. Lapidge, J. Blair, S. Keynes, and D. Scragg (eds.), *The Blackwell Encyclopaedia of Anglo-Saxon England*. Oxford: Blackwell, 185–6.

Bonde, N. 2007. Dendrochronological dates from Kaupang. In Skre (ed.), *Kaupang*, 273–82.

Bone, P. 1989. The development of Anglo-Saxon swords from the fifth to the eleventh century. In Chadwick Hawkes (ed.), *Weapons and Warfare*, 63–70.

Bonser, M. 1998. Single finds of ninth-century coins from southern England: a listing. In Blackburn and Dumville (eds.), *Kings, Currency and Alliances*, 199–240.

Borger, H. and Oediger, F. 1969. *Beiträge zur Frühgeschichte des Xantener Viktorstiftes*. Düsseldorf: Rheinland-Verlag.

Bourke, C. 2010. Antiquities from the River Blackwater IV. Early medieval non-ferrous metalwork. *Ulster Journal of Archaeology* 69: 24–133.

Bradley-Lovekin, T. 2003. *Archaeological Evaluation of Land at Star Lane, Stamford Lincolnshire*. Archaeological Project Services Report 122/03. York: Archaeology Data Service. https://doi.org/10.5284/1015144

Brink, S. and Price, N. (eds.) 2008. *The Viking World*. Abingdon and New York: Routledge.

Brinklow, D. 1986. A pre-Conquest structure at Clementhorpe. In J. Moulden and D. Tweddle (eds.), *Anglo-Scandinavian Settlement South-west of the Ouse*. Archaeology of York 8/1. York: Council for British Archaeology, 57–61.

Broadley, R. 2014. The vessel glass assemblage from Anglo-Saxon occupation at West Heslerton, North Yorkshire. In D. Keller, J. Price, and C. Jackson (eds.), *Neighbours and Successors of Rome: traditions of glass production and use in Europe and the Middle East in the later 1st millennium AD*. Oxford and Philadelphia: Oxbow Books, 22–31.

Brooks, N.P. and Graham-Campbell, J. 1986. Reflections on the Viking-age silver hoard from Croydon, Surrey. In Blackburn (ed.), *Anglo-Saxon Monetary History*, 91–110.

Brown, D. 2003. Bound by tradition: a study of pottery in Anglo-Saxon England. *Anglo-Saxon Studies in Archaeology and History* 12: 21–7.

Brown, M.P. and Okasha, E. 2009. The inscribed objects. In Evans and Loveluck (eds.), *Life and Economy at Early Medieval Flixborough*, 138–41.

Brown, R. and Popescu, E. 2020. Discussion and conclusions. In Brown *et al.* (eds.), *Stoke Quay*, 414–47.

Brown, R., Teague, S., Loe, L., Sudds, B., and Popescu, E. (eds.) 2020. *Excavations at Stoke Quay Ipswich: southern Gipewic and the parish of St Augustine*. East Anglian Archaeology Report 172. Oxford and London: Oxford Archaeology South and Pre-Construct Archaeology.

Bruce-Mitford, R. 1987. Ireland and the hanging-bowls—a review. In M. Ryan (ed.), *Ireland and Insular Art: proceedings of a conference at University College Cork, 31 October–3 November 1985*. Dublin: Royal Irish Academy, 30–9.

Brunning, S. 2019. *The Sword in Early Medieval Northern Europe: experience, identity, representation*. Anglo-Saxon Studies 36. Woodbridge: The Boydell Press.

Buckberry, J., Montgomery, J., Towers, J. *et al.* 2014. Finding Vikings in the Danelaw. *Oxford Journal of Archaeology* 33: 413–34.

Byrne, F.J., Jenkins, W., Kenny G., and Swift, C. 2008. *Historical Knowth and its hinterland*. Excavations at Knowth, vol. 4. Dublin: Royal Irish Academy.

Cameron, K. and Insley, J. 2010. *The Place-names of Lincolnshire. Part 7, Lawress Wapentake.* Nottingham: English Place Name Society.

Campbell, A. 1962. *The Chronicle of Æthelweard.* London: Nelson.

Capelle, T. 1976. *Die frühgeschichtlichen Metallfunde von Domburg Auf Walcheren,* 2 vols. Nederlandse Oudheden 5. The Hague: Rijksdienst voor het Oudheidkundig Bodemonderzoek.

Capelle, T. 2003. Fünf Miniaturen. In B. Hårdh (ed.), *Fler fynd i centrum: Materialstudier i och kring Uppåkra.* Uppåkrastudier 9, Acta Archaeologica Lundensia 45. Stockholm: Almqvist & Wiksell International, 165–71.

Capelle, T. 2006. Die Wikinger auf dem westeuropäischen Kontinent: Normannische Aktionen und karolingische Reaktionen—eine historisch-archäologische Spurensuche entlang von Flüssen. *Deutsches Schiffahrtsarchiv* 29: 7–58.

Cardon, T., Moesgaard, J.C., Prot, R., and Schiesser, P. 2008. Le premier trésor monétaire de type Viking en France. Denier inédit d'Eudes pour Beauvais. *Revue Numismatique* 164: 21–40.

Carhart, L. 2014. *An Iron Hoard from Torksey, Lincolnshire: identification and analysis.* MSc dissertation, University of Sheffield. https://doi.org/10.5284/1038398

Carver, M.O.H. 2010. *The Birth of a Borough. An archaeological study of Anglo-Saxon Stafford.* Woodbridge: The Boydell Press.

Cessford, C. and Dickens, A. 2005a. The manor of Hintona: the origins and development of Church End, Cherry Hinton. *Proceedings of the Cambridge Antiquarian Society* 94: 51–72.

Cessford, C. and Dickens, A. 2005b. Cambridge Castle Hill: excavations of Saxon, medieval and postmedieval deposits, Saxon execution site and a medieval coin hoard. *Proceedings of the Cambridge Antiquarian Society* 94: 73–101.

Cessford, C., Dickens, A., Dodwell, N., and Reynolds, A. 2007. Middle Anglo-Saxon justice: the Chesterton Lane Corner execution cemetery and related sequence, Cambridge. *Archaeological Journal* 164: 197–226.

Chadwick Hawkes, S. (ed.) 1989. *Weapons and Warfare in Anglo-Saxon England.* Oxford: Oxford University Committee for Archaeology.

Clark, A.J., Tarling, D.H., and Noel, M. 1988. Developments in archaeomagnetic dating in Britain. *Journal of Archaeological Science* 15: 645–67.

Clarke, H.B. and Johnson, R. (eds.) 2015. *The Vikings in Ireland and Beyond.* Dublin: Four Courts Press.

Clarke, H.B., Ní Mhaonaigh, M., and Ó Floinn, R. (eds.) 1998. *Ireland and Scandinavia in the Early Viking Age.* Dublin: Four Courts Press.

Clarke, R.R. and Dolley, M. 1958. The Morley St. Peter hoard. *Antiquity* 32: 100–3.

Clason, A.T. 1980. Worked bone and antler objects from Dorestad, Hoogstraat I. In W.A. Van Es and W.J.H. Verwers (eds.), *Excavations at Dorestad 1. The harbour: Hoogstraat I.* Nederlandse Oudheden 9. Amersfoort: Rob, 238–47.

Clinton, M. 2013–14. The Viking longphort of Linn Duachaill: a first report. *Peritia* 24–5: 123–40.

Coatsworth, E. 2008. *Corpus of Anglo-Saxon Stone Sculpture. Volume VIII. Western Yorkshire.* Oxford: British Academy.

Coatsworth, E. and Pinder, M. 2002. *The Art of the Anglo-Saxon Goldsmith. Fine metalwork in Anglo-Saxon England: its practice and practitioners.* Anglo-Saxon Studies 2. Suffolk: The Boydell Press.

Cooijmans, C. 2020. *Monarchs and Hydrachs: the conceptual development of Viking activity across the Frankish realm (c.750–940).* Abingdon: Routledge.

Cooijmans, C. 2021. Down by the river: exploring the logistics of Viking encampment across Atlantic Europe. In F. Iversen and K. Kjesrud (eds.), *Viking Wars.* Viking Special Volume 1. Oslo: Universitetet i Oslo, 187–206.

Cooijmans, C. (trans.) 2022. *Annales Fontanellenses.* Apardjón Journal for Scandinavian Studies, Special Volume II. Aberdeen: University of Aberdeen.

Cooijmans, C. 2023. Hostile in tent: reconsidering the roles of Viking encampment across the Frankish realm. In Hedenstierna-Jonson and García Losquiño (eds.), *Viking Camps,* 147–67.

Cook, B. and Williams, G. (eds.) 2006. *Coinage and History in the North Sea World, c.AD 500–1250: essays in honour of Marion Archibald.* Leiden: Brill.

Cooper, L.P. and Ripper, S. 2017. *Fishing and Managing the Trent in the Medieval Period (7th–14th Century): excavations at Hemington Quarry (1998–2000), Castle Donington, UK.* BAR British Series 633. Oxford: BAR.

Coppack, G. 1987. Saxon and early medieval pottery. In Beresford, *Goltho,* 134–69.

Corder, P. 1961. *The Roman Town and Villa at Great Casterton, Rutland. Third report for the years 1954–1958.* Nottingham: University of Nottingham.

Coupland, S. 1985. L'article XI de l'édit de Pitres du 25 juin 864. *Bulletin de la Société Française de Numismatique* 40(9): 713–14.

Coupland, S. 1988. Dorestad in the ninth century: the numismatic evidence. *Jaarboek voor Munt- en Penningkunde* 75: 5–26.

Coupland, S. 1990. Money and coinage under Louis the Pious. *Francia* 17(1): 23–54.

Coupland, S. 1991. The fortified bridges of Charles the Bald. *Journal of Medieval History* 17: 1–12.

Coupland, S. 1995. The Vikings in Frankia and Anglo-Saxon England to 911. In R. McKitterick (ed.), *The New Cambridge Medieval History.* Cambridge: Cambridge University Press, 190–201.

Coupland, S. 1998. From poachers to gamekeepers: Scandinavian warlords and Carolingian kings. *Early Medieval Europe* 7(1): 85–114.

Coupland, S. 2001. The coinage of Lothar I (840–855). *Numismatic Chronicle* 161: 157–98.

Coupland, S. 2004. The Carolingian army and the struggle against the Vikings. *Viator* 35: 49–70.

Coupland, S. 2006. Between the devil and the deep blue sea. Hoards in ninth-century Frisia. In Cook and Williams (eds.), *Coinage and History,* 241–66.

Coupland, S. 2011. Raiders, traders, worshippers and settlers: the continental perspective. In Graham-Campbell *et al.* (eds.), *Silver Economies,* 113–31.

Coupland, S. 2014. Holy ground: the plundering and burning of churches by Vikings and Franks in the ninth century. *Viator* 44: 73–97.

Coupland, S. 2016. Recent finds of imitation gold solidi in the Netherlands. *The Numismatic Chronicle* 176: 261–9.

Coupland, S. 2021. A Carolingian coin hoard from Wirdum (Friesland, the Netherlands) and the Dorestad mint. In Willemsen and Kik (eds.), *Dorestad and its Networks,* 119–34.

Cowie, R. 1988. A gazetteer of Middle Saxon sites and finds in The Strand/Westminster area. *Transactions of the London & Middlesex Archaeological Society* 39: 37–46.

Craddock, P.T. 1989. Metalworking techniques. In S. Youngs (ed.), *'The Work of Angels': masterpieces of Celtic metalwork, 6th to 9th centuries A.D.* London: British Museum Press, 170–213.

Cramp, R. 1964. An Anglo-Saxon pin from Birdoswald. *Transactions of the Cumberland and Westmorland Antiquarian and Archaeological Society* 64: 90–3.

Croom, A. and Youngs, S. 2021. An insular horse-harness fitting from South Shields Roman fort, Tyne and Wear. *Medieval Archaeology* 65: 224–37.

Cross, P.J. 2011. Horse burial in first millennium AD Britain: issues of interpretation. *European Journal of Archaeology* 14: 190–209.

Crumlin-Pedersen, O. 1997. *Viking-Age Ships and Shipbuilding in Hedeby/Haithabu and Schleswig.* Ships and Boats of the North Volume 2. Roskilde: The Viking Ship Museum.

Crumlin-Pedersen, O. 2010. *Archaeology and the Sea in Scandinavia and Britain: a personal account*. Maritime Culture of the North 3. Roskilde: The Viking Ship Museum.

Crummy, N. 2010. Metalwork. In Atkins and Connor, *Farmers and Ironsmiths*, 42–59.

Dallas, C. 1993. *Excavations in Thetford by B.K. Davison between 1964 and 1970*. East Anglian Archaeology 62. Gressenhall: Norfolk Museums Service.

Darrah, R. 1982. Working unseasoned wood. In S. McGrail (ed.), *Woodworking Techniques before A.D.1500: papers presented to a Symposium at Greenwich in September, 1980, together with edited discussion*. National Maritime Museum, Greenwich, Archaeological Series No. 7. BAR International Series 129. Oxford: BAR, 219–30.

Darrah, R. 2014. Timber. In Tester *et al.*, *Staunch Meadow, Brandon*, 133–9.

Dass, N. 2007. *Viking Attacks on Paris: the Bella Parisiacae urbis of Abbo of Saint-Germain-des-Prés*. Paris: Peeters.

Daubney, A.J. 2016. *Portable Antiquities, Palimpsests, & Persistent Places: a multi-period approach to Portable Antiquities Scheme data in Lincolnshire*. Leiden: Sidestone Press.

Davies, G. 2010. *Settlement, Economy and Lifestyle: the changing social identities of the coastal settlements of West Norfolk, 450–1100 AD*. PhD thesis, University of Nottingham. https://eprints.nottingham.ac.uk/id/eprint/12002

Davies, G., Knight, D., Lomax, S., and Loveluck, C. 2019. From 'House of Caves' to nexus of central England: Nottingham, c.AD 650–1250—future research directions. *Transactions of the Thoroton Society* 123: 55–75.

Deckers, P. 2022a. The long history of early medieval urbanism on the island of Walcheren (Netherlands). Towards a biography of urban continuity. *Journal of Urban Archaeology* 5: 191–210.

Deckers, P. 2022b. Site formation and artefact assemblages. In Sindbæk (ed.), *Northern Emporium: Vol. 1*, 271–300.

Dent, J., Loveluck, C., and Fletcher, W. 2000. The early medieval site at Skerne. In S. Ellis and R. van der Noort (eds.), *Wetland Heritage of the Hull Valley: an archaeological survey*. Hull: Centre for Wetland Archaeology, University of Hull, 217–42.

Deutsch-Dumolin, C. 2023. Viking wintering in Frankish territory. In Hedenstierna-Jonson and García Losquiño (eds.), *Viking Camps*, 168–88.

Dickinson, T.M. 1982. Fowler's Type G penannular brooches reconsidered. *Medieval Archaeology* 26: 41–68.

Dobat, A.S. 2017. From Torksey to Füsing and Hedeby: gambling warriors on the move? In B.V. Eriksen, A. Abegg-Wigg, R. Bleile, and U. Ickerodt (eds.), *Interaction without Borders: exemplary archaeological research at the beginning of the 21st century*, Volume 2. Schleswig: Stiftung Schleswig-Holsteinische Landesmusee, 597–605.

Dobat, A.S. 2022. Finding Sliesthorp? The Viking Age settlement at Füsing. *Danish Journal of Archaeology* 11: 1–22.

Dobat, A.S., Christiansen, T., Henriksen, M.B. *et al.* 2019. The DIME project—background, status and future perspectives of a user driven recording scheme for metal detector finds as an example of participatory heritage. *Danish Journal of Archaeology* 8: 1–15.

Dodd, A., Goodwin, J., Griffiths, S., Norton, A., Poole, C., and Teague, S. 2014. Excavations at Tipping Street, Stafford, 2009–10. *Transactions of the Staffordshire Archaeological & Historical Society* 47: 1–115.

Dolley, R.H.M. 1954. A Piedfort lead trial-piece of Edward the Confessor. *British Numismatic Journal* 27: 175–8.

Dolley, R.H.M. 1961. The 1871 Viking-age find of silver coins from Mullaghboden as a reflection of Westfalding intervention in Ireland. *Årbok Universitetets Oldsaksamling 1960/61*: 49–62.

Downham, C. 2004. The historical importance of Viking-Age Waterford. *Journal of Celtic Studies* 4: 71–96.

Downham, C. 2007. *Viking Kings of Britain and Ireland: the dynasty of Ívarr to A.D. 1014.* Edinburgh: Dunedin Academic Press.

Downham, C. 2013. Vikings' settlements in Ireland before 1014. In J.V. Sigurdsson and T. Bolton (eds.), *Celtic-Norse Relations in the Irish Sea in the Middle Ages 800–1200.* Leiden: Brill, 1–21.

Downham, C. 2017. The earliest Viking activity in England. *The English Historical Review* 132(554): 1–12.

Du Chatellier, P. and Le Pontois, L. 1908–9. A ship burial in Brittany. *Saga-Book* 6: 123–62.

Duczko, W. 1985. *Birka V: the filigree and granulation work of the Viking period.* Stockholm: Almqvist & Wiksell International.

Dumont, A. and Mariotti, J.-F. (eds.) 2013. *Archéologie et histoire du fleuve Charente. Taillebourg-Port d'Envaux: une zone portuaire du haut Moyen Âge sur le fleuve Charente.* Dijon: Universitaires de Dijon.

Dunning, G. 1959. IV. Pottery of the Late Anglo-Saxon period in England. In Dunning *et al.*, Anglo-Saxon pottery, 31–78.

Dunning, G. and Evison, V. 1961. The Palace of Westminster sword. *Archaeologia* 98: 123–58.

Dunning, G., Hurst, J., Myres, J.N.L., and Tischler, F. 1959. Anglo-Saxon pottery: a symposium. *Medieval Archaeology* 3: 1–78.

Düwel, K. Jankuhn, H., Siems, H., and Timpe, D. (eds.) 1987. *Untersuchungen zu Handel und Verkehr der vor- und frühgeschichtlichen Zeit in Mittel- und Nordeuropa. Teil IV: der handel der Karolinger- und Wikingerzeit.* Göttingen: Der Akademie der Wissenschaften in Göttingen.

East, K. 1986. A lead model and a rediscovered sword, both with gripping beast decoration. *Medieval Archaeology* 30: 1–7.

Edwards, J.F. and Hindle, B.P. 1991. The transportation system of medieval England and Wales. *Journal of Historical Geography* 17: 123–34.

Edwards, N. 1990. *The Archaeology of Early Medieval Ireland.* London: B.T. Batsford.

Egan, G. 2007. Weights for fishing. In Griffiths *et al.* (eds.), *Meols,* 284–6.

Eisenschmidt, S. 2011. The Viking Age graves from Hedeby. In Sigmundsson (ed.), *Viking Settlements and Society,* 83–102.

Ellis Davidson, H.R. 1962. *The Sword in Anglo-Saxon England.* Woodbridge: The Boydell Press.

Emery, P.A. (ed.) 2007. *Norwich Greyfriars: pre-Conquest town and medieval friary.* East Anglian Archaeology 120. Gressenhall: Norfolk Museums Service.

Eogan, G. 2012. *The Archaeology of Knowth in the First and Second Millennia.* Excavations at Knowth, vol. 5. Dublin: Royal Irish Academy.

Eriksen, M.H., Pedersen, U., Rundberget, B., Axelsen, I., and Berg, H.L. (eds.) 2015. *Viking Worlds: things, spaces and movement.* Oxford: Oxbow Books.

Evans, D.H. and Loveluck, C. (eds.) 2009. *Life and Economy at Early Medieval Flixborough, c.AD 600–1000: the artefact evidence.* Excavations at Flixborough, vol. 2. Oxford and Oakville: Oxbow Books.

Everson, P. and Stocker, D. 2022. The Late-Saxon graveyard at Cambridge castle and the origins of urbanism in Cambridge. In G. Byng and H. Lunnon (eds.), *Medieval Art, Architecture and Archaeology in Cambridge: college, church and city.* British Archaeological Association Conference Transactions 43. Abingdon: Routledge, 38–68.

Evison, V. 1969. A Viking grave at Sonning, Berks. *Antiquaries Journal* 49: 330–45.

Fabech, C. 2006. Centrality in Old Norse mental landscapes: a dialogue between arranged and natural places? In A. Andrén, K. Jennbert, and C. Raudvere (eds.), *Old Norse Religion in*

Long-term Perspectives: origins, challenges, and interactions. Lund: Nordic Academic Press, 26–32.

Fanning, T. 1994. *Viking Age Ringed Pins from Dublin*. Medieval Dublin Excavations 1962–81, Series B, Volume 4. Dublin: Royal Irish Academy.

Feveile, C. 2008. Ribe. In Brink and Price (eds.), *Viking World*, 126–30.

Fleming, R. 2012. Recycling in Britain after the fall of Rome's metal economy. *Past and Present* 217: 3–45.

Foot, S. 1996. The making of *Angelcynn*: English identity before the Norman Conquest. *Transactions of the Royal Historical Society* (6th series) 6: 25–49.

Ford, D. 1998–9. A Late Saxon pottery industry in Staffordshire: a review. *Medieval Ceramics* 22–3: 11–36.

Frantzen, A. 2014. *Food, Eating and Identity in Early Medieval England*. Woodbridge: The Boydell Press.

Fryer, V. 1998. The lead weights. In G. Lucas (ed.), A medieval fishery on Whittlesea Mere, Cambridgeshire. *Medieval Archaeology* 42: 19–44.

Gaimster, M. 1991. Money and media in Viking Age Scandinavia. In R. Samson (ed.), *Social Approaches to Viking Studies*. Glasgow: Cruithne Press, 113–22.

Gaimster, M. with and Popescu, A. and Waxenberger, G. 2020. Small finds from the settlement. In Brown et al. (eds.), Stoke Quay, 195–225.

Gannon, A. 2004. North Yorkshire area: Anglo-Saxon gold cross pendant (2004 T291). *Treasure Report 2004*. London: Department for Culture, Media and Sport, 83–4.

Gardeła, L. 2015. Vikings in Poland. A critical overview. In Eriksen et al. (eds.), *Viking Worlds*, 211–32.

Gardeła, L. 2021. Miniature swords in the Viking Age. *Acta Archaeologica* 92: 42–51.

Gardeła, L., Pentz, P., and Price, N. 2022. Revisiting the 'Valkyries'. Armed females in Viking Age figurative metalwork. *Current Swedish Archaeology* 30: 95–151.

Garwood, P. forthcoming. The north area of Stamford Castle site EE XII: pre-Conquest and later medieval activity. In Mahany (ed.), *Stamford Castle*.

Gaut, B. 2011. Vessel glass and evidence of glassworking. In Skre (ed.), *Things from the Town*, 169–280.

Geake, H. 2000. A Viking-period Scandinavian strike-a-light handle from Norfolk. *Medieval Archaeology* 44: 223–4.

Geake, H. 2010. Viking-Age cubo-octahedral weights recorded on the PAS database: weights and weight-standards. *Medieval Archaeology* 54: 393–6.

Giertz, W. 1996. Middle Meuse valley ceramics of Huy type: a preliminary analysis. *Medieval Ceramics* 20: 33–61.

Giertz, W. 2000. Reliefbandamphoren aus St. Quirin im Kontext karolingischer Keramik. In M. Tauch (ed.), *Quirinus von Neuss. Beiträge zur Heiligen-, Stifts- und Münstergeschichte*. Cologne: Wienand, 222–71.

Giles, J.A. 1849. *Roger of Wendover's Flowers of History. Volume I*. London: Henry G. Bohn.

Glørstad, Z.T. and Røstad, I.M. 2021. Echoes of the past: memories and disc-on-bow brooches in Vendel- and Viking-period Scandinavia. *European Journal of Archaeology* 24: 89–107.

Goldberg, M. and Davis, M. 2021. *The Galloway Hoard: Viking-age treasure*. Edinburgh: NMS Enterprises Limited Publishing.

Goodall, A.R. 1984. Non-ferrous metal objects. In Rogerson and Dallas, *Excavations in Thetford*, 68–75.

Goodall, I.H. 1981. The medieval blacksmith and his products. In D.W. Crossley (ed.), *Medieval Industry*. Council for British Archaeology Research Report 40. London: Council for British Archaeology, 51–62.

Goodall, I.H. 1984. Iron objects. In Rogerson and Dallas, *Excavations in Thetford*, 77–106.

Goodall, I.H. 1987. Objects of iron. In Beresford, *Goltho*, 117–87.

Goodall, I.H. 1990a. Metal-working tools. In Biddle (ed.), *Medieval Winchester*, 198–9.

Goodall, I.H. 1990b. Iron domestic implements. In Biddle (ed.), *Medieval Winchester*, 818–22.

Goodall, I.H. 2011. *Ironwork in Medieval Britain: an archaeological study*. Society for Medieval Archaeology Monograph 31. London: The Society for Medieval Archaeology.

Goodall, I.H., Ellis, B., and Gilmour, B. 1984. Iron objects. In Rogerson and Dallas, *Excavations in Thetford*, 76–106.

Goodburn, D.M. 1994. Anglo-Saxon boat finds from London. Are they English? In C. Westerdahl (ed.), *Crossroads in Ancient Shipbuilding: proceedings of the Sixth International Symposium on Boat and Ship Archaeology Roskilde 1991*. ISBSA 6. Oxbow Monograph 40. Oxford: Oxbow Books, 97–104.

Goustard, V. 2015. Les ateliers Carolingiens et post-Carolingiens de Saint-Maurice-Montcouronne (Essonne). In Thuillier and Louis (eds.), *Tourner Autour du Pot*, 163–81.

Graham-Campbell, J. 1973. A fragmentary bronze strap-end of the Viking period from the Udal, North Uist, Inverness-shire. *Medieval Archaeology* 17: 128–31.

Graham-Campbell, J. 1980. *Viking Artefacts: a select catalogue*. London: The Trustees of the British Museum.

Graham-Campbell, J. 1995. *The Viking-Age Gold and Silver of Scotland (AD 850–1100)*. Edinburgh: National Museums of Scotland.

Graham-Campbell, J. 2001. Pagan Scandinavian burial in the central and southern Danelaw. In Graham-Campbell *et al.* (eds.), *Vikings and the Danelaw*, 105–23.

Graham-Campbell, J. 2002. The dual economy of the Danelaw. The Howard Linecar Memorial Lecture 2001. *British Numismatic Journal* 71: 49–59.

Graham-Campbell, J. 2004. The archaeology of the 'Great Army' (865–79). In E. Roesdahl and J.P. Schjødt (eds.), *Beretning fra treogtyvende tværfaglige vikingesymposium*. Højbjerg: Århus Universitet, 30–46.

Graham-Campbell, J. (ed.) 2011. *The Cuerdale Hoard and Related Viking-Age Silver and Gold from Britain and Ireland in the British Museum*. London: British Museum.

Graham-Campbell, J. 2015. An early medieval horse-harness mount, of Irish manufacture, from Yorkshire. In Purcell *et al.* (eds.), *Clerics, Kings, and Vikings*, 247–50.

Graham-Campbell, J. 2020. Harness mount. In Williams (ed.), *A Riverine Site Near York*, 64.

Graham-Campbell, J. and Batey, C. 1998. *Vikings in Scotland: an archaeological survey*. Edinburgh: Edinburgh University Press.

Graham-Campell, J., Hall, R.A., Jesch, J., and Parsons, D.N. (eds.) 2001. *Vikings and the Danelaw. Select papers from the proceedings of the Thirteenth Viking Congress, Nottingham and York, 21–30 August 1997*. Oxford: Oxbow Books.

Graham-Campbell, J. and Kidd, D. 1980. *The Vikings*. London: The Trustees of the British Museum.

Graham-Campbell, J. and Okasha, E. 1991. A pair of inscribed Anglo-Saxon hooked tags from the Rome (Forum) 1883 hoard. *Anglo-Saxon England* 20: 221–9.

Graham-Campbell, J. and Sheehan, J. 2011. Classification and discussion of the objects. Part 2: rings. In Graham-Campbell (ed.), *Cuerdale Hoard*, 87–110.

Graham-Campbell, J. and Williams, G. (eds.) 2007. *Silver Economy in the Viking Age*. Walnut Creek: Left Coast Press.

Graham-Campbell, J.A., McCord, M.E.A., Ottaway, P.J., Sanderson, R.W., Shearman, F.N., and Winsor, P.R. 2002. Tenth-century graves: the Viking-age artefacts and their significance.

In D. Freke, *Excavations on St Patrick's Isle, Peel, Isle of Man 1982–88: prehistoric, Viking, medieval and later*. Centre for Manx Studies Monographs 2. Liverpool: Liverpool University Press, 83–98.

Graham-Campbell, J.A., Sindbæk, S.M., and Williams, G. (eds.) 2011. *Silver Economies, Monetisation and Society in Scandinavia AD 800–1100*. Århus: Århus University Press.

Gräslund, A.-S. 1980. *The Burial Customs: a study of the graves on Björkö*. Birka Studies 4. Stockholm: Almqvist & Wiksell.

Grieg, S. 1928. *Osebergfundet Bind II: Kongsgaarden*. Oslo: Universitetets Oldsaksamling.

Grieg, S. 1940. *Viking Antiquities in Great Britain and Ireland Part II: Viking antiquities in Scotland*. Oslo: H. Aschehoug & Co.

Grieg, S. 1947. *Gjermundbufunnet: En Høvdingegrav fra 900–Årene fra Ringerike*. Norske Oldfunn VIII. Oslo: John Griegs Boktrykkeri.

Griffiths, D. 1988. A group of Late Anglo-Saxon hooked tags from Cheshire. *Journal of the Chester Archaeological Society* 70: 39–49.

Griffiths, D. 2007. Early medieval material: AD 400–450 to 1050–1100. In Griffiths *et al.* (eds.), *Meols*, 58–77.

Griffiths, D. 2010. *Vikings of the Irish Sea: conflict and assimilation AD 790–1050*. Stroud: The History Press.

Griffiths, D., Philpott, R.A., and Egan, G. (eds.) 2007. *Meols, the Archaeology of the North Wirral Coast. Discoveries and observations in the 19th and 20th centuries with a catalogue of collections*. Oxford University School of Archaeology Monograph Series 68. Oxford: Oxford University.

Groothedde, M. 2004. The Vikings in Zutphen (Netherlands): military organisation and early town development after the Viking raid in 882. In R. Simek and E. Engel (eds.), *Vikings on the Rhine: recent research on early medieval relations between the Rhinelands and Scandinavia*. Vienna: Fassbaender, 111–32.

Grueber, H.A. 1903. A find of coins of Alfred the Great at Stamford. *Numismatic Chronicle* (4th series) 3: 347–55.

Gurney, D. 1994. Archaeological finds in Norfolk 1993. *Norfolk Archaeology* 42(1): 104–15.

Gurney, D. 1996. Archaeological finds in Norfolk 1995. *Norfolk Archaeology* 42(3): 387–96.

Gurney, D. 1999. Archaeological finds in Norfolk 1998. *Norfolk Archaeology* 43(2): 358–68.

Gurney, D. 2000. Archaeological finds in Norfolk 1999. *Norfolk Archaeology* 43(3): 516–21.

Gurney, D. 2005. Archaeological finds in Norfolk 2004. *Norfolk Archaeology* 44(4): 736–50.

Gustin, I. 2004. Coins and weights from the excavations 1990–1995. An introduction and presentation of the material. In Ambrosiani (ed.), *Excavation in the Black Earth 1990–1995. Eastern connections*, 11–25.

Gustin, I. 2011. Coin stock and coin circulation in Birka. In Graham-Campbell *et al.* (eds.), *Silver Economies*, 227–44.

Gustin, I. 2015. Trade and trust in the Baltic Sea area during the Viking Age. In J.H. Barrett and S.J. Gibbon (eds.), *Maritime Societies of the Viking and Medieval World*. Society for Medieval Archaeology Monograph 37. Leeds: Maney Publishing, 25–40.

Hadley, D.M. 2020. The archaeology of migrants in Viking-age and Anglo-Norman England: process, practice, and performance. In M. Ormrod, J. Story, and E. Tyler (eds.), *Migrants in Medieval England, c.500–c.1500*. London: British Academy, 175–205.

Hadley, D.M. and Richards, J.D. (eds.) 2000. *Cultures in Contact: Scandinavian Settlement in England in the Ninth and Tenth Centuries*. Turnhout: Brepols.

Hadley, D.M. and Richards, J.D. 2000. Introduction: interdisciplinary approaches to the Scandinavian settlement. In Hadley and Richards (eds.), *Cultures in Contact*, 3–15.

Hadley, D.M. and Richards, J.D. 2016. The winter camp of the Viking Great Army, AD 872–3, Torksey, Lincolnshire. *Antiquaries Journal* 96: 23–67.

Hadley, D.M. and Richards, J.D. 2018. In search of the Viking Great Army: beyond the winter camps. *Medieval Settlement Research* 32: 1–7.

Hadley, D.M. and Richards, J.D. 2020. Changing places: tracing the Viking Great Army in the Anglo-Saxon countryside. In A. Pedersen and S. Sindbæk (eds.), *Viking Encounters: proceedings of the Eighteenth Viking Congress*. Århus: Århus University Press, 112–33.

Hadley, D.M. and Richards, J.D. 2021. *The Viking Great Army and the Making of England.* London: Thames & Hudson.

Hadley, D.M. and Richards, J.D. 2023. Beyond the D-shaped enclosure: winter camps of the Viking Great Army in England. In Hedenstierna-Jonson and García Losquiño (eds.), *Viking Camps*, 78–95.

Hadley, D.M., Richards, J.D., Craig-Atkins, E., and Perry, G. 2023. Torksey after the Vikings: urban origins in England. *Antiquaries Journal* 103: 102–34.

Hadley, D.M., Richards, J.D., Groothede, M., and Fermin, B. 2020. The Viking Great Army moves on: new evidence. *Newsletter of the Society for Medieval Archaeology*, 63: 2–3.

Hadley, D.M. and Ten Harkel, L. (eds.) 2013. *Everyday Life in Viking Towns: social approaches to towns in England and Ireland, c.800–1100.* Oxford: Oxbow Books.

Hagen, A. 2006. *Anglo-Saxon Food and Drink.* Ely: Anglo-Saxon Books.

Haldenby, D. 1992. Anglo-Saxon strap-ends—readers' finds part 3. *Treasure Hunting*, June, 27.

Haldenby, D. 2012. *Early Medieval 'Collared' Pins.* Datasheet 44, The Finds Research Group AD 700–1700.

Haldenby, D., Hadley, D.M., and Richards, J.D. 2022. Casting cultural identity in early Viking-age Northumbria. *Yorkshire Archaeological Journal* 94: 94–118.

Haldenby, D. and Kershaw, J. 2014. Viking-Age lead weights from Cottam. *Yorkshire Archaeological Journal* 86: 106–23. Haldenby, D. and Richards, J.D. 2009. Settlement shift at Cottam, East Riding of Yorkshire, and the chronology of Anglo-Saxon copper alloy pins. Medieval Archaeology 53: 309–14.

Haldenby, D. and Richards, J.D. 2016. The Viking Great Army and its legacy: plotting settlement shift using metal-detected finds. *Internet Archaeology* 42. https://doi.org/10.11141/ia.42.3

Hall, M.A. 2021. Trading games? Playing with/without the Vikings in Dorestad. In Willemsen and Kik (eds.), *Dorestad and its Networks*, 35–46.

Hall, M.A., Graham-Campbell, J., and Petts, D. (forthcoming). Dress pins, bosses and pegged playing pieces: changing identities of some early medieval glass objects.

Hall, R.A. 1984. *The Viking Dig.* London: The Bodley Head.

Hall, R.A. 1989. The Five Boroughs of the Danelaw: a review of present knowledge. *Anglo-Saxon England* 18: 149–206.

Hall, R.A. 1994. *Viking Age York.* London: B.T. Batsford/English Heritage.

Hall, R.A. 2000. Anglo-Scandinavian attitudes: archaeological ambiguities in late ninth- to mid-eleventh-century York. In Hadley and Richards (eds.), *Cultures in Contact*, 311–24.

Hall, R.A. (ed.) 2004. *Aspects of Anglo-Scandinavian York.* The Archaeology of York: Anglo-Scandinavian York 8/4. York: Council for British Archaeology.

Hall, R.A. 2020a. Introduction. In Williams (ed.), *A Riverine Site Near York*, 3–4.

Hall, R.A. 2020b. Geophysical survey. In Williams (ed.), *A Riverine Site Near York*, 9–11.

Hall, R.A. 2020c. Archaeological excavations. In Williams (ed.), *A Riverine Site Near York*, 65–75.

Hall, R.A. with D.T. Evans, K. Hunter-Mann, and A.J. Mainman. 2014. *Anglo-Scandinavian Occupation at 16–22 Coppergate: defining a townscape.* Archaeology of York 8/5. York: Council for British Archaeology.

Hall, R.A. and Williams, G. 2020. A riverine site near York: a possible Viking camp? In Williams (ed.), *A Riverine Site Near York*, 3–102.

Halpin, A. 2008. *Weapons and Warfare in Viking and Medieval Dublin*. Medieval Dublin Excavations 1962–81, Series B, 9. Dublin: National Museum of Ireland.

Halpin, A. 2010. Weapons and warfare in Viking-age Ireland. In J. Sheehan and D. Ó Corráin (eds.), *The Viking Age: Ireland and the West. Papers from the proceedings of the Fifteenth Viking Congress, Cork, 18–27 August 2005*. Dublin: Four Courts Press, 124–35.

Halsall, G. 2000. The Viking presence in England? The burial evidence reconsidered. In Hadley and Richards (eds.), *Cultures in Contact*, 259–76.

Hamerow, H., Bogaard, A., Charles, M., *et al.* 2020. An integrated bioarchaeological approach to the medieval 'Agricultural Revolution': a case study from Stafford, England, c.AD 800–1200. *European Journal of Archaeology* 23(4): 585–609.

Hamilton, D., Cook, G., Finlayson, R., Hall, R., and Marshall, P.D. 2020. Radiocarbon dating. In Williams (ed.), *A Riverine Site Near York*, 75–9.

Hårdh, B. 1996. *Silver in the Viking Age: a regional-economic study*. Acta Archaeologica Lundensia Series in 8°, No. 25. Stockholm: Almquist & Wiksell International.

Hårdh, B. 2007. Oriental-Scandinavian contacts on the Volga, as manifested by silver rings and weight systems. In Graham-Campbell and Williams (eds.), *Silver Economy in the Viking Age*, 151–64.

Hårdh, B. 2008. Hacksilver and ingots. In Skre (ed.), *Means of Exchange*, 95–118.

Hårdh, B. 2011a. Viking-age silver from hoards and cultural layers. In Graham-Campbell *et al.* (eds.), *Silver Economies*, 281–96.

Hårdh, B. 2011b. Jewellery and ornamentation. In Skre (ed.), *Things from the Town*, 29–63.

Hårdh, B. 2016. *The Perm'/Glazov Rings: contacts and economy in the Viking Age between Russia and the Baltic region*. Acta Archaeologica Lundensia Series in 8°, No. 67. Stockholm: Almqvist & Wiksell.

Harrison, S. 2014a. Historical background. In Russell and Hurley (eds.), *Woodstown*, 11–19.

Harrison, S. 2014b. Weapons and grave-goods. In Russell and Hurley (eds.), *Woodstown*, 155–71.

Harrison, S. and Ó Floinn, R. 2014. *Viking Graves and Grave-Goods in Ireland*. Medieval Dublin Excavations 1962–81, Series B, Volume 11. Dublin: National Museum of Ireland.

Haslam, J. 1987. The second burh of Nottingham. *Landscape History* 9(1): 45–51.

Haslam, J. 2017. The territorial and strategic context of Stamford, Lincolnshire, in the early tenth century. *Journal of Historical Geography* 58: 23–38.

Hayeur Smith, M. 2004. *Draupnir's Sweat and Mardöll's Tears: an archaeology of jewellery, gender and identity in Viking Age Iceland*. BAR International Series 1276. Oxford: BAR.

Hayeur Smith, M. 2015. Weaving wealth: cloth and trade in Viking age and medieval Iceland. In A.L. Huang and C. Jahnke (eds.), *Textiles and the Medieval Economy: production, trade, and consumption of textiles, 8th–16th centuries*. Oxford: Oxbow Books, 23–40.

Hayfield, C. 1982. *Medieval Pottery from North Lincolnshire*, 2 vols. PhD thesis, University of Nottingham. https://eprints.nottingham.ac.uk/id/eprint/14076

Hedenstierna-Jonson, C. 2006. *The Birka Warrior: the material culture of a martial society*. Theses and Papers in Scientific Archaeology 8. Stockholm: University of Stockholm.

Hedenstierna-Jonson, C. and García Losquiño, I. (eds.) 2023. *Viking Camps: studies and comparisons*. Oxford and New York: Routledge.

Hedenstierna-Jonson, C., Kjellström, A., Zachrisson, T. *et al.* 2017. A female Viking warrior confirmed by genomics. *American Journal of Physical Anthropology* 164(4): 853–60.

Heen-Pettersen, A.M. 2014. Insular artefacts from Viking-age burials from mid-Norway. A review of contact between Trøndelag and Britain and Ireland. *Internet Archaeology* 38. https://dx.doi.org/10.11141/ia.38.2

Heen-Pettersen, A.M. 2018. Objects from a distant place: transformation and use of insular mounts from Viking age burials in Trøndelag Central Norway. *Anglo-Saxon Studies in Archaeology and History* 21: 60–74.

Heen-Pettersen, A.M. 2021. Evidence of Viking trade and 'Danelaw' connections? Inset lead weights from Norway and the western Viking World. *Internet Archaeology* 56. https://doi.org/10.11141/ia.56.10

Hennius, A. 2018. Viking age tar production and outland exploitation. *Antiquity* 92: 1349–61.

Henry, P. 1999. Development and change in Late Saxon textile production: an analysis of the evidence. *Durham Archaeological Journal* 14–15: 69–76.

Hiett, R. 2020. *An Examination of Viking-Age Inset Lead Weights and their Association with the Viking Great Army*. MA thesis, University of York.

Hilberg, V. 2009. Hedeby in Wulfstan's days: a Danish *emporium* of the Viking Age between East and West. In A. Englert and A. Trakadas (eds.), *Wulfstan's Voyage: the Baltic Sea region in the early Viking Age as seen from shipboard*. Maritime Culture of the North 2. Roskilde: The Viking Ship Museum, 79–113.

Hilberg, V. 2011. Silver economies of the ninth and tenth centuries AD in Hedeby. In Graham-Campbell *et al.* (eds.), *Silver Economies*, 203–25.

Hincker, V. and Husi, P. (eds.) 2006. *La céramique du haut Moyen Âge (Ve–Xe siècles) dans le nord-ouest de l'Europe. Bilan et perspectives dix ans après le colloque d'Outreau, Actes du colloque de Caen, 18–20 mars 2004*. Caen: CRAHM.

Hincker, V., Jardel, K., Savary, X., and Delacampagne, F. 2006. Un atelier de potier Carolingien à Subles et éléments de comparaison avec l'atelier de la rue de Verdun à Bayeux (Calvados). In Hincker and Husi (eds.), *La céramique du haut Moyen Âge*, 75–92.

Hines, J., Lane, A., and Redknap, M. (eds.) 2004. *Land, Sea and Home: settlement in the Viking period*. Society for Medieval Archaeology Monograph 20. Leeds: Maney Publishing.

Hinton, D.A. 1974. *A Catalogue of the Anglo-Saxon Ornamental Metalwork 700–1100 in the Department of Antiquities, Ashmolean Museum*. Oxford: Clarendon Press.

Hinton, D.A. 1996. *The Gold, Silver and Other Non-Ferrous Alloy Objects from Hamwic*. Southampton Archaeology Monographs 6. Stroud: Alan Sutton.

Hinton, D.A. 2000. *A Smith in Lindsey: the Anglo-Saxon grave at Tattershall Thorpe, Lincolnshire*. Society for Medieval Archaeology Monograph 16. London: The Society for Medieval Archaeology.

Hinton, D.A. and Parsons, A.L. 1996. Pins. In Hinton, *The Gold, Silver and Other Non-Ferrous Alloy Objects from Hamwic*, 14–37.

Hjardar, K. and Vike, V. 2016. *Vikings at War* (translated from the Norwegian by F. Stewart). Oxford: Casemate Publishers.

Hodges, R. 2023. In praise of Tating Ware (and high-definition archaeology). *The Past*. https://the-past.com/review/travel/in-praise-of-tating-ware-and-high-definition-archaeology/ (last accessed 29 November 2023)

Hoffmann, V.E. 2021. *All That Glitters: a comparative analysis of Late Iron Age non-ferrous metalworking at Kaupang, Ribe, and Birka*. MA thesis, University of Bergen. https://hdl.handle.net/11250/2759130

Holland, L. 1986. Islamic bronze weights from Caesarea Maritima. *Museum Notes (American Numismatic Society)* 31: 171–201.

Holm, P. 1986. The slave trade of Dublin, ninth to twelfth centuries. *Peritia* 5: 317–45.

Hooke, D. 2010. *Trees in Anglo-Saxon England: literature, lore, and landscape*. Anglo-Saxon Studies 13. Woodbridge: The Boydell Press.

Horne, T. 2022. *A Viking Market Kingdom in Ireland and Britain*. Abingdon: Routledge.

Hougen, E.K. 1969. Glassmaterialet fra Kaupang. *Viking* 33: 119–37.

Hoverd, T., Reavill, P., Stevenson, J., and Williams, G. 2020. The Herefordshire Viking hoard. *Current Archaeology* 361: 47–51.

Howard, A.J. 2020. Geoarchaeological assessment of the site. In Williams (ed.), *A Riverine Site Near York*, 4–6.

Hurst, J.G. 1956. Saxo-Norman pottery in East Anglia. Part I. General discussion and St Neots ware. *Proceedings of the Cambridge Antiquarian Society* 49: 43–70.

Hurst, J.G. 1958. Saxo-Norman pottery in East Anglia. Part III. Stamford ware. *Proceedings of the Cambridge Antiquarian Society* 51: 37–65.

Hurst, J.G. 1959. III. Middle-Saxon pottery. In Dunning *et al.*, Anglo-Saxon pottery, 13–31.

Hurst, J.G. 1976. The pottery. In Wilson (ed.), *The Archaeology of Anglo-Saxon England*, 283–348.

Hurst, J.G. and West, S.E. 1957. Saxo-Norman pottery in East Anglia. Part II. Thetford ware. *Proceedings of the Cambridge Antiquarian Society* 50: 29–60.

Husi, P. 2010. Red-painted and glazed ware of the early medieval period in western France: new data for previous interpretations, an assessment for northwestern Europe. In K. De Groote, D. Tys, and M. Pieters (eds.), *Exchanging Medieval Material Culture: studies on archaeology and history presented to Frans Verhaeghe*. Brussels: Vlaams Instituut voor het Onroerend Erfgoed, 81–91.

IJssennagger-van der Pluijm, N. 2021. Vikings beyond Dorestad: Rethinking some metal finds in, around and after the emporium. In Willemsen and Kik (eds.), *Dorestad and its Networks*, 24–39.

Innes, M. 2000. Danelaw identities: ethnicity, regionalism, and political allegiance. In Hadley and Richards (eds.), *Cultures in Contact*, 65–88.

Jacques, A. 1976. Un four de potier du Haut Moyen-Âge à Baralle. *Revue du Nord* 58: 73–86.

Jagodziński, M.F. 2010. *Between Weonodland and Witland*. Elbląg: Archaeological and Historical Museum in Elbląg.

Jamieson, E. and Pearson, T. 2021. *An Archaeological Survey of an Earthwork at Aldby Park, Buttercrambe, North Yorkshire*. Scarborough Archaeological and Historical Society Report 54. York: Archaeology Data Service. https://doi.org/10.5284/1113099

Jansson, I. 1984a. Kleine Rundspangen. In Arwidsson (ed.), *Birka II*, 58–74.

Jansson, I. 1984b. Grosse Rundspangen. In Arwidsson (ed.), *Birka II*, 75–84.

Jansson, I. 1985. *Ovala spännbucklor: en studie av vikingatida standardsmycken med utgångspunkt från Björkö-fynden*. Uppsala: Institute for Archaeology.

Jarman, C. 2018. Resolving Repton: has archaeology found the great Viking camp? *British Archaeology* 159: 28–35.

Jarman, C. 2019. Resolving Repton: a Viking Great Army winter camp and beyond. *Current Archaeology* 352: 18–25.

Jarman, C. 2021. *River Kings: a new history of the Vikings from Scandinavia to the Silk Roads*. London: William Collins.

Jarman, C., Biddle, M., Fullagar, M., and Horton, M. 2019. Viking age Repton: strontium evidence for the mobility and identity of the charnel dead. *Church Archaeology* 19: 73–90.

Jarman, C., Biddle, M., Higham, T., and Bronk Ramsey, C. 2018. The Viking Great Army in England: new dates from the Repton charnel. *Antiquity* 92: 183–99.

Jennings, A. and Kruse, A. 2009. One coast–three peoples: names and ethnicity in the Scottish West during the Early Viking period. In A. Woolf (ed.), *Scandinavian Scotland: twenty years after*. St John's House Papers 12. St Andrews: Committee for Dark Age Studies, 75–102.

Jensen, B. 2010. *Viking Age Amulets in Scandinavia and Western Europe*. BAR International Series 2169. Oxford: BAR.

Jessop, O. 1996. A new artefact typology for the study of medieval arrowheads. *Medieval Archaeology* 40: 192–205.

Johnson, C. 2014. Ferrous and non-ferrous metal. In Russell and Hurley (eds.), *Woodstown*, 115–25.

Johnson, P.G. 2002. *Cemetery Excavations at Village Farm, Spofforth, North Yorkshire. Archaeological post-excavation assessment*. Unpublished report by Northern Archaeological Associates.

Johnson South, T. (ed. and trans.) 2002. *Historia de Sancto Cuthberto: a history of Saint Cuthbert and a record of his patrimony*. Anglo-Saxon Texts 3. Woodbridge: Brewer.

Jones, L.A. 2002. Overview of hilt and blade classifications. In I.G. Peirce, *Swords of the Viking Age*. Woodbridge: The Boydell Press, 15–24.

Jørgensen, L. 2008. Manor, cult and market at Lake Tissø. In Brink and Price (eds.), *Viking World*, 77–82.

Kalmring, S. 2011. The harbour of Hedeby. In Sigmundsson (ed.), *Viking Settlements and Society*, 245–59.

Kelleher, R. and Williams, G. 2020. The coins. In Williams (ed.), *A Riverine Site Near York*, 36.

Kelly, E. 2015. The *longphort* in Viking age Ireland: the archaeological evidence. In Clarke and Johnson (eds.), *The Vikings in Ireland*, 55–92.

Kershaw, J. 2013. *Viking Identities. Scandinavian jewellery in England*. Oxford: Oxford University Press.

Kershaw, J. 2014. Viking-age silver in north-west England: hoards and single finds. In S.E. Harding, D. Griffiths, and E. Royles (eds.), *In Search of Vikings. Interdisciplinary approaches to the Scandinavian heritage of north west England*. London: CRC Press, 149–64.

Kershaw, J. 2017. An early medieval dual-currency economy: bullion and coin in the Danelaw. *Antiquity* 91: 173–90.

Kershaw, J. 2019. Gold as a means of exchange in Scandinavian England (*c*.AD 850–1050). In Kershaw and Williams (eds.), *Silver, Butter, Cloth*, 227–50.

Kershaw, J. 2022. The non-numismatic objects of the Watlington hoard. In Naylor and Standley (eds.), *The Watlington Hoard*, 118–36.

Kershaw, J., Jarman, C., Weber, H., and Horton, M. 2023. The Viking Great Army north of the Tyne: a Viking camp in Northumberland? In Hedenstierna-Jonson and García Losquiño (eds.), *Viking Camps*, 96–116.

Kershaw, J. and Merkel, S.W. 2022. Silver recycling in the Viking Age: theoretical and analytical approaches. *Archaeometry* 64: 116–33.

Kershaw, J. and Williams, G. (eds.) 2019. *Silver, Butter, Cloth: monetary and social economies in the Viking Age*. Oxford: Oxford University Press.

Kershaw, P. 2000. The Alfred-Guthrum treaty: scripting accommodation and interaction in Viking Age England. In Hadley and Richards (eds.), *Cultures in Contact*, 43–64.

Keynes, S. and Lapidge, M. 1983. *Alfred the Great: Asser's Life of King Alfred and other contemporary sources*. Harmondsworth: Penguin.

Kilger, C. 2008a. Kaupang from afar: aspects of the interpretation of dirham finds in northern and eastern Europe between the late 8th and early 10th centuries. In Skre (ed.), *Means of Exchange*, 197–252.

Kilger, C. 2008b. Wholeness and holiness: counting, weighing and valuing silver in the early Viking period. In Skre (ed.), *Means of Exchange*, 253–326.

Kilmurry, K. 1980. *The Pottery Industry of Stamford, Lincolnshire, A.D. 850–1250. Its manufacture, trade and relationship with continental wares, with a classification and chronology*. BAR British Series 84. Oxford: BAR.

Kilmurry, K. and Mahany, C. 1977. The production of red-painted pottery at Stamford, Lincs. *Medieval Archaeology* 21: 180–6.

Klassen, L. 2010. The finds and their interpretation. In J.S. Madsen and L. Klassen (eds.), *Fribrødre Å: a late 11th century ship-handling site on Falster*. Jutland Archaeological Society Publications 69. Moesgaard: Jutland Archaeological Society.

Kleingärtner, S. and Williams, G. 2014. Contacts & exchange. In G. Williams, P. Pentz, and M. Wemhoff (eds.), *Vikings: life and legend*. London: The British Museum, 30–69.

Koktvedgaard Zeitzen, M. 2002. Miniaturanker aus Haithabu und Schleswig. In B. Von Hayo Vierck, M. Koktvedgaard Zeitzen, B.R. Armbruster, and K. Schietzel (eds.), *Berichte über die Ausgrabungen in Haithabu: das archäologische Fundmaterial VII*. Neumünster: Wachholtz Verlag, 69–84.

Krause, G. 2020. *Archäologische Zeugnisse zur frühen Geschichte Duisburgs*. Duisburg: Niederrheinische Gesellschaft für Vor- und Frühgeschichtsforschung Duisburg.

Kruse, S.E. 1986. The Viking-age silver hoard from Scotby; the non-numismatic element. *Transactions of the Cumberland and Westmorland Antiquarian and Archaeological Society* (series 2), 86: 79–84.

Kruse, S.E. 1988. Ingots and weight units in Viking age silver hoards. *World Archaeology* 20(2): 285–301.

Kruse, S.E. 1992. Late Saxon balances and weights from England. *Medieval Archaeology* 36: 67–95.

Kruse, S.E. 1993. Silver storage and circulation in Viking-age Scotland. In C. Batey *et al.* (eds.), *The Viking Age in Caithness*, 187–203.

Kruse, S.E. and Graham-Campbell, J. 2011. Classification and discussion of the Cuerdale objects part 1: ingots. In Graham-Campbell (ed.), *The Cuerdale Hoard*, 73–86.

Kruse, S.E., Smith, R.D., and Starling, K. 1988. Experimental casting of silver ingots. *Historical Metallurgy* 22: 87–92.

Laing, L. 1993. *A Catalogue of Celtic Ornamental Metalwork in the British Isles c AD 400–1200*. Nottingham Monographs in Archaeology No. 5. BAR British Series 229. Oxford: Tempus Reparatum.

Lang, J. and Ager, B. 1989. Swords of the Anglo-Saxon and Viking periods in the British Museum: a radiographic study. In Chadwick Hawkes (ed.), *Weapons and Warfare*, 85–122.

Langdon, J. 1993. Inland water transport in medieval England. *Journal of Historical Geography* 19: 1–11.

Langouët, L. 2006. La sépulture viking à barque de l'île de Groix (Morbihan). *Bulletin de l'A.M.A.R.A.I.* 19: 87–108.

Lathe, R. and Smith, D. 2015. Holocene relative sea-level changes in western Scotland: the early insular situation of Dun Add (Kintyre) and Dumbarton Rock (Strathclyde). *The Heroic Age. A Journal of Early Medieval Northwestern Europe* 16. https://www.heroicage.org/issues/16/ (last accessed 30 July 2023)

Le Maho, J. 1994. Les fouilles de la cathédrale de Rouen de 1985–1993: esquisse d'un premier bilan. *Archéologie médiévale* 24: 17–21.

Leahy, K. 2003. *Anglo-Saxon Crafts*. Stroud: Tempus Publishing.

Leahy, K. 2007. *The Anglo-Saxon Kingdom of Lindsey*. Stroud: Tempus Publishing.

Leahy, K. 2013. A deposit of early medieval iron objects from Scraptoft, Leicestershire. *Medieval Archaeology* 57: 223–37.

Leahy, K. 2014. A bit of blarney? *The Searcher* 342 (February): 36–8.

Leahy, K. and Paterson, C. 2001. New light on the Viking presence in Lincolnshire. In Graham-Campbell *et al.* (eds.), *Vikings and the Danelaw*, 181–202.

Lefèvre, A., Bourgeau, L., Brut, C., *et al.* 2015. Premier aperçu sur l'artisanat potier en Île-de-France au Haut Moyen Âge. In Thuillier and Louis (eds.), *Tourner Autour du Pot*, 139–47.

Lefèvre, A. and Peixoto, X. 2015. Les ateliers de potiers de la rue Gaudray à Vanves (Hauts-de-Seine). In Thuillier and Louis (eds.), *Tourner Autour du Pot*, 149–61.

Lentowicz, I. 2007. Late Saxon, medieval and post-medieval pottery. In Emery (ed.), *Norwich Greyfriars*, 164–86.

Leonard, A. 2015. *Nested Negotiations: landscape and portable material culture in Viking-Age England*. PhD thesis, University of York. https://etheses.whiterose.ac.uk/11142/

Lewis, H. 2019. *Pattern and Process in the Material Culture of Anglo-Saxon Non-elite Rural Settlements*. BAR British Series 649. Oxford: BAR.

Linford, P. 2006. *Archaeomagnetic Dating: guidelines on producing and interpreting archaeomagnetic dates*. Swindon: English Heritage.

Löffelmann T., Snoeck C., Richards, J.D., Johnson, L.J., Claeys, P., and Montgomery, J. 2023. Sr analyses from the only known Scandinavian cremation cemetery in Britain illuminate early Viking journey with horse and dog across the North Sea. *PLoS ONE* 18(2): e0280589. https://doi.org/10.1371/journal.pone.0280589

Louis, E. 2015. Ateliers céramiques du Douaisis au Haut Moyen Âge (vie–xiie siècles): un bilan. In Thuillier and Louis (eds.), *Tourner Autour du Pot*, 51–81.

Loveluck, C.P. 1996. The development of the Anglo-Saxon landscape, economy and society 'On Driffield', East Yorkshire, 400–750 AD. *Anglo-Saxon Studies in Archaeology and History* 9: 25–48.

Loveluck, C.P. 2007. *Rural Settlement, Lifestyles and Social Change in the Later First Millenium AD: Anglo-Saxon Flixborough*. Excavations at Flixborough 4. Oxford: Oxbow Books.

Loveluck, C.P. and Atkinson, D. 2007. *The Early Medieval Settlement Remains from Flixborough, Lincolnshire: the occupation sequence, c. AD 600–1000*. Excavations at Flixborough 1. Oxford: Oxbow Books.

Lund, J. 2010. At the water's edge. In M. Carver, S. Semple, and A. Sanmark (eds.), *Signals of Belief in Early England: Anglo-Saxon paganism revisited*. Oxford: Oxbow Books, 49–66.

Mac Airt, S. and Mac Niocaill, G. (eds. and trans.) 1983. *The Annals of Ulster, to AD 1131*. Dublin: Dublin Institute for Advanced Studies.

McCarthy, M. and Brooks, C. 1988. *Medieval Pottery in Britain AD 900–1600*. Leicester: Leicester University Press.

McCormick, M. *et al.* 2013. Roman road network (version 2008). *DARMC Scholarly Data Series, Data Contribution Series #2013–5*. Cambridge MA: DARMC, Center for Geographic Analysis, Harvard University.

McDonnell, J. 1981. *Inland Fisheries in Medieval Yorkshire 1066–1300*. Borthwick Papers no. 60. York: University of York.

McGrail, S. 1987. *Ancient Boats in N.W. Europe: the archaeology of water transport to AD 1500*. Harlow: Longman Group.

MacGregor, A. 1982. *Anglo-Scandinavian Finds from Lloyds Bank, Pavement, and Other Sites*. The Archaeology of York: The Small Finds 17/3. London: Council for British Archaeology.

MacGregor, A. 1985. *Bone, Antler, Ivory & Horn. The technology of skeletal material since the Roman period*. Beckenham: Croom Helm.

MacGregor, A., Mainman, A.J., and Rogers, N.S.H. 1999. *Craft, Industry and Everyday Life: bone, antler, ivory and horn from Anglo-Scandinavian and medieval York*. The Archaeology of York: The Small Finds 17/12. York: Council for British Archaeology.

MacKay, W.A. 2015. The coinage of Burgred of Mercia 852–874. *British Numismatic Journal* 85: 101–237.

MacKay, W.A. 2018. A small hoard of Lunettes pennies from South Cambridgeshire. *British Numismatic Journal* 88: 194–6.

MacLean, S. 2009. *History and Politics in Late Carolingian and Ottonian Europe: the Chronicle of Regino of Prüm and Adalbert of Magdeburg*. Manchester: Manchester University Press.

McLeod, S. 2006. Feeding the *micel here* in England, *c.*865–878. *Journal of the Australian Early Medieval Association* 2: 141–56.

McLeod, S. 2014. *The Beginning of Scandinavian Settlement in England*. Turnhout: Brepols.

McLeod, S. 2023. Between the winter camps. Logistics of the Viking Great Army. In Hedenstierna-Jonson and García Losquiño (eds.), *Viking Camps*, 206–21.

Mahany, C.M. (ed.) forthcoming. *Excavations at Stamford Castle, Lincolnshire, 1971–1976*.

Mahany, C.M. and Roffe, D.R. 1983. Stamford: the development of an Anglo-Scandinavian borough. *Anglo-Norman Studies* 5: 197–219.

Mainman, A.J. 1990. *Anglo-Scandinavian Pottery from 16–22 Coppergate*. The Archaeology of York: Pottery 16/5. London: Council for British Archaeology.

Mainman, A. 2019. *Anglian York*. Pickering: Blackthorn Press.

Mainman, A. 2020. The emergence of professional pottery production: York, a case study. In Ashby and Sindbaek (eds.), *Crafts and Social Networks*, 59–82.

Mainman, A.J. and Rogers, N.S.H. 2000. *Craft, Industry and Everyday Life. Finds from Anglo-Scandinavian York*. Archaeology of York 17/14. York: Council for British Archaeology.

Maixner, B. 2005. *Die gegossenen kleeblattförmigen Fibeln der Wikingerzeit aus Skandinavien*. Universitätsforschungen zur Prähistorischen Archäologie Band 116. Bonn: Rudolf Habelt Gmbh.

Malcolm, G., Bowsher, D., and Cowie, R. (eds.), Middle Saxon London: Excavations at the Royal Opera House 1989–99. MoLAS Monograph 16. London: Museum of London.

Maldonado, A. 2021. *Crucible of Nations: Scotland from Viking Age to medieval kingdom*. Edinburgh: National Museums of Scotland.

Mariotti, J.-F., Dumont, A., Arles, A., and Téreygeol, F. 2013. Conclusion sur les plombs. In Dumont and Mariotti (eds.), *Archéologie et histoire du fleuve Charente*, 215–23.

Martin, E., Pendleton, C., and Plouviez, J. 1999. Archaeology in Suffolk 1998. *Suffolk Archaeology and History* 39(2): 353–86.

Maxwell, H. 1913. Notes on a hoard of personal ornaments, implements, and Anglo-Saxon and Northumbrian coins from Talnotrie, Kirkcudbrightshire. *Proceedings of the Society of Antiquaries of Scotland* 47: 12–16.

Medieval Pottery Research Group. 2010. *Alan Vince Archive*. York: Archaeology Data Service. https://doi.org/10.5284/1000382

Menghin, W. 1983. *Das Schwert im Frühen Mittelalter*. Stuttgart: Konrad Theiß Verlag.

Mepham, L. and Brown, L. 2007. The Broughton to Timsbury pipeline, part 1: a Late Saxon pottery kiln and the production centre at Michelmersh, Hampshire. *Proceedings of the Hampshire Field Club Archaeological Society* 62: 35–68.

Merkel, S.W. 2013. The relationship of hacksilver and minting in 10th century southern Scandinavia. *Metalla* 20(2): 75–9.

Merkel, S.W. 2016. *Silver and the Silver Economy at Hedeby*. Raw Materials, Innovation, Technology of Ancient Cultures RITaK 2. Bochum: VML Verlag Marie Leidorf.

Metcalf, D.M. and Northover, J.P. 1985. Debasement of the coinage in southern England in the age of King Alfred. *The Numismatic Chronicle* 145: 150–76.

Mikkelsen, E. 1998. Islam and Scandinavia during the Viking Age. In E. Plitz (ed.), *Byzantium and Islam in Scandinavia: Acts of a symposium at Uppsala University June 15–16 1996.* Jonsered: Paul Åströms Förlag, 39–51.

Miles, P., Young, J., and Wacher, J. 1989. *A Late Saxon Kiln Site at Silver Street Lincoln.* Archaeology of Lincoln 17:3. London: Council for British Archaeology.

Mileson, S. and Brookes, S. 2014. A multi-phase Anglo-Saxon site in Ewelme. *Oxoniensia* 79: 1–29.

Mitchell, J. 1994. Fashion in metal: a set of sword-belt mounts and bridle furniture from San Vincenzo al Volturno. In D. Buckton and T.A. Heslop (eds.), *Studies in Medieval Art and Architecture presented to Peter Lasko.* Stroud: Alan Sutton Publishing in association with the Trustees of the British Museum, 127–56.

Morris, C.A. 1983. A Late Saxon hoard of iron and copper-alloy artefacts from Nazeing, Essex. *Medieval Archaeology* 27: 27–39.

Morris, C.A. 2000. *Craft, Industry and Everyday Life: wood and woodworking in Anglo-Scandinavian and Medieval York.* The Archaeology of York: The Small Finds 17/13. York: Council for British Archaeology.

Morris, S. and Walsh, T. 2008. *Archaeological Watching Brief at Wharf Road Stamford, Lincolnshire March 2007.* Northamptonshire Archaeology Report 08/142. York: Archaeology Data Service. https://doi.org/10.5284/1026473

Mortimer, C. 2020. Metalworking. In Williams (ed.), *A Riverine Site Near York,* 48.

Mortimer, P. 2019. Pattern-welding. In P. Mortimer and M. Bunker (eds.), *The Sword in Anglo-Saxon England from the 5th to the 7th Century.* Ely: Anglo-Saxon Books, 93–130.

Mortimer, R. and Hall, D.N. 2000. Village development and ceramic sequence: the Middle to Late Saxon village at Lordship Lane, Cottenham, Cambridgeshire. *Proceedings of the Cambridge Antiquarian Society* 89: 5–34.

Mortimer, R., Regan, R., and Lucy, S. 2005. *The Saxon and Medieval Settlement at West Fen Road, Ely: the Ashwell site.* East Anglian Archaeology 110. Cambridge: Cambridge Archaeological Unit.

Müller-Wille, M. 1976. *Das Bootkammergrab von Haithabu.* Neumünster: Karl Wachholtz Verlag.

Mustchin, A. and Walker, J. 2016. *Land off Lime Avenue, Oulton, Suffolk.* Hertford: Archaeological Solutions. York: Archaeology Data Service. https://doi.org/10.5284/1053465

Musty, J. 1993. The Thetford pottery kilns: an appraisal and overview. In Dallas, *Excavations in Thetford by B.K. Davison,* 70–5.

Naismith, R. 2005. Islamic coins from early medieval England. *Numismatic Chronicle* 165: 193–222.

Naismith, R. 2017. *Medieval European Coinage with a Catalogue of the Coins in the Fitzwilliam Museum, Cambridge 8: Britain and Ireland c.400–1066.* Cambridge: Cambridge University Press.

NASA JPL. 2013. *NASA Shuttle Radar Topography Mission Global 1 arc second.* NASA EOSDIS land processes distributed active archive center. https://doi.org/10.5067/MEaSUREs/SRTM/SRTMGL1.003

Naylor, J. 2001. York and its region in the eighth and ninth centuries AD: an archaeological study. *Oxford Journal of Archaeology* 20: 79–105.

Naylor, J. 2015. The deposition and hoarding of non-precious metals in early medieval England. In J. Naylor and R. Bland (eds.), *Hoarding and the Deposition of Metalwork from the Bronze Age to the 20th Century. A British perspective.* BAR British Series 615. Oxford: BAR, 125–46.

Naylor, J. 2022a. The coinage of Wessex and Mercia, c.875–79: a re-assessment of the Two Emperors and Cross-and-Lozenge types. In Naylor and Standley (eds.), *The Watlington Hoard*, 66–97.

Naylor, J. 2022b. The Watlington hoard in context. In Naylor and Standley (eds.), *The Watlington Hoard*, 150–69.

Naylor, J. and Coupland, S. 2022. The coins of the Watlington hoard. In Naylor and Standley (eds.), *The Watlington Hoard*, 98–117.

Naylor, J. and Standley, E. (eds.) 2022. *The Watlington Hoard. Coinage, kings and the Viking Great Army in Oxfordshire, AD 875–880*. Oxford: Archaeopress.

Nelson, J.L. 1991. *The Annals of St Bertin*. Manchester: Manchester University Press.

Nelson, J.L. 1997. The Frankish empire. In P.H. Sawyer (ed.), *The Oxford Illustrated History of the Vikings*. Oxford: University Press, 19–47.

Nelson, J.L. 2003. England and the continent in the ninth century II: the Vikings and others. *Transactions of the Royal Historical Society* (6th series) 13: 1–28.

Neuray, B. 2020. L'incendie du monastère de Stavelot par les vikings, mythe ou réalité? *Archaeologia Mediaevalis Chronique* 43: 70.

Newman, J. 1993. *Three Antler Moulds from Ipswich*. Datasheet 17, The Finds Research Group AD 700–1700.

Newman, J., Allen, M., and Minter, F. 2004. Mildenhall area, Suffolk: three Late Anglo-Saxon silver pennies (2004 T115). *Treasure Annual Report*. London: DCMS, 185.

Nicholson, A. 1997. Metalwork and sculpture: design and patronage in *c.*900 AD. In P. Hill (ed.), *Whithorn & St Ninian: the excavation of a monastic town 1984–91*. Gloucestershire: Sutton Publishing, 621–3.

Nicolardot, J.-P. and Guigon, P. 1991. Une forteresse du Xe siècle: le camp de Péran à Plédran (Côtes d'Armor). *Revue archéologique de l'ouest* 8: 123–57.

Nicolaysen, N. 1877. Udgravninger i Fjære 1876. Foreningen til Norske Fortidsminnesmerkers bevaring. *Aarsberetning* 1876: 117–39.

Ó Cróinín, D. 2013. *Early Medieval Ireland, 400–1200*. London and New York: Routledge.

O'Donovan, E. 2008. The Irish, the Vikings and the English: new archaeological evidence from excavations at Golden Lane, Dublin. In S. Duffy, *Medieval Dublin 8*. Dublin: Four Courts Press, 37–130.

Ó Floinn, R. 1989. Secular metalwork in the eighth and ninth centuries. In S. Youngs (ed.), 'The Work of Angels': masterpieces of Celtic metalwork, 6th to 9th centuries A.D. London: British Museum Press, 72–124.

Ó Floinn, R. 1998. The archaeology of the early Viking Age in Ireland. In Clarke *et al.* (eds.), *Ireland and Scandinavia*, 131–65.

Ó Floinn, R. 2014. Cast and gilt copper alloy. In Russell and Hurley (eds.), *Woodstown*, 172–93.

O'Meadhra, U. 1993. Viking-age sketches and motif-pieces from the northern Earldoms. In Batey *et al.* (eds.), *The Viking Age in Caithness*, 423–40.

Ottaway, P. 1992. *Anglo-Scandinavian Ironwork from Coppergate*. Archaeology of York 17/6. London: Council for British Archaeology.

Ottaway, P. 1999. Iron objects. In Richards, Cottam, 72–8.

Ottaway, P. 2009a. Iron brooches. In Evans and Loveluck (eds.), *Life and Economy at Early Medieval Flixborough*, 6–7.

Ottaway, P. 2009b. Weapons and armour. In Evans and Loveluck (eds.), *Life and Economy at Early Medieval Flixborough*, 123.

Ottaway, P. 2009c. Agricultural tools. In Evans and Loveluck (eds.), *Life and Economy at Early Medieval Flixborough*, 245–9.

Ottaway, P. 2009d. Woodworking tools. In Evans and Loveluck (eds.), *Life and Economy at Early Medieval Flixborough*, 253–5.

Ottaway, P. 2013. 'All shapes and all sizes': Anglo-Saxon knives *c.*700–1100. In Reynolds and Webster (eds.), *Early Medieval Art and Archaeology*, 111–38.

Ottaway, P. 2016. *The Products of the Blacksmith in Mid-Late Anglo-Saxon England.* https://www.pjoarchaeology.co.uk/ (last accessed August 2021)

Ottaway, P., Barber, L., and Thomas, G. 2010. Cultivation, crop processing, and food procurement. In G. Thomas, *The Later Anglo-Saxon Settlement at Bishopstone: a Downland manor in the making.* Council for British Archaeology Research Report 163. York: Council for British Archaeology, 130–3.

Ottaway, P. and Cowgill, J. 2009. Woodworking, the tool hoard and its lead containers. In Evans and Loveluck (eds.), *Life and Economy at Early Medieval Flixborough*, 253–77.

Ottaway, P., Starley, D., and Loveluck, C. 2009. Ironworking. In Evans and Loveluck (eds.), *Life and Economy at Early Medieval Flixborough*, 317–28.

Owen, O. and Dalland, M. 1999. *Scar: a Viking boat burial on Sanday, Orkney.* East Linton: Tuckwell Press.

Owen-Crocker, G.R. 2011. Weapons and armour. In M. Clegg Hyer and G.R. Owen-Crocker (eds.), *The Material Culture of Daily Living in the Anglo-Saxon World.* Liverpool: Liverpool University Press, 201–30.

Øye, I. 2011. Textile-production equipment. In Skre (ed.), *Things from the Town*, 339–72.

Øye, I. 2015. Technology and textile production from the Viking Age and the Middle Ages: Norwegian cases. In A.L. Huang and C. Jahnke (eds.), *Textiles and the Medieval Economy: production, trade, and consumption of textiles, 8th–16th Centuries.* Oxford and Philadelphia: Oxbow Books, 41–63.

Øye, I. 2022. *Tracing Textile Production from the Viking Age to the Middle Ages: tools, textiles, texts and contexts.* Oxford: Oxbow Books.

Pagan, H.E. 1965. Coinage in the age of Burgred. *British Numismatic Journal* 34: 11–27.

Pagan, H.E. 1966. The Gainford hoard. *British Numismatic Journal* 35: 190–1.

Pagan, H.E. 1986. Presidential address 1986. *British Numismatic Journal* 56: 207–9.

Pagan, H.E. 1987. Some thoughts on the hoard evidence for the Northumbrian styca coinage. In D.M. Metcalf (ed.), *Coinage in Ninth-Century Northumbria: the tenth Oxford Symposium on Coinage and Monetary History.* BAR British Series 180. Oxford: BAR, 147–58.

Pagan, H.E. 2020. The Laxfield hoard: some puzzles explained but not yet resolved. *British Numismatic Society Research Blog.* https://britnumsoc.files.wordpress.com/2020/05/74-hugh-pagan-laxfield-hoard.pdf (last accessed November 2023)

Parsons, J. 1992. A linked pin from Thorpe Salvin, South Yorkshire. *Medieval Archaeology* 36: 169–75.

Paterson, C. 1997. The Viking Age trefoil mount from Jarlshof: a reappraisal in the light of two new discoveries. *Proceedings of the Society of Antiquaries of Scotland* 127: 649–57.

Paterson, C. 2021. Dress and dress fasteners from the pagan Norse graves of Scotland: origins and identity. *The Scottish Historical Review* 100: 314–34.

Paterson, C., Parsons, A.J., Newman, R.M., Johnson, N., and Howard Davis, C. 2014. *Shadows in the Sand: excavation of a Viking-Age cemetery at Cumwhitton, Cumbria.* Lancaster Imprints 22. Oxford: Oxbow Books.

Paterson, C. and Tweddle, D. 2014. Copper-alloy. In M. McCarthy (ed.), A post-Roman sequence at Carlisle Cathedral. *The Archaeological Journal* 171: 185–257.

Pedersen, A. 2012. Viking weaponry. In Brink and Price (eds.), *Viking World*, 204–11.

Pedersen, U. 2008. Weights and balances. In Skre (ed.), *Means of Exchange*, 119–95.

Pedersen, U. 2016. *Into the Melting Pot: non-ferrous metalworking in Viking-period Kaupang.* Kaupang Excavation Project Publication Series Volume 4, Norske Oldfunn XXV. Denmark: Narayana Press.

Pedersen, U. 2017. Viking-period non-ferrous metalworking and urban commodity production. In Z.T. Glørstad and K. Loftsgarden (eds.), *Viking-Age Transformations.* Abingdon: Routledge, 1–27.

Pedersen, U. and Rødsrud, C.L. 2013. Nye vektlodd fra Vestfold. *Nicolay* 119, 53–9.

Pelteret, D. 1980. Slave raiding and slave trading in early England. *Anglo-Saxon England* 9: 99–114.

Périn, P. 1990. Les objets vikings du musée des antiquités de la Seine-Maritime, à Rouen. *Annales de Normandie* 23: 166–88.

Perring, D. 1981. *Early Medieval Occupation at Flaxengate.* Archaeology of Lincoln 9/1. London.

Perry, G. 2016. Pottery production in Anglo-Scandinavian Torksey (Lincolnshire): reconstructing and contextualising the *chaîne opératoire. Medieval Archaeology* 60: 72–114.

Perry, G. 2019. Situation vacant: potter required in the newly founded late Saxon burh of Newark-on-Trent, Nottinghamshire. Antiquaries Journal 99: 33–61.

Perry, G. forthcoming. Aceramic revolution? Understanding technological continuity and change in Viking Age England.

Pestell, T. 2004. *Landscapes of Monastic Foundation: the establishment of religious houses in East Anglia, c.650–1200.* Woodbridge: The Boydell Press.

Pestell, T. 2013. Imports or immigrants? Reassessing Scandinavian metalwork in Late Anglo-Saxon East Anglia. In D. Bates and R. Liddiard (eds.), *East Anglia and its North Sea World in the Middle Ages.* Woodbridge: The Boydell Press, 230–55.

Pestell, T. 2017. The kingdom of East Anglia, Frisia and continental connections, c.AD 600–900. In J. Hines and N. IJssennagger (eds.), *Frisians and their North Sea Neighbours: from the fifth century to the Viking Age.* Woodbridge: The Boydell Press, 193–222.

Pestell, T. 2019. *Viking East Anglia.* Norfolk Museums Service. Shaftesbury: Blackmore Group.

Pestell, T. 2023. Runic finds from the kingdom of East Anglia and their archaeological contexts. In G. Waxenberger and K. Kazzazi (eds.), *Old English Runes: interdisciplinary perspectives on approaches and methodologies.* Berlin: De Gruyter, 137–77.

Petersen, J. 1919. *De Norske Vikingesverd: En Typologisk-Kronologisk Studie Over Vikingetidens Vaaben.* Kristiania: Vindenskapsselskapet Skrifter II.

Pettersson, A.-M. (ed.) 2009. *The Spillings Hoard: Gotland's role in Viking Age world trade.* Visby: Gotlands Museum.

Phillips, P. (ed.) 1989. *Archaeology and Landscape Studies in North Lincolnshire,* 2 vols. British Archaeological Report 208. Oxford: BAR.

Pickle, T. 2018. *Kingship, Society, and the Church in Anglo-Saxon Yorkshire.* Oxford: Oxford University Press.

Pilø, L. 2007. The settlement: character, structures and features. In Skre (ed.), *Kaupang,* 191–247.

Pirie, E.J.E. 1986. *Post-Roman Coins from York Excavations 1971–81.* The Archaeology of York: The Coins 18/1. London: Council for British Archaeology.

Pirie, E.J.E. 2000. *Thrymsas, Sceattas and Stycas of Northumbria: an inventory of finds recorded, to 1997.* Northumbrian Numismatic Studies 2. Llanfyllin: Galata Print.

Piton, D. (ed.) 1993. *Travaux du Groupe de Recherches et d'Etudes sur la Céramique dans le Nord -Pas-de-Calais: Actes du Colloque d'Outreau (10–12 Avril 1992).* Numéro hors-série de Nord-Ouest Archéologie. Imprimerie du Moulin: Saint-Josse-sur-Mer.

Pol, A. 2011. A square madelinus from Katwijk: trial piece of die cleaner? In T. Abramson (ed.), *Studies in Early Medieval Coinage Volume 2: new perspectives*. Woodbridge: The Boydell Press, 183–90.

Poole, C. 2020. Ipswich ware kiln. In Brown *et al.* (eds.), *Stoke Quay*, 59–68.

Porter, J.E. 2021. *Vikings, Currency and Power: an interdisciplinary assessment of the late ninth- and early tenth-century St Edmund 'memorial' coinage*, 2 vols. PhD thesis, University of East Anglia.

Pourmomeni, S. 2022. *Forming Techniques of Lincoln Gritty Wares: a milestone moment of ceramic production in England's 9th century*. MSc dissertation, University of York.

Price, N.S. 1989. *The Vikings in Brittany*. London: Viking Society for Northern Research.

Price, N.S. 2014. Ship-men and slaughter-wolves: pirate polities in the Viking Age. In S.E. Amirell and L. Müller (eds.), *Persistent Piracy: maritime violence and state-formation in global historical perspective*. Basingstoke: Palgrave Macmillan, 51–68.

Price, N.S. 2016. Pirates of the North Sea? The Viking ship as political space. In L. Melheim, H. Glørstad, and Z.T. Glørstad (eds.), *Comparative Perspectives on Past Colonisation, Maritime Interaction, and Cultural Integration*. Sheffield: Equinox, 149–71.

Pritchard, F. 1991. Tools. In A. Vince (ed.), *Aspects of Saxo-Norman London: II, finds and environmental evidence*. London: London and Middlesex Archaeological Society, 135–8.

Purcell, E. 2015. The first generation in Ireland, 795–812: Viking raids and Viking bases? In Clarke and Johnson (eds.), *The Vikings in Ireland*, 41–54.

Purcell, E., MacCotter, P., Nyhan, J., and Sheehan, J. (eds.) 2015. *Clerics, Kings, and Vikings: essays on medieval Ireland in honour of Donnchadh Ó Corráin*. Dublin: Four Courts Press.

Raffield, B. 2014. 'A river of knives and swords': ritually deposited weapons in English watercourses and wetlands during the Viking Age. *European Journal of Archaeology* 17: 634–55.

Raffield, B. 2016. Bands of brothers: a re-appraisal of the Viking Great Army and its implications for the Scandinavian colonization of England. *Early Medieval Europe* 24: 308–37.

Raffield, B. 2022. Bound in captivity: intersections of Viking raiding, slaving, and settlement in western Europe during the ninth century CE. *Scandinavian Journal of History* 47(4): 414–37.

Raffield, B., Greenlow, C., Price, N., and Collard, M. 2016. Ingroup identification, identity fusion and the formation of Viking warbands. *World Archaeology* 48(1): 35–50.

Raffield, B., Price, N., and Collard, M. 2017. Male-biased operational sex ratios and the Viking phenomenon. An evolutionary anthropological perspective on late Iron Age Scandinavian raiding. *Evolution and Human Behaviour* 38: 315–24.

Randerson, M.J. 2023. *'A Winter's Tale': a comparative analysis of the artefact assemblages from the winter camps of the Viking Great Army at Torksey and Aldwark*. MPhil thesis, University of York.

Ratican, C. 2020. *The Other Body: persons in Viking Age multiple burials in Scandinavia and the western diaspora*. PhD thesis, University of Cambridge. https://doi.org/10.17863/CAM.54718

Ravn, M. 2016. *Viking-Age War Fleets: shipbuilding, resource management and maritime warfare in 11th-century Denmark*. Maritime Culture of the North 4. Roskilde: Viking Ship Museum.

Redknap, M. 2004. Viking-age settlement in Wales and the evidence from Llanbedrgoch. In Hines *et al.* (eds.), *Land, Sea and Home*, 139–75.

Redknap, M. 2013. Ring rattle on swift steeds: equestrian equipment from early medieval Wales. In Reynolds and Webster (eds.), *Early Medieval Art and Archaeology*, 177–210.

Redknap, M. 2019. Lead objects of uncertain date. In A. Lane and M. Redknap (eds.), *Llangorse Crannog: the excavation of an early medieval royal site in the kingdom of Brycheiniog*. Oxford: Oxbow Books, 388–95.

Redmond, A. 2007. *Viking Burial in the North of England: a study of contact, interaction and reaction between Scandinavian migrants with resident groups, and the effect of immigration on aspects of cultural continuity.* BAR British Series 429. Oxford: BAR.

Reuter, T. (ed. and trans.) 1992. *The Annals of Fulda.* Manchester: Manchester University Press.

Reynolds, A. and Semple, S. 2011. Anglo-Saxon non-funerary weapon depositions. In S. Brookes, S. Harrington, and A. Reynolds (eds.), *Studies in Early Anglo-Saxon Art and Archaeology: papers in honour of Martin Welch.* BAR British Series 527. Oxford: BAR, 14–22.

Reynolds, A. and Webster, L. (eds.) 2013. *Early Medieval Art and Archaeology in the Northern World: studies in honour of James Graham-Campbell.* The Northern World 58. Leiden: Brill.

Reynolds, R.V. 2015. *Food for the Soul: the dynamics of fishing and fish consumption in Anglo-Saxon England: c.A.D. 410–1066.* PhD thesis, University of Nottingham. https://eprints.nottingham.ac.uk/id/eprint/29001

Richards, J.D. 1999. Cottam: an Anglian and Anglo-Scandinavian settlement on the Yorkshire Wolds. *Archaeological Journal* 156: 1–110.

Richards, J.D. 2003. Pagans and Christians at a frontier: Viking burial in the Danelaw. In M.O.H. Carver (ed.), *The Cross Goes North: processes of conversion in Northern Europe, AD 300–1300.* York: York Medieval Press, 383–95.

Richards, J.D. 2013. Cottam, Cowlam and environs: an Anglo-Saxon estate on the Yorkshire Wolds. *Archaeological Journal* 170: 201–71.

Richards, J.D. with contributions by P. Beswick, J. Bond, M. Jecock, J. McKinley, S. Rowland, and F. Worley. 2004. The Viking barrow cemetery at Heath Wood, Ingleby. *Antiquaries Journal* 84: 23–116.

Richards, J.D. and Hadley, D.M. 2016. *Archaeological Evaluation of the Anglo-Saxon and Viking Site at Torksey, Lincolnshire.* York: Archaeology Data Service. https://doi.org/10.5284/1018222

Richards, J.D. and Hadley, D.M. 2020. *Metal-Detector Survey of Land South of Sand Lane, Torksey, Lincolnshire 2020.* Department of Archaeology, University of York unpublished report series. https://doi.org/10.5284/1097744

Richards, J.D., Hadley, D.M., and Randerson, M. 2023a. *Torksey Viking Camp: illustrated artefact catalogue 2024.* York: Archaeology Data Service. https://doi.org/10.5284/1115932

Richards, J.D., Hadley, D.M., and Randerson, M. 2023b. *Aldwark Viking Camp: illustrated artefact catalogue.* York: Archaeology Data Service. https://doi.org/10.5284/1115933

Richards, J.D. and Haldenby, D. 2018. The scale and impact of Viking settlement in Northumbria. *Medieval Archaeology* 62: 322–50.

Richards, J.D. and Naylor, J. 2012. Settlement, landscape and economy in early medieval Northumbria: the contribution of portable antiquities. In D. Petts and S. Turner (eds.), *Early Medieval Northumbria: kingdoms and communities.* Studies in the Early Middle Ages. Turnhout: Brepols, 129–49.

Richards, J.D., Naylor, J., and Holas-Clark, C. 2009. Anglo-Saxon landscape and economy: using portable antiquities to study Anglo-Saxon and Viking Age England. *Internet Archaeology* 25. https://dx.doi.org/10.11141/ia.25.2

Riddler, I. 2014. The Middle and Late Saxon sequence. In Tester *et al.*, *Staunch Meadow, Brandon*, 353–5.

Riddler, I., Evison, V., and Rogers, N. 2014. Dress accessories. In Tester *et al.*, *Staunch Meadow, Brandon*, 219–44.

Riddler, I., Trzaska-Nartowski, N., and Hatton, S. 2023. *An Early Medieval Craft: antler and bone working from Ipswich.* East Anglian Archaeology 181. Gressenhall: Archaeological Service Suffolk County Council.

Rispling, G. 2004. Catalogue and comments on the Islamic coins from the excavations 1990–1995. In Ambrosiani (ed.), *Excavations in the Black Earth 1990–1995. Eastern connections*, 26–60.

Rispling, G. 2014. Numismatic evidence: Islamic silver dirham fragments. In Russell and Hurley (eds.), *Woodstown*, 259–61.

Robak, Z. 2018a. The sword and sword-belt in Carolingian times: the warrior burial 23 from Závada reconsidered. *Študijné Zvesti Archeologického Ústavu Sav* 64: 149–77.

Robak, Z. 2018b. Two Carolingian strap-ends on exhibition in Želiezovce (Okr. Levice/SK). *Archäologisches Korrespondenzblatt* 48: 417–35.

Roesdahl, E. 2008. The emergence of Denmark and the reign of Harald Bluetooth. In Brink and Price (eds.), *Viking World*, 652–64.

Roesdahl, E. 2014. Agricultural and fishing tools. In Roesdahl *et al.* (eds.), *Aggersborg*, 313–16.

Roesdahl, E., Sindbæk, S.M., Pedersen, U., and Wilson, D.M. (eds.) 2014. *Aggersborg: the Viking-Age settlement and fortress*. Jutland Archaeological Society Publications 82. Højbjerg: Jutland Archaeological Society in Association with The National Museum of Denmark.

Roffe, D.R. and Garwood, P. forthcoming. The ninth-century defensive work. In Mahany (ed.), *Stamford Castle*.

Rogers, N. 1993. *Anglian and other Finds from 46–54 Fishergate: the small finds*. Archaeology of York 17/14. York: Council for British Archaeology.

Rogers, N. 2020a. Folding balance. In Williams (ed.), *A Riverine Site Near York*, 19–20.

Rogers, N. 2020b. Woodworking. In Williams (ed.), *A Riverine Site Near York*, 49.

Rogers, N. 2020c. Household equipment. In Williams (ed.), *A Riverine Site Near York*, 49–65.

Rogers, N., O'Connor, S., Ottaway, P., and Panter, I. 2009. The pins. In Evans and Loveluck (eds.), *Life and Economy at Early Medieval Flixborough*, 249–52.

Rogers, N. and Ottaway, P. 2014. Weaponry. In Tester *et al.*, *Staunch Meadow, Bransdon*, 265–7.

Rogerson, A. 1995. *A Late Neolithic, Saxon and Medieval Site at Middle Harling, Norfolk*. East Anglian Archaeology 74. Gressenhall: Norfolk Museums Service, and The British Museum.

Rogerson, A. and Ashley, S. 2013. A selection of finds from Norfolk recorded in 2013 and earlier. *Norfolk Archaeology* 4(4): 554–68.

Rogerson, A. and Dallas, C. 1984. *Excavations in Thetford, 1948–59 and 1973–80*. East Anglian Archaeology 22. Gressenhall: Norfolk Museums Service.

Roxburgh, M., IJssennagger, N., Huisman, H., and van Os, B. 2018. Where worlds collide. A typological and compositional analysis of the copper-alloy mounts from Viking-age Walcheren. *The Medieval Low Countries* 5: 1–33.

Russell, I.R. 2023. The Woodstown enigma: a discussion of the ninth- and tenth-century Viking winter camps at Woodstown, Co. Waterford, Ireland. In Hedenstierna-Jonson and García Losquiño (eds.), *Viking Camps,* 132–46.

Russell, I.R. and Hurley, M. (eds.) 2014. *Woodstown: a Viking-age settlement in Co. Waterford*. Dublin: Four Courts Press.

Salisbury, C.R. 1988. Primitive British fishweirs. In G.L. Good and R.H. Jones (eds.), *Waterfront Archaeology: Proceedings of the Third International Conference, Bristol*. Council for British Archaeology Research Report 74. London: Council for British Archaeology, 76–87.

Sawyer, P.H. 1998. *Anglo-Saxon Lincolnshire*. History of Lincolnshire III. Lincoln: History of Lincolnshire Committee.

SCCAS (Suffolk County Council Archaeological Service) 2015a. *Ipswich 1974–1990 Excavation Archive*: Pottery database (IAS COREDATA: IAS_Pottery). York: Archaeology Data Service. https://doi.org/10.5284/1034376

SCCAS 2015b. *Ipswich 1974–1990 Excavation Archive*: Non-ferrous metalwork database (IAS COREDATA: IAS_ObjectsNonFerrousMetal). York: Archaeology Data Service. https://doi.org/10.5284/1034376

SCCAS 2015c. *Ipswich 1974–1990 Excavation Archive*: Worked bone database (IAS COREDATA: IAS_BulkFinds). York: Archaeology Data Service. https://doi.org/10.5284/1034376

SCCAS 2020. *Ipswich 1974–1990 Excavation Archive*. York: Archaeology Data Service. https://doi.org/10.5284/1034376

Schietzel, K. 2014. *Spurensuche Haithabu*. Neumünster/Hamburg: Wachholtz Verlag-Murmann Publishers.

Schoenfelder, M. and Richards, J.D. 2011. Norse bells—a Scandinavian colonial artefact. *Anglo-Saxon Studies in Archaeology and History* 17: 151–68.

Schulze-Dörrlamm, M. 2009. Gegossene gürtel- und riemenbeschläge mit Karolingischem pflanzendekor aus Andalusien. *Jahrbuch des Römisch-Germanischen Zentralmuseums* 56: 743–88.

Scully, Ó. 2014. Ferrous and non-ferrous metal. In Russell and Hurley (eds.), *Woodstown*, 125–40.

Shearman, J.F. 1872. Discovery of Carolingian coins at Mullaboden, Ballymore Eustace. *Journal of the Kilkenny Archaeological Society* 2: 13–16.

Sheehan, J. 1998. Early Viking Age silver hoards from Ireland and their Scandinavian elements. In Clarke *et al.* (eds.), *Ireland and Scandinavia*, 166–202.

Sheehan, J. 2007. The form and structure of Viking-age silver hoards: the evidence from Ireland. In Graham-Campbell and Williams (eds.), *Silver Economy in the Viking Age*, 141–54.

Sheehan, J. 2008. The longphort in Viking-age Ireland. *Acta Archaeologica* 79: 282–95.

Sheehan, J. 2009. The Huxley hoard and Hiberno-Scandinavian arm-rings. In J. Graham-Campbell and R. Philpott (eds.), *The Huxley Hoard: Scandinavian settlement in the North West*. Liverpool: National Museums Liverpool, 58–69.

Sheehan, J. 2011. Bullion-rings in Viking-age Britain and Ireland. In Sigmundsson (ed.), *Viking Settlements and Society*, 393–406.

Sheehan, J. 2013. Viking raiding, gift-exchange and insular metalwork in Norway. In Reynolds and Webster (eds.), *Early Medieval Art and Archaeology*, 809–23.

Sheehan, J. 2014. Silver. In Russell and Hurley (eds.), *Woodstown*, 194–222.

Sheehan, J. 2015. Fighting with silver: the Woodstown assemblage. In Clarke and Johnson (eds.), *The Vikings in Ireland*, 161–76.

Sheehan, J. 2018. Reflections on kingship, the Church and Viking-age silver in Ireland. In Kershaw and Williams (eds.), *Silver, Butter, Cloth*, 104–22.

Sheppard, T. 1939. Viking and other relics at Crayke. *Yorkshire Archaeological Journal* 34: 273–81.

Sherlock, R.J. 1956. A nineteenth-century manuscript book on coins. *British Numismatic Journal* 28: 394–9.

Sigmundsson, S. (ed.) 2011. *Viking Settlements and Society: papers from the proceedings of the Sixteenth Viking Congress*. Reykjavík: Hið íslenzka fornleifafélag and University of Iceland Press.

Simpson, L. 2005. Viking warrior-burials: is this the *longphort*? In E. Duffy (ed.), *Medieval Dublin Symposium 2004*. Dublin: Four Courts Press, 11–62.

Sindbæk, S. 2001. An object of exchange: brass bars and the routinization of Viking Age long-distance exchange in the Baltic area. *Offa* 58: 49–60.

Sindbæk, S. 2008. Local and long-distance exchange. In Brink and Price (eds.), *Viking World*, 150–7.

Sindbæk, S. (ed.) 2022. *Northern Emporium: Vol. 1. The making of Viking-age Ribe*. Jutland Archaeological Society Publications. Århus: Århus University Press.

Skre, D. (ed.) 2007. *Kaupang in Skiringssal.* Kaupang Excavation Project Publication Series 1. Århus: Århus University Press.

Skre, D. (ed.) 2008. *Means of Exchange: dealing with silver in the Viking Age.* Kaupang Excavation Project Publication Series 2. Århus: Århus University Press.

Skre, D. 2008. The development of urbanism in Scandinavia. In Brink and Price (eds.), *Viking World*, 83–93.

Skre, D. (ed.) 2011. *Things from the Town: artefacts and inhabitants in Viking-age Kaupang.* Kaupang Excavation Project Publication Series 3, Norske Oldfunn XXIV. Århus: Århus University Press.

Sloane, B., Swain, H., and Thomas, C. 1995. The Roman road and the river regime. *London Archaeologist* 7: 359–70.

Smedley, N. and Owles, E.J. 1963. Some Suffolk kilns: iv. Saxon kilns in Cox Lane, Ipswich, 1961. *Proceedings of the Suffolk Institute of Archaeology and History* 29: 304–55.

Smyth, A. 1977. *Scandinavian Kings in the British Isles, 850–880.* Oxford: Oxford University Press.

Solberg, B. 2007. Pastimes or serious business? Norwegian graves with gaming objects *c.*200–1000 AD. In B. Hårdh, K. Jennbert, and D. Olausson (eds.), *On the Road: studies in honour of Lars Larsson.* Acta Archaeologica Lundensia in 4°, No. 26. Stockholm: Almqvist & Wiksell International, 265–9.

Somerville, A.A. and McDonald, R.A. (eds.) 2014. *The Viking Age. A reader.* Toronto: University of Toronto Press.

Sørensen, A.C. 2001. *Ladby: a Danish ship-grave from the Viking Age.* Ships and Boats of the North 3. Roskilde: The Viking Ship Museum.

Sperber, E. 2004. Metrology of the weights from the Birka excavations 1990–1995. In Ambrosiani (ed.), *Excavation in the Black Earth 1990–1995. Eastern connections,* 61–95.

Spoerry, P. 2016. *The Production and Distribution of Medieval Pottery in Cambridgeshire.* East Anglian Archaeology 159. Gressenhall: Norfolk Museums Service.

Stalsberg, A. 2017. Swords from the Carolingian Empire to the Baltic Sea and beyond. In J. Callmer, I. Gustin, and M. Roslund (eds.), *Identity Formation and Diversity in the Early Medieval Baltic and Beyond: communicators and communication.* The Northern World 75. Leiden: Brill, 259–80.

Standley, E.R. 2016. Spinning yarns: the archaeological evidence for hand spinning and its social implications, *c.*AD 1200–1500. *Medieval Archaeology* 60: 266–99.

Standley, E.R. 2022. The non-numismatic objects. In Naylor and Standley (eds.), The Watlington Hoard, 170–81.

Steane, K. (ed.) 2016. *The Archaeology of the Lower City and Adjacent Suburbs.* Oxford: Oxbow.

Steane, K. 2016a. Flaxengate 1972 (f72). In Steane (ed.), *The Archaeology of the Lower City,* 11–62.

Steane, K. 2016b. Saltergate 1973 (LIN73). In Steane (ed.), *The Archaeology of the Lower City,* 198–245.

Steedman, K. 1994. Excavation of a Saxon site at Riby Crossroads, Lincolnshire. *Archaeological Journal* 151: 212–306.

Stein, S. 2014. *Understanding Torksey, Lincolnshire: a geoarchaeological and landscape approach to a Viking overwintering camp.* PhD thesis, University of Sheffield, https://etheses.whiterose.ac.uk/9616/

Steuer, H. 1987. Gewichtsgeldwirtschaften im frühgeschichtlichen Europa: Feinwaagen und Gewichte als Quellen zur Währungsgeschichte. In Düwel *et al.* (eds.), *Untersuchungen zu Handel und Verkehr,* 405–527.

Stocker, D. 1989. Review of *Goltho: the development of an early medieval manor, c.850–1150.* By G. Beresford. *Archaeological Journal* 146: 627–9.

Stocker, D. (ed.) 2003. *The City by the Pool: assessing the archaeology of the City of Lincoln.* Oxford: Oxbow.

Stone Gaines, J. 2007. Eel fishing. *Spritsail* 21(1): 6–10.

Story, J. 2003. *Carolingian Connections: Anglo-Saxon England and Carolingian Francia, c. 750–870.* Aldershot: Ashgate.

Stos-Gale, S. 2004. Lead isotope analyses of the lead weights from Birka, Sweden. In I. Gustin (ed.), *Mellan gåva och marknad: handel, tillit och materiell kultur under vikingatid.* Stockholm: Almqvist & Wiksell, 324–32.

Stylegar, F.-A. 2007. The Kapuang cemeteries revisited. In Skre (ed.), *Kaupang*, 65–101.

Sudds, B. 2016. Pottery. In C. Jackson (ed.), *Land North of Church Road, Wreningham, Norfolk; a post-excavation assessment.* Unpublished report no. 12683, Pre-Construct Archaeology, 76–87.

Sudds, B. 2020. The pottery. In Brown *et al.* (eds.), *Stoke Quay*, 121–94.

Swanton, M.J. 1973. *The Spearheads of the Anglo-Saxon Settlements.* Leeds: The Royal Archaeological Institute.

Swanton, M.J. 1975. *Anglo-Saxon Prose.* London: Dent.

Swift, C. 2008. The early history of Knowth. In Byrne *et al.*, *Historical Knowth*, 5–42.

Symonds, L. 2003. *Landscape and Social Practice: the production and consumption of pottery in 10th century Lincolnshire.* BAR British Series 345. Oxford: John and Erica Hedges.

Taylor, J. and Webster, L. 1984. A Late Saxon strap-end mould from Carlisle. *Medieval Archaeology* 28: 178–81.

Ten Harkel, L. 2018. Ethnic identity or something else? The production and use of non-ferrous dress-accessories and related items from early medieval Lincoln. *Anglo-Saxon Studies in Archaeology and History* 21: 1–27.

Tester, A., Anderson, S., Riddler, I., and Carr, R.J.M. 2014. *Staunch Meadow, Brandon, Suffolk: a high status Middle Saxon settlement on the Fen Edge.* East Anglian Archaeology 151. Gressenhall: Norfolk Museums Service.

Thomas, C., Cowie, R., and Sidell, J. 2006. *The Royal Palace, Abbey and Town of Westminster on Thorney Island: archaeological excavations (1991–8) for the London Underground Limited Jubilee Line Extension Project.* MoLAS Monograph 22. London: MoLAS.

Thomas, G. 1997. *Specialist Report: Late Anglo-Saxon strap-ends from excavations at Ipswich.* York: Archaeology Data Service. https://doi.org/10.5284/1034376

Thomas, G. 2000a. *A Survey of Late Anglo-Saxon and Viking-Age Strap-ends from Britain.* PhD thesis, Institute of Archaeology, University College London. https://discovery.ucl.ac.uk/id/eprint/1317562

Thomas, G. 2000b. Anglo-Scandinavian metalwork from the Danelaw. In Hadley and Richards (eds.), *Cultures in Contact*, 237–55.

Thomas, G. 2001. Strap-ends and the identification of regional patterns in the production and circulation of ornamental metalwork in Late Anglo-Saxon and Viking-age Britain. In M. Redknap, N. Edwards, S. Youngs, A. Lane, and J. Knight (eds.), *Pattern and Purpose in Insular Art.* Oxford: Oxbow Books, 39–48.

Thomas, G. 2006. Reflections on a '9th-century' Northumbrian metalworking tradition: a silver hoard from Poppleton, North Yorkshire. *Medieval Archaeology* 50: 143–64.

Thomas, G. 2009. The hooked tags. In Evans and Loveluck (eds.), *Life and Economy at Early Medieval Flixborough*, 17–21.

Thomas, G. 2012. Carolingian culture in the North Sea world: rethinking the cultural dynamics of personal adornment in Viking-age England. *European Journal of Archaeology* 15: 486–517.

Thomas, G., McDonnell, G., Merkel, J., and Marshall, P. 2016. Technology, ritual and Anglo-Saxon agriculture: the biography of a plough coulter from Lyminge, Kent. *Antiquity* 90: 742–58.

Thomas, G. and Ottaway, P. 2008. The symbolic lives of Late Anglo-Saxon settlements: a cellared structure and iron hoard from Bishopstone, East Sussex. *The Archaeological Journal* 165: 334–98.

Thomas, G., Payne, N., and Okasha, E. 2008. Re-evaluating base-metal artefacts: an inscribed lead strap-end from Crewkerne, Somerset. *Anglo-Saxon England* 37: 173–81.

Thomas, G., Youngs, S.M., Edwards, G., and Watson, J. 2009. Strap-ends. In Evans and Loveluck (eds.), *Life and Economy at Early Medieval Flixborough*, 7–16.

Thuillier, F. 2006. Étude synthétique des fours de potiers du Haut Moyen Âge dans le Nord de la France, en Belgique et aux Pays-Bas. In Hincker and Husi (eds.), *La céramique du haut Moyen Âge*, 17–26.

Thuillier, F. 2015. L'atelier de potiers Carolingien de la Rue de Cassel à Racquinghem (Pas-de-Calais). In Thuillier and Louis (eds.), *Tourner Autour du Pot*, 123–37.

Thuillier, F. and Louis, E. (eds.) 2015. *Tourner Autour du Pot…Les Ateliers de Potiers Médiévaux du Ve au XIIe Siècle dans l'Espace Européen*. Caen: Presses Universitaires de Caen.

Thuillier, F., Routier, J., Bocquet-Liénard, A., and Harnay, V. 2015. L'atelier de potiers Carolingien de la Fontaine aux Linottes, à La Calotterie (Pas-de-Calais). In Thuillier and Louis (eds.), *Tourner Autour du Pot*, 103–22.

Thurborg, M. 1988. Regional economic structures: an analysis of the Viking Age silver hoards from Öland, Sweden. *World Archaeology* 20(2): 302–24.

Tweddle, D. 1986. *Finds from Parliament Street and other Sites in the City Centre*. The Archaeology of York: The Small Finds 17/4. London: Council for British Archaeology.

Tweddle, D. 2004. Art in pre-Conquest York. In Hall (ed.), *Aspects of Anglo-Scandinavian York*, 446–58.

Ulbricht, I. 1992. Bars. In E. Roesdahl and D.M. Wilson (eds.), *From Viking to Crusader: the Scandinavians and Europe 800–1200*. New York: Rizzoli, 252.

Van den Bossche, B. 2022. De zaak Hasloa zoektocht naar een winterkamp van het grote leger. *Archeologie in Limburg* 125. Roermond: Koninklijk.

Vince, A. 1993. Forms, functions, and manufacturing techniques of late 9th- and 10th-century wheelthrown pottery in England and their origins. In Piton (ed.), *Travaux du Groupe de Recherches et d'études sur la Céramique dans le Nord-Pas-De-Calais*, 151–64.

Vince, A. 2001. Lincoln in the Viking Age. In Graham-Campbell *et al.* (eds.), *Vikings and the Danelaw*, 157–79.

Vince, A. 2003. Lincoln in the early medieval era, between the 5th and 9th centuries. In Stocker (ed.), *The City by the Pool*, 141–6.

Vince, A. 2004. *Characterisation of Medieval Pottery from Thorner, West Yorkshire*. Alan Vince Archaeological Consultancy Report 2004/161. York: Archaeology Data Service. https://doi.org/10.5284/1010684

Vince, A. 2006. Coinage and urban development: integrating the archaeological and numismatic history of Lincoln. In Cook and Williams (eds.), *Coinage and History*, 525–44.

Vince, A. and Jones, M. 2016. Discussion. In Steane (ed.), *The Archaeology of the Lower City*, 470–516.

Vince, A. and Young, J. 2009. The Anglo-Saxon pottery. In Evans and Loveluck (eds.), *Life and Economy at Early Medieval Flixborough*, 392–401.

Vlasatý, T. 2018. Bronze Anglo-Saxon sword pommels. *Projekt Forlǫg—Reenactment a věda*. https://sagy.vikingove.cz/bronze-anglo-saxon-sword-pommels/ (last accessed 12 August 2023)

Von Ackermann, M. 2018. *Early Medieval Locks and Keys in England and Scandinavia*. PhD thesis, University of York. https://etheses.whiterose.ac.uk/25951/

Wade, K. 1980. The pottery. In P. Wade-Martins (ed.), *Excavations in North Elmham Park 1967–72*. East Anglian Archaeology 9. Gressenhall: Norfolk Museums Service, 413–77.

Wade, K. 1988. Ipswich. In R. Hodges and B. Hobley (eds.), *The Rebirth of Towns in the West AD 700–1050*. Council for British Archaeology Research Report 68. London: Council for British Archaeology, 93–100.

Wade, K. 1993. The urbanisation of East Anglia: the Ipswich perspective. In J. Gardner (ed.), *Flatlands & Wetlands: current themes in East Anglian archaeology*. East Anglian Archaeology 50. Gressenhall: Norfolk Museums Service, 144–51.

Wade, K. 2013a. The chronological framework. *Ipswich 1974–1990 Excavation Archive*. York. Archaeology Data Service. https://doi.org/10.5284/1034376

Wade, K. 2013b. IAS3601: site summary. *Ipswich 1974–1990 Excavation Archive*. York: Archaeology Data Service. https://doi.org/10.5284/1034349

Wade, K. 2014a. IAS 3104: site summary. *Ipswich 1974–1990 Excavation Archive*. York: Archaeology Data Service. https://doi.org/10.5284/1034342

Wade, K. 2014b. IAS4801: site summary. *Ipswich 1974–1990 Excavation Archive*. York: Archaeology Data Service. https://doi.org/10.5284/1034354

Wade, K. 2014c. IAS5003: site summary. *Ipswich 1974–1990 Excavation Archive*. York: Archaeology Data Service. https://doi.org/10.5284/1034356

Wade, K. 2014d. IAS4310: site summary. *Ipswich 1974–1990 Excavation Archive*. York: Archaeology Data Service. https://doi.org/10.5284/1034348

Wallace, P. 1987. The economy and commerce of Viking Age Dublin. In Düwel *et al.* (eds.), *Untersuchungen zu Handel und Verkehr*, 200–45.

Wallace, P. 1998. Line fishing in Viking Dublin: a contemporary explanation for archaeological evidence. In C. Manning (ed.), *Dublin and Beyond the Pale: studies in honour of Patrick Healy*. Wicklow: Wordwell, 3–15.

Wallace, P. 2013. Weights and weight systems in Viking Age Ireland. In Reynolds and Webster (eds.), *Early Medieval Art and Archaeology*, 302–16.

Wallace, P. 2014. Weights. In Russell and Hurley (eds.), *Woodstown*, 222–55.

Wallace, P. 2015. Meagre lead: the ubiquity of lead in Hiberno-Scandinavian Dublin. In Purcell *et al.* (eds.), *Clerics, Kings, and Vikings*, 263–75.

Wallis, H. 2005. *Excavations at Mill Lane, Thetford*. East Anglian Archaeology 108. Gressenhall: Norfolk Museums Service.

Walton Rogers, P. 1997. *Textile Production at 16–22 Coppergate*. The Archaeology of York: The Small Finds 17/11. London: Council for British Archaeology.

Walton Rogers, P. 2007. Cloth and Clothing in Early Anglo-Saxon England AD450–700. Council for British Archaeology Research Report 145. York: Council for British Archaeology

Walton Rogers, P. 2014. Textile production and treatment. In Tester *et al.*, *Staunch Meadow, Brandon*, 85–94.

Walton Rogers, P. 2020a. Copper-alloy pin. In Williams (ed.), *A Riverine Site Near York*, 47–8.

Walton Rogers, P. 2020b. Textile production. In Williams (ed.), *A Riverine Site Near York*, 48–9.

Walton Rogers, P. 2020c. Textile networks in Viking-age towns of Britain and Ireland. In Ashby and Sindbaek (eds.), *Crafts and Social Networks*, 83–122.

Wamers, E. 1985. *Insularer Metallschmuck in wikingerzeitlichen Gräbern Nordeuropas. Untersuchungen zur skandinavischen Westexpansion*. Neumünster: Karl Wachholtz Verlag.

Wamers, E. 1997. Hammer und Kreuz. Typologische Aspekte einer nordeuropäischen Amulettsitte aus der Zeit des Glaubenswechsels. In M. Müller-Wille (ed.), *Rom und Byzanz im Norden. Mission und Glaubenswechsel im Ostseeraum während des 8.–14.* Stuttgart: Franz Steiner Verlag, 83–107.

Wamers, E. 1998. Insular finds in Viking Age Scandinavia. In Clarke *et al.* (eds.), *Ireland and Scandinavia*, 37–72.

Wamers, E. 2005a. Die Zusammensetzung des Schatzes. In Wamers and Brandt (eds.), *Die Macht des Silbers*, 129–41.

Wamers, E. 2005b. Imitatio Imperii—Silber verändert den Norden. In Wamers and Brandt (eds.), *Die Macht des Silbers*, 149–81.

Wamers, E. 2011. Continental and insular metalwork. In Skre (ed.), *Things from the Town*, 65–97.

Wamers, E. and Brandt, M. (eds.) 2005. *Die Macht des Silbers: Karolingische Schätze im Norden.* Regensburg: Schnell & Steiner.

Wastling, L.M. 2009. Evidence for fishing and netting birds. In Evans and Loveluck (eds.), *Life and Economy at Early Medieval Flixborough*, 249–52.

Waterman, D.M. 1959. Late Saxon, Viking, and early medieval finds from York. *Archaeologia* 97: 59–105.

Webster, L. 2000. Sword fittings. In P.A. Stamper and R.A. Croft (eds.), *Wharram: a study of settlement on the Yorkshire Wolds VIII: the South Manor area.* York University Archaeological Publications 10. York: University of York, 138–9.

Webster, L. 2001. Metalwork of the Mercian supremacy. In M.P. Brown and C.A. Farr (eds.), *Mercia: an Anglo-Saxon kingdom in Europe.* London: Leicester University Press, 263–78.

Webster, L. 2012. *The Franks Casket.* British Museum Objects in Focus. London: Trustees of the British Museum.

Webster, L. and Backhouse, J. (eds.) 1991. *The Making of England: Anglo-Saxon art and culture AD 600–900.* London: The British Museum Press.

Weetch, R. 2014. *Brooches in Late Anglo-Saxon England within a North West European Context: a study of social identities between the eighth and eleventh centuries.* PhD thesis, University of Reading. https://ethos.bl.uk/OrderDetails.do?uin=uk.bl.ethos.655741

West, S.E. 1963. Excavations at Cox Lane (1958) and at the Town Defences, Shire Hall Yard, Ipswich (1959) (with reports by G.C. Dunning, R.H.M. Dolley, and D. Charman). *Proceedings of the Suffolk Institute of Archaeology and History* 29: 233–303.

West, S.E. 1998. *A Corpus of Anglo-Saxon Material from Suffolk.* East Anglian Archaeology 84. Gressenhall: Norfolk Museums Service.

Westholm, G. 2009. Gotland and the surrounding world. In Pettersson (ed.), *The Spillings Hoard*, 109–52.

Wheeler, R E.M. 1927. *London and the Vikings.* London Museum Catalogues: No. 1. London: Lancaster House.

Whitelock, D. (ed. and trans.) 1961. *The Anglo-Saxon Chronicle.* London: Eyre and Spottiswoode.

Whitelock, D. (ed. and trans.) 1979. *English Historical Documents, Vol. I.* London: Routledge.

Whitfield, N. 1998. The manufacture of ancient beaded wire: experiments and observations. *Jewellery Studies* 8: 57–86.

Wiechmann, R. 1996. *Edelmetalldepots der Wikingerzeit in Schleswig-Holstein* (Offa-Bücher 77). Neumünster: Wachholtz Verlag.

Wilkinson, A. and Batt, C. 2022. *Archaeomagnetic Investigation of a Kiln at Castle Field, Torksey, Lincolnshire.* In J.D. Richards, D. Hadley, E. Craig-Atkins, and G. Perry, *Digital Archive from an Investigation into the Early Medieval Town at Torksey, Lincolnshire 2012-2021.* York: Archaeology Data Service. https://doi.org/10.5284/1083529

Willemsen, A. 2021. Mixed emotions: the swords of Dorestad. In Willemsen and Kik (eds.), *Dorestad and its Networks*, 101–15.

Willemsen, A. and Kik, H. (eds.) 2021. *Dorestad and its Networks: communities, contact and conflict in early medieval Europe*. Papers on Archaeology of the Leiden Museum of Antiquities 25. Leiden: Sidestone Press.

Williams, G. 1999. Anglo-Saxon and Viking coin weights. *British Numismatic Journal* 69: 19–36.

Williams, G. 2007. Kingship, Christianity and coinage: monetary and political perspectives on silver economy in the Viking Age. In Graham-Campbell and Williams (eds.), *Silver Economy in the Viking Age*, 177–214.

Williams, G. 2011. Silver economies, monetisation and society: an overview. In Graham-Campbell *et al.* (eds.), *Silver Economies*, 337–72.

Williams, G. 2013. Towns and identities in Viking England. In Hadley and Ten Harkel (eds.), *Everyday Life in Viking Towns*, 27–49.

Williams, G. 2014. Coins and currency in Viking England, AD 865–954. In R. Naismith, M. Allen, and E. Screen (eds.), *Early Medieval Monetary History. Studies in memory of Mark Blackburn*. Farnham: Ashgate, 13–38.

Williams, G. 2015. Viking camps and the means of exchange in Britain and Ireland in the ninth century. In Clarke and Johnson (eds.), *The Vikings in Ireland*, 93–116.

Williams, G. (ed.) 2020. *A Riverine Site Near York: a possible Viking camp?* London: British Museum Research Publications.

Williams, G. 2020a. The coins. In Williams (ed.), *A Riverine Site Near York*, 11–13.

Williams, G. 2020b. Copper-alloy weights. In Williams (ed.), *A Riverine Site Near York*, 15.

Williams, G. 2020c. Lead weights. In Williams (ed.), *A Riverine Site Near York*, 15–16.

Williams, G. 2020d. Trade and exchange at ARSNY. In Williams (ed.), *A Riverine Site Near York*, 19.

Williams, G. 2020e. Weights. In Williams (ed.), *A Riverine Site Near York*, 20–33.

Williams, G. 2020f. The coins, weights and bullion: discussion and interpretation. In Williams (ed.), *A Riverine Site Near York*, 36–45.

Williams, G. 2020g. Dating. In Williams (ed.), *A Riverine Site Near York*, 79–82.

Williams, G. 2020h. The site in context. In Williams (ed.), *A Riverine Site Near York*, 84–92.

Williams, G. 2020i. Viking camps and the *micel here*. In Williams (ed.), *A Riverine Site Near York*, 92–9.

Williams, G. 2020j. Viking hoards from Yorkshire, c.866–954: a survey. In Williams (ed.), *A Riverine Site Near York*, 104–12.

Williams, G. 2023. Viking camps: a historiographical overview. In Hedenstierna-Jonson and García Losquiño (eds.), *Viking Camps*, 11–65.

Williams, G. and Ager, B. 2010. *The Vale of York Hoard*. London: The British Museum Press.

Williams, G. and Hall, R.A. 2020. Character of the site and comparators elsewhere. In Williams (ed.), *A Riverine Site Near York*, 82–4.

Williams, G. and Naylor, J. 2016. *King Alfred's Coins. The Watlington Viking hoard*. Oxford: Ashmolean Museum.

Williams, J., Shaw, M., and Chapman, A. 2021. Anglo-Saxon Northampton revisited. *Northamptonshire Archaeology* 41: 25–77.

Willmott, H. and Daubney, A. 2019. Of saints, sows or smiths? Copper-brazed iron handbells in early medieval England. *Archaeological Journal* 177: 63–82.

Wilson, D.M. 1964. *Anglo-Saxon Ornamental Metalwork 700–1100 in the British Museum*. Catalogue of the Antiquities of the Later Saxon Period Volume I. London: Trustees of the British Museum.

Wilson, D.M. 1965. Some neglected Anglo-Saxon swords. *Medieval Archaeology* 9: 32–54.

Wilson, D.M. (ed.) 1976. *The Archaeology of Anglo-Saxon England*. London: Methuen.

Wilson, D.M. 1976. Craft and industry. In Wilson (ed.), *The Archaeology of Anglo-Saxon England*, 253–81.

Wilson, D.M. 1984. *Anglo-Saxon Art from the Seventh Century to the Norman Conquest*. London: Thames & Hudson.

Wilson, D.M. and Blunt, C.E. 1961. The Trewhiddle hoard. *Archaeologia* 98: 75–122.

Wilthew, P. 1996. Metallurgical analyses of pins and other mid-Saxon copper-alloy objects from Saxon Southampton. In Hinton, *The Gold, Silver and Other Non-Ferrous Alloy Objects from Hamwic*, 66–73.

Winterbottom, J. 1972. *Three Lives of English Saints*. Toronto: Pontifical Institute of Medieval Studies.

Woods, A. 2020. Viking economies and the 'Great Army': interpreting the precious metals from Torksey, Lincolnshire. In J. Gruszczynski, M. Jankowiak, and J. Shepard (eds.), *Viking Age Trade: silver, slaves and Gotland*. London: Routledge, 396–414.

Woolf, A. 2007. *From Pictland to Alba 789–1070*. The New Edinburgh History of Scotland. Edinburgh: Edinburgh University Press.

Wrathmell, S. 2020. Sharing out the land of the Northumbrians. Exploring Scandinavian settlement in eastern Yorkshire through -*by* place-names and township boundaries, part one. *Medieval Settlement Research* 35: 163–26.

Young, J. and Vince, A. 2009. The Anglo-Saxon pottery from Flixborough within the context of the East Midlands of England. In Evans and Loveluck (eds.), *Life and Economy at Early Medieval Flixborough*, 392–401.

Young, J., Vince, A., and Nailor, V. 2005. *A Corpus of Anglo-Saxon and Medieval Pottery from Lincoln*. Oxford: Oxbow.

Young, T. 2014a. Discussion of metalworking evidence. In Russell and Hurley (eds.), *Woodstown*, 103–13.

Young, T. 2014b. Ceramics: crucibles and cupels. In Russell and Hurley (eds.), *Woodstown*, 267–85.

Youngs, S. 2001. Insular metalwork from Flixborough, Lincolnshire. *Medieval Archaeology* 45: 210–20.

Ystgaard, I. 2021. Warfare and recruitment in Iron Age central Norway. In H.L. Aanestad, U. Pedersen, M. Moen, E. Naumann, and H. Lund Berg (eds.), *Vikings Across Boundaries: Viking-age transformations*. Abingdon: Routledge, 285–303.

Index